TEXAS
WOMEN
WRITERS

5/2/04

TO MY FAVORITE TEXAS WOMAN WRITER...

TODD

NUMBER EIGHT:
Tarleton State University
Southwestern Studies in the Humanities

TEXAS WOMEN WRITERS

A Tradition of Their Own

EDITED BY

Sylvia Ann Grider & Lou Halsell Rodenberger

Texas A&M University Press
College Station

The paper used in this book meets the minimum requirements
of the American National Standard for Permanence
of Paper for Printed Library Materials, Z39.48-1984.
Binding materials have been chosen for durability.

Library of Congress Cataloging-in-Publication Data

Texas women writers : a tradition of their own / edited by Sylvia Ann
    Grider and Lou Halsell Rodenberger. — 1st ed.
        p.   cm. — (Tarleton State University southwestern studies in
the humanities ; no.8)
        Includes bibliographical references and index.
        ISBN 0-89096-752-0 (cloth : alk. paper). — ISBN 0-89096-765-2
(paper : alk. paper)
        1. American literature—Texas—History and criticism.
        2. American literature—Women authors—History and criticism.
        3. Women and literature—Texas—History.   4. Texas—In literature.
    I. Grider, Sylvia Ann.   II. Rodenberger, Lou Halsell.   III. Series.
PS266.T4T49   1997
810.9'9287'09764—dc21   97-7048
                                                                                    CIP

Dedicated to the memory of
Bill Shearer,
Suzanne Comer,
and
Joyce Thompson

CONTENTS

PREFACE

Women armed only with pen and paper have been capturing the Texas experience for more than 150 years. The first were women who came to the state as visitors and stayed long enough to record their impressions of the landscape and the colonists' lives. Those who lived in the early settlements after Texas had declared its independence, perceiving that they were history makers, scribbled diaries or later wrote their reminiscences, usually at the request of family members. By the middle 1880s, reflections on life in the new state, written by women who had acquired a strong sense of Texas as place, were appearing in newspaper stories, periodical articles, short stories, and novels. But Texas's border, interminable though it may be, rarely has fenced in its women writers. Several early native-born writers were educated in eastern universities. Others traveled widely, often abroad or to Mexico. None, it seems, thought of themselves as "good ol' girls" from Big Texas, as did many of their men counterparts.

Our definition of Texas women writers includes women who have lived in the state long enough to develop a sense of place and to acquire an understanding of the state's complex regional and cultural diversity, who reflect that knowledge in what they have written. Many can be classified as regionalists, but none should be regarded as provincial. Not all were born in Texas, nor have many made Texas their home for life, but their accomplishments have been recognized, statewide and nationally, as Texas-connected. Texas women writers are highly individualistic, usually ignoring the prevalent image of Texas as a masculine state intrigued only by the so-called Texas Mystique, which raises to sacred status such icons as the cowboy, the oil derrick, and the Alamo. Included here are fiction and nonfiction writers, poets, and dramatists who have developed a literary tradition of their own, apart from the interests and subject matter of Texas men's writing. The materials covered in this book are grounded in the Texas experience from the point of view of women who are cultural insiders.

For many years, we have discovered, women's writing in Texas was considered a separate genre from the works that men writers produced. Particularly in the 1920s and 1930s, when provincial regionalist J. Frank Dobie and his admirers considered themselves arbiters of literary matters in the state, women writers depended largely on other women for readership. Nevertheless, women writers have never assumed the role of reactionaries in the state's literary establishment. During the Dobie years, Texas women polished their professionalism and gained critical attention outside the state as novelists and producers of short fiction for popular magazines.

As the twenty-first century approaches, women writers associated with Texas enjoy increasing recognition nationally, even internationally, and many have received prestigious awards for their novels, nonfiction books, poetry, and short-story collections. There is an extraordinary degree of literary activity in Texas, even as this book goes into production. New women authors and books constantly emerge as the contributors and editors are busy researching and compiling. We acknowledge this creative ferment but cannot include all the women authors working in Texas today. In some ways, then, this book is a work in progress. We must add, too, that the burgeoning body of creative work by contemporary Texas women encompasses literary genres beyond the scope of this study, including fantasy, romance, lesbian writing, cookbooks, and perhaps other topics. For the time being we leave research in these fields to other scholars. Most encouraging for all has been the acknowledgment and rapid development of a distinct literary tradition that showcases the accomplishments and world views of Tejana and African-American women in the state.

Nevertheless, even though in the last two decades scholarly interest in past lives and contributions of Texas women has accelerated, no comprehensive history of the development of a woman's literary tradition in the state has been written. From the establishment of an independent literary tradition by Mary Austin Holley, whose account of her observations on a visit to her cousin Stephen F.'s colony on the Brazos was published in 1833, to the flourishing careers of Texas women writers today, what women writers in the state have accomplished is a distinct and often untold story. This volume, which includes a summary history of the field and an anthology of essays on major writers and genres, focuses on the historical development of Texas women's writing. It has been written both to inform and entertain scholars and general readers and to provide the stimulus for further research.

Contributors to the anthology—some of whom are subjects of critical essays elsewhere in the volume—were asked only to provide lively guides for all readers or would-be readers interested in Texas women writers. As editors we suggested they include biographical sketches, summaries of major works, and brief critical evaluations of individual authors, but essayists were urged to "think of these suggestions as a starting gate, not a corral." We encouraged a variety of styles to increase readability. Documentation styles and formats therefore vary from contributor to contributor.

Essays on writers within each genre are arranged chronologically. Discussion of some authors in several essays is inevitable because so many women writers in Texas are working in several genres. Fiction and nonfiction writers appear in the first division. Following are chronologically organized summaries on writers of short fiction, creative nonfiction, and children's literature, on Tejana and African-American writers, and on dramatists and poets. The history of the remarkable accomplishments of ethnic women writers in the state is a unique story, deserving, we believe, separate accounts in this study to emphasize their growing influence on the tradition as a whole. The essays devoted to African-Americans are brief, but that is because only in the past twenty years or so have these women developed a distinctive literary presence in Texas. We are convinced that African-American women writers in the state are in the process of creating a strong new tradition, and we earnestly hope that the brief essays included here will provide the impetus for further research and documentation. The Tejana tradition in Texas is much older but is also in the midst of a creative flowering. The lengthy essay on their accomplishments is the first attempt to gather what is known about this exciting literary development. Even during the time our book has been in progress, some of these writers, such as Sandra Cisneros and Denise Chavez, have attained national recognition. Definitive biographical/critical essays on these writers have yet to be written.

The volume concludes with a symposium of discussions, by women active in publishing in Texas, on the status and future of women writers in the state. A selective bibliography of both primary and secondary materials provides sources for further reading and research.

Regrettably we cannot include the names or extensive coverage of contemporary writers in the state who are publishing useful, interesting, and often scholarly nonfiction. Although many of their works are informed by the Texas experience and therefore receive cursory treatment in this book, the whole field of nonfiction by contemporary Texas women deserves separate treatment.

One problem in conducting research into this emerging field is the dearth of collected materials. Many libraries throughout the state have invaluable special collections of Texana, but no single library has extensive and complete holdings covering Texas women writers (although the Texas Federation of Women's Clubs Historical Foundation in Austin does have a special collection of books by and about Texas women). In the course of our research for the book, therefore, Lou Rodenberger has developed one of the most comprehensive libraries on Texas women writers, including books and articles as well as extensive vertical files of clippings, pamphlets, ephemera, and correspondence. This private collection, with support from Texas Woman's University's library and other libraries throughout the state, has been the basis of our research. One aim of this book is to provide guidelines enabling libraries to increase their special collections and general holdings regarding works by and about Texas women writers.

Readers interested in further research into the work of Texas women writers can utilize the essays included in this volume in various ways. Although each essay can stand independently, many are also complementary. For example, the essay on Jewel Gibson provides extensive biographical information, and the essay on Texas women dramatists provides a critical evaluation of her dramas. The general bibliography contains publication data on all secondary sources cited in the various essays. The separate author section of the bibliography contains a selected listing of primary and secondary works by and about the authors. Used in combination with the bibliographies and comprehensive index, the essays not only should help most readers find whatever information they seek but also should provide for them a point of departure for further research.

We are indebted to family, friends, and colleagues for their encouragement as we worked on this book. The project began in the Woman's Collection at Texas Woman's University with the generous support of Elizabeth Snapp, director of TWU libraries, and her able assistants, Kim Grover-Haskins and Peg Rezac. We express our gratitude to the Texas Foundation for Women's Resources, which sponsored the research for the Texas Women's History Project. The project archives, now in the TWU Woman's Collection, provided much useful information on early Texas women writers. We are indebted as well to the McMurry University Faculty Development Fund, which provided financial support for initial research. The sustained support of Sandra Harper will always be appreciated.

To Margaret Waring, librarian of the Comanche Public Library, whose optimism and knowledge fired our flagging enthusiasm, we owe a special thanks. Our gratitude goes also to our friends Betty Wiesepape, Lawrence Clayton, Paula Mitchell Marks and Al Lowman, who have been generous with their knowledge and encouragement. Two former secretary-treasurers of the Texas Institute of Letters, John Edward Weems and James Hoggard, generously provided recent TIL programs and other information. Our thanks to both. Other friends, too numerous to list, have shared information and given encouragement, and we appreciate their sustaining support. We are grateful to Myra Dorris Hall, who kindly provided us with a copy of her informative dissertation on Laura V. Hamner, and to Antoinette Franklin, who diligently collected information on African-American women writers in San Antonio for us. Norma Rutledge Grammer's master's thesis, "Texas Women Writers before 1865," provided much useful information. We particularly appreciate the careful reading of our manuscript by Kathryn Lang and Tom Pilkington, who willingly and competently provided much-needed editing advice. We thank and admire our contributors, all scholars with remarkable patience. For Charles Rodenberger's generous assistance with printouts of first drafts, his unfailing belief in this project, and his daily encouragement, we shall always remain grateful.

We also acknowledge permission to reprint from poems published by Arte Público Press, Milkweed Editions, Southern Methodist University Press, and University of North Texas Press, and from poems by Naomi Shihab Nye which appeared in *Yellow Glove* (1988), published by Breitenbush.

We are indebted greatly to Becky Jobling, who spent many tedious hours organizing the bibliography. Without the careful, masterful work of Charlene Archer, who made a polished manuscript of our smudged, heavily edited copy, we could not have completed this project. Lastly, we remember the late Suzanne Comer, whose dream it was to provide this story of women writers in Texas for their readers.

TEXAS
WOMEN
WRITERS

INTRODUCTION

Texas Women Writers, 1830–1995:
A Tradition of Their Own

SYLVIA ANN GRIDER
AND LOU HALSELL RODENBERGER

The first comprehensive survey of women writers in Texas appeared in the *Galveston Daily News* in 1893, more than a century ago. Bride N. Taylor, Austin journalist and literary critic, compiled brief profiles of sixty-seven writers that the *News* published in two installments, on June 18 and 25. Taylor's candid conclusion to "The Women Writers of Texas" includes her assessment of the status of women writers in the state's literary establishment:

> Some of our earliest writers were women of noble talents, who failed of more than local recognition solely because they were isolated here in Texas too far away from the centers of literary life to make themselves heard. They did receive, however, a respectful and often enthusiastic appreciation in their own circle, which was frequently coextensive with the state boundaries. In this they were more fortunate than their successors of our own day. These last work almost without exception in hopeless bitterness of spirit, recognizing that their only chance lies in the forlorn hope of gaining the notice of the far away critics and readers of the eastern and northern centers of thought, after which their neighbors will be ready enough with their superfluous meed [sic] of praise.

One can infer from Taylor's guarded but grim tone that women writers in the state yearned for recognition of their contribution to Texas letters. She sees better times for women writers, however, if they unite. Her tone brightens as she concludes the essay with a description of the purposes of the newly organized Texas Woman's Press Association, commending its organization on May 10, 1893, under the leadership of Aurelia Hadley Mohl, a Houston journalist.

Known well across the state, Mohl had a clear purpose in mind when she invited the women journalists attending the annual meeting of the Texas Press Association to meet with her at the Windsor Hotel in Dallas. She had established her reputation as a writer in 1865 when the Houston *Tri-Weekly Telegraph* published her short story "An Afternoon Nap," which predicted a number of later inventions, including the telephone—an accomplishment noted both in Bride Taylor's "The Women Writers of Texas" and in Elizabeth Brooks's *Prominent Women of Texas* (1896). She had begun her career as a journalist in 1856 when she took over the literary department of the widely read *Houston Telegraph*. Later she lived in Washington for thirteen years, where she served as correspondent to newspapers in Dallas, San Antonio, Houston, and Waco. In Washington she also was corresponding secretary of the Woman's National Press Association. Mohl initiated plans to organize a Texas chapter of the association when she returned to Houston as editor of the "Woman's World" department at the *Houston Post*.

Thirty-eight women assembled to hear Mohl's proposal that they organize themselves into the Texas Woman's Press Association, and ultimately forty-three "enthusiastic" supporters became charter members of the chapter. Because only journalists were eligible for membership in the Texas Press Association, Mohl saw clearly the need to include all women writers in a separate organization offering both fellowship of the like-minded and opportunities for professional development. Furthermore, as Mrs. M. R. Walton reveals in her fifteenth-anniversary history of the association, women members of the Texas Press Association were relegated to the balcony as spectators rather than participants in the social events enjoyed by male members. Aurelia Mohl was determined to bring the women down from the balcony. It was time for women writers to receive the recognition they deserved.

The Texas Woman's Press Association sponsored meetings in which the members mapped out plans for entry into mainstream literary life. Nevertheless, descent from the balcony did not occur suddenly. Significantly, in that same hotel on that same spring day, Aurelia Mohl attended another meeting, in which she helped found the Texas Equal Rights Association. For the next three decades, Texas women spent most of their creative energies in support of suffrage. Today, a century after she championed the unification of women writers, Aurelia Mohl would be gratified to see the status of Texas women writers.

THE PIONEERS, 1830–1920

Despite Bride Taylor's sometimes pessimistic view of their situation, members of the association already had a developing literary tradition uniquely their own. In 1833, Stephen F. Austin's cousin, Mary Austin Holley, published a collection of letters containing her observations of Texas life. This work Holley titled *Texas. Observations Historical, Geographical, and Descriptive. In a Series of Letters, Written during a Visit to Austin's Colony, with a view to a permanent Settlement in that country, in the Autumn of 1831.* Holley gained even more attention nationally with her second book, *Texas,* a guide for those contemplating settlement in Texas. Published in July, 1836, this volume also includes one of the earliest accounts of the Texas Revolution. According to historian Marilyn McAdams Sibley, in her introduction to the 1985 edition, the book drew "favorable notice" and became a readers' favorite because of its informal style.

Books were not yet a priority with most colonists, but readers outside Austin's colony found that Holley's narratives satisfied their curiosity. In 1854, New York traveler Frederick Law Olmsted, hungry for reading material, was willing to pay an Austin druggist twice the eastern price to purchase a Putnam's Semi-Monthly Library edition of *Eagle Pass: or Life on the Border.* A best-seller of the time, the book was Jane Cazneau's 1852 account of her two-year stay on the Rio Grande, written under the pseudonym "Cora Montgomery." Olmsted seems pleased to have found a good book in Austin. In *A Journey through Texas or, a Saddle-Trip on the Southwestern Frontier* (1857) he complains that during his stopover there, he found "a very remarkable number of drinking and gambling shops, but not one book-store."

In 1855, despite the dearth of bookstores in Texas, Augusta J.

Evans, who had lived in Texas as a child, gained numerous readers with her conventionally sentimental novel of the Texas Revolution, *Inez: A Tale of the Alamo.* In 1888, Amelia Barr's novel *Remember the Alamo,* on the same subject but more realistic in its treatment of Spanish-Anglo relationships, became standard in home libraries. Some years later, Barr, who lived in Austin between 1856 and 1866, published her autobiography, *All the Days of My Life: An Autobiography. The Red Leaves of a Human Heart* (1913), which provided a detailed record of Austin social life during that time and of the city's upheaval during the Civil War.

Other autobiographical narratives of women who settled early in Texas convey the authors' sense of history—their sure knowledge that their experiences are unique and illuminating. Several of these narratives, which would furnish rich materials for future historical fiction, unveil as well the captivating personalities of the writers themselves. A number of strong-minded, independent women writers captured the attention of readers in mid-nineteenth century Texas. Among the most interesting of these women was Jane McManus Storms Cazneau. Jane Storms, the recently divorced mother of a son, came to Texas with a brother in 1832 as a land speculator but returned to Manhattan after her family's efforts to establish a colony of German settlers on the Texas coast failed. During the Mexican War, however, she served as correspondent to the *New York Sun* and became an avid lobbyist for Mexican and Cuban annexation. In the late 1840s she married Matagorda merchant and politician William Cazneau, and in 1850 she moved to the Rio Grande Valley. Her life there is recorded in *Eagle Pass,* the book Olmsted had purchased so dearly. She died in 1878 in a shipwreck on her way to Jamaica, after spending her last years lobbying for annexation of several Caribbean Islands to the United States.

In 1851, soon after Jane Cazneau moved to Eagle Pass, Teresa Viele followed her army lieutenant to Ringgold Barracks on the Rio Grande, where she took careful note of both army and native life. Her account, in *"Following the Drum": a Glimpse of Fontier Life* (1858), reflects frontier life in detail, but the story of the writer herself makes the best tale. In the early 1870s, Viele divorced and took her eight-year-old son to France. Later she returned to the United States, but only to kidnap her young daughter and return to Paris. There, according to Sandra L. Myres in her foreword to the 1984 edition of Viele's book, she became known for her literary salon, wrote a pamphlet on "Islam and Islamism," and returned to Chicago to lecture on "Moslemism" during the 1893 Columbian Exposition. Her son, Francis Griffin-Viele, became a prominent writer associated with the French symbolist school.

According to C. Harvey Gardiner, who wrote the introduction to the 1966 abridged edition of Fanny Chambers Gooch's *Face to Face with the Mexicans: the Domestic Life, Educational, Social, and Business Ways, Statesmanship and Literature* (1887), when William Dean Howells reviewed the book in *Harper's*, he deemed the book to have a "value that only a quick, intelligent, sympathetic woman could give her study of a foreign people's life." Her biographers portray her as a lively organizer of Austin social life, who married three times and who actively promoted more amicable Texas-Mexican relations during the presidency of Porfirio Diaz. Diaz is said to have greatly approved of Gooch's sensitive account of Mexican life and society as she experienced it while living in Mexico between 1880 and 1887. C. W. Raines, in his 1896 *Bibliography of Texas,* calls the book "an agreeable pen picture of the domestic life of the Mexicans," and adds, "The tendency of the book is to weaken, if not destroy, the prejudice which exists on either bank of the Rio Grande." That same year, Elizabeth Brooks included Gooch's biography in *Prominent Women of Texas* and reported that the book won for Gooch such avid attention abroad that she was made a fellow of the Royal Society of Science, Letters, and Art in London. In Texas, however, she and her book seem to have been ignored. Gardiner says Gooch was aggressive in obtaining endorsements for her book from prominent politicians in Washington, where she lived when her work was published. She received no reply, however, from Texas governor Lawrence S. Ross when she wrote urging him to invite the Mexican cadets of Chapultepec to participate in a drill competition as a way of promoting better Texas-Mexican relationships.

As with these three remarkable women, almost every writer's personality proves as fascinating as her work in this period. Adah Isaacs Menken, a Jewish poet, dancer, and actress, who came to Texas as a fifteen-year-old circus tightrope performer, returned a few years later to live in Liberty, where she wrote articles for the *Liberty Gazette* and was named an assistant editor. She left Texas after marrying Isaac Menken, an orchestra conductor, in Galveston, and achieved dubious fame the world over, consorting with the likes of the elder Alexandre Dumas in Paris and Mark Twain's circle in Virginia City. She was married for a time to Robert Henry Newell, a journalist known for his satirical articles written under the name Orpheus C. Kerr. As a writer, Menken is best-known for her poetry collection *Infelicia* (1868). Algernon Swinburne, rumored once to have had an affair with Menken, owned a copy of her poetry in which he wrote, "Lo, this is she that was the World's delight."

Another strong-minded woman writer, Elise Waerenskjold, who had broken tradition as editor of a Norwegian periodical, divorced her seaman husband and immigrated to America in 1847. She settled in Van Zandt County, where she raised her three sons alone after her second husband was murdered. Her letters detailing her life and supporting the abolition of slavery were the glue that held Texas Norwegian communities together and encouraged immigration of other Norwegians. Modern readers can learn much about pioneer farm life from her letters written between 1851 and 1895 and collected in *The Lady with the Pen* (1961) by the Norwegian-American Historical Association.

At the turn of the century, several Tejana writers gained admiration in towns along the Texas border. A Laredo resident, Jovita Idar, proved her courage the day she stood in the door and faced down Texas Rangers who had come to close down the newspaper, *El Progreso,* which she served as society editor. Objecting to an editorial against the arrival of U.S. troops on the border, the Rangers arrested the workers and destroyed the building the next day. Idar, who was an accomplished teacher and journalist, joined her brother to write and publish the family newspaper, *La Cronica,* after her father's death. She was best known for organizing women educators into La Liga Femenil Mexicanista, the first Mexican feminist organization, in 1911.

Not until the closing decades of the nineteenth century did a Texas woman novelist gain national critical attention. Augusta Evans and Amelia Barr had limited experience in Texas. Each is remembered for only one novel with a Texas setting. Mollie E. Moore Davis, by contrast, grew up on the San Marcos River near Austin in the 1850s. Her novels, *Under the Man-Fig* (1895) and *The Wire Cutters* (1899), are based on knowledge of Texas life acquired through observation and experience. After the writer's marriage to Galveston businessman Thomas E. Davis, she moved with him to New Orleans in 1879, where he became an associate editor of the *New Orleans Times*. Mollie, who suffered from lung problems, found New Orleans summers unhealthy and spent many of them with her brother Tom's family near Comanche, on the western edge of central Texas. There she collected material she would use in *The Wire Cutters*, which reflects the human suffering brought on by West Texas water-rights disputes.

Literary historians of the West have yet to notice Davis's believable exploration of the complex motives behind the infamous Fence Cutting Wars that erupted in many Central Texas counties during the 1880s. Even though her novel realistically depicts the lives of pioneer women and would-be cattlemen during this turbulent era, she is seldom mentioned except as a chronicler of "the plantation tradition," as J. Frank Dobie classified her. Many consider Owen Wister's *The Virginian: a Horseman of the Plains* (1902) the first western and Andy Adams's *Log of a Cowboy: A Narrative of the Old Trail Days* (1903) the first fiction to portray cowboy and range life realistically. Nevertheless, despite the author's adherence to sentimental plot conventions and occasional plantation settings, *The Wire Cutters* is the first western novel to treat seriously the life of the would-be Texas cowman.

THE INNOVATORS, 1920–60

The novels of Mollie E. Moore Davis won status for her as an important Southern writer before 1900, but women writers as significant contributors to Texas literature did not gain much notice until the 1920s, when several women Texans received national attention for fiction couched in social commentary.

Ruth Cross's novel, *The Golden Cocoon* (1924), which went through five printings in the first year after publication, reflects Cross's knowledge of the sterile lives of North Texas tenant farmers trying to survive on hardscrabble cotton farms. The young woman protagonist in Cross's novel declares, "I hate men, I hate marrying, I hate children." Her determination drives her actions, and finally she escapes the hard, unrewarding farm work that her mother accepts as her lot in life.

A year later, Dorothy Scarborough created an uproar in West Texas with her powerful novel *The Wind*. Published anonymously for publicity value, the novel depicted the Rolling Plains around Sweetwater as hostile to any but the toughest of women. Wind, heat, and unending space are the conquering enemies in this narrative. Because the account is forceful and brutal, readers assumed the author was a man.

Scarborough, who lived in West Texas as a young child, described the unfriendly climate as her mother remembered it. Winifred Sanford's stories, by contrast, originated in her own keen observations as a curious newcomer to Wichita Falls during the 1920s when an oil boom energized that North Texas town. One of the most exemplary women writers of the twenties, Sanford, a Phi Beta Kappa graduate of the University of Michigan, became the first southwestern author to examine in fiction the alternate joy and despair that the discovery of oil could precipitate in human lives. Sanford's work appealed to H. L. Mencken, who published nine of her stories in *The American Mercury.*

During this decade, too, Texas's most respected author, Katherine Anne Porter, began her career as short-story writer. Before 1930, Porter had published "María Concepción," "He," and "The Jilting of Granny Weatherall." Early in life, Porter rejected traditional roles of women as too confining and began to explore women's interior lives in short fiction. In 1939 the Texas Institute of Letters, strongly influenced by Dobie, chose his *Apache Gold and Yaqui Silver* instead of Porter's *Pale Horse, Pale Rider* as the best Texas book of the year. According to TIL historian William H. Vann, "The judges felt that because of Dobie's residence in Texas and the indigenous nature of his material, the award should go to him." Dobie, the self-appointed leader of Texas literati, remained indigenous; Porter went on to national acclaim.

Several other fiction writers merited critical attention as "new women" whose work looked squarely at life in Texas during this era. Anne Austin's novel, *Jackson Street,* seems to have gained short-lived attention in 1927, when publishers released *The Younger Generation,* by Austin's precocious daughter, Elizabeth Benson, at the same time. Benson was only thirteen and already a student at Barnard College. In her novel, Austin develops the same theme as Ruth Cross in *The Golden Cocoon* except her protagonist works her way out of the slums on the wrong side of the tracks. Reared in Waco, Austin based this first novel on her own experiences.

Another novel gained short-lived notice in this decade. Miriam

"Ma" Ferguson had served her first term in 1925–26 as puppet governor when journalist Clare Ogden Davis's *The Woman of It* (1929) was published. Set in the early twenties, Davis's novel explores the life of a competent woman governor of Texas who has been elected by women exercising their power as recently franchised voters.

At the turn of the decade, short-story writer and Democratic political campaigner Evelyn Miller Pierce caught critics' attention with *Hilltop* (1931), her novel about a young woman social climber in an early Texas town. Margaret Bell Houston, Sam Houston's granddaughter, wrote steadily during this era, producing romantic novels and gaining considerable attention for her poetry. Her novel *Hurdy-Gurdy* (1932), in which a young woman moves to New York to escape narrow Texas town life, echoes Cross's and Austin's themes.

By the end of the decade of the 1930s, women's fiction in Texas had already turned away from the Texas Mystique that Dobie and his followers continued to celebrate. Like Winifred Sanford, Karle Wilson Baker, already well-known for her poetry, perceived the impact of oil booms on Texas communities as a likely subject for fiction. Like Sanford, Baker gained firsthand knowledge of the drilling process by going on the well site. Her novel *Family Style* (1937) explores how East Texas families coped with the upheaval an oil boom brings to a region. In 1942, Baker's *Star of the Wilderness: A Novel*, set during the Texas Revolution, was a Book of the Month Club selection.

Early in the 1940s, two historical novels by Laura Krey were best-sellers. Krey, who grew up on a Brazos River cotton farm, once a plantation, located the action of *And Tell of Time* (1938) on a plantation during Reconstruction days in Texas. *On the Long Tide* (1940) recaptures the days of the Texas Revolution in the adventures of Jeffrey Fentress, a cousin of Thomas Jefferson who comes to Texas in time to participate in all the excitement. Other novels of note during this period include *Quincie Bolliver* (1941) by Mary King and *Mr. George's Joint* (1941) by Elizabeth Wheaton. *Quincie Bolliver*, which won a Houghton Mifflin Fellowship, reflects the turbulent life of Texas oil boomtowns through the eyes of an adolescent girl. The life and times of African-Americans who gather daily in a Texas City beer joint during the Great Depression provide a focus for the narrative in Elizabeth Wheaton's novel.

Anne Pence Davis and Norma Patterson, popular fiction writers, published a number of novels in this period. In *The Customer Is Always Right* (1940), Davis wove her narrative through the seasonal activities of a small-city department store. Patterson, who set an example for women writers of the 1940s as a successful professional with stories appearing regularly in periodicals in the United States, Canada, and England, served as mentor for George Sessions Perry, who dedicated *My Granny Van: The Running Battle of Rockdale, Texas* to her. In 1930, Patterson's second novel, *The Gay Procession*, set in the early days of the century and culminating in the tragedies of World War I, was one the most popular of several romances she wrote during this decade.

Texas's colorful history offered several novelists ample material for fiction in the forties and fifties. Texas contemporary author and critic A. C. Greene's literary grandmother, Maude E. Cole, published *Wind Against Stone: A Texas Novel* (1941), which follows a Georgia-born protagonist through her difficult life as a pioneer in West Texas. Cleo Dawson, perceiving possibilities in the story of her family's pioneer life in the Rio Grande Valley, wrote *She Came to the Valley: A Novel of the Lower Rio Grande Valley, Mission, Texas* (1943), based on her mother's experiences. In 1979 the novel was filmed, starring Scott Glenn, Dean Stockwell, and Ronee Blakely.

In 1950, Loula Grace Erdman, who came to the Panhandle to teach English, published her popular novel, *The Edge of Time*, which captures the spirit and experience of women who came with their husbands to the Panhandle plains as homesteaders. Its focus on "sodbusters" instead of cowboys was a complete departure from the norm for Texas fiction.

In 1952, Elithe Hamilton Kirkland, journalist and radio script writer, developed further the theme Amelia Barr had explored in *Remember the Alamo*. Set in the days of the Texas Republic, *Divine Average* examines a family tragedy that results when a bigoted cattleman discovers his wife's racially mixed Mexican heritage. Kirkland's best-known novel, *Love Is a Wild Assault* (1959), is the loosely fictionalized story of Harriet Potter, whose handwritten memoir inspired Kirkland to immortalize the life of this real but legendary Texas woman.

Although late in the nineteenth century Mollie E. Moore Davis often smiled at the foibles of early Texas citizens in her novels and short fiction, women fiction writers in the early twentieth-century exhibit a sense of humor only occasionally. However, in his survey, *Southwest Humorists* (1969), Elton Miles says that, by the 1940s, Mary Lasswell had become an important southwest humorist. Lasswell, who grew up in Brownsville, is creator of three feisty, irreverent old women characters, Mrs. Rasmussen, Mrs. Feeley, and Miss Tinkham, who roam from California to New York in a series of four novels chronicling their adventures. Their saga begins in *Suds in Your Eye* (1942), which sold a phenomenal three hundred thousand copies, and concludes in *Tooner Schooner* (1953). Along the way they solve problems of troubled people they encounter, usually in some unconventional way. Miles says, "Like O. Henry, Mrs. Lasswell has created humor that is invariably sound and good-natured in its understanding of ordinary people." Lasswell's narrative of her tour of her native state, *I'll Take Texas* (1958), emphasizes the state's regional diversity in colorful anecdotes notable for their precise description. Lasswell relishes the story of how she autographed two battered copies of her novels at the isolated Study Butte store in Big Bend.

One other novelist demonstrated a remarkable sense of the comic in this era. In 1946, east Texan Jewel Gibson was praised for her novel *Joshua Beene and God*, which follows Joshua Beene through his last year of life as chief elder in a country church. A funny but gentle satire, the novel reveals much about the culture of East Texas during the first half of this century.

Still another writer among the creators of humorous fiction in this era is Alma Stone, a witty octogenarian who grew up in East Texas and now lives in New York. She has written four novels, each of which she says has "substantial Texas underpinnings." One novel, *The Harvard Tree* (1953), is set in Texas. Stone, whose sharp wit spices all her fiction, has published a number of short stories, including "The Ride," first published in *The Yale Review*. Set in East Texas, the story is also included in Suzanne Comer's collection of Texas short stories, *Common Bonds: Stories by and about Modern Texas Women* (1990).

During the shaping era for Texas writing, 1920–60, Texas women writers did not limit themselves to fiction. One astonishing nonfiction work that came out of this period was Gertrude Beasley's autobiographical account of her early life in the Abilene area. Published in 1925, the same year Scarborough's first edition of

The Wind came out anonymously, Beasley's *My First Thirty Years* was judged even more scandalous in its criticism of life in West Texas. Unusually frank for a writer of that time, Beasley recreated the bleak life she led growing up as a member of a trashy rural family in the early 1900s. Few copies of the book were sold, and novelist Larry McMurtry, who wrote the afterword to the 1989 Book Club of Texas edition of this graphic personal history, was unable to find Beasley family connections in the Abilene area. In his informed commentary, McMurtry cites H. L. Mencken's review in *American Mercury,* which declares that the book is "the profoundly serious and even indignant story of a none too intelligent woman."

As informative and astute as McMurtry's assessment of Beasley's work proves, his acknowledgement of two other women writers as worthy of a reader's attention is even more revealing. In his much-cited but curiously titled essay on the state of Texas literature, "Ever a Bridegroom: Reflections on the Failure of Texas Literature," published first in the *Texas Observer* (October 23, 1981), McMurtry gives little space to Texas women writers, mentioning Katherine Anne Porter in passing and praising only the poet Vassar Miller. He concludes his commentary on Beasley's autobiography with an admission: "Reading *The Wind* and *My First Thirty Years* now should be a mildly embarrassing corrective to critics (myself among them) who have acted as if even semi-serious Texas writing began with Dobie, whose first book didn't arrive until 1929, the year in which *The Wind* was made into a memorable silent film, starring Lillian Gish." With Beasley, McMurtry names Dorothy Scarborough and Sallie Reynolds Matthews as the "three lonely bluebonnets" representing "a modest South Plains flowering" in this era.

When Sallie Reynolds Matthews, author of *Interwoven* (1936), set out to record the history of the Reynolds and Matthews families, early-day ranchers in the Albany area, she had her large extended family in mind as its readers. In *Basic Texas Books* (1983), bibliophile John H. Jenkins, designated *Interwoven* "the best book on Texas ranch life from a woman's perspective." Earlier even Dobie acknowledged that "*Interwoven,* more than any other ranch chronicle that I know, reveals the family life of the old-time ranchers."

Sallie Reynolds Matthews has garnered much of the critical attention accorded women authors of prose nonfiction during this era. Anita Brenner, however, has the most fascinating background. Born to American-Jewish parents in Aguascalientes, Mexico, in 1905, she took classes from Dobie at the University of Texas, returned to Mexico to study anthropology and archaeology at the National University of Mexico, and, under the direction of Franz Boas, received a Ph.D. in anthropology at Columbia University. By 1930 she had won a Guggenheim Fellowship to study ancient American art in Mexico. A prolific writer, Brenner is best known for her work *Idols Behind Altars* (1929), her account of the superstitions and folkways that her family never quite understood during their Mexican residency.

Brenner's niece, Marie Brenner, refers to her aunt's book in a *New Yorker* essay (September 13, 1993) to illustrate that the dilemmas of modern Texas-Mexican border relationships are as complicated as those her aunt described sixty years earlier. Brenner's essay, which explores causes behind the murder of her eighteen-year-old cousin in Brownsville, describes her family's Mexican connections as powerful and deeply rooted in central Mexico, where her ancestors settled in the nineteenth century. Her aunt is one of the few women writers J. Frank Dobie praised.

Dobie, whose critical opinions mattered to Texas writers during the three decades beginning in the 1920s, created the impression that mainstream fiction during that time came from the pens of men writers. He established the Texas literary canon for many readers in 1929 with the publication of his *Guide to Life and Literature of the Southwest,* which appeared first as a bibliography for the English course of the same name that he taught at the University of Texas. Two years later, John William Rogers included a revised version of Dobie's guide in *Finding Literature on the Texas Plains.* By 1942, Dobie published the annotated bibliography in book form, denying in the introduction that the guide is more than "fragmentary, incomplete," and warning that it is "in no sense a bibliography." In 1928, a year before the first appearance of Dobie's guide, Professor Leonidas W. Payne, Jr., published *A Survey of Texas Literature.* Payne's survey is more literary history than criticism, and Payne never updated it, so teachers and readers of Southwestern literature turned to Dobie for guidance, ignoring his admitted selectivity and biases.

Dobie's bibliography includes but few women writers. Neither Ruth Cross nor Winifred Sanford is mentioned. Dobie's two-line appraisal of Dorothy Scarborough points out that *The Wind* "excited the wrath of chambers of commerce and other boosters in West

Texas—a tribute to its realism." And, for Dobie, Katherine Anne Porter worked on "small canvases" and "appeals only to cultivated tastes." Dobie devoted one short chapter of his guide to "Women Pioneers," but it seems clear that he, like many other male critics of his time, seldom read what women wrote.

Whether Dobie acknowledged their work or not, other women writers exhibited superior talent in their production of nonfiction during the 1920s and 1930s. Mary Ann Maverick, wife of early Texas politician Samuel Maverick, published her *Memoirs of Mary A. Maverick, Arranged by Mary A. Maverick and Her Son, Geo. Madison Maverick* in 1921. In *Basic Texas Books,* Jenkins cited it as the best source of information about the Council House Fight, the infamous and bloody confrontation in early-day San Antonio between Texans and Comanche Indians, which Maverick witnessed in 1840. In 1927, Mattie Austin Hatcher, a University of Texas archivist, published *The Opening of Texas to Foreign Settlement,* the "seminal study of the beginning of foreign immigration," according to Jenkins. Hatcher also collected, edited, and wrote the introduction to *Letters of an American Traveller: Mary Austin Holley, Her Life and Her Works, 1784–1846* (1933).

Jenkins included two other women authors of 1920s nonfiction in his bibliography. Basing her account on her pioneer father's experiences, Alice Jack Shipman recounted the early history of the Big Bend in *Taming the Big Bend: A History of the Extreme Western Portion of Texas from Fort Clark to El Paso* (1927). Annie Doom Pickrell's *Pioneer Women in Texas* (1929) is a compilation of seventy-seven biographies of prominent pioneers. Reprinted in 1991 by State House Press with an introduction by women's historian Ann Fears Crawford, this book, according to Jenkins, is "one of the best sources of authentic grass roots history of [Texas] social life." Dobie's succinct annotation with his citation of Pickrell's compilation reads, "Too much lady business but valuable." Dobie's infelicitous epithet notwithstanding, careful attention to this volume will furnish readers with details of early Texas daily life.

In the 1930s a Fort Worth schoolteacher, Julia Kathryn Garrett, wrote a well-researched account of the decline of Spanish power in Texas, *Green Flag Over Texas: A Story of the Last Years of Spain in Texas* (1939), and Lota Mae Spell, a musician who, after receiving her Ph.D., became director of the Latin American Library at the University of Texas, published *Music in Texas: A Survey of One Aspect of Cultural Progress* (1936), a history of Texas music, including Indian, Spanish mission, Mexican folk, and Mexican war music.

A gifted linguist, who spoke German, French, Italian, and Spanish, Spell was well-known at the time for her articles on music and history in major journals.

During this developmental period for Texas women writers, between 1930 and 1960, two librarians at the University of Texas made major contributions to translation and historical writing in the state. Fannie Ratchford, for years director of the Rare Books Collection, wrote the introduction to the first known novel about Texas, *L'Heroine du Texas* (1819), which Donald Joseph translated from the French for The Book Club of Texas in 1937. Ratchford wrote numerous essays and edited several books in her lifetime, including a compilation of the Brontes' early writings. Llerena Friend, first librarian of the Eugene C. Barker Texas History Center, is best known for the biography, *Sam Houston: The Great Designer* (1954), still considered to be one of the most scholarly accounts of Sam Houston's life. Friend reveals considerable talent as a memoirist in her personal essay in the Encino Press's compilation *Growing Up in Texas: Recollections of Childhood* (1972).

In 1940, Dora Neill Raymond, an El Paso native who became a history professor, was the first woman to win the Texas Institute of Letters award for best book. Her biography, *Captain Lee Hall of Texas* (1940), narrates the life story of Texas Ranger Hall, who furnished O. Henry with much of his Texas material while the writer recovered from tuberculosis at Hall's ranch.

One writer beloved in the Panhandle but less well-known in the literary centers of Texas, was late-bloomer Laura V. Hamner, a former country schoolteacher who began writing seriously when she was Potter County superintendent of schools. Before her death in 1968 at age ninety-two, Hamner had written five books, published poetry and essays on pioneer life, written and broadcast a weekly advice column for teens, and founded the Panhandle Pen Women.

Now praised for her early gathering of oral history of the Panhandle, Hamner published two books based on her research. *Short Grass and Long Horns* (1943) records the region's ranch history in the 1870s and 1880s. In 1958 she compiled fifty sketches featured on her radio show, "Light 'n Hitch," which furnished the title for her book. A pioneer in grass-roots research into the folk culture and ranch life of the Panhandle, Hamner narrates the history of the region in the introductory chapter. In a dissertation study definitive in its exploration of Hamner's life and literary contributions, scholar Myra Dorris Hall says Hamner "would never have agreed with [Walter Prescott] Webb that this land overwhelmed women." Hamner frequently pointed out the "feeling of freedom" that living on the Texas plains gave her.

Another writer of note during this period was Julia Nott Waugh, journalist and freelance writer, whom Dobie praises for her monograph, *Castroville and Henry Castro* (1934). In 1955, Waugh published *The Silver Cradle: Las Posadas, Los Pastores, and Other Mexican Traditions,* a collection of religious folk practices that she gathered in the Mexican-American community in San Antonio. In *Southwest Review* (Spring, 1956), Charles Ramsdell comments that Waugh "shows sympathy and humor that never go sticky with sentimentality or sour with condescension."

Although they published nonfiction, two women writers of this period gained more attention with the plays they wrote. Jan I. Fortune, who published poetry as well as *Fugitive* (1934), the story of outlaws Clyde Barrow and Bonnie Parker, also wrote fifty-two Texas history plays, and broadcast over radio station WFAA in Dallas in the 1930s. Also publishing plays was novelist Mollie E. Moore Davis's niece, Mollie Moore Godbold. Several of her plays, including *The Flapper Grandmother* (1924) and *The Love Cure: A Comedy in One Act* (1926), were produced nationally and performed in both Canada and Jamaica.

Early in the 1920s, with the organization of the Poetry Society of Texas and numerous pen women clubs, including the long-lived Manuscript Club, in Wichita Falls, and the Panhandle Pen Women, women writers began to provide the support and encouragement that Aurelia Mohl envisioned when she inspired the organization of the Texas Woman's Press Association. In 1923 the *Dallas News* began running a weekly page of literary news and book reviews under the editorship of John H. McGinnis. As early as 1926, Goldie Capers Smith, Dallas poet and essayist, collected biographies of contemporary writers, composers, sculptors, and artists in *The Creative Arts in Texas: A Handbook of Biography* but included only brief profiles of writers.

By 1935, however, an independent scholar, Florence E. Barns, had compiled and published *Texas Writers of Today*, one of the most valuable sources of information for readers interested in the origins of the Texas literary tradition. Barns includes informative biographies and short excerpts from each writer's work, as well as bibliographic data. In her introduction, "The Growth of a Literature in Texas," Barns analyzes Texas writing in a brief history of literary activity in the state. She sensed the problems that writers attempting to portray the Texas experience realistically might have with the intrusion of dominant Texas myths: "The essence of Texas is romantic, and a realistic treatment of romanticism is subject to a paradoxical complex."

A Chicago native who held a Ph.D. from the University of Chicago, Barns had traveled widely, conducting research in major European libraries. The American Council of Learned Societies funded her research with grants in 1932 and 1933. An essayist and journalist as well, Barns spent a number of years in Texas, where she co-edited with Hilton Ross Greer a collection of Texas poetry, *New Voices of the Southwest* (1934). It is possible that Barns's exhaustive biographical study of Texas writers stimulated major writers in 1936 to consider a statewide organization of writers who had achieved some measure of fame. The Texas Institute of Letters was organized that year, but even though the original purpose of the organization was "the promotion and recognition of literature in Texas," Barns seems never to have been considered for membership.

In the same year that the Texas Institute of Letters was initiated, an opinionated, articulate Catholic nun, Sister Agatha (Mary Louise Sheehan) published *Texas Prose Writings: A Reader's Digest* (1936), a readable but idiosyncratic survey of major prose works. In the foreword to his *Survey of Texas Literature*, Payne says Sister Agatha's "judgments in this little book may not always be sound, but certainly they are honest and sincere, and it is this honest, sincere, nonpartisan kind of criticism that American local literature is sorely in need of, if we may judge by the examples too frequently met with in print." Certainly Sister Agatha's assessment of the mystique surrounding Dobie hits the mark. He is, "a leader in the indigenous type of literary art of Texas," she wrote, "leading a cult that is interested in [Texas] local color and in the rich lode of Texas folk-lore." Sister Agatha's literary history appeared in bookstores as Texas celebrated its Centennial with much pageantry.

At the 1935 annual meeting of Sigma Tau Delta, national honorary English fraternity, in Georgetown, several members suggested that they invite major Texas writers to their 1936 meeting, to be held at Mary-Hardin Baylor College. There they would organize, for presentation at the Centennial Exposition in Dallas that fall, a program honoring these writers. Rebecca Smith, head of the English Department at Texas Christian University, encouraged other members to support the project. Several writers, including Walter Prescott Webb and Karle Wilson Baker, attended the 1936 meeting and joined in planning the Dallas meeting in November of that year. The Texas Institute of Letters became a reality that summer, and charter members held their first meeting at the Dallas Centennial Exposition.

Dobie immediately disliked the notion of organizing Texas writers, and William H. Vann, who wrote the thirty-year history of the Institute in 1966, describes Dobie's response to an invitation to attend the Dallas meeting as "brief—a swipe at one of the members of the committee and the statement that he did not expect to attend." Apparently, Dobie began to realize that the organization might succeed despite his boycott. That fall, Vann reports, Dobie wrote eight letters objecting to many of the plans and proposed members. One possible member he thought "a pedagogical nonentity"; another, "a mere compiler." Finally, after he had been convinced that the Institute would not be a gathering of "pink-tea poets or sentimental scribblers," he acknowledged that such an organization could "do some good for Texas culture."

In spite of his earlier grousing, Dobie addressed the TIL inaugural meeting. According to a report of the meeting in the *Dallas Morning News* (November 10, 1936), he took "a sharp dig at the superficial writing that was produced by followers of the H. L. Mencken school." Among the seventeen writers who attended the meeting was Winifred Sanford, whose short stories had appeared regularly in Mencken's *The American Mercury*.

Among other women who attended that first meeting of the organization were Rebecca Smith, Karle Wilson Baker, Lexie Dean Robertson, Olive McClintock Johnson, and Jan Fortune. Karle Wilson Baker served as president in 1938. And women dominated the "outstanding" program that year: Laura Krey and Helen Topping Miller participated in the fiction workshop, Grace Noll Crowell read for the poetry group, Mabel Major chaired the folklore session, and that evening, Laura Krey gave the major address to an overflow crowd in the Cokesbury Auditorium. In spite of Dobie's condescension, Texas women obviously were holding their own.

Poet and novelist Karle Wilson Baker was honored as one of the first three Fellows of the Institute. In 1941, Rebecca Smith as president hosted the meeting at TCU. The poet Lexie Dean Robertson presided in 1945. For the next fifteen years, women writers were active as judges and on planning committees, but the presidency of the organization went to men. Nevertheless, Rebecca Smith Lee, then married and living in Kentucky, was the keynote speaker for the TIL twentieth-anniversary meeting, in Dallas in 1956.

Within three years TIL began to reward writers for superior work. At the same time, writers' groups being established across the state offered women writers workshops and encouragement. The Manuscript Club of Wichita Falls could boast that among its members were short-story writer Winfred Sanford, novelist Anne Pence Davis, and poets Fay Yauger and Fania Kruger. According to Betty Wiesepape, whose essay chronicling the history of the group appears in the *Southwestern Historical Quarterly* (April, 1994), members of the Manuscript Club, many of whom published regularly, shared editors' advice and marketing news generously. Wiesepape also points out that former members of the organization with whom she corresponded "stressed the informality of meetings, the intelligence of the participants, and the excellence of criticism."

With such strong support from regional groups, it was inevitable that regional chauvinism would come under fire during the reign of J. Frank Dobie and the heyday of the Texas Folklore Society in the 1930s and 1940s. In 1924 the *Texas Review,* founded by Stark Young in 1915 at the University of Texas, moved to Southern Methodist University to become the *Southwest Review.* The new editor-in-chief, Jay B. Hubbell, believed that the journal should serve the "new Southwest." In his discussion of purposes and policies, the editor makes clear that he has little use for any further romanticizing of Texas's colorful past. Nevertheless, although the journal will be "national in its outlook . . . it will especially encourage those who write on Western themes, for it is a magazine for the Southwest."

Hubbell then chose Dobie, already developing his talents as a self-trained folklorist and dedicated regionalist, to serve as one of twelve members of the advisory board. Other board members who promoted writers in Texas included Hilton Ross Greer, who had just published an anthology of Texas poetry, and in 1928 and 1930 edited anthologies he called *Best Short Stories of the Southwest*. Thus began what a later editor, Margaret Hartley, describes in her introduction to an anthology of essays from the journal as "the problem of regionalism." Regionalism presented "one of the most difficult questions of choice" for the editorial staff through the years.

Because of this renewed interest in the culture and lore of place, editors and critics perceived a need to distinguish between provincialism and regionalism in fiction reflecting a writer's knowledge of place. In 1930, Carey McWilliams published a chapbook defining what he and other scholars then called "the New Regionalism." In his measured examination of this forceful declaration of pride in origins and place—particularly in the works of Texas, Oklahoma, and New Mexico writers—McWilliams foresees the perspective from which critics can recover and reconsider the remarkable literary heritage of Texas. In *The New Regionalism in American Literature*, he advises:

> To see the issues involved in contemporary movements, one must dissociate the ideas supplied by partisan critics and historians to give coherence and direction to the formless stuff of movements, from the real problems, which are those of motivation.

Recognizing the diversity of subject matter in Texas experience and the importance of motivation to both character development and theme, women writing fiction and nonfiction were innovators from the 1920s through the 1950s.

THE PROFESSIONALS, 1960–95

By 1960, many women writing in Texas came to the full realization of the richness of their materials, drawing on the sources that Katherine Anne Porter describes in "Three Statements about Writing": "All my past is 'usable,' in the sense that my material consists of memory, legend, personal experience, and acquired knowledge." Beginning to consider writing as a profession and unconcerned with propagating Texas myths, women writing in Texas perceived that what they shaped from their personal experiences in the state could have universal appeal.

Novelist Shelby Hearon, who has set eight of her thirteen novels in Texas, admits in her introduction to the 1983 edition of her first novel, *Armadillo in the Grass* (1968), that she learned one of the early reviews by heart. Her elation came from knowing, after five years of writing and rewriting and submitting her manuscript "over the transom," that "they, up there, had *understood*. That it would be all right: you could sit down in Texas and try to figure it out, and send your message off, and they would get it." "They" were the literary arbiters and editors in New York.

As early as the 1920s, Texas women writers sent their messages off to eastern publishers and had the pleasure of discovering that "they, up there" got it. They proved themselves persistent, and although less than a dozen writers each decade until the 1960s distinguished themselves by publishing nationally, several, such as Ruth Cross, Winifred Sanford, and Dorothy Scarborough, gained more than regional attention for their courageous debunking of the Texas Mystique. They saw the isolation and drudgery associated with ranch life, the sleaziness overshadowing the development of the oil industry, and the bigotry underlying race relations in the state. Women writers' stories illuminated life as it really was in a state that still revered the bold and brassy "good ol' boy."

By the 1960s, Texas women were developing a literary tradition based on recognition of the almost unlimited fictional possibilities inherent in the state's diversity of regions and cultures. Several writers have focused on the complexities of life in Texas in the 1960s. Miriam Merritt, reared on a ranch near Robstown, captures that experience in *By Lions, Gladly Eaten* (1965). Merritt examines the nature of South Texas prejudices when a rancher hedges in defending his Mexican ranch hand wrongly accused of causing a fatal car wreck. The author understands the intricacies of human interaction in a small town where ethical decisions are influenced by townsmen's background and bigotry. The rancher John Horne remembers his father's describing the oldtimers who came before them: "Those were men! Wouldn't *be* no state of Texas if it hadn't been for them. They had to believe they were extraordinary. They had to tell each other they were bigger and stronger and braver and more righteous than anybody else or look at their own puniness set out in a country so wild and big and dangerous they'd want to hightail it back to safety." Merritt, it seems, understands clearly the motivation of those men who became the Texas heroes to whom these modern citizens turn for example. The author, who studied at Stanford on a Creative Writing Fellowship, received the 1965 Theta Sigma Phi Award for Fiction for this book.

Sherry Kafka, who has written two children's books and who, with psychologist Robert Coles, edited a collection of writings by migrant children, published her only novel, *Hannah Jackson*, in 1966. As in Merritt's novel, the setting of Kafka's narrative is a small Texas ranching town. Rancher Terrell Jackson's strong-willed second wife creates the tensions. Although her son, Mark, is drawn to the life his rancher father lives, Hannah battles her husband for Mark's soul, willing that he become the preacher she had promised God he would be. Again the relationship of rancher and Mexican worker affects the novel's events. Texas Writers Roundup, sponsored by Theta Sigma Phi, and Friends of American Writers both presented awards to Kafka for this novel.

A third notable novel of the 1960s is Georgia McKinley's *Follow the Running Grass* (1969), which won for its author the Houghton Mifflin Literary Fellowship. Set in Dallas in the mid-1960s, the narrative traces the efforts of a civil-rights activist home from New York who tries to spring his ailing mother from the nursing home she has been committed to for life by his rich uncle, who controls the family fortune. What he learns in his futile quest is that this family, still proud of its frontier heritage, will never yield to a disaffected member with newfangled ideas. Perhaps the most enlightening undercurrent in this narrative is McKinley's examination of the relationship between the aged, invalid mother, who is a racist, and the black woman who cares for her. Three decades before this novel appeared, Katherine Anne Porter foresaw the implications of such a connection when she describes the longtime friendship of the grandmother, Sophia Jane, and her former slave, Aunt Nannie, who becomes her companion in "The Old Order."

In the 1960s, three major Texas women writers, Jane Gilmore Rushing, Carolyn Osborn, and Shelby Hearon, began publishing works that both reflect and illuminate the experiences of women in Texas. These women have distinguished themselves by publishing extensively for three decades. Rushing, who grew up on the Rolling Plains, the harsh setting of Scarborough's *The Wind,* began her career in 1964 with the publication of *Walnut Grove,* which narrates pioneer life on the plains from the point of view of a sensitive boy. In five subsequent novels, however, Rushing introduces women protagonists whose stories reflect the history of this region from homesteading days to modern farm life.

Carolyn Osborn, best-known for her entertaining and skillfully crafted short stories, initiated her career in the early 1960s when she began publishing in major literary journals. Osborn's strength as a writer lies in her ability to share diverse experiences, often set in Texas. Most often she writes perceptively about the modern-day cowboys, post-hippie life in Austin, or eccentric old men and women who have lived interesting lives.

Shelby Hearon, whose fiction is strong in its portrayal of place and character, traces the many changes occurring in women's lives since the sixties. Beginning with *Armadillo in the Grass* (1968), the story of a restless wife and mother who finds fulfillment in developing her creative talents, Hearon explores divorce, second marriages, career choice, widowhood, and other changes affecting women's lives in the last quarter of the twentieth century.

Influential among Texas women writers since the 1970s is novelist and short-story writer Beverly Lowry. Not until 1981 did Lowry's fiction reflect her knowledge of Texas life. Her 1994 novel, *The Track of Real Desires* (1994), probes the dark side of small-town Mississippi life. Along with Rushing, Hearon, and Osborn, Lowry has set the norm for contemporary Texas women writers: steady productivity and continuous national recognition.

In the decade of the 1950s, novels exemplified the best of Texas women's writings, the Texas Institute of Letters flourished, and women writers began to receive occasional recognition at awards time. For two decades after Dora Neill Raymond won the Institute's 1940 prize for the best Texas book, women authors were cited only for children's books and collections of poetry. Outstanding children's writers during this period included Elizabeth Baker, Carol Hoff (whose *Johnny Texas* [1950] remains in print), Siddie Joe Johnson, Charlotte Baker Montgomery, Irmengarde Eberle, and Camilla Campbell. Women poets receiving awards were Vaida Montgomery, Frances Alexander, Mary Poole, Eloise Roach (for her translation of Nobel Prize winner Juan Ramon Jimenez's *Platero and I* [1957]), and Vassar Miller (twice during this period). Then Frances S. Mossiker received the best book award in 1961 for *The Queen's Necklace* and in 1964 for *Napoleon and Josephine,* both studies of French history. In 1962, Rebecca Smith Lee was honored with the award for her *Mary Austin Holley: A Biography.*

The 1963 award went to *Washington Wife: Journal of Ellen Maury Slayden from 1897–1919,* coedited by Terrell Maverick Webb and Walter Prescott Webb. This was the last book Dobie's historian friend Walter Prescott Webb would be involved with before his untimely death in a car accident in March, 1963. He had married Terrell Maverick, widow of Congressman Maury Maverick, in 1961 and had found among the Maury Maverick papers (which Terrell planned to give to the University of Texas) the journal Terrell's aunt wrote as a congressman's wife at the turn of the century. Both Walter Webb, who provides the historical background, and Terrell Webb, who shares her personal connections with the journal's author, introduce the book, and both autographed it at signing parties. Walter Webb's biographical sketch of Ellen Slayden reveals her to be a spunky rebel. Webb, however, could not resist the adjective "feminine" when describing Ellen's "war" against Woodrow Wilson's cabinet members' wives, who had declared they would not return social calls of wives of representatives. Hers is also "feminine realism" when she describes Washington politics, says Webb. Ellen Slayden, however, is more feminist than "feminine" in her rapier-sharp criticisms of Washington society, including the incumbent president. A quick-witted observer and professional writer, she not only kept this journal but also contributed to *Century,* wrote for New York papers, and was the first society editor of the *San Antonio Express.* Her recognition as a gifted Texas woman writer came posthumously but deservedly.

Only once during the sixties did a woman writer receive the Texas Institute of Letters best-book award for fiction. In 1962 the Institute belatedly honored Katherine Anne Porter for *Ship of Fools.* The year before, Larry McMurtry had insulted a prominent Texas woman editor when he accepted his best-fiction award for *Horseman, Pass By.* The editor had praised the literary excellence of the novel but criticized what she felt was the author's gratuitous inclusion of obscenities. McMurtry declared that Texas literature suffered from the domination of "old lady reviewers in crinolines." It seems fair to surmise that Dobie's disdain for "pink tea poets" and McMurtry's aversion to "old lady reviewers" reflect stereotypical images of this era, which may have clouded objective assessment of what Texas women were producing as writers.

In 1973, Shelby Hearon shared the fiction award as a co-winner for *The Second Dune,* and in 1978 she received the honor for *A Prince of a Fellow.* In the eighties, Laura Furman, Beverly Lowry, and Rosalind Wright received awards for their fiction. In this decade, too, Shelby Hearon, Beverly Lowry, Kaye Northcott, and Laura Furman led the Institute as presidents.

Perhaps the most beneficial support the Texas Institute of Letters has given women writers is the Dobie-Paisano Fellowship, established after Dobie's death in 1964. The University of Texas and TIL purchased Dobie's ranch, where Dobie-Paisano Fellows live for six months and are provided living expenses. Among the women Fellows are novelists Kathryn Marshall, Laura Furman, and Sarah Glasscock. Poets Harryette Mullen, Sandra Lynn, Rosemary Catacalos, and Sheryl St. Germain and short-story writers Pat Ellis Taylor, Lisa Fahrenthold, Catherine Agrella, and Sandra Cisneros have also been recipients of the Fellowship.

Accelerated publication of Texas women's fiction in the last two decades suggests that Texas women can claim a literary tradition approaching maturity. Although not often winners of coveted national awards, many women writers have been published by major publishers, and several have seen their books reviewed in the *New York Times* and the *Washington Post.* Subjects vary widely, and the state's regional diversity provides a variety of settings—from Houston's urban tangle to the Panhandle's small-town isolation. Almost every novel seeks to provide insights into Texas experience socially or psychologically. Character development emphasizes individual eccentricities and complexities. In this era, writers began to experiment with narrative techniques. As early as 1978, Elizabeth Forsythe Hailey created a narrator whose letters reveal her personality and her story in *A Woman of Independent Means.*

The city of Houston furnishes rich material for fiction writers, and as early as 1979, the poet and biographer Louise Horton attempted to build credible fiction set both in Wales and Houston. In *Houston: A Novel,* Horton narrates the efforts of a suicidal widow to bow out of life. In his review, Robert Flynn admires Horton's many poetic passages but finds the narrative flawed by an uncertain point of view and a superficial sense of place. Laura Furman captures modern Houston graphically in her first novel, *The Shadow Line* (1982).

Depiction of the life and times of the old order in Houston, however, flows best from the pen of one of its own, who lived that life during the heyday of Houston's powerful. Perhaps one of the most daring of Texas women writers in the 1980s, June Arnold co-established the feminist press Daughters, Inc., in Vermont in 1972 and then came home to Houston in 1982 to write her mother's story. In the novel *Baby Houston* (1987), Baby narrates her life as a young widow who brings her children back to Houston to grow up among Houston's elite during the 1940s. Baby depends for support on her brother Oscar who, as the only son of the family, is in charge of the fortune his father made. He doles money out with a reluctant hand until Baby's daughters begin to question his authority.

Life among the River Oaks socialites from the 1930s through the 1950s—as Houston grows from easy-going town to sprawling city— is delineated as only a native could draw it. Oscar lives in the hotel he owns and feels at ease with both national and state politicians. His sister strives to raise her girls to be proper Houstonians. Beverly Lowry says the author's "intent was not to comment on her mother's time but recreate it. She meant to enter the realm of her own mother's dreams." Arnold died before publication of her story, but the novel was praised in a *New York Times Book Review* for its "evocation of a time and social milieu"—although the reviewer questioned the author's ambiguous portrayal of the mother-daughter relationship.

June Arnold and Laura Furman reflect a sure knowledge of Texas urban settings in their fiction. On the other hand, A. G. Mojtabai's stark portrayal of a remote Panhandle town she calls Durance in *Ordinary Time* (1989) provides a key to understanding both Texas small-town life and regional differences in this diverse state. As far from Houston as it is from California, the fictional Durance, near Amarillo, is a town where, reviewer Leila Levinson says in the *Texas Observer* (October 13, 1989), "Everyone . . . is wanting, needing, and waiting."

The novel poignantly develops the texture of life in a small town near extinction, tenuously held together by its religious life. Brother Shad, pastor of the Rooftree Pentecostal Church, warns his flock daily to get ready for Judgment Day, but near-blind Father Gilvary, serving his last priestly appointment, wants only to survive each day, depending on daily ritual to give his waning days meaning. At the Three Square Meals Restaurant, most often called the Cemetery Restaurant because of its location, the widow Henrietta, who has "the eye of discernment," fights loneliness with routine. She belongs to Brother

Shad's church but is more akin to Father Gilvary, as they both doggedly make the best of every day—ordinary time, Father Gilvary notes, so designated on the Roman Catholic calendar as the time between Pentecost and the First Sunday of Advent. No other novel about Texas examines small-town religious life with such clear-eyed understanding. Mojtabai, who teaches at the University of Tulsa, has made her permanent residence in Amarillo for the last decade. She gained Texans' attention first in 1986 when she published *Blessed Assurance: At Home with the Bomb in Amarillo, Texas,* a nonfiction study of Pantex, a nuclear bomb factory. Her most recent novel, *Called Out* (1994), examines how a shocking airliner crash in a rural Texas field affects local citizens who become involved in the aftermath.

Critics who prefer neat classifications of genres are sure to be frustrated when they attempt generalizations about the works of women writers in Texas during the last two decades. However, it is clear that West Texas spaces and history have inspired several recent fictional settings. Katie Breeze, a native of Texas, set her first novel, *Nekkid Cowboy* (1982), in West Texas, where an octogenarian remembers her life as wife of a lively cowboy whose pranks, destined to become community legend, lead finally to tragedy. Breeze, who possesses a keen ear for turn of speech, creates believable characters and events. The narrator's ability to view her hard life with humor as she reminisces captures the spirit of many pioneer women who survived hardships because they could see the comic in the tragic.

Margot Fraser, who lives in Odessa, sets her novel, *The Laying Out of Gussie Hoot* (1990), in a West Texas border town, and like Breeze she creates both a comedy and a mystery in her tale of the strong-willed Gussie, whose murder begins the tale. One reviewer praises Fraser's ability to create "caricatures without exaggerating the stereotype" in this tale exploring small-town quirkiness.

Sarah Glasscock, who grew up in Big Bend country, writes of modern life in the area's major town, Alpine. With great sensitivity to dark undercurrents that often pull at spirits living in one of the state's most isolated regions, Glasscock recreates the daily give-and-take at a small-town beauty shop in *Anna L.M.N.O.* (1988). Anna takes pride in her talents as a hairdresser and dreams of owning the shop. A product of an unsteady family, Anna is really looking for her own identity. Both comic and compassionate, original and realistically representative of a region not much explored in fiction, the novel drew praise nationally. A reviewer for the *Los Angeles Times* compares Glasscock to Pat Ellis Taylor, Barbara Kingsolver, and Clyde Edgerton, all of whom are producing "fine new southern writing."

Like Glasscock, novelist Olive Hershey admits to a "fascination with a region, namely Texas, specifically West Texas," and adds, "I am drawn to people who live on the edge." In Hershey's first novel, *Truck Dance* (1989), Wilma Hemshoff, like Anna L.M.N.O., is uncertain of her future. Wilma works in a truck-stop cafe in El Campo but longs to see the West. Weary of her inept, unfaithful husband and rebellious adolescent sons, she takes to the road driving an eighteen-wheeler, and there she discovers that life is as complicated as ever but offers considerably more variety in associates and events. Hershey received a Ph.D. from the University of Texas after completing the University of Houston Creative Writing Program. A poet as well as a novelist, she has taught fiction writing at Rice University.

In the last decade, several writers have won national media attention with first novels. Neither Karleen Koen, former editor of *Houston Home and Garden,* nor Linda Lay Shuler, a Brownwood resident, writes novels connected with Texas experience, but it is interesting to note their success. Both women received record-setting advances for their historical novels. Koen's *Through a Glass Darkly* (1986), is set in eighteenth-century England and France. Shuler's *She Who Remembers* (1988), the first in her Time Circle Series, fictionalizes the research she conducted into the history of the Anasazi Indians.

Although not so dramatically promoted as Koen and Shuler, Elizabeth Crook of Austin has received considerable praise from historians for her careful research into Sam Houston's mysterious first marriage to Eliza Allen, which ended after eleven weeks.

Before Crook published her fictionalized version of the relationship in *The Raven's Bride* (1991), her carefully documented scholarly essay, "Sam Houston and Eliza Allen: The Marriage and the Mystery," appeared in *Southwestern Historical Quarterly* (July, 1990). Crook, who took creative-writing courses with writer Max Apple at Rice University, says of her novel's protagonist, Eliza, "She is not a minor figure in history if you look at the ramifications of her actions but she is a minor figure in literature because no one has ever dealt with her in any realistic way." Texan and PBS host Bill Moyers, longtime friend of Crook's family, called this novel to editor Jackie Onassis's attention at Doubleday, which resulted in a first printing of fifteen thousand copies. Southern Methodist University Press published the novel in a paperback edition that includes the scholarly essay. Onassis edited Crook's second novel, *Promised Lands: A Novel of the Texas Rebellion* (1994), which, like earlier novels by Amelia Barr and Elithe Hamilton Kirkland, explores the conflicts for both Hispanic and Anglo families during the Texas Revolution. Crook, daughter of a former U.S. Ambassador to Australia, grew up in San Marcos and on her family's Hill Country ranch.

Since 1985, several other fiction writers' first novels have rated critics' attention. Novelist Kate Lehrer, who grew up in McKinney before she married TV personality and author Jim Lehrer, says Mabel Major, one of her professors at Texas Christian University, encouraged her writing. Kate Lehrer began her fiction-writing career with her novel *Best Intentions,* which was a bestseller in 1987. Set in Washington, the novel explores the intricacies of a struggle for power in the capital. Texas is the setting for her second novel, *When They Took Away the Man in the Moon* (1993), which brings a political consultant home from Washington to face both a family emergency and her past.

The most outstanding novel produced by a writer with Texas connections in 1986 won the TIL award that year for Best Book of Fiction. *Veracruz* (1986) by Rosalind Wright, who lived both in Abilene and Dallas during her twelve-year residency in Texas, examines the lives of Anglos living in Veracruz when the city was occupied by U.S. forces during the upheaval of the Mexican Revolution in 1912. Wright's first novel, *Rocking* (1975), is an episodic account of the tragicomic lives of residents in a Texas nursing home. Not often set in Texas nor connected with Texas experience, works by women nevertheless were winning TIL awards more often in the 1980s.

Robin McCorquodale, daughter of a Houston judge, began her career as a music teacher. In 1986 she published *Dansville,* the story of a young World War II widow trying to put her life back together in Texas ranch country near Victoria. In 1992, McCorquodale published a second novel, *Stella Landry,* the story of strong woman dealing with a scandalous past.

As early as 1979, Houston writer Guida Jackson chose an East Texas small-town social climber who discovers she has African-American ancestors as protagonist for her novel *Passing Through* (1979). Susan Clark Schofield returns to the Big Bend of Texas as the setting for *Refugio, They Named You Wrong* (1990). Schofield, who lived in Texas several years, tells the story of Pete, a footloose cowboy, dodging the law in the 1880s. One reviewer says Schofield's tale is "a marvelous study in character and in a time and place that are often misunderstood, usually misrepresented."

Although first novels during the last decade have introduced a number of promising women fiction writers with Texas connections, several Texas writers have won even wider recognition as award-winning and prolific storytellers. In 1984, Judy Alter won the TIL Best Book for Young People award for *Luke and the Van Zandt County War,* a historical novel. Since then, Alter has published the Maggie books, a series for young readers, and in 1988 her novel *Mattie* won a Spur Award from Western Writers of America. A meticulous researcher, Alter tells the story of the ambitious Mattie's challenges as a woman doctor on the frontier.

In a later novel, *A Ballad for Sallie* (1992), Alter recreates Hell's Half Acre, the bawdy district of Fort Worth where cowboys on the trail blew off steam and their pay during the late 1800s. Again a strong-willed young woman brings about change. Known widely as the director of Texas Christian University Press, Alter also continues to publish critically acclaimed novels. In 1994 she chose the life of Elizabeth Custer, faithful wife of General George Custer, as the basis for her novel *Libbie.*

"That wry Bird humor" is the way writer Thomas Zigal describes a major trait of Sarah Bird, one of Texas's liveliest contemporary writers. After serving an apprenticeship as a romance writer, Bird proved in 1986 that she could make readers grin at the absurdities in life while they winced at the painful truths her humor masks. In *Alamo House: Women without Men, Men without Brains* (1986), Bird reshapes her own experiences as a graduate student into a tragicomic running battle between residents of a graduate women's co-op house and a neighboring men's fraternity. The Sigma Upsilon Kappas (SUKS) came to the University of Texas to party and bedevil the grad students. The women are marvelously triumphant in the end, when the ex-governor father of a fraternity member shows up and, after asking, "Son, when are you going to break the factory seal on your brain?" puts the frat brothers—overindulged yahoos Bird has called them—to work.

In *The Boyfriend School,* selected by the New York Public Library as one of twenty-five Books to Remember for 1989, an Austin photojournalist covers the Luvboree, a romance writers' convention in Dallas, determined to make fun of its participants. Instead the narrator decides to write her own romance novel and finally recognizes her own life as grist for such fiction. The film version of this novel, *Don't Tell Her It's Me,* starred Shelley Long and Steve Guttenberg. Bird's latest fiction includes *The Mommy Club* (1991), the story of Trudy, a San Antonio surrogate mother-to-be who sorts out her life while she waits for the baby, and *Virgin of the Rodeo* (1993), the history of Sonja "Son Hozro," who sets out to find her rodeo trickroper father. What Sonja finds is an identity that needs no paternal validation as she travels from African-American rodeo to Native American rodeo. Bird's earlier unpublished research and photographs of alternative rodeos gave this novel authenticity.

Other contemporary novelists include Patricia Browning Griffith, an award-winning short-story writer and playwright who grew up in DeKalb, and Kathryn Marshall, who has written nonfiction in recent years. Griffith's latest novel, *The World Around Midnight* (1991), narrates the adventures of a big-city girl compelled to come back to small-town Texas and take over her late father's weekly newspaper. The novel was named an American Library Association Notable Book. Marshall, who was a Dobie-Paisano Fellow, has written two novels, *My Sister Gone* (1975) and *Desert Places* (1977), which realistically depict life in East Texas small towns and West Texas oil fields.

Although many male writers in the state wrote rebuttals to Larry McMurtry's *Texas Observer* essay criticizing Texas literature, Kathryn Marshall's lead essay in the April 9, 1982, issue of the journal is one of few replies by women writers. Laconically she explains her residency in New Hampshire at the time, "I write with less anxiety when a fat chunk of the map separates me from a letters [sic] that doesn't really believe women in general, and women writers in particular exist." Now more interested in producing nonfiction, Marshall published *In the Combat Zone: An Oral History of American Women in Vietnam, 1966–1975* in 1987.

Suzanne Morris, a Houston resident, has been most praised for her historical novel *Galveston* (1976), which received the Literary East Texas Award in 1979. Another historical novel, *Keeping Secrets* (1979) was followed by *Skychild* (1981), Morris's poignant exploration of a mother and her son, who may be autistic.

In 1982 a college professor, Janis Stout, won the Frank Wardlaw

Prize for her first novel, *A Family Likeness*. This is a tale of three generations of women, whose roots are put down in East Texas by the grandmother and where the granddaughter returns to find out the truths behind the myths of family history. An October 28, 1983, *Texas Observer* review concludes that the novel's "blend of penetrating sadness and humor compares favorably to the best of early McMurtry." The author, who grew up in Fort Worth, set her next novel, *Eighteen Holes* (1985), on the Gulf Coast. This novel recounts the adventures of four longtime friends who meet every fall to play golf. Stout's latest novel, *Home Truth* (1992), looks squarely at the problems of the dutiful mother who also assumes care of a handicapped sister.

Jeanne Williams, who has written historical Western novels for a number of years, no longer lives in the state but was resident long enough to establish Texas connections. In 1957 she won the TIL award for Best Texas Children's novel with *Tame the Wild Stallion*. The book appeared under the name J. R. Williams because, for years, fiction about the West sold better if the author seemed to be male. In 1985, TCU Press republished the hardcover edition, and the book has been published in England and translated into German and Dutch. Williams's juveniles have won awards, been serialized in New Zealand and published in Europe. Since the early 1960s, Williams has published a number of novels based on the history of the West, usually exploring the roles of women. In 1988, St. Martin's published *Lady of No Man's Land*, the story of an ambitious young Swedish immigrant who aims to homestead in the West and becomes one of the little-known "sewing women" of that era, visiting homesteads as a seamstress. *No Roof But Heaven* (1990) chronicles the adventures of a frontier schoolteacher who must deal with isolation and community leaders' feuds as she struggles to teach their children.

Another novel about a pioneer schoolteacher in West Texas gained national attention for author Jane Roberts Wood, who is a third-generation Texan. *The Train to Estelline* (1987) takes Lucy Richards, a very young East Texan, to teach her first school on a lonesome West Texas ranch. Her adventures proved so intriguing that the book remained on the Dallas-area bestseller list for seven months. A sequel, *A Place Called Sweet Shrub* (1990), was followed by *Dance A Little Longer* (1993), the final volume in the Lucy trilogy, which returns Lucy with her husband Josh to teach in West Texas. Wood has also published several short stories.

Fiction writer Marj Gurasich, who imagined the life of German girl just arrived in Texas, drew critical acclaim for *Letters to Oma: A Young Girl's Account of Her First Year in Texas 1847* (1989). The book proved so popular with readers that Gurasich wrote its sequel, *A House Divided* (1994), which narrates the trials of a German family living in Texas during the Civil War.

One of the most poignant fictionalized autobiographies published recently is Dulce Moore's *A Place in Mind* (1992). Moore's novel reflects the experiences of those who grew up in Texas during the Great Depression knowing what it was like to have a restless father and an enduring mother coping with the exigencies of an uncertain future.

As the twenty-first century approaches, Texas women writers have become the professionals that Bride Taylor foresaw when she compiled and published "The Women Writers of Texas" in 1893. Many have attracted national publishers, won awards for their books, enjoyed generous fellowships, and been inducted into national professional writers' organizations. Women writers with connections to the state have been particularly successful with publication of their short-fiction collections.

Among fiction writers recently reviewed extensively, Carol Dawson, who lives in Mt. Calm, has received considerable attention since publication of *Body of Knowledge* in 1994. Set in a small town in East Texas, this novel is a family saga as enormous as its 600-pound narrator. The novel is Dawson's second to be published, although she has been writing since 1979. Her first novel, *The Waking Spell* (1992), explores reasons for ghostly encounters in the old house in East Texas where their grandmother has lived most of her marriage, a life not without its own mysteries.

Sandra Scofield, now an Oregon resident, is a West Texas native who has won several awards for her fiction. She sets her fifth novel, *Opal on Dry Ground* (1994), in Lubbock. Opal, a grandmother in her fifties who has just remarried, finds herself entangled in her daughters' collapsing marriages. Scofield's first novel, *Gringa* (1989), nominated for the First Fiction Award sponsored by the American Academy of Arts and Letters, was selected by the National Endowment for the

Arts for a 1990 New American Writing Award. In the novel a Texas woman named Abilene Painter participates in student protests during the 1968 Summer Olympics in Mexico City. *Beyond Deserving* (1991), which chronicles a dissatisfied Texas woman's life in Oregon, won a 1992 American Book Award and was finalist for the 1991 National Book Award. In *Walking Dunes* (1992) a teenage boy grows up among the sand dunes of West Texas, learning along the way how to cope with the poverty in his family and in his own spirit. He longs for sustenance he may never find, and in the final scene he weeps "for all the sadness, the cruelty, the awful *resolution* of his friends' lives." Scofield's memory of small-town West Texas life in the 1950s recalls the truth for those who have experienced it.

A Corpus Christi native, Cindy Bonner, creates a memorable young woman in two novels that introduce a promising talent among young Texas women writers. In *Lily* (1992) a courageous, sometimes rash young woman narrates events that have led up to the final scene, when she buys a pistol to smuggle to the man she loves, an outlaw who barely escaped a shootout and hanging when vigilantes destroyed his gang. In an afterword, Bonner describes her research into the 1883 Christmas lynchings in McDade, near Bastrop, which inspired this novel. Her second novel, *Looking After Lily* (1994), develops Lily's relationship with Haywood, a brother of Lily's still-jailed husband, who has promised to take care of the pregnant Lily. Lily soon becomes for him more than a fifteen-year-old girl in need of care. Haywood falls in love with her. In *Review of Texas Books* (Summer, 1994), Ernestine Sewell Linck declares: "We have great expectations for their [Lily's and Haywood's] further adventures. Bonner's star continues to rise."

The career of Janis Arnold, a San Antonio writer and native Houstonian, escalated in the 1990s with the publication of two novels. She set the first, *Daughters of Memory* (1991), in a town near Houston. Experimenting successfully with dual points of view, Arnold gradually reveals the sources of conflict between two sisters. *Excuse Me for Asking* (1994) is set in Cypress Springs. Several of the characters narrate the story from a first-person point of view. Speakers are designated by their names as subheads, a technique William Faulkner and, later, the Native American writer Louise Erdrich have employed successfully. Handling this story-telling method skillfully, she tells the story of the entwined lives of two former Texas Tech University roommates.

When Janice Woods Windle of El Paso sat down with her mother in 1984 to sort through recipes saved by her Seguin family since the days of the Texas Revolution, she meant to make a scrapbook for her soon-to-be-married son. What she did instead, after hearing voluminous anecdotes from her family history, was write *True Women* (1993), declared by one of its many reviewers to be "a female *Lonesome Dove*." After almost a decade of intensive research into the history of her family, and of Texas, Windle transformed the stories of three courageous, feisty women ancestors into fiction that is both informative and entertaining. The narrative covers life in Texas from the time of the Runaway Scrape through the trials of the Civil War and Reconstruction in the state. Windle's title originates in a minority report against woman suffrage delivered at a 1868 Reconstruction Convention. The report concludes: "We are opposed to it [suffrage] . . . because we believe that the good sense of every true woman in the land teaches her that granting them the power to vote is a direct open insult to their sex by the implication that they are so unwomanly as to desire the privilege." Windle's independent, often bold female ancestors had already defined a very different "true woman."

Mystery writers have proliferated in Texas in the last decade. Of those who reflect the Texas experience in their mystery stories, Amarillo resident Doris Meredith, who has published a dozen novels under the name D. R. Meredith, and Mary Willis Walker, who sets her stories in Austin, are perhaps the best known. Meredith has received critical praise for her tales starring Sheriff Charles Matthews. In 1984 *The Sheriff and the Panhandle Murders* was designated a best novel by the American Library Association and received the Oppie Award for Best Mystery Novel that year. *The Sheriff and the Folsom Man Murders* (1987) was a selection of the Detective Book Club. John Lloyd Branson, an eccentric attorney, solves the cases in another series of novels by Meredith, who is married to a lawyer. Branson's latest adventures in Canadian and Amarillo are chronicled in *Murder by Sacrilege* (1993). Meredith also has written several historical novels set in the Panhandle.

Mystery writers covet the Edgar Awards presented annually by the Mystery Writers of America. Mary Willis Walker won the Edgar in 1994 for best first mystery novel. Walker sets *The Red Scream* in Austin, where she is an active member of the Heart of Texas Chapter of Sisters in Crime, a supportive writers' group (which accepts male writers for membership as well). Another Austin mystery writer, Susan Wittig Albert, has created China Bayles, an herbalist, to solve mysteries set in the Hill Country. Albert and her husband coauthor a series of Victorian mysteries under the pseudonym Robin Paige.

A former English teacher at Texas A&M University, Virginia Stem Owens, winner of the TIL nonfiction award in 1991 for *If You Do Love Old Men,* is author of *At Point Blank* (1992), a suspense novel set in a small Texas town and starring an eccentric old woman, Miss Mineola. In her latest work, *A Multitude of Sins* (1993), a young woman reporter teams up with an Episcopal priest to solve a mystery in a Texas town near a prison.

In the last two decades, nonfiction books by Texas women writers, many published by university presses, have equaled fiction production, in both number and quality. Although much of their work deals with Texas, many of these versatile writers, such as Paula Mitchell Marks, have expanded their vision to include wider western, southwestern, and universal topics and themes. Since 1970, several women writers have won the TIL Nonfiction Book award. The 1975 award went to Elizabeth A. H. John for *Storms Brewed in Other Men's Worlds: The Confrontation of Indians, Spanish, and French in the Southwest, 1540–1795.* Celia Morris, who was co-winner in 1984 for her biography of a nineteenth-century feminist, *Fanny Wright: Rebel in America,* has published a study of the campaigns of two women governors in *Storming the Statehouse: Running for Governor with Ann Richards and Dianne Feinstein* (1992). Morris's work, the product of meticulous scholarship and lucid prose, is both informative and readable.

Ernestine Sewell and Joyce Gibson Roach received the 1989 award for *Eats: A Folk History of Texas Foods.* Both Sewell and Roach have published critical articles and numerous reviews. Sewell's most recent book, *How the Cimmaron River Got Its Name and Other Stories About Coffee* (1995), is a collection of stories, lore, and recipes about coffee. In 1990, TCU Press published a new edition of Roach's 1977 history of cowgirls in Texas, *The Cowgirls.* As editor of *This Place of Memory: A Texas Perspective* (1992), Roach includes essays on place by a number of Texas writers.

Two biographers have won TIL awards for nonfiction. Emily Fourmy Cutrer won her award for *The Art of the Woman: The Life and Work of Elizabet Ney* (1988), published by the University of Nebraska Press. Betsy Colquitt calls this biography of an early eccentric Texas woman sculptor "a distinguished contribution to Nebraska's Distinguished Women of the West series." Earlier, in 1965, Lois Wood Burkhalter won a TIL award for her biography of an early Texan, *Gideon Lincecum, 1793–1874: A Biography*. Burkhalter also wrote *Marion Koogler McNay: A Biography* (1968). McNay's San Antonio mansion is now an art museum.

General interest in the lives of pioneer women in Texas increased in the eighties, particularly after Jo Ella Powell Exley's publication of *Texas Tears and Texas Sunshine: Voices of Frontier Women* in 1985. Now in its seventh printing, this collection of writings by pioneer women, carefully organized, edited, and introduced by Exley, includes excerpts from the diaries, memoirs, and biographies of sixteen nineteenth-century Texas women. The book has received a number of awards, including the Texas Historical Commission T. R. Fehrenbach Award, the Sons of the Republic of Texas Summerfield G. Roberts Award, and the English Speaking Union Books Across the Sea Program. Citations have been presented by the Colonial Dames of America and the San Antonio Conservation Society. An honors English teacher at Mayde Creek High School, Exley continues her research into the lives of pioneer Texas women. Inspired by Exley's collection, the University of Texas Press published *Ella Elgar Bird Dumont: An Autobiography of a West Texas Pioneer* (1988), a life history edited by Tommy J. Boley that had remained a long time in manuscript form.

Among the memoirs reflecting the valiant lives Texas ranch women have lived is Mamie Sypert Burns's *This I Can Leave You: A Woman's Days on the Pitchfork Ranch* (1986), which tells of her life as the wife of a ranch manager from 1942 to 1965. Other Texas ranch women's autobiographies include longtime Big Bend resident Hallie Stillwell's *I'll Gather My Geese* (1991) and Willie Newbury Lewis's *Willie, a Girl from a Town Called Dallas* (1984), which begins with the marriage of Dallas debutante Willie Newbury to a rancher who brought her to the Spur Ranch as a bride. Willie lived most of her married life in Dallas, however, while her husband ranched in the Panhandle. Lewis's first book was *Tapadero: The Making of a Cowboy* (1972), a biography of her husband, Will. In 1976 she followed with *Between Sun and Sod: An Informal History of the Texas Panhandle,* a revised and expanded version of her informal 1938 history of the Panhandle based on her many interviews with oldtimers in the area after 1912.

Many other personal accounts by Texas women provide knowledge of the state's varied regional cultures. Among these are *Gay as a Grig: Memories of a North Texas Girlhood* (1963) by Ellen Bowie Holland; *The Golden Free Land: The Reminiscences and Letters of Women on an American Frontier* by Crystal Sasse Ragsdale (1976); *Dorothy's World: Childhood in Sabine Bottom, 1902–1910* (1977) by pioneer folklorist Dorothy Howard; *Boardin' in the Thicket* (1990) by Wanda Landrey; *Oil Field Child* (1989) by Estha Briscoe Stowe; and *Walking Backward in the Wind* (1995) by Helen Mangum Fields. A twentieth-century pioneer, Bess Whitehead Scott narrates her experiences as the first woman reporter for the city desk at the *Houston Post,* where she began her long career as a journalist in 1915. *You Meet Such Interesting People* (1989) shares the author's memoirs at the age of ninety-seven.

In 1969 the nonfiction book that received the TIL award is said to have caused consternation among some of the members and several critics. After long hours of interviewing C. C. White, an East Texas African-American preacher, Ada Morehead Holland, unknown at the time, wrote his biography, *No Quittin' Sense.* Recently reprinted, the book now is praised for its candid portrayal of a remarkable man. Holland has published two other biographies based on her careful gathering of information through interviews and archives. *Mr. Claude* (1984), life of an obscure early-day East Texan, and *Brush Country Woman* (1988), story of a long-time ranch woman, demonstrate Holland's particular talent as a biographer.

As Holland recognized in her choice of a ranchwoman as subject for her most recent book, the cattle industry furnishes rich materials for historical studies. Newspaperwoman Mary Whatley Clarke's numerous histories of early-day Texans and ranch life include *The Swenson Saga and the SMS Ranches* (1976) and *The Slaughter Ranches and Their Makers* (1979). She also published *A Century of*

Cow Business (1976), a history of the Texas and Southwestern Cattle Raisers Association. J'Nell L. Pate provides an interesting supplement to Whatley's history in her prize-winning study, *Livestock Legacy: The Fort Worth Stockyards,* named outstanding book by the Texas State Historical Association in 1988.

Other studies of ranch life include Kathy Greenwood's memoir of growing up on a ranch, *Heart-Diamond* (1990); Frances Mayhugh Holden's early history of Sallie Reynolds Matthews's home territory, *Lambshead before Interwoven: A Texas Range Chronicle, 1848–1878* (1982); Louise O'Connor's *Crying for Daylight: A Ranching Culture in the Coastal Bend* (1989); and Dulcie Sullivan's *The L. S. Brand: The Story of a Texas Panhandle Ranch* (1968) with an introduction by novelist Loula Grace Erdman.

Barney Nelson shares her knowledge of the Big Bend ranch country in *The Last Campfire: The Life Story of Ted Gray, a West Texas Rancher* (1984). Jane Pattie provides a history of one of the main items of cowboy paraphernalia in *Cowboy Spurs and Their Makers* (1991), which went into a second printing soon after publication.

Deborah Lightfoot Sizemore won the 1988 Texas-Wide Writer's Competition for her manuscript of *The LH7 Ranch: In Houston's Shadow* (1991) and was finalist in the 1989 C. L. Sonnichsen Book Award competition. A well-written history of a ranch now swallowed up by Greater Houston, Sizemore's account was named Editor's Choice by *Review of Texas Books.* Sizemore frequently publishes periodical articles and is author of nonfiction for juvenile readers.

Texas women history writers have provided well-researched, readable background on many subjects during this era. Among the most often cited are Sandra Myres's *Westering Women and the Frontier Experience, 1800–1915* (1982). Myres was one of the first historians to recognize the rich materials to be found in women's personal accounts of experiences on the Western frontier.

Marilyn McAdams Sibley published *Travelers in Texas, 1761–1860* in 1967 and *Lone Star and State Gazettes: Texas Newspapers before the Civil War* in 1983. Elizabeth Silverthorne, biographer and historian, has received considerable critical attention for her books *Ashbel Smith of Texas: Pioneer, Patriot, Statesman* (1982) and *Plantation Life in Texas* (1986) and particularly for her definitive examination of Texas holiday traditions in *Christmas in Texas* (1990).

Martha Anne Turner of Huntsville wrote several historical studies during her lifetime but is probably best known for her study of the African-American woman who allegedly distracted Santa Anna to Sam Houston's advantage during the Texas Revolution. Turner tells her story as she traces the origins of the song in *The Yellow Rose of Texas: Her Saga and Her Song* (1976).

Three writers have made careful studies of Texas Jews. Ruthe Winegarten, who published *Texas Women, A Pictorial History, From Indians to Astronauts* (1985), is author with Cathy Schechter of *Deep in the Heart: The Lives and Legends of Texas Jews* (1990). Natalie Ornish's history, *Pioneer Jewish Texans: Their Impact on Texas and American History for 400 Years, 1590–1990*, received first place in the national Benjamin Franklin Awards competition for best book of history, was cited by the Publishers Marketing Association at the 1990 American Booksellers Association meeting in Las Vegas, and was presented the National Conference of Christian and Jews Mass Media Award. The *New York Times* also reviewed the book.

An American Studies professor at St. Edward's University in Austin has won awards for each of her three histories. Paula Mitchell Marks received the Kate Broocks Bates Award for best book on Texas before 1900 from the Texas State Historical Association in 1991, as well as the T. R. Fehrenbach Book Award, for *Turn Your Eyes Toward Texas: Pioneers Sam and Mary Maverick* (1989). Drawn from family archives and journals, this narrative of the daily lives of two strong Texas pioneers illuminates much of the social history of early Texas. *And Die in the West: The Story of the O.K. Corral Gunfight* (1989), Marks's second history, which sets the record straight on what happened that day at the O.K. Corral, was one of three finalists in the Western Writers of America 1989 nonfiction book competition for the Spur Award. Five years later, Marks won the Spur Award for her much-reviewed history of gold rushes in the West, *Precious Dust: The American Gold Rush Era: 1848–1900* (1994). Her most recent book tells the stories of nineteenth-century Texas women spinners and weavers in *Hands to the Spindle: Texas Women and Home Textile Production, 1822–1880* (1995).

Among the many memoirists published in recent years are four well-known Texas women whose reminiscences appear in *Growing Up in Texas* (1972) a collection of memoirs by Texas writers. Two are by Dobie's and Webb's talented wives, Bertha McKee Dobie and Terrell Maverick Webb. Third is historian and librarian Llerena Friend.

Professor Lorece Williams, an African-American who recalls her early life in Caldwell County, is fourth. These women are featured with nine men, including John Graves and A. C. Greene. The Encino Press book is illustrated with remarkable woodcuts by Barbara Mathews Whitehead, who with her late husband, Fred, created award-winning book designs in Texas for several decades.

Mary Karr's *The Liar's Club: A Memoir* reached the bookstores in 1995. Reviewers were lavish in their praise of this autobiographical account of Karr's young life growing up in a dysfunctional family in the refinery regions southeast of Houston. The *New York Times* review (July 9, 1995) concludes, "Not the least of [Karr's] assets in this quest [to recapture her past] is her haunting, often exquisite phrasing of states of being and qualities of mind that resonate long after a page is turned."

Texas has produced few successful agents, but Evelyn Oppenheimer, longtime book reviewer and an author herself, has represented several Texas women writers successfully, including Elithe Hamilton Kirkland. In recent years she has conducted a weekly radio program in Dallas called "Book Talk." In 1991 she published the biography *Gilbert Onderdonk, The Nurseryman of Mission Valley: Pioneer Horticulturist,* and in 1995 her lively autobiography, *A Book Lover in Texas.*

Inspired by the Texas Woman's History Project set up by the Texas Foundation for Women's Resources in 1978, research into the lives of Texas women of note accelerated. Directed by Mary Beth Rogers, the project resulted in a Sesquicentennial traveling exhibit, *Texas Women: A Celebration of History.* Archival materials from the project are now housed in the Texas Woman's University Women's Collection.

Three writers have published studies of Texas women's lives that have proven helpful to researchers. Patricia Lasher and Beverly Bentley include interviews with Shelby Hearon and Liz Carpenter in *Texas Women: Interviews and Images* (1980). In Ann Fears Crawford and Crystal Sasse Ragsdale's *Women in Texas: Their Lives, Their Experiences, Their Accomplishments* (1982) the biographies of thirty women from early-day Texas to modern times are narrated.

In *Gentle Giants: Women Writers in Texas* (1983), Iva Nell Elder includes, among biographies of seventeen women writers, insights into the lives of Suzanne Morris, Elizabeth Silverthorne, Margaret Cousins, Joan Lowery Nixon, and Jane Gilmore Rushing. *Women in*

Early Texas, a compilation of biographies edited in 1975 by Evelyn M. Carrington, includes these recorders of nineteenth-century Texas life: Dilue Rose Harris, Fannie Baker Darden, and Elise Waerenskjold. The Texas State Historical Association published a new edition of this book in 1994 with an introduction by historian Debbie Mauldin Cottrell. Cottrell won the 1994 Liz Carpenter Award for best work by a Texas woman for her biography, *Pioneer Woman Educator: The Progressive Spirit of Annie Webb Blanton* (1993).

Although no comprehensive literary history of Texas writing has been attempted, *Southwest Heritage,* an ambitious survey of southwestern writers, includes brief summaries of many major works by Texas writers. As early as 1938, Mabel Major and Rebecca Smith, both professors at Texas Christian University collaborated with University of New Mexico professor T. M. Pearce to produce what even then was a formidable task, a literary history of the Southwest. The three updated the history and published a second edition in 1948. After achieving the status of professor emeritus, both Major and Pearce produced yet another revision, in 1972. At that time the editors noted that "in the past twenty-two years literary activity in the southwest has accelerated with more books in the field published in a year than during decades in earlier times." Surveying all literary genres, this edition mentions most Texas literary works written before 1970. The authors' knowledgeable interpretations of these works, even though they are presented in the context of regional literature, provide readers with a comprehensive, useful history of Texas writing.

Among the more comprehensive surveys of Texas literature by men writers, which include discussions of works by Texas women writers, are William T. Pilkington's *Imagining Texas: The Literature of the Lone Star State* (1981), A. C. Greene's *The Fifty Best Books on Texas* (1982), Don Graham's *Texas: A Literary Portrait* (1985), and James Ward Lee's *Classics of Texas Fiction* (1987). Although these surveys provide commentary and helpful bibliographies on several Texas women writers, none attempts to trace fully the development of a Texas literary tradition.

Now in print, however, after ten years' intensive research is a volume that will greatly stimulate and aid those wishing to research the history of Texas women, including its writers. Elizabeth and Harry F. Snapp's *Read All About Her!* (1995), subtitled *Texas Women's His-*

tory: A Working Bibliography, includes entries numbered in the thousands, and arranged in easy-to-use cross-indexed listings.

Much of what Texas women have written for almost two centuries reflects their insights into those areas of Texas life ignored by the true believers in the Texas Mystique, epitomized by J. Frank Dobie and his admirers. Except in occasional witty satire, the state's women writers have valued individuality over stereotype, and unlike many men authors in the state, women have ignored the prevalent image of the state as a masculine domain, dominated by cowboys, rednecks, and rich businessmen.

Texas women writers have responded with sensitivity and a sense of the real to those events and periods affording continuity and contributing to change in Texas culture. When Jane Gilmore Rushing chose cowboy life as her subject in *Mary Dove* (1974), she created a redheaded cowpoke overwhelmed by his love for a mulatto girl. In her much-anthologized short story, "My Brother Is a Cowboy," Carolyn Osborn portrays the modern-day "windshield" cowboy as a faithful believer in the Mystique, who demonstrates his belief by driving out daily from his home in town to check his livestock. Like these writers, who depart in their themes from overworked cliche, women authors in every period of the state's literary development exemplify their ability to prod the Texas Mystique until they expose its less glittery underside.

Katherine Ann Porter, whose life and work transcend her Texas experience but whose roots remained deep in her native state, once wrote novelist Andrew Lytle that the "riddle of the universe" asks why Man cannot "face the truth of his own motives." From the beginnings, what women have written about the Texas experience considers not the typical but the individual. Texas women writers have faced "the truth" of motive in that experience.

Part 1
PROSE WRITERS

The Pioneers, 1830–1920

When Frances Trask arrived in Texas in the early 1830s, she already possessed the skills to survive in frontier Texas: she could ride well and shoot straight. According to early historian Elizabeth Ellet, Trask "had accustomed herself to firing at a mark, and was considered one of the best shots in the country, besides being able to ride a horse with any racer." Back in her home state of Michigan she never passed up the opportunity to make a "smart or satirical speech," and she was admired for her learning and wit. She was criticized, however, for her "unfeminine defiance of general opinion in many trifling matters."

When her cousin's family, with whom Trask lived, was obliged after financial failure to move to Texas, Trask was the "nerve" of the family, calmly packing up, dressing the children, and making arrangements for the family's travel. Her first act upon arriving in the colony in 1834 was to establish a boarding school for Texas girls at Cole's Settlement. The indomitable Trask also established a tradition. As on every American frontier, literate women with wit and courage soon became crusaders for schools, libraries, churches, and societies as civilizing influences in embryonic Texas communities.

Inevitably, women writers were called upon to employ the power of their pens to advance worthy causes. Often isolated as colonists, at first they chose to express their experiences in diaries and letters, but even before the Civil War, women writers were submitting short stories, sketches, poems, and letters to Texas newspapers. Often they signed their work with only their first name or with "Anonymous" or a pseudonym, and frequently they found themselves defending their authorship to skeptical editors, who believed no woman could write so well. In her thesis, "Writings by Women in Texas before 1865," Norma Rutledge Grammer, candidate for an M.A. at Texas Christian University in 1937, quotes the spirited response of one letter writer to an editor's incredulity. In reply to the editor of the *Huntsville Dispatch* on March 22, 1854, "Alice" writes:

> How erroneous the generally received opinion that it is only necessary for females to receive a limited education. For instance, study a little geography, grammar, elementary branches of arithmetic, and then a little of the ornamental, such as music, drawing, and a finishing touch in novel reading; which, of course, qualifies them only to idle away time, and to entertain such of those "Masterpieces" of creation, in the parlor, as may visit them.
>
> Now, Mr. Editor, permit me to ask those lordly would-be superiors of ours, if they were going to select a companion, if they would not like to gain the favor of one with a highly cultivated mind, if so I entreat them to come out and advocate female rights.

It was as crusaders for "female rights" that many Texas women writers took up their pens during the last two decades of the nineteenth century—and until they won the right to vote, in 1920. In 1893, during the so-called Progressive Era, S. Isadore Miner was appointed the first woman's editor of the *Dallas Morning News,* and for two decades, writing under the name Pauline Periwinkle, she provided a stellar example of a leader bringing about numerous civic improvements and social reforms through her newspaper column.

From Mary Austin Holley's publication of her observations and experiences in Texas to the appearance of Amelia Barr's reminiscences of life in Austin during the Civil War, Texas women demonstrated their abilities as both observers and writers. Early fiction and poetry presage the accomplishments of writers to come, but Texas women writers accomplished the most for future women writers in the state in their forceful defense of their profession and in their ambitious efforts to gain attention equal to that received by men writers of the time.

"THE ASTONISHING PROPORTIONS"

Nonfiction Literature, 1830–1920

FANE DOWNS

In the June 18, 1893, issue of the *Galveston Daily News,* Bride Neill Taylor observed that from time to time works by Texas women appeared in out-of-state journals. According to Taylor, "Such being the case, it seemed likely that more good work than anyone suspected might be coming to light in the papers of the state itself. . . . No one—least of all the writer herself—suspected that the number would, upon investigation, assume the astonishing proportions which the following [article] reveals." Texas women's literary productions during the nineteenth century include memoirs, diaries, letters, travel accounts, history, science, religious works, and news and feature articles.[1]

This essay is limited to two broad categories of nonfiction: works written or edited and published between 1830 and 1920, and works written or edited during that period and published later. Works focused on the period before 1920 but written later are not included, nor are works written during the period and not published at all, such as manuscript or typescript diaries in archives or private collections.[2] The essay will treat published nonfiction by Texas women; many of the authors, of course, also produced fiction, poetry, and drama.

The best-known category of Texas women's writing is the personal memoir. The experience of settling the Texas frontier (and some parts of Texas can be classified as "frontier" throughout this entire period) called forth many chronicles—most of which were written for families and descendants, not for publication. The largest body of early Texas women's literature, however, is historical writing. Among the first to preserve and record Texas history were several women who, having traveled through Texas or lived there briefly, recorded their impressions and adventures. These works are not *Texas* women's writing; nevertheless, they are women's books *about* Texas. The writers are almost all white women; apparently very few Hispanic or Black women published works during this period. Moreover, apart from journalists and newspaperwomen, very few women made their living by their pen.

MEMOIRS PUBLISHED BEFORE 1920

Historians and students of Texas history are indebted to the many women who recorded their experiences of life in Texas. This body of work adds texture and flavor to the past, gives us insight into commonplace events or circumstances—the "stuff" of social history, which women recorded more often than men: food, clothing, furnishings, how people related to one another, health practices, and so forth. About half of the works cited below were published before 1920, many of them in the *Quarterly of the Texas State Historical Association,* renamed *Southwestern Historical Quarterly.*

The first book published in English about Texas was Mary Austin Holley's *Texas. Observations, Historical, Geographical and Descriptive. In a Series of Letters, Written during a Visit to Austin's Colony, with a view to a permanent Settlement in that country, in the Autumn of 1831*[3] (1833). Intended for persons curious about Texas, the book included information about topography, natural features, towns, political organization, and other material of general interest to emigrants. Holley published a more formal work, *Texas,* in 1836. Holley praises the hardiness of the Texas settlers she has met and notes:

> Living in a wild country under circumstances requiring constant
> exertion, forms the character to great and daring enterprise. Women
> thus situated are known to perform exploits which the effeminate
> men of populous cities might tremble at.

Holley, Stephen F. Austin's cousin, was an early and enthusiastic publicist for Texas; her works combine features of an emigrant guide, personal memoir, and history. Her diary, edited by J. P. Bryan, was published in 1965. Bryan called her the "first credible historian" of Texas. Rebecca Smith Lee, in *Mary Austin Holley: A Biography*, provides details and interpretation of the life of this resourceful and intelligent woman.

One of the most often cited reminiscences is that of Dilue Harris, "The Reminiscences of Mrs. Dilue Harris." Harris was a young woman during the 1830s and 1840s, and her memoir reflects the exuberance of youth. Memoirs describing German experiences in early Texas settlement are Rosa Kleberg's "Some of My Early Experiences in Texas," Caroline von Hinueber's "Life of German Pioneers in Early Texas," and Marie Bennet Urwitz's "Early Days in Texas." Other memoirs from the antebellum period include Harriet Durst's *Early Days in Texas*. Durst's work is principally about her husband, John Durst, but includes a brief reminiscence of her life during the period 1827–36. She, like so many early memoirists and historians, wanted to keep alive the memoirs of "our brave pioneers . . . [in order] to imbue coming generations with the patriotic fire that stirred the breasts of their forefathers." Mary Sherwood Helm in *Scraps of Early Texas History, by Mrs. Mary S. Helm who with her First Husband, Elias R. Wightman, Founded the City of Matagorda, in 1828–29* recalled her experiences during the years prior to the Texas Revolution. About one-half the book is devotional writing reflecting her religious sensibilities and prejudices. Mrs. A. J. Lee's "Some Recollections of Two Pioneer Texas Women," about Mrs. M. E. Kenney and Lydia McHenry, focuses on the same period.

Two writers who brought a distinctive point of view to their works are Melinda Rankin and Jane McManus Cazneau. The former, a Presbyterian missionary, came to Texas at mid-century and began to evangelize the Mexicans on both sides of the border. Her *Texas in 1850* and *Twenty Years among the Mexicans: A Narrative of Missionary Labor* are as much religious treatise as memoir. In *Twenty Years* she wrote that God works through women as well as men, but she was quick to explain, "To a very great extent the prevailing sentiment among Christ's people has been, that woman's work should be necessarily circumscribed, lest she transcend the delicacy of her sex. To unwomanly aspirations I am as much opposed as anyone. But had public sentiment been my guide some forty years ago, I should have probably settled down in my New England home." She believed Protestant Christianity was the most effective means of the moral uplift of all people, particularly Roman Catholics. She wrote to encourage others to evangelize Mexicans. Jane Cazneau, writing under the name Cora Montgomery, in *Eagle Pass: or Life on the Border* describes her life in Texas 1850–52. Cazneau was a well-traveled, intelligent, sophisticated woman of firm political and social opinions and wide acquaintance; hers is a "significant contribution to an understanding of thinking women in 19th Century Texas."[4]

Two captivity narratives are Rebecca Fisher's, *Captured by Comanches* also published as "Capture and Rescue of Mrs. Rebecca J. Fisher, nee Gilleland," and Rachael Plummer's *Rachael Plummer's Narrative of Twenty-one Months Servitude as a Prisoner among the Comanchee [sic] Indians.*

Perhaps the most prolific Texas woman writer was Amelia Barr, who lived in Texas 1856–67. Her nonfiction literature consists of her autobiography *All the Days of My Life: An Autobiography. The Red Leaves of a Human Heart,* which reads much like one of her numerous novels, and several articles published in the *North American Review,* during 1889–92. Her work indicates that she held rather unconventional ideas and opinions for her day; in fact in the introduction to her autobiography, she wrote, "I write mainly for the kindly race of women. I am their sister, and in no way exempt from their sorrowful lot. I have drank [sic] the cup of their limitations to the dregs, and if my experience can help any sad or doubtful woman to outleap her own shadow, and to stand bravely out in the sunshine to meet her destiny, . . . I shall have done well; I shall not have written this book in vain."

MEMOIRS PUBLISHED AFTER 1920

Several memoirs and collections of letters written between 1820 and 1920 were not published until much later. Two useful collections are Jo Ella Powell Exley's *Texas Tears and Texas Sunshine: Voices of Frontier Women* and Crystal Sasse Ragsdale's *The Golden Free Land: The Reminiscences and Letters of Women on an American Frontier.* Exley includes excerpts from women's published reminiscences written between 1821 and 1905; the volume is dependable but of course no substitute for the full published versions. Ragsdale includes memoirs and letters of German women in Texas, some of which have not been published previously. Together these volumes constitute a significant study of acculturation and adaptation in a new environment.

Other memoirs include Millie Richards Gray's *The Diary of Millie Gray, 1832–1840*; L. W. Kemp's edition of "Early Days in Milam County: Reminiscences of Susan Turnham McCown," dictated in 1913 but covering the period 1840–65; Mary Crownover Rabb's *Travels and Adventures in Texas in the 1820s: Being the Reminiscences of Mary Crownover Rabb*, a spirited and charming account; *Victorian Lady on the Texas Frontier: The Journal of Anne Raney Coleman*, edited by C. Richard King, which relates Coleman's personal experiences, made difficult by an abusive husband and limited resources; Mary Taylor Bunton's *A Bride on the Old Chisholm Trail in 1886*, the written version of a well- and often-told tale; and "Emma Altgelt's Sketches of Life in Texas," edited by Henry B. Dillmann, the memoir of a German girl who came to Texas in 1854.

The Maverick family participated in or witnessed a great deal of nineteenth-century Texas history. In 1881, Mary Maverick wrote her memoirs for her children who, she says, had often asked that she put into shape the notes and memoranda she jotted down during the early days. Her *Memoirs of Mary A. Maverick, Arranged by Mary A. Maverick and Her Son, Geo. Madison Maverick*, edited by Rena Maverick Green, reveal a woman of keen religious feelings, deep commitment to her family, and courage and resourcefulness in coping with life during Sam Maverick's frequent absences. Helpful also to understanding the Mavericks' life is Paula Mitchell Marks's *Turn Your Eyes Toward Texas: Pioneers Sam and Mary Maverick* (1989), a dual biography of the public life of Sam Maverick and the private life of Mary Maverick.

Illuminating personal portraits and observations are found in letters. *Lucadia Pease and the Governor: Letters, 1850–1857*, edited by Katherine Hart and Elizabeth Kemp, includes intimate, literate, informative letters from a self-confident woman and loving wife; in *Letters from Fort Sill, 1886–1887*, Marion T. Brown (daughter of journalist-historians John Henry and Mary Brown) reveals rich details of social life at the fort; "Lydia Ann McHenry and Revolutionary Texas," edited by George R. Nielson, shows the challenges of life as a single woman, the "maiden aunt." Among the more perceptive and interesting letters are those of Elise Waerenskjold, who emigrated to Texas in 1847 and lived in Van Zandt County until her death in 1895. The letters, addressed to her friends in Norway, include practical advice for emigrants, details of life and customs of Texas, and news of ordinary events. This valuable correspondence from an unusually gifted and intelligent woman was edited by C. A. Clausen and published as *The Lady with the Pen*. A few letters from Rebecca Adams to her husband are contained in *The Hicks-Adams-Bass-Floyd-Patillo and Collateral Lines with Family Letters, 1840–1868*, edited by Gary Doyle Woods.

The writings of Jane Y. McCallum, suffragist and civic leader, fall largely in the period following this essay. However, Janet G. Humphrey's *A Texas Suffragist: Diaries and Writings of Jane Y. McCallum*, comprising two "write and run" diaries from the years 1916–19, is a compelling work by this incredibly busy wife, mother, and reformer.

HISTORICAL WRITING

Because women traditionally have been charged with the task of preserving values and traditions, it is not surprising that the largest body of published work by women writers is historical writing. Although none of these women could be classified as professional historians, many produced competent historical works. The most widely read and best known, Anna J. Hardwick Pennybacker's *New History of Texas for Schools*, was published privately in Tyler in 1888, when the author was twenty-seven years old. Pennybacker taught history in the Tyler public schools, and several persons—including her husband, the superintendent of schools—encouraged her to write a history of Texas for school children. In 1898 the Pennybacker history was adopted for use in the schools, and it remained the standard textbook for four decades. Vividly written, the book appealed to youngsters' imagination. She was not unmindful of the opportunity to instill patriotism in her students. Her biographer noted, "Through Anna Pennybacker's eyes they [students] saw Texas for the first time as a great commonwealth, formed by the struggle of heroic forces. The book awakened in these children the resolution to bring to the future of Texas the same industry and high courageous spirit which had animated their fathers."[5]

Anna Pennybacker was among several women charter members

of the Texas State Historical Association. In fact three women—Dora Fowler Arthur, Julia Lee Sinks, and Bride Neill Taylor—attended the first gathering, in 1897, at which this historical association was conceived. Some of the men present were reluctant to allow women full membership, but the women took their places and served the association well. Sinks was a vice president; Arthur and Taylor were members of the executive council. Besides Arthur, Sinks, and Taylor, women charter members who were writers of history included Adele Briscoe Lubbock Looscan (who served as president 1915–25) and Adina de Zavala.[6]

In many ways, Adele Looscan typified women historians of her day. The daughter of early Texans Andrew Briscoe and Mary Jane Harris, she was active as a club woman, founder of the Daughters of the Republic of Texas, and historian. Her writings include contributions on homemaking to the *Ladies' Messenger,* the organ of the Woman's Exchange. Principally, however, she wrote history.[7] Of particular interest in the context of this essay is her article, "The Women of Pioneer Days in Texas—Domestic and Social Life in the Periods of the Colonies, the Revolution, and the Republic" in Dudley Wooten's *Comprehensive History of Texas, 1685–1897.* The subtitle of this piece provides a summary of its contents and hints at its point of view: "A Graphic and Detailed Account of the Daily Life, Social Customs, Domestic Experiences, and great Trials and Privations of the Heroic Woman of Early Texas, a Personal Notice of the Most Famous of those Women, the Gradual Growth of Civilization in the Wilderness, Primitive Festivities of Pioneer Society, Modes of Dress, the Gay and Melancholy Sides of Women's Lives in those Times." Despite the uncritical, celebratory tone of this passage, Looscan produced competent social history. Not surprisingly it focuses on white women only, but it is not an unqualified panegyric to the "founding mothers" of Texas.

Looscan contributed two additional articles to Wooten's history: "The History and Evolution of the Texas Flag" and "Tombs and Monuments of Noted Texans." Her other historical writings, published in the *Quarterly of the Texas State Historical Association,* include "The Old Mexican Fort at Velasco," "Elizabeth Bullock Huling: A Texas Pioneer," "Sketch of the Life of Oliver Jones and of His Wife Rebecca Jones," and "Micajah Autry: A Soldier of the Alamo."

Julia Lee Sinks's major work is *Chronicles of Fayette: The Remi-*

niscences of Julia Lee Sinks. The Fayette County Centennial Committee asked Sinks to compile the history. She responded with admirable diligence and objectivity, but apparently the manuscript was not published during her lifetime. Of her work, Sinks said: "I think I have done my full duty towards Fayette, and have nothing more to say. I have written the history of its formation, collected its chronicles, preserved the names from oblivion of those who stood in the vanguard when heroism was needed, and by their heroism prepared the way for its present progress." The work is somewhat celebratory, but Sinks did attempt to reclaim the experiences of all the people (white people, that is), including women. She interviewed old settlers and pioneers and attempted to reconcile conflicting accounts. She also contributed "Editors and Newspapers of Fayette County" to the *Quarterly of the Texas State Historical Association*.

An early attempt to chronicle the deeds of women in Texas is Elizabeth Brooks's *Prominent Women of Texas*, a collection of short, celebratory biographies. Brooks categorized her subjects in this manner: wives of presidents, wives of military heroes, pioneers—harbingers of civilization, Indian experiences, well-known vocalists, prominent authors, educators, physicians, temperance leaders, dramatic (actresses), wives of prominent men, representative women, and women well-known in social life. She wrote, "The bibliography of Texas is bright with female names. Whether in the domain of history, travels, romance, adventure, poetry, or other learning, women have equally shared the laurels with the other sex."

Mary M. Brown's *A School History of Texas from its Discovery in 1685 to 1893, for the use of Schools, Academies, Convents, Seminaries, and all Institutions of Learning* was "compiled with scrupulous care" from *History of Texas from 1685 to 1892* by John Henry Brown, her husband. In the introduction, John Henry Brown wrote, "Without prejudice or partiality, the writer has been able to turn a strong light upon portions of the history otherwise obscure."

Minnie G. Dill's *Footprints of Texas History*, a story book for the third grade, asserts that "every child should read history stories at an early age, because they have great value in forming the character of the young." Mollie E. Moore Davis said of her *Under Six Flags: The Story of Texas*: "I have endeavored to sketch, in rather bold outlines, the story of Texas. It is a story of knightly romance, which calls the poet even as in earlier days, the Land of Tehas called across its borders dreamers of dreams. But the history of Texas is more than romantic legend." Davis wrote voluminously—plays, poetry, stories, novels—but this is her only attempt at history.

Adina de Zavala, granddaughter of Lorenzo de Zavala, first vice president of the Republic of Texas, and prominent member of the Daughters of the Republic of Texas, wrote *History and Legends of the Alamo and Other Missions in and Around San Antonio.* This probably should be classified as folklore rather than history inasmuch as she sought to preserve the legends of early Texas history. Fannie Baker Darden, another descendant of prominent early settlers, wrote *Romances of the Texas Revolution* in addition to a large volume of fiction, poetry, and contributions to the state's newspapers.[8]

At the American Historical Association, Mrs. Lee Cohen Harby read a paper, "The Earliest Texas," in which she described the earliest Spanish settlement in Texas. Although she lauded the Spanish heritage of Texas, she exhibited the common anti-Mexican bias of the late nineteenth century. She published "The City of a Prince," about New Braunfels, in the *Magazine of American History* in 1888 and "The Old Stone Fort at Nacogdoches" in the *American Magazine.* Harby wrote short stories and essays as well as poetry.[9]

Another woman of considerable versatility was Katie Daffan— clubwoman, journalist, historian, novelist. Her historical works include *History of the United States; My Father as I Remember Him; Texas Heroes: A Reader for the Schools; Texas Hero Stories: an Historical Reader for the Grades; Women in History* (a collection of biographies of famous women); and "United Daughters of the Confederacy." She clearly states that the purpose of the Texas heroes reader is "to create in the mind of the child a love for those men who gave their strength, their talent, and their life blood for Texas, and to stimulate a desire to dip deeper into the wonderful history of the state." Her Texas history collections are celebratory, uncritical, and pro-South.[10]

Other publications by Texas women include Bonnie Ponton and Bates H. McFarland's "Alvar Nunez Cabeza de Vaca: A Preliminary Report on his Wanderings in Texas," in the *Quarterly of the Texas State Historical Association;* Bella French Swisher's *History of Austin, Travis County, Texas, with a Description of its Resources,* and, as editor and publisher, *The American Sketch Book: Historical and Home Journal;* Kate Scurry Terrell's "Terry's Texas Rangers" and "The

Runaway Scrape" in Wooten's *Comprehensive History of Texas, 1685–1897*; Mrs. A. V. Winkler's "Hood's Texas Brigade," in Wooten; Maude Fuller Young's "Stephen F. Austin, the Father of Texas," in *Writers and Writings of Texas*; Dora Fowler Arthur's "Jottings from the Old Journal of Littleton Fowler"; Ellen B. Ballou's "Scudder's Journey to Texas, 1859"; Fannie McAlpine Clarke's "The Indians of Young Territory" in the *Quarterly of the Texas State Historical Association*; and *Letters from an Early Texas Settler to a Friend,* written by Cara Cardelle (whose pseudonym was Emaretta C. Kimball) and edited by William B. Dewees. Other early writers of history include Laura V. Hamner of Amarillo and Nannie Smith Thaxton.[11]

Mattie Austin Hatcher began her work during the period under consideration. One of the few professionally trained women historians, she received her degrees from the University of Texas. A specialist in the Spanish period of Texas history, Hatcher titled her thesis "The Municipal Government of San Fernando de Bexar, 1731–1800." Named archivist of the University of Texas in 1906, she remained associated with the university throughout her professional career. Most of her published work appeared after 1920. Another historian-librarian-archivist was Elizabeth Howard West. When she was archivist at the Texas State Library, she selected and supervised the transcription of documents from archives in Mexico and Cuba. Like Hatcher, West published most of her work after 1920. She spent the balance of her professional career as a librarian at Texas Technological College, in Lubbock.[12]

This survey indicates that women's contributions to the historiography of Texas are considerable. As researchers, writers, editors, and compilers, they helped preserve and transmit the historical heritage of the state.

OTHER WRITING

In addition to history, women have treated a variety of subjects. Mrs. William E. Fisher published a spirited scriptural defense of women's preaching in *Woman's Right to Preach: A Sermon.* A related work is Maria Beulah Woodworth's *Acts of the Holy Ghost, or the Life, Work, and Experiences of Mrs. M. B. Woodworth-Etter, Evangelist.* In *A Southerner among the Spirits: A Record of Investigation into the Spiritual Phenomenon,* on the other hand, Mary Dana Shindler employs a different approach to spiritual matters: she relates her own experiences communicating with the dead and presents her firm convictions about the practice.

Texas women produced works of science as well as religion. The first botany textbook used in Texas, *Familiar Lessons in Botany with Flora of Texas,* was the work of Maude J. Young. In a classic statement, Young explained her reason for writing the book:

> The book is an outgrowth of the wants of her own classroom, and was first used there without any thought of publication. Finding the primary works too primary, and therefore, not awakening the proper interest—the more advanced too scientific, thus at the very outset disheartening the pupil—she prepared these lessons, endeavoring to combine simplicity of diction with some degree of technical and scientific knowledge, thereby leading the pupil gradually on to where he should get such glimpses of the wonders and beauties of Vegetable Physiology . . . as to become willing to go with earnest zeal into advanced work.

Eliza Griffin Johnston produced another work of botany, though she intended it more as paintings for her husband Albert Sidney Johnston than a reference work. *Texas Wildflowers with a Biography of Mrs. Johnston by Mildred Pickle Mayhall* consists of nearly one hundred watercolor paintings of Texas wildflowers with informative texts about each.[13]

Another science teacher and writer was the geologist Augusta Hasslock Kemp. She published several articles in geological journals, but she also wrote essays, poems, and stories. These works, which she called her "idiot children," were published as *Pegasus Limping.* Most of her published work appeared after 1920. Helen Selina Lewis, classics scholar and entomologist, produced scientific papers on "phosphorescent insects."[14]

Fanny Chambers Gooch wrote a combination memoir, travel account, and descriptive essay in *Face to Face with the Mexicans: the Domestic Life, Educational, Social, and Business Ways, Statesmanship and Literature, Legendary and General History of the Mexican People.* While relatively sympathetic to Mexicans and very complimentary of President Porfirio Diaz, Gooch exhibited a patronizing attitude nonetheless. Her other published work is *The Boy Captive of the Texas Mier Expedition.* In recounting the story of John C. C.

Hill, "one of the most romantic and tragic military episodes known in the annals of Texas history," she hoped to instill patriotism in boys and girls.

Emma Elizabeth Pirie published books and articles on topics of particular interest to women in homemaking, including *A Sewing Course* and *Science of Home Making*. This long-time San Antonio teacher contributed to newspapers and magazines as well.

Women also were active in the collection, publication, and preservation of Texas folklore. Ruth Dodson published articles in *Publications of the Texas Folk-Lore Society, Frontier Times,* and *Southwest Review* on both Anglo-American and Mexican folklore. Amanda Julia Estill, a Fredericksburg teacher and principal, also contributed to *Publications of the Texas Folk-Lore Society* as well as to San Antonio newspapers.[15]

TRAVEL ACCOUNTS

Women's travel accounts have long provided historians with significant primary sources. These works include Martha Isabella Hopkins Barbour's *Journals of the Late Brevet Major Philip Norbourne Barbour . . . and his Wife Martha Isabella Hopkins Barbour, Written During the War with Mexico, 1846* (edited by Rhoda van Bibber Tanner Doubleday); Ellen McGowan Biddle's *Reminiscences of a Soldier's Wife*; Elizabeth Bacon Custer's *Tenting on the Plains: or General Custer in Kansas and Texas*; Matilda Charlotte (Jesse) Fraser Houstoun's *Hesperos: or Travels in the West* and *Texas and the Gulf of Mexico: or, Yachting in the New World*; Mary J. Jaques's *Texas Ranch Life: With Three Months through Mexico in a "Prairie Schooner"*; Lydia Spencer (Blaney) Lane's *I Married a Soldier: or, Old Days in the Old Army*; Amelia Matilda Murray's *Letters from the United States, Cuba and Canada*; Lou Conway Roberts's *Mrs. D. W. Roberts, A Woman's Reminiscences of Six Years in Camp with the Texas Rangers*; Teresa (Griffin) Viele's *"Following the Drum": a Glimpse of Frontier Life*; Eliza (Griffin) Johnston's "The Diary of Eliza (Mrs. Albert Sidney) Johnston: The Second Cavalry Comes to Texas" in *Southwestern Historical Quarterly*. A travel account by a well-known Texas woman is Cornelia R. Adair's *My Diary: August 30th to November 5th, 1874.*

JOURNALISM

Journalism attracted many talented nineteenth-century women writers. There are at least three categories of these journalists: those who were also publishers and/or editors; professional journalists; and "contributors," those not employed by a particular newspaper or magazine but who contributed material to several, for which they may or may not have been compensated. Among those women who were publishers and editors is Bella French Swisher, who published *American Sketchbook,* a monthly magazine devoted to historical and contemporary subjects. She first established a newspaper, *Western Progress,* in Brownville, Minnesota, in 1868 and began *American Sketch book* in 1874. She moved the magazine to Texas in 1877. She published *American Sketch book* until 1882 and was a frequent contributor.[16]

Women frequently assumed their husbands' responsibilities in business. Lydia Starr McPherson became owner and editor of the *Whitesboro Democrat* when her husband died in 1877. She moved the paper to Sherman and published the *Democrat* there for several years. Likewise, Mrs. F. L. Denison assumed editorship of her husband's paper, the *Belton Reporter,* when he died. Because his health had been failing, Mrs. Denison had worked closely with him for several years. Annie C. Bridges assumed responsibility for the *Luling Signal* when her husband died.[17] Sally Boner worked closely with her husband Charles on weekly newspapers in Montague and Clay counties; after they moved to Austin she concentrated on writing fiction. Mary Winn Smoots contributed to the *Dallas News, Semi-Weekly Farm News,* and *Galveston News* before establishing the first woman's paper in Texas, *Texas Woman,* which later merged with *American Home Journal,* which she edited. Smoots wrote widely in politics and contemporary events.[18] Laura Bibb Foute wrote for newspapers before she founded the *Ladies' Messenger* in Houston; she moved the paper to San Antonio and renamed it *Gulf Messenger* in 1889. Sara E. Hartman was her associate in this enterprise.[19]

Several women could be classified as professional journalists because they either were employed by newspapers or received compensation for their work. Aurelia Hadley Mohl began with the Houston *Telegraph* in 1856 in the literary department. During her residency in Washington, she served as correspondent for several Texas newspapers. She returned to Texas and joined the staff of the Houston *Post.* The society editor of the paper, she wrote on a variety of local and national topics. Active in the Women's National Press association, Mohl was an organizer of the Texas Women's Press Association. Mrs. M. R. Walton served as literary editor of the *Fort Worth Gazette* but was considered an all-around journalist. She too was active in the Texas Women's Press Association. Another professional journalist, Bessie Agnes Dwyer, served on the staff of the *National Economist* in Washington, D.C.; as correspondent for several southern newspapers, she contributed to several Texas publications.[20]

Isadora Miner served as society and assistant literary editor of the *Dallas News* and editor of the woman's and children's columns of the paper. Bride Neill Taylor wrote widely on literary, historical, and educational topics as well as women's issues. At the conclusion of her two-part *Galveston News* series on women writers of Texas, the editor noted, "She writes for publication for the same reason that other bright people write—ideas possess her and she must give them expression; but she has a dignified view of woman's field in literature and journalism and thinks they ought to be paid the full value of their services—not so much, she says, for the sake of the pay as for the injustice of working for nothing."[21]

Molly Connor Cook began her journalism career early by establishing the first school newspaper in the one-room, one-teacher school in Eagle Lake. "I was editor-in-chief, reportorial staff, poet." In the 1920s, Cook was editor of the *Austin-American* woman's department. For twelve years during this period, Bess Murphy Drew, society editor of the *Denison Herald*,[22] wrote a daily column, "From the Feminine Viewpoint."

The largest category of women journalists comprises women who were "contributors" to various newspapers, magazines, and journals in Texas and beyond. The first woman journalist in the state, according to Bride Neill Taylor, was Eva Lancaster. In 1849, Lancaster moved to Texas with her husband, who began publication of the *Texas Ranger* in Washington-on-the-Brazos. A regular contributor, she oversaw the operations of the paper and its successor in Brenham during her husband's absences. Alice McGowan, something of an adventurer, wrote for popular journals an account of her horseback trip in the Tennessee mountains.[23] Mamie Folsom Wynne began her journalism career as editor of the *Atlanta Constitution* organized-labor page; in Georgia she edited *Fraternal Age*. After coming to Texas, in 1890, she contributed to *Dallas Dispatch* and the *Dallas News* on a variety of topics, apparently not including organized labor. She also wrote travel articles following trips to Europe, Mexico, Bermuda, Alaska, Panama, and Central America. This versatile writer produced fiction, poetry, and plays, and works on music appreciation.[24]

Two women focused on religious topics. Mrs. C. C. Armstrong, wife of a minister, wrote extensively on women's missionary work, "before the women of her church were as fully aroused as they have since become." She contributed to the *Texas Christian Advocate* and other religious publications. Mary C. Billings, the wife of a minister in Hico, was a preacher as well, beginning in 1885. "The arduous duties of her double vocation have not prevented her from being also an industrious writer." She published in denominational journals as well as the secular press.[25]

Three other contributors are May Eddins Welborn, Mrs. H. C. L. Gorman (who frequently wrote under the pen name of Clara LeClerc), and Emma Holmes Jenkins.[26]

At least three Texas women wrote in the field of literary criticism. Angelina Virginia Winkler, who contributed widely to southern literary journals, established the *Prairie Flower,* "an authority upon matters pertaining to southern literature" during its short existence in the 1880s. Virginia Quitman Goffe contributed works of literary criticism to various journals. Her "Jefferson Davis and the Old South" has been judged an example of her very best work. Some enthusiastic critics declared that "a man might have done it." She was associated with the *Dallas Times Herald.* Nettie Thompson Grove, also of Dallas ("descended exclusively from a southern ancestry"!), devoted herself to a study of southern literature and contemporary southern writers. She observed "we are prone to run after false gods when it comes to literature, overlooking or underrating the talent of our own people, while lifting our eyes to that which bears the seal of New England." Grove was determined to eliminate that tendency.[27]

This survey of nineteenth- and early twentieth-century Texas women's nonfiction suggests that they contributed significantly to both the historical record of and intellectual life in Texas. Considering the size and diversity of the state, the fact that its women wrote on a variety of topics in a number of genres is not surprising. Few, however, supported themselves by their writing; most produced one or just a few works. Moreover they were not specialists. Many wrote poetry, fiction, and drama as well as nonfiction. Nonfiction writing was a career open to only a few, and most of these were employed by newspapers. In this period a woman who supported herself by freelance writing was rare indeed. Nevertheless the contributions of women to the Texas literary tradition are significant.

NOTES

1. Useful reference works include Bride Neill Taylor, "The Women Writers of Texas," *Galveston Daily News,* June 18 and 25, 1893; Davis Foute Eagleton, *Writers and Writings of Texas,* though most of the women writers are poets; Florence Elberta Barns, *Texas Writers of Today,* an encyclopedic collection; Sister M. Agatha Sheehan, *Texas Prose Writings: A Reader's Digest;* Sinclair Moreland, *The Texas Women's Hall of Fame,* a classic example of Victorian sentimentality but useful for the women writers he includes. Collections of short biographies provide sketches of a few women writers: Evelyn M. Carrington, ed., *Women in Early Texas,* largely uncritical; Ann Fears Crawford and Crystal Sasse Ragsdale, *Women in Texas: Their Lives, Their Experiences, Their Accomplishments;* and Annie Doom Pickrell, *Pioneer Women in Texas.* Also helpful are Ann Patton Malone, "Women in Texas History," in Light Cummins and Alvin Bailey, Jr., eds., *A Guide to the History of Texas,* a survey of historical writing on Texas women; Ruthe Winegarten, *Finder's Guide to Texas Women: A Celebration of History Exhibit Archives;* Ruthe Winegarten, ed., *Texas Women's History Project Bibliography;* Bessie Malvina Pearce, "Texas Through Women's Eyes, 1823–1868"; Carol Wolf, "A Study of Prose by Nineteenth Century Texas Women"; Marilyn McAdams Sibley, *Travelers in Texas, 1761–1860;* Mattie Lloyd Wooten, *Women Tell the Story of the Southwest;* and Martha Mitten Allen, *Traveling West: Nineteenth Century Women on the Overland Routes.*

2. Readers interested in archival material should consult Harriette Andreadis, "True Womanhood Revisited: Women's Private Writing in Nineteenth-Century Texas," in *Journal of the Southwest* 31 (Summer, 1989): 170–204, and the extensive notes in Sandra Myres, *Westering Women and the Frontier Experience, 1800–1915.*

3. Taylor, "The Women Writers of Texas," 13–14.

4. Wolf, "A Study of Nineteenth Century Prose," 106.

5. Rebecca Richmond, *A Woman of Texas: Mrs. Percy V. Pennybacker,* 68. Pennybacker's history went through several editions and revisions until the 1920s.

6. Dorman H. Winfrey, *Seventy-five Years of Texas History: The Texas State Historical Association, 1897–1972,* 2–6.

7. "Adele Looscan," in Texas State Historical Association, *Handbook of Texas* (1952) 2:81; Moreland, *Texas Woman's Hall of Fame,* 194–97.

8. Jeanette Hastedt Flachmeir, "Frannie Baker Darden," in Carrington, *Women*

in Early Texas, 59–63; this author did not find references to the two works in the card catalog in the Barker Texas History Center at the University of Texas.

9. Taylor, "Women Writers of Texas."

10. See *Handbook of Texas,* 1:452–53.

11. Barns, *Texas Writers of Today,* 222, 437.

12. Barns, *Texas Writers of Today,* 230, 462.

13. Of the bluebonnet, Johnston wrote, "The Lupin, called by the people of the country 'Bonnet flower' grows in such profusion that the prairie in a distance, often closely resembles the blue waters of a lake, and again on the horizon, one can scarcely tell where earth and sky meet." Johnston lived in Texas during the 1840s and 1850s. See also Charles P. Roland and Richard C. Robbins, "The Diary of Eliza (Mrs. Albert Sidney) Johnston, the Second Cavalry Comes to Texas," *SHQ* 60 (April, 1957): 463–500.

14. Brooks, *Prominent Women of Texas,* 107–11.

15. Barns, *Texas Writers of Today,* 362, 155, 173.

16. *Handbook of Texas* 1:699.

17. Taylor, "Women Writers of Texas", 5–6, 10, 13.

18. Barns, *Texas Writers of Today,* 84, 423.

19. Taylor, "Women Writers of Texas," 10; Eagleton, *Writers and Writings of Texas,* 127.

20. Taylor, "Women Writers of Texas," 2, 6, 10.

21. Taylor, "Women Writers of Texas," 14, 17.

22. Barns, *Texas Writers Today,* 119, 159.

23. Taylor, "Women Writers of Texas," 1–2, 6.

24. Barns, *Texas Writers of Today,* 483.

25. Taylor, "Women Writers of Texas," 11.

26. Taylor, "Women Writers of Texas," 5–6, 12.

27. Taylor, "Women Writers of Texas," 13–14.

FICTION BY TEXAS WOMEN, 1846–1920

CAROLE WOLF

Discovering the Texas women who wrote fiction in English before 1920 presents many challenges, the first of which is to determine who can be considered Texan. Because Texas was not officially open to Anglo settlers until the 1820s, and because published fiction generally waits for some degree of civilization and refinement to arrive, pinpointing an exact beginning is difficult. Some immigrants were only temporary Texans, and some native Texans left the state to reside elsewhere. The following survey is limited to those who resided here for a period of years and/or wrote about a distinctive Texas event, setting, or character in at least one work. Until recently, bibliographic sources have been scarce and sketchy, and even though an interest in these writers has been revived, many will remain lost or long undiscovered. Some works are so obscure that they are known only by title. The survey in this chapter, then, provides a beginning for those who want to join the search for the works these women created. Identifying representative writers and their works, it attempts to show their connections to broader trends of the times.

For the most part, Texas women who wrote fiction in English before 1820 wrote in the sentimental style prevalent in popular fiction at that time; a few, however, moved in the direction of the realism being established by major American writers, and some local colorists captured the flavor of the Texas that was southern and the Texas that was western. Those in the sentimental school sometimes seemed to equate themselves as writers with heroines in a novel. They seldom alter the basic melodramatic formulas, offering all their ideas, lessons, characters, and vocabulary in one or two grand gestures. The typical sentimental novel includes a great deal of narration, elaborately entangled plots, stock characters (often with exotic names), syrupy sentimentality, "purple" prose, and heavy-handed morality, all culminating in one of two ways—tragically or happily-ever-after. Generally they provide readers with an escape into a world of intensity and, frequently, a lesson in morality as well. A few, mixing sentimental plots with historical events and settings, make a token move toward realism. Although the sentimentalists embrace melancholia, espouse causes, and flaunt erudition, other writers accept the challenge of creating a world closer to life. For those writers, dramatic presentation rather than narration is the norm, and plot is often subordinated to characters who express believable feelings in their own voices. Their details mirror life instead of glamorizing it, and in the works of local writers, those details preserve the life of a particular area, Texas.

For the more extreme sentimentalists, whose works depend upon stock characters and melodramatic tragedy, brief biographical sketches appear below.

Bella French Swisher, who lived in Austin at one time, was a poet and journalist who developed a journal entitled *A Sketch Book*. The *New Union Catalog* (cited hereafter as *NUC*) shows the publication dates as 1874–76, but Swisher continued editing the journal (also cited as *American Sketch Book*) when she came to Texas in 1877. Her novel, *Struggling Up to the Light* (1876), is little more than a catalog of the heroine's grief (complete with the standard fever and an attempted suicide)—except for one rather surprising deviation: the heroine pursues a career, albeit as a poet, and succeeds after a separation from a brutish husband named Harry Mann. Davis Foute Eagleton, in his *Writers and Writings of Texas,* mentions *Rocks and Shoals in the River of Life: A Novel* (1889) and includes one of her poems, "The San Antonio River." The *NUC* lists two other works: *Florecita* (1889) and *The Sin of Edith Dean* (1890).

Susanna Pinckney published under the name Sue Pinckney and used the pen name Miss McPherson. Though Eagleton mentions only

Douglas: Tender and True (1892), the *NUC* also lists *Darcy Pinckney* (1906) and *In the Southland* (1906). Pinckney squeezes as many conventions as she can into *Douglas: Tender and True*: a crippled daughter of a Confederate soldier falls in love with a Yankee soldier who rescued her father on the field of battle, and before the book ends, the widowed father has found love with a second wife and baby while the crippled daughter has married the Yankee who has taken her to Europe, cured her of her lameness with skills learned on the battlefield, and given her a child as well. In *Texas Prose Writings: A Reader's Digest,* Sister M. Agatha Sheehan describes the novel as an "oversentimental love story . . . in which the characters seemingly live on love alone. Money comes from unknown sources; struggles or desires from any cause, other than the emotions of the heart, are unheard of." According to the *NUC,* Pinckney was born in 1843, and her full name was Susanna Shulrick Hayne Pinckney.

Iona Oakley Gorham of Austin or Galveston wrote "Auf Wiedersehen," a short story published in *The Dallas and Galveston News* around 1891. Her interest in the exotic is apparent in the name she gives the heroine of her novel, *Naval Cadet Carlyle's Glove* (1894): Viva Van Vessler. After secretly marrying a young cadet who dies, the heroine finds love again but later chooses suicide (decked in a white evening gown with white hyacinths in her hair) instead of confessing the previous marriage to her prospective bridegroom. Gorham is noted in both Taylor and Eagleton, and according to both, she wrote another novel, *The Paces of Three Seasons,* though it is not listed in the *NUC.* Eagleton indicates that Gorham was on the staff of the *New York Evening Telegram.*

Hilda C. Collins wrote *My Guardian: A Novel* (1902), which, according to Sister M. Agatha, features "domestic scenes without regard for plot and with little or no universality of appeal." According to the *NUC,* Collins also wrote *Nadia Grey, A Novel* (1909).

Although some sentimentalists seemed content to revel in melodrama for its own sake, others apparently felt the need to champion a cause, speak out against vice, preach about Christian virtue, or offer their readers food for thought.

Kate Alma Orgain, is described by Sister M. Agatha as a member of the sentimental school whose *Waif from Texas* (1901) is "didactic in tone." According to the *NUC,* Orgain also published *Southern Writers in Poetry and Prose* (1908), which includes a citation of

Augusta Jane Evans Wilson, and a *Supplementary Reader* (n.d.) printed in Temple.

Mrs. H. C. L. Gorman of Fort Worth, like several others, sometimes used a pen name. According to Taylor, her earliest, "Clay Ligon," is mentioned in Ida Raymond's *Southland Writers*. Native to Alabama and educated in Georgia, Gorman first published a short story in the *Temperance Crusader* of Atlanta at the age of fifteen. When she moved to Texas in 1873 with her husband, she did some editing in 1883 for the *Fort Worth Gazette*. In 1892, under the pen name Clara LeClerc, she published a collection of short stories entitled *Uncle Plenty,* named for one of the characters who represents the "faithful old darky" typical in much of the literature romanticizing the Old South. A passion for the maudlin is clear in one story, "True Heroism; or Only Waiting": a long-suffering, lame child dies, and the details of the funeral, complete with "myrtle bordered walk" and a "snow-white pall," are offered in lavish detail. Taylor and Eagleton (who misspells Gorman as "Gorham" and LeClerc as "Leclere") mention a collection of stories entitled *Aunt Clara's Friday Afternoon Stories,* but there is no such listing in the *NUC*.

Annie Jefferson Holland of Austin, also identified by Taylor, is another champion of the Old South. She wrote *The Refugees: A Sequel to "Uncle Tom's Cabin"* and intended "to show . . . where a refined and cultivated people were thrown down into extreme poverty in the midst of a coarse African race, whom slavery barely rescued from cannibalism." According to Sister M. Agatha, "The book, imitating all the faults and none of the virtues of Mrs. Stowe's novel, is a vigorous feminine attack on the work of the Northern feminine Abolitionist." The novel is based on Holland's own experiences as a Civil War refugee from Louisiana. Another exotically named heroine, Oizelle Carrington, is reduced to sewing for the Negroes and loses her mind. She decks herself in the proverbial white and hangs herself in a tree by a river.

Mary Richardson Lesesne moved to Texas from North Carolina sometime before 1868, when she married and moved to Centerville with her husband. According to Taylor she sometimes wrote under the pen name Annie Norland. Whereas Gorman's and Holland's cause was the Old South, Lesesne preaches against the godless life of gambling and drink in her novel, *Torpedoes: or Dynamite in Society* (1883). Adele Reese, the heroine, loves a gambler who dies ignominiously on the gallows while she lives happily ever after because she learns to love a man of virtue. According to Sister M. Agatha, Lesesne's too-blatant purpose failed to impress the literary public.

Emily Davant Embree, writing in the early twentieth century, espouses religious piety. Though a native of Arkansas, Embree came to Texas in 1884 with her parents. The daughter of a Beaumont pastor, she attended Baylor College in Belton, where she later resided. Embree was a frequent contributor of short stories to the *Baptist Standard* and had a few short articles published in *Ladies Home, Country Gentlemen,* and *Modern Priscilla.* In *A Lesser Light* (1904) and *Mine Inheritance* (1907), Embree presents pious heroines who devote their lives to visiting the sick, saving souls, and teaching Sunday school. Both combine biblical citations with typical sentimental romances.

Margaret Olive Jordan wrote about the "movements of grace" in *God's Smiles and a Look into His Face* (1901). The NUC lists two other works by Jordan: *Wine for the Soul in Prose and Verse* (1919) and a collection of poetry, *Scattered Rose Leaves* (1903).

Ida Carmichael was another advocate of the religious life. Sister M. Agatha notes that Carmichael claims to have written the book *Beware! or, Irma's Life* (1901) "on her knees" and that each chapter ends with BEWARE!

Willie Williamson Rogers promotes erudition instead of religion in her novel *The House by the Side of the Road* (1912). Instead of biblical citations, Rogers offers literary allusions. Her characters congregate at a mansion designed and built by the heroine as a place of refuge for intellectuals to meditate, browse through its extensive library, engage in stimulating conversations, participate in little dramatic presentations, and attend inspiring lectures. Though the flaunting of scholarship is oppressive, the book does offer a glimpse of contemporary ideas and issues as well as a couple of sentimental romances. Rogers was a native of McKinney, but she lived in San Marcos for the most part. She became active in the women's suffrage movement, wrote a book on the history of Methodism in Texas, and coauthored a history textbook entitled *Flashlights of Texas* (1929) with Lillie T. Shaver.

Ada Cornelius Brannon was another writer interested in improving the minds of her readers. Sister M. Agatha remarks on the heroine's love of Shakespeare and the author's deliberate show of her own knowledge of Shakespeare in *A Noble Girl. A Book Devoted to The Uplift of Character and Modern Society* (1905).

These writers, though connected to Texas, did not offer anything distinctly Texan in their works, with the possible exception of Holland and Embree, whose settings are in Texas. Other sentimentalists, however, did make use of the romance of the Texas experience itself. Alice Cleveland in two early novelettes, *Lucy Morley, or, the Young Officer: A Tale of the Texan Revolution* (1846) and *The Haunted Castle* (1846), demonstrates an interest in both the exotic and the local. *The Haunted Castle* is set in France in the distant past, but *Lucy Morley* is set during the Texas Revolution. Though the plot is melodramatic, Cleveland does include Texan characters. For example, the heroine Lucy is saved from a forced marriage to a Mexican villain when the Texas scout whom she loves arrives in the nick of time with her father and a troop of Texans.

Maud Mason Austin, who according to Eagleton wrote real life stories, also wrote the novel *'Cension: A Sketch from Paso del Norte* (1896). Though the plot is thin and dull, the book is distinctive because the characters are Mexican peasants and the setting is El Paso.

Augusta Jane Evans [Wilson], a native of Columbus, Georgia, was a temporary resident who lived in Galveston, Houston, and San Antonio during the mid-1840s before moving to Mobile, Alabama, in 1849. As a result of her interest in Texas, she wrote the novel *Inez: A Tale of the Alamo* (1855) when she was about fifteen. It is the only one of her nine novels that is related to Texas at all and is principally an attack on Catholicism. Sister M. Agatha remarks that the heroines are typical orphans, and "their bereavement is typically and everlastingly sad." Commenting on the religious didactism, she adds: "The book in its entirety is little more than the conversation of these two girls who say all that Mrs. Wilson, who was herself at this time a mere girl, can put into their young minds in the way of theological disputation." Evans [Wilson] does set the story during the flight of San Antonio residents from the city and Santa Anna's assault. There is the usual romance and melodrama, complete with the deaths of two heroines and the happy ending for another, but the mention of historic events and places offers some relief. Evans [Wilson] also wrote *Beulah* (1859), *Macaria, or, Altars of Sacrifice* (1864), *St. Elmo* (1866), *Vashti: or "Until Death Do Us Part"* (1869), *Infelice* (1875), *At the Mercy of Tiberius* (1887), *A Speckled Bird* (1902), and *Devorta* (1907).

William Perry Fidler's *Augusta Evans Wilson 1835–1909: A Biography* (1951) also includes an epilogue on the sentimental novel.

Readers of this sentimental fiction apparently expected and enjoyed an escape from ordinary life into extraordinary tragedy and/or romance. Whether the ending was tragic or happy, a sense of completion was important. With the usual heavy dose of morality such fiction offered, writer and reader alike could regard it as instructive and enjoyable without a question of its being frivolous.

Several writers, however, either by design or accident, moved closer to creating fiction that mirrors life. These writers seemed to recognize the need to interject artificial feelings and lessons into their stories because both they and their readers could be affected by what was almost real. Freed from devising intricate plots to entangle their characters' lives in moral lessons leading to happy endings, these writers became less panoramic in scope and more focused on character development. For some of the writers, this move toward realism was evident in a more extensive use of local events, settings and dialect.

Belle Hunt Shortridge employs local attitudes, dialect, and setting in her short story "Texas Thanksgiving" (1892), which Eagleton includes in his collection. The story is set in Decatur, near where she was born, and it is delivered in an unpretentious, tongue-in-cheek tone, the writer admitting in the text that it is a conventional love story. Later in her career, Shortridge lived for some time in New York. She apparently was noted for her collection of poems *Lone Star Lights* (1891) because of its distinctive Texas flavor. Both Eagleton and Taylor mention a novel, *Held in Trust* (1892), and Eagleton also mentions another, *Circumstance* (1892); however, the NUC lists neither.

Fanny Chambers Gooch [Iglehart] wrote a "historical story for youth," *The Boy Captive of the Texas Mier Expedition* (1909). Sister M. Agatha says, "the author drops naturally into the pioneer expressions and into the easy freedom of boys out for a hike," and she notes a move "toward conciliation of any ill feeling between Texas and Mexico" and mentions Gooch's *Face to Face with the Mexicans: the Domestic Life, Educational, Social, and Business Ways, Statesmanship and Literature, Legendary and General History of the Mexican People* (1887).

Amelia Edith Huddleston Barr was one of the better-known and more prolific writers associated with Texas, though *Remember the Alamo* (1888) is the only Texas book among her fifty-nine novels.

Taylor makes no mention of Barr, but there is a significant entry about her in *American Women Writers*. Eagleton identifies her as a Texas writer. A native of England, she came to the United States from Scotland with her husband in 1850 and resided in Austin for ten years before moving to Galveston. After her husband and three sons died of yellow fever, she moved to New York City with her three daughters, and soon after, she began her career as a writer. The *NUC* lists more than seventy-five works, in addition to short stories and essays, that appeared in *Christian Union, Illustrated Christian Weekly, Harper's Weekly, Harper's Bazaar, Frank Leslie's Magazine,* and *Advance.*

In *Remember the Alamo,* Barr makes better use of the Texas Revolution than Evans [Wilson], though she too attacks Catholicism and involves her characters in the flight from San Antonio and Santa Anna. She is less sentimental and develops more distinct characters. For example, her heroine is a strong young woman whose father is Anglo and whose mother is from an elite Mexican family. By using this conflict of loyalties within a family, Barr introduces a problem evident in historical families' lives. In addition to using history, Barr develops characters who grow from spoiled petulance to maturity, and she refrains from the all-or-nothing happy or tragic ending. Sister M. Agatha wonders about Barr's enthusiastic attack on Mexican Catholicism, given her English background, but acknowledges the book's popularity and concludes: "A little less theme and a little more fiction would have saved the story element and made the book a work of art." Barr's *All the Days of My Life: An Autobiography. The Red Leaves of a Human Heart* (1913), which offers a good picture of the Texas of her times, also reveals her as a strong woman who was an activist for women's rights.

Emma Nelson Hood of Austin is the author of *Bob Dean; or, Our Other Boarder* (1882). The novel, though flawed in places by excessive editorial comment and too-sweet passages, does deal less with plot and more with the interactions of characters than most sentimental pieces do. Hood deviates in using a man as the main character and gives him something else to do besides be in love. In particular, Hood elevates this plot above the ordinary melodramatic love story by means of extensive dialogue and by probing the characters' thoughts and motivations, and she also uses these thoughts as vehicles for developing other characters.

Julia Truitt Bishop had her own publication, *Texas Home-Corner.* She came to Texas in 1877 and, in addition to the magazine, she published stories in the *Houston Post* and other Texas papers, as well as papers in Philadelphia and St. Louis. Her poetry is collected in *Birds of Passage* (1890), and she also published the novel *Kathleen Douglas* (1890). Written in first person, the novel features an internalized view of the character, and though it is a romance, female education and independence seem to be focal points of equal value. Bishop integrates character development with plot.

Mollie E. Moore Davis, rightfully claimed by both Texas and Louisiana, is perhaps the best of these early fiction writers. Certainly she is the most widely cited by literary historians. According to *American Woman Writers,* Davis was born in 1852. Other sources place her birthdate in 1847 or 1844, which seems more likely. As a child she moved from her home in Alabama to San Marcos. Initially she was recognized for her poetry, which first appeared in the *Tyler Reporter* in 1860. Following that beginning, she spent half her time in Tyler and half in Houston, writing for the papers, before moving to Galveston in 1867. Her first collection of poetry, *Minding the Gap, And Other Poems,* was published in 1867. In 1879 she moved to New Orleans with her husband, who was on the staff of the *New Orleans Times.* He became editor of the *Picayune* in 1889. Her first prose work, *In War Times at La Rose Blanche Plantation* (1888), is noted in *American Women Writers* as her "best-known work, . . . a semiautobiographical story sequence." Gaston and Sister M. Agatha, however, regard *Under the Man-Fig* (1895) as her best-known work; *American Women Writers,* acknowledging it to be the "most fully realized" of her novels, praises her "deft use of regional dialect, historical detail, and humorous characters."

In 1897, Davis published *An Elephant's Track, and Other Stories,* which shows her at her technical best. The collection includes stories set in both Texas and Louisiana. *The Wire-Cutters* (1899) is distinctly Southwestern in flavor, since the vehicle of the plot is controversy over the fencing of ranch lands. *Jaconetta: Her Loves* (1901), a first-person reminiscence of one looking back on childhood fascinations with special people and things, may be somewhat autobiographical since it is set on a plantation like Davis's girlhood home. The last two novels Davis wrote are *The Little Chevalier* (1903), "a historical novel regarded as her best," and *The Price of Silence* (1907), "her most popular." Both focus on the Creole culture of Louisiana. Although Davis sometimes works with intricate plots, touches of mystery and voodoo, and some standard romance elements, she illustrates the movement away from narrated, sentimental novels toward more dramatic, realistic works. In fact, Davis also wrote some dramatic works that are included in complete lists of her published works.

The writers presented here are merely representative; there are others waiting to be rediscovered and introduced to modern readers. The short-story writers of the period in particular are difficult to discover because the proliferation of popular magazines and other periodicals, as well as hometown newspapers, provided so many opportunities to publish. Individual writers' works may not be collected anywhere, however, and indexes to the more local publications are not always available.

THE INNOVATORS, 1920–60

In Katherine Anne Porter's short story "The Old Order," Miranda's grandmother, Sophia Jane, widowed and responsible for an extended family, has come to Texas to make a new life. Here she has "all of the responsibilities of man but with none of the privileges." Hard though her life is, Sophia Jane remains true in spirit to her southern-bred notion of "true womanhood." She broods over her pampered youngest son's choice of a bride:

> [T]here was something about her new daughter-in-law, a tall, handsome, firm-looking young woman, with a direct way of speaking, walking, talking, that seemed to promise that the spoiled Baby's days of clover were ended. . . . [S]he was altogether too Western, too modern, something like the "new" woman who was beginning to run wild, asking for the vote, leaving home and going out in the world to earn her own living.

That Sophia Jane, self-sufficient matriarch, would criticize the perceived independence of a younger woman is an irony on which Porter develops her theme: the grandmother is of the "old order," but her description of the "new woman" mirrors the author's own image.

Porter led the "new women" writers of Texas in the 1920s. Her fame has been more lasting than that of other Texas women novelists and short-story writers of her time, but she exemplifies in her themes most clearly what other Texas women writers had begun to explore. New women themselves, they sought to demystify some of the treasured notions of a woman's place in society carried over from the nineteenth century. Newly enfranchised as voters and often encouraged by their membership in literary clubs where other women writers critiqued and criticized their work, Texas women writers began to demonstrate that for them writing was not a hobby but a profession.

Beginning in the late 1920s, two talented university teachers were loyal advocates of Texas writers, particularly women writers. For three decades the inimitable Mabel Major and Rebecca Smith made Texas Christian University a center for study of southwestern literature, competing no doubt with Dobie for recognition as knowledgeable critics. Rebecca Smith joined the faculty at Texas Christian University in 1919. From 1931 to 1943 she served as head of the English Department. Mabel Major came to the same department in the same year as Smith and retired in 1963. Both professors were active in the Texas Folklore Society as well as the Texas Institute of Letters. Major was president of TFS in 1936–37. Smith was instrumental in the organization of TIL, publicizing its organization with a series of articles in *The Texas Outlook.*

Both professors were forceful promoters of southwestern literature, collaborating as editors of several books, and writing numerous essays about southwestern writers. In *The Southwest in Literature* (1929), an anthology for high schools, Smith and Major included an excerpt from Bride Taylor's biography of sculptor Elisabet Ney, Julia Beazley's narration of a Jean Lafitte legend, Adina de Zavala's retelling of San Antonio mission legends, an excerpt from Dorothy Scarborough's *On the Trail of Negro Folksong,* and poetry by Karle Wilson Baker and Lexie Dean Robertson.

In the 1920s and 1930s, Smith edited a literary page in *The Texas Outlook,* reviewing books by Texans, as well as nationally known authors, under the title "Books and Branding Irons." One interesting comment in her January, 1929, column is that the Texas Folklore Publication for that year is "edited by the Society's invaluable secretary, J. Frank Dobie, and—we want to add—his wife, Bertha McKee Dobie, who seems to be the unofficial genius of the volume." Smith's concept of Bertha's role in J. Frank's career is clear here.

In 1936, Smith collaborated with William H. Vann to publish

"Texas Centennial Literature Programs" in *The Texas Outlook*. In 1937 she was among the editors of the southwestern edition of *American Literature,* published for high school juniors by Scribners. Texas women writers' works appearing in the textbook include those by Laura Krey, Karle Wilson Baker, Berta Hart Nance, Goldie Capers Smith, Margaret Bell Houston, Dorothy Scarborough, Grace Noll Crowell, Fay Yauger, and Lexie Dean Robertson. The only male authors from Texas included among such well-knowns as Emerson, Whitman, and Twain are J. Frank Dobie, Walter Prescott Webb, and Larry Chittenden. Obviously, Smith influenced choices for this edition, which served as a textbook through the early 1940s.

George Sessions Perry concludes his 1943 collection of Southwestern writings, *Roundup Time,* with Smith's "The Southwest in Fiction," which had appeared the year before in the *Saturday Review of Literature* (May 16, 1942). Admitting that "except in the stories of Katherine Anne Porter and in the literary circles of Santa Fe and Taos, there has been little sophistication" in southwestern writing, Smith nevertheless includes commentary on Ruth Cross's *The Golden Cocoon,* which she calls "an indictment of North Texas tenant farm life," and on Dorothy Scarborough's *The Wind,* which she says is "no conventional 'Western'." She devotes paragraph-long discussions to novels by Laura Krey, Karle Wilson Baker, Mary King, and Elizabeth Wheaton, and mentions Anne Pence Davis's fiction.

Smith's chief criticism of novels produced in the Southwest during the twenties and thirties is that they lack "psychological intensity." She perceives what Florence Barns, author of *Texas Writers of Today* (1935), discusses earlier in "The Novel in Texas" in *The Southwester* (Summer, 1935). Barns comes to the conclusion that "no specific trend has even hinted its conception until recently." She perceives the Texas novel as still in the "embryonic state."

Whatever the inadequacies of Texas women writers in the twenties and thirties, their innovative approaches to subject and theme promised that their work would soon move out of the embryonic stage. There is evidence of a developing literary maturity and independence in what these women chose to write. Most were unimpressed with the rapidly coalescing Texas Mystique that influenced Dobie's admirers for years. Dorothy Scarborough stirred up readers with her realistic version of West Texas pioneer life, Loula Grace Erdman saw that homesteaders' lives in the Panhandle were as interesting as those of the range cowboys, and Jewel Gibson proved that a Texas woman could write humorous satire, even about fundamental religion. Ruth Cross portrayed the hard life of the tenant-farmer's wife, and Elithe Hamilton Kirkland perceived the dynamic fictional possibilities in the personal history of a remarkable early-Texas woman. Karle Wilson Baker and Winifred Sanford described oil-boomtown life as it really was. These writers, with Katherine Anne Porter setting the pace, were the trail breakers. By 1960, Texas women as professional writers were recognized as a vital part of the mainstream in Texas letters.

Such diversity of theme and subject in Texas women's writing as well as that of all southwestern writers of this era inspired the most useful collaboration of Rebecca Smith and Mabel Major. With T. M. Pearce, a University of New Mexico professor, they produced *Southwest Heritage: A Literary History with Bibliographies* in 1938 and a revised edition in 1948. The third edition, published in 1972, was edited by Pearce and Major only. In the 1940s Smith had married and moved to Kentucky, where, as Rebecca Smith Lee, she wrote a biography of Mary Austin Holley in 1962. Mabel Major continued to encourage the study of southwestern literature until her retirement.

MABEL MAJOR

JOYCE GIBSON ROACH

Mabel Irmyn Major (1894–1974) was not, according to her own assessment and judgment, a writer. Others bestowed that label on her, she said. Yet there are credits to support the claim that Mabel Major (no *s* on my last name, please) was a southwestern writer. Numerous articles, book reviews, and poems appeared in leading quarterlies, magazines, and newspapers over the years of her career. "British Ballads in Texas" was a significant contribution to *Tone the Bell Easy,* the 1932 volume of the *Publications of the Texas Folklore Society.* She wrote a biography of Susan Elston (Mrs. Lew) Wallace, but it was never published. Her significant publications were coauthored or coedited. In 1929, Rebecca Smith appeared as her coeditor in *The Southwest in Literature: An Anthology for High Schools.* T. M. Pearce, of the University of New Mexico, was added as coeditor for the 1938 and 1948 editions of a survey entitled *Southwest Heritage: A Literary History with Bibliographies.* The 1972 edition appeared under the names of Major and Pearce only. *Early Times in Texas, or, The Adventures of Jack Dobell* (1936) by John C. Duval, contained a preface and commentary on the life of Duval by Major and Smith. *My Foot's in the Stirrup,* by W. S. Bartlett as told to Major and Smith, appeared soon after. An edition of *The Adventures of Big-Foot Wallace* by John C. Duval was edited by Major and Smith. In 1949 an anthology of southwestern poetry, *Signature of the Sun: Southwest Verse, 1900–1950,* listed Major and Pearce as coeditors.

"I am not a creative writer; not a novelist, short story writer, not even a good poet. I write instead about others who write," insisted Mabel.

If she was not, by her own admission, a "real" writer, she was, without a doubt and on good testimony, a teacher. In teaching about literary research about the Southwest, she became a leading figure on the subject. The recipient of the Piper Professorship in 1959 and an emeritus professorship in 1964, Mabel Major influenced hundreds of students during her forty-five years of teaching at Texas Christian University. And she inspired countless others through her association with the Texas Folklore Society and the Texas Institute of Letters and as a lifetime member of the Poetry Society of Texas.

I cannot speak of Mabel Major in other than personal terms. Although she died several years ago, I have the feeling that she is still in the English office on the TCU campus; or in the auditorium listening to a concert or seeing a play; or at the library reaching on tiptoes while calling for help to "get it down for me please; I am still too short." Mabel was first my teacher and eventually my friend. Probably—no, decidedly—Mabel became my friend in the very process of establishing a student-teacher relationship.

Because Mabel instructed in Chaucer, Shakespeare, Browning, and the Romantics at one time or another and in southwestern literature as well, she was delighted when her students found connections between English literature and western writing. When reading one of Tennyson's treatments of the Arthurian cycle one day, I said, "Miss Major, it isn't very far from Camelot to the cow lot is it?" "You are right," she responded. The next weekend she took me—rather, I took her—to the meeting of the Texas Folklore Society, where I met J. Frank Dobie and Walter Prescott Webb and a great gathering of people ready to talk about anything from the cow lot to Camelot as long as the discussions could be related to the great state of Texas.

Mabel Major did not discuss English literature with me much after that. She pushed a variety of interesting southwestern subjects and people in my path and urged me to write. Early on she convinced me that a small, rural town such as the one I grew up in had as much to offer in subject matter and characters as any other place on earth. In addition she kept filling my ear with fascinating information about southwestern subjects. She spoke of visiting the widow of D. H. Lawrence in New Mexico and of eating a squash-blossom omelet prepared by Mrs. Lawrence and listening to stories about D. H.'s celebrated ashes (which were kept in an urn on the ranch grounds). Mary Austin, whom Mabel considered the brightest female star in the southwestern literary sky, fascinated her. A snapshot of Major, Smith, and probably Austin encourages me to believe the three met at least once.

Mabel's favorite story concerned a trip Mary Austin made to some pueblo in New Mexico. Residents of the pueblo, who knew of Austin's importance and value to their way of life, wished to honor her and to defer to her customs. The elders inquired and learned that white people slept in beds with covers over them. The bed was a problem, but heavy, woollen blankets were plentiful. A makeshift bed was constructed and coverings collected. Austin arrived. The month was August. After celebration, ceremony, gourd rattling, and chanting far into the night, Austin was shown to her quarters, a typical pueblo cubicle with no windows. She climbed up the ladder of the pueblo walls and down into her sleeping quarters deep inside the many-layered apartment. She was not alone, however. Following close behind her were four tribal members who took up a respectful vigil, one in each corner of the tiny room.

It was hot. It was dark. But no person or spirit would disturb the rest of the woman in the sacred innards of the communal dwelling that August night. Whether the four held ceremonial feather or pipe, the guest could not tell. Where the bed was she could not tell except by feeling. What to do? She must honor the customs that they thought were proper for her.

Mary lay down. Silently some or all of the guardians moved to the end of her bed and gently drew the woollen covers over her body and up to her neck. After a suffocating time, slowly and quietly Mary drew the covers down. In a few moments, kind hands drew the covers back up again and tucked her in. All night the ritual was repeated. When morning finally came, Mary gratefully climbed from her guarded oven into the air. She was followed by her four guardians, puzzled yet sure that the proper rituals had been observed.

It may well be that southwestern events, characters, and writers were a source of interest for Mabel Major because her own background was very different. Mabel was, in her own words, "by birth a

Utahan, by rearing a Missourian, but by choice a Texan." Her growing-up years were spent in Paris and Columbia, Missouri. She received the A.B. and B.S. in education and an M.A. in English from
the University of Missouri. She taught at Higginsville, Missouri, for
a short time and then asked for an assignment as far away from home
as possible. The assignment turned out to be in Texas, in Big Spring.
Little is known about her time in Big Spring or what she thought of
the place, except that she fell in love with one of her students. They
planned to be married, but wedding plans were canceled by the
groom's family. In 1919, Mabel joined the English staff at Texas Christian University, where she remained until her retirement, in 1963.
Later she taught at Baylor University and established a course in southwestern literature.

As a member of a university faculty and of a professional organization, Mabel felt obligated to stake a claim on a subject that might
be enriched by her research. If anyone cried, "Publish or perish!" in
her ear, she could say with assurance, "I am deep in research." Mabel
chose not Browning or Shakespeare but, instead, a simple southwestern poem by a then-unknown author. The verses tell of a cowboy
who loves a Mexican beauty by the name of Lasca. Lasca saves the
cowboy from a wild cattle stampede by throwing her body across his
as the cowboy pulls his horse's carcass down on top of them both.

The poem is melodramatic. I asked Mabel once if she thought
"Lasca" a good poem. "No," she confided, "but it is memorable,
and it keeps everybody from bothering me about scholarly projects. I
just keep telling them I am researching 'Lasca.'" I reminded her that
she had been researching "Lasca" for thirty years. She chuckled.

From students whom she had put to work on "Lasca," Mabel
found that the poem was written by Frank Desprez, an Englishman
who had spent two years along the Rio Grande but who worked in
the theater business most of his life and wrote "Lasca" and similar
poems for recitation during play intermissions. Only a few years before her death, Mabel went to England, found Frank Desprez's daughter, Sylvia Wakefield, and made a recording of her reading "Lasca."
Mabel's favorite line from the poem was, "One does not drink in
little sips / In Texas down by the Rio Grande." Mabel never drank in
little sips either, nor would she allow any of her students to love
Texas in any way except in enormous gulps.

Mabel Major's course in literature of the Southwest caused some comment, mainly in the English Department, but in other places too. The course contained much folklore and concentrated on the depth, breadth, and height of the life as well as the literature of three cultures—Indian, Mexican, and Anglo in the states of Texas, Oklahoma, New Mexico, and Arizona and parts of a few states hanging around the edges. Such a study was in sharp contrast to courses in Shakespeare's plays or surveys in Victorian literature. At the time the very term *folklore* smacked of something low, perhaps vulgar, and certainly unworthy of attention at the university level. Nobody taught folklore. Mabel, however, insisted that all good art, music, literature, and drama has folklore as its base. She encouraged the learning of folklore as a springboard to fine arts. Mabel was never in love with folklore for its own sake, but rather because it pointed out the possibilities for better forms of expression. Her thinking was a curious mixture of almost Victorian correctness, love of scholarship, fine detail, and right technique blended with admiration for dancing gods, Texas cowboy rigging, bright and gaudy colors, mystic communion with the desert, and coyotes howling at the moon. Fortunate were those who learned the lessons of both her worlds.

KARLE WILSON BAKER
AND CHARLOTTE
BAKER MONTGOMERY

PAMELA LYNN PALMER

KARLE WILSON BAKER

When Karle Wilson (1878–1960) joined her parents in Nacogdoches in 1901, she never imagined she would live there for most of the rest of her life. Born in Little Rock, Arkansas, on October 13, 1878, she had seen her hometown grow into a bustling community of nearly thirty-five thousand by the time she left in 1898. After two summers and an academic year at the University of Chicago, she had grown to adore large cities. Her two years of teaching French and English at Southern Virginia Institute in tiny Bristol had reinforced her preference for big-city energy over small-town lethargy. Although her partiality toward urban life was strong, familial devotion drew her to Nacogdoches, and romantic love kept her there.

Karle's mother, Kate Florence ("Floy") Montgomery Wilson, had suffered from frail health since about 1884 and was for many years an invalid. Karle's father, William Thomas Murphy Wilson, and her younger brother, Benjamin Taylor Wilson, were busy trying to establish a wholesale grain business centered in Nacogdoches. Her older half-sisters had more firmly established lives of their own in Little Rock. As the only unattached daughter, Karle felt a responsibility to care for her mother. Hired help was expensive, and finding someone able to endure Floy's fiery temperament and demands for perfection was difficult. While staying with her mother, Karle drafted a juvenile novel based on Floy's childhood experiences as the daughter of a Union officer assigned to the former Confederate capital of Washington, Arkansas, during Reconstruction. Titled "The Little Carpet-bagger," the manuscript suffered from a diffuse point of view, the story being that of a child viewed through adult hindsight. Karle also had trouble portraying Yankees because her own sympathies were stronger for the South. She never found a publisher for this work.

By 1903, Floy's health had improved enough to allow Karle to return to Little Rock to teach at Peabody High for two years. She found the job rewarding but emotionally and physically exhausting. During the summers she returned to Nacogdoches and pursued a free-lance writing career. By 1907 she had published poems, short stories, and essays in *Harper's Magazine, Cosmopolitan, Redbook,* and *Atlantic Monthly.* She was earning enough money to support herself, especially with the sale of a story, "The Accidental Saint," to *Collier's* for $300.

Marriage and children slowed but did not disrupt Karle's literary development. On August 8, 1907, she married Thomas E. Baker of Nacogdoches, a businessman with an interest in a local drugstore. He soon turned to banking and eventually became president of Commercial National Bank. Their son, Thomas Wilson Baker, was born December 1, 1908, and a daughter, Charlotte, arrived on August 31, 1910. In her new roles as wife and mother, Baker expanded her exploration of male-female relationships to include the repercussions of family life. Always sensitive to her surroundings, she absorbed the imagery and color of her adopted region and captured its dialects, folklore, and history on paper. While the children were young, she found it difficult to concentrate on anything longer than poems and brief essays, mostly on homemaking topics. After they started school, however, she turned to more ambitious projects.

In 1914, Baker began sending poetry and essays to *Yale Review,* where she found a sympathetic reader in editor Wilbur L. Cross. This connection led to the publication of her first collection of poetry, *Blue Smoke: A Book of Verses,* by Yale University Press in 1919. The volume received numerous positive reviews in periodicals throughout the United States and in England. Soon after submitting her poetry collection, Baker sent her volume of allegorical tales, *Old Coins.*

The stories were similar in style and content to the *Fifty-One Tales* of Irish playwright Lord Dunsany, but she was unaware of their affinity until after she had completed her own manuscript. *Old Coins* was accepted for publication but delayed to allow the appearance of Baker's fantasy for children, *The Garden of the Plynck.* Eager to have the children's book ready in time for Christmas sales in 1920, Yale rushed the book into production and, in so doing, cut corners. The result was unfortunate flaws in the book design. Color illustrations were out of the question, except for the cover and title page, and the number of black-and-white drawings, produced by Florence Minard, had to be reduced. The print was small and allowed no italics, and unattractive gray boards were used to back the cover design. Because its main character was female, reviewers could not resist comparing the book to *Alice in Wonderland,* even though, as Karle insisted, her Sara was a feminine creation and her world, a poet's.

By 1922, *Blue Smoke* had nearly gone out of print, and rather than reprint it, Yale urged Baker to bring out a new collection. *Burning Bush,* which consisted mainly of poems composed over the two or three years preceding publication, was not as strong as *Blue Smoke,* which represented the distillation of nearly twenty years of labor. In 1923, *Old Coins* finally appeared, but falling between the usual spring and fall lists, it dropped into an abyss of neglect.

With four published books to her credit, Baker was called upon with increasing frequency to lecture and read her works before women's clubs, literary societies, schools, and colleges in Texas and as far away as Atlanta, Boston, and New York. In the summer of 1924 she was invited to teach a course in contemporary poetry at the newly opened Stephen F. Austin State Teachers College. Having acquired an honorary Litt.D. from Southern Methodist University, she was asked to join the English faculty at Stephen F. Austin permanently. She accepted and, except for a year's leave to study at the University of California at Berkeley, stayed until 1934. Her influence on campus as a teacher, and as a leader in the cultural vanguard of the Southwest, was chronicled in the SFA newspaper, *The Pine Log.*

In 1930, dissatisfied with the failure of Yale University Press to take full advantage of her increasing renown in Texas, Baker turned to Southwest Press of Dallas to publish *The Birds of Tanglewood,* a group of four nature essays. Southwest Press also brought out Baker's

Dreamers on Horseback (Collected Verse) (1931), which reprinted portions of *Blue Smoke* and *Burning Bush* as well as later poems. The volume was a nominee for the Pulitzer Prize for Poetry.

In 1923, Baker's friend at the World Book Company, John Rosser, approached her with the idea of writing a children's reader based on Texas material. Baker's *Texas Flag Primer* was adopted for use in public schools by the State Textbook Commission for 1926–29. This book was Baker's most successful financially: her income from the 110,000 copies printed for statewide distribution was about $3,000. A rival textbook publisher soon came out with a competing line of Texas readers, however, and Baker's book failed to make the list a second time. Furthermore, because the Great Depression caused a drastic retrenchment in state expenditures, her second reader, *Two Little Texans* (1932), was never adopted.

By the time Baker retired from college teaching, in 1934, she had completed two novels and started a third. "The White Elephant," about a young widow who fixes up houses for sale to the *nouveau riche* of the oil industry, was never published. For thirty years, Baker and her family made frequent trips to oil rigs, and they even invested in some mineral leases, always hoping for a strike near Nacogdoches. These experiences lent remarkable technical detail and verisimilitude to *Family Style,* a novel about the impact of the 1930s oil boom upon several East Texas families, and in 1937 Coward-McCann published the novel. Baker's third novel, published by Coward-McCann in 1942, became a Book of the Month Club selection. *Star of the Wilderness: A Novel* emphasized the role of Dr. James Grant in the Texas Revolution and detailed the hardships and adventures of his cousin's family from Ohio to Nacogdoches. Focusing on lesser-known events of the period, such as the Battle of Nacogdoches and the successful siege of the Bexar fortress in San Antonio (later known as the Alamo), the novel was much admired by historians for its authenticity. A fourth novel, "It Blows from the Spanish Country," about the abortive Magee-Gutiérrez Expedition, which attempted to free Texas from Spanish rule in 1812–14, never saw print.

Disappointed with the rejection of her final, nearly six-hundred-page novel, and suffering from ill health, Baker wrote only sporadically during her last decade. She began an autobiography, "Full Circle," but being a private soul who disliked displays of self-absorption, she soon digressed into observations on birds and weather. Her son, her daughter, and two grandchildren lived in Nacogdoches, and she spent much of her time with them. After an illness that kept her hospitalized for most of her last year, she died on November 8, 1960, at the age of eighty-two.

Baker's last work to be published, *The Reindeer's Shoe and Other Stories,* was issued by Ellen C. Temple in cooperation with Stephen F. Austin State University in 1988. Consisting of four children's stories probably written in the 1920s, the book is illustrated with black-and-grey silhouettes that were created by her daughter, Charlotte, in the 1930s. The stories are a unique blend of regional imagery with fairy-tale fantasy, and the volume is superbly designed.

Although Karle Wilson Baker never intended to be known as a poet, that label, once bestowed, stuck. She wrote little poetry after 1930, but after helping found the Poetry Society of Texas, she became its first elected vice president, and she retained the office in an honorary capacity long after she became only peripherally involved. In 1936, Baker also helped organize the Texas Institute of Letters, and she served as president from 1938 to 1939. Her highest recognition as a writer came in 1952, when she was named the third Fellow of the Institute, an honor she shared with J. Frank Dobie and Walter Prescott Webb. She was the first woman thus honored. One of the first Texas writers to forge a reputation in a literary world dominated by eastern publishers, Baker deserves to be remembered not only for her diverse literary accomplishments, but also as an inspiration to other women attempting to juggle a career and homelife.

CHARLOTTE BAKER MONTGOMERY

Charlotte Baker (b. 1910) inherited her mother's literary talent and added artistic skills to become a highly successful author and illustrator. Graduating from Mills College in 1929, she received her M.A. degree the following year at the University of California at Berkeley. She taught in the Kilgore public schools from 1931 to 1934 and at Ball State Teachers College in Muncie, Indiana, in 1934 and 1935. From 1940 to 1942 she was acting head of the Art Department at Texas College of Arts and Industries in Kingsville, and from 1945 to 1950 she served as docent and acting director of the Portland Art

Museum in Oregon. She married Robert Montgomery on October 23, 1942, but retained her maiden name as her signature on most of her published works.

Charlotte Baker's first two novels, *A Sombrero for Miss Brown* (1941) and *House of the Roses* (1942), suspense novels with hints of Nazi intrigue, were set in Mexico. Published by Dutton, both received good reviews from *The New York Times*. Her first juvenile, *Hope Hacienda,* a Pro Parvula Book Club selection published by Crowell in 1942, was also set in Mexico. *Necessary Nellie* (1945), *Nellie and the Mayor's Hat* (1947), and *The Green Poodles* (1956) all became Junior Literary Guild selections. *Magic for Mary M* (1953), a child's view of the East Texas oil boom, and *The Best of Friends* (1966) received the Cokesbury Award from the Texas Institute of Letters. Inspired by her experiences and research in Portland, where her husband practiced law, *The House on the River* (1948), *Kinnery Camp: A Story of the Oregon Woods* (1951), *Sunrise Island: A Story of the Northwest Coast Indians before the Coming of the White Man* (1952), *The Venture of the Thunderbird* (1954), *The Return of the Thunderbird* (1954), and *Thomas, the Ship's Cat* (1958), a *Parents Magazine* Book Club selection, were set in the Pacific Northwest.

Charlotte Baker's writings, like her mother's, reflect a regional consciousness that immerses the reader in the geographical setting through the use of unique speech patterns and sensitivity to natural surroundings. Animal themes, already a prominent feature of Charlotte Baker's work, became her focal point in 1959, when she and her husband became cofounders of the Humane Society of Nacogdoches County. That year saw the publication of *Little Brother* and *An ABC of Dog Care for Young Owners.* These were followed by *The Best of Friends* (1966) and *The Kittens and the Cardinals* (1969). *Cockleburr Quarters,* her most acclaimed work to date was published by Prentice-Hall in 1972 and reissued by Avon and Methuen. The book received first prize at Book World Children's Spring Book Festival, the Lewis Carroll Shelf Award from the University of Wisconsin, and the Kerlan Collection Award from the University of Minnesota. In addition it was nominated for the Newbery Award.

Since becoming active in the humane-society movement, Charlotte Baker has devoted most of her talents to interpreting, particularly for young people, the humane ethic of reverence for life. Defining humane education as "bringing out the best in human nature," she has written various instructional materials. *A Visit to a Humane Society Animal Shelter: A Teacher's Guide Grades 3–4* (1967) and *Meeting Animal Friends: A Humane Education Handbook* (1972) were distributed through the National Humane Education Center. Parameter Press published her *Return to Eden: A Play about Ecology* in 1973. She has written the text for a coloring book on dog and cat care for the National Association for Humane Education and Ecology.

For her work as an animal-rights advocate, Charlotte Baker received the Society for Animal Protection Poag Award as "Humanitarian of the Year" for 1960–61, the Humane Society of the United States certificate of appreciation in 1969, and the Joseph Wood Krutch Medal "for significant contribution towards the improvement of life and environment" in 1983. From July 1960 until July 1996 she wrote a weekly column about animal welfare, "Noah's Notebook," for the Nacogdoches *Daily Sentinel*. She was instrumental in the development of an annual humane education workshop at Stephen F. Austin State University in 1978. In 1984 she founded the Roger Montgomery Humane Education Fund as a tribute to her late husband's contribution to animal welfare, to support the program at SFA, which is a pioneer effort to educate teachers about animal rights.

In addition to illustrating her own works, Charlotte Baker contributed the drawings and endpaper designs for her mother's *Birds of Tanglewood* and illustrated Frances Alexander's *Mother Goose on the Rio Grande* (1944). In 1982 her adult short story, "Hands of Horror," was included in *Her Work: Stories by Texas Women*. Her latest children's book, *The Trail North: Stories of Texas' Yesterdays*, portraying life from ancient days to the present in and about her home on North Street in Nacogdoches, was published by Eakin Press in 1990. It received the Texas Institute of Letters Young People's Book Award in 1991.

RUTH CROSS

SYLVIA WHITMAN

Like so many protagonists in her novels, Mattie Ruth Cross (1887–1981) drew from her Texas roots the gumption to transcend them. Born near Paris on Christmas Day, 1887, she grew up in rural Sylvan, which she rechristened "Law's Chapel" in her fiction. Her writing ambitions drew her far afield. Yet even after she had traveled from coast to coast and then settled in rural Connecticut, Sylvan continued to people her imagination. As Cross told an interviewer in 1928, "Everything I have written had its origin in characters and environments that I knew in my youth . . . not cowboy Texas, but the cotton area and Austin, where I went to college."

Cross's parents inspired in their oldest daughter a love of learning and of people. A high school principal, Walter D. Cross had packed up his young family in order to study medicine in the Southeast. Once he returned to Sylvan to practice, the four children attended public school; the teacher boarded at their colonial house. But for her academic head start, Cross always credited her mother, Willie Alta (Cole) Cross, a music teacher and scholar of Greek and Latin. The family moved into town so that Ruth could study at Paris High School, from which she graduated with highest honors in English. In 1904 she entered the University of Texas.

On the modest income of a country doctor, the Crosses could

afford one servant and just one year of Ruth's college education. To pay the rest of her way, she worked as a bank cashier and as a schoolteacher in small Texas towns and on an Oklahoma Indian reservation. An eye malady aggravated her struggles. Her mother enrolled as a UT student to assist Ruth with her course work. After her mother's sudden death, Ruth depended upon friends to read and take notes for her. Despite this temporary handicap, in 1911 she received her M.A. in creative writing—Phi Beta Kappa.

Although Cross resumed teaching Latin and German in a Longview high school, she longed to publish the stories she had been penning since age thirteen. Full of resolve, she left Texas. After a summer studying in Chicago and a period of writing and visiting maternal relatives in Winnfield, Louisiana, she landed in New York. Steeled against rejections, Cross supported her artistic endeavors with jobs as a housekeeper, interior decorator, traveling companion, typist, teacher, and real-estate agent. In 1915 she sold her first short story for $15.20.

Popular periodicals, such as the *Saturday Evening Post*, began to accept her work. *Holland's Magazine* of Texas published her "cottonfield tales," which explored themes she later developed in her novels—the sacrifices of a rural doctor, the rebellion of a creative son, the love of a black servant for her employer's family. "In all the hurry and bustle and nerve-strain of modern life, these quiet village stories are like a breath of country air," Cross once said. She aspired to the nostalgic local color of New Englander Mary E. Wilkins and New Orleanian G. W. Cable.

Still writing, she nurtured a friend through a divorce in Reno and moved on to Los Angeles. Success followed. After World War I, First National studio based a movie on her serial "A Question of Honor," which had appeared in the *People's Home Journal* in 1917. Cross had expanded another short story into a book, and she entered it in Harper's Ten Thousand Dollar Novel Contest. Even though *The Golden Cocoon* did not win a prize, Harper's published it in 1924. Five printings and less than a year later, Warner Brothers bought the movie rights for $25,000 and cast Helene Chadwick as the spunky Molly Shannon.

In *The Golden Cocoon*, farm girl Molly overcomes the tendencies of those "shiftless Shannons" by excelling at the University of Texas. The glamorous social life of the state capital snares her, but after a heartbreaking affair with the governor, Molly discards the empty glitter of Austin and starts from scratch as an aspiring novelist in New York—destined for success, of course. According to a 1924 review in *The New York Times,* "In the major portion of her story, the author writes entertainingly and gives the reader a sense of conviction, notwithstanding a certain saccharine quality which crops out."

With a novel selling well, at least two short stories in "best-of" anthologies, and a one-act play—*Just a Little Souvenir*—on the Keith vaudeville circuit, Cross married and moved back to New York. But she found time to make a thirty-five-day victory tour of Texas (she counted sixty-one turkey dinners) and accept the $500 D. A. Frank award for best novel by a UT graduate. Cross's national recognition thrilled local journalists, who emphasized her rags-to-riches path to fame in their profiles.

With her husband, horticulturalist-businessman George W. Palmer, Cross bought "Edendale," forty acres "of fine woods and hills" about thirty miles northwest of Hartford, Connecticut. Together they remodeled the 250-year-old farmhouse—the how-tos of which Cross detailed in *Eden on a Country Hill* (1938). They liked solitude but occasionally missed the city. "Radio is a great invention," Cross said, "for when we sit down to a meal there is nothing to talk about." Writer friends visited, however, particularly the other expatriate Texans in the neighborhood—Annie Laurie Williams, Maurice Crain, and Dorothy Scarborough.

Cross established a working routine: breakfast, stack the dishes, work from 9 to 12, fix leftovers for lunch, stack the dishes, work three more hours, make the beds, sweep, bake, dust, work in the garden (one hour in the spring), prepare dinner. After she washed the dishes, her husband dried them. Although Cross enjoyed cooking and entered her cakes, pies, and jellies in country fairs, she remarked that "men are luckier than women when it comes to having their domestic path cleared for writing." She did not have children.

The Unknown Goddess (1926)—a novel featuring Noel Higgins, the daughter of a social-climbing Texas merchant—flopped. According to a Dallas reviewer, Cross "unwittingly alienated a part of her audience by venturing into the wasteland of modernism." Although Harper's had signed her to a three-book contract, the company did not bring out her next novel.

When Longmans, Green published *Enchantment* in 1930, Cross

"won back some of those who had deserted her." Although born on the wrong side of the tracks in Goshen, heroine Rosemary Mooney wins the love of a visiting New York producer. As a condition of marriage, she agrees to bury her acting ambitions. In New York she dazzles society with her wit and charm, but she cannot live up to the Puritan expectations of the husband she adores or his haughty family. After an avalanche of misunderstandings, they divorce. Ill and penniless, Rosemary returns to Goshen in defeat:

> Rose began to suspect why she had returned with unerring instinct to this place. That braver, more dauntless self had drawn her. Out of her vast reservoirs of youth and strength, of a certain rash egotism and audacity, she could re-create her.

The novel closes with Rosemary's name in footlights and marital reconciliation possible.

One critic argued that Cross did not qualify as a Texas author because she used the state "as a place which her characters must leave in order to achieve success." But most reviewers did not quibble about a label. In general they admired Cross's realistic portrayal of small-town wretchedness but panned her romantic plots and conventional descriptions of the big city.

Perhaps in response to this criticism, Cross returned to Law's Chapel in *The Big Road* (1931). Bullied by his brutish father and nurtured by his passionate mother and the kindly general practitioner who secretly loves her, sensitive David Strawn comes of age in a town outgrowing the pioneer code. Inured to hardship, Texans like David's father resist the encroachment of sissified culture:

> The sight of the rich, black land which had only to be ploughed, planted and cultivated—mostly with horse or mule power—in order to produce crops of almost incredible luxuriance drove them after a fashion crazy. . . . They shared with Hector Strawn his hunger for land and more land. They could never get enough of it.
>
> Many of the men got up regularly at three in the morning to go out on the prairie and start work. . . . They paused in the inhuman heat of midday only to snatch a bite of lunch. They worked until dark drove them from the fields, then went home to do their chores by lantern light. It was the spirit that built states and empires; good for the whole, but merciless on the individual.

Thanks to the bequest of one of his mother's pining lovers, David pursues his dream of playing the piano professionally. In the end he forgives Hector.

Although one Dallas critic proclaimed Cross "a Texas and an American novelist of distinction," *The Big Road* did not generate the kudos of *The Golden Cocoon*. Five years passed before she produced *Soldier of Good Fortune* (1936), a historical novel about the exploits of Louis Juchereau-Duchesnay de St. Denis (1675–1744)—of Beaumont, Quebec, Paris, Louisiana, Texas, and Mexico. First published by the young Dallas house of Banks Upshaw and Company, it remained in print in deference to Cross's research rather than the finesse of her storytelling.

Back Door to Happiness (1937) confirmed the critical appraisal of Cross's fiction as "light reading." Once again a talented ingenue—this time a Mississippi-born opera singer—breaks into the artistic circles of New York. But unlike Rosemary Mooney, Jessica Marsh prizes love above any sense of self and masquerades as a middle-aged housekeeper for most of the novel. The plot turns on a melodramatic shooting, robbery, and vacation in Bermuda rather than on revelations of character.

Cross did not publish another novel for almost forty years. During the 1930s, however, her short stories continued to appear in such magazines as *Pictorial Review* and *American Liberty*. Deeply involved with her flowers and vegetables, she wrote essays on horticulture, contributed advice to Heinz's "Magazine of the Air," broadcast an original radio program, "Your Garden and Home," and compiled a national guide, *Wake Up and Garden! The Complete Month-by-Month Gardener's Manual* (1942).

Just before her husband's death in 1947, Cross sold Edendale and moved to New York. Nine years later she relocated to Winnfield, Louisiana, to live near her sister. A local celebrity, she presided over such civic organizations as the Readers Review Club and devoted her time to reading (Bertrand Russell, for instance, in 1976), writing, and religion. According to Pamela Jones—whose 1986 master's thesis probes the swift decline in popularity of Cross's fiction—nothing disappointed the writer more than her thirty-year failure to publish "The Book of Life," a condensation of the Bible.

Yet Cross never retired. In 1975 she donated her papers to Northwestern State University in Natchitoches, which in 1976 published her final novel, a revised manuscript from the 1930s. In *The Beautiful and the Doomed: A Novel in Defense of Natural Beauty*, a noble but unlikely couple—a slightly crippled woman and her unhappily married lover—sort out their relationship in an idyllic New England village soon to be sullied by a four-lane highway and the attendant gift shops and gas stations. "I wrote this book to sort of enshrine the New England life I knew and loved so well" Cross said. She dedicated it to Lady Bird Johnson, "who has done so much in defense of natural beauty."

Committed to her craft, Cross was a professional. At eighty-nine she outlined for a reporter her two current projects—a novel based on her psychic experiences and a play about the British Brontes. "I could no more stop writing than I could stop breathing," she once said. She died in Winnfield on September 30, 1981.

LOULA GRACE ERDMAN

ERNESTINE SEWELL

Loula Grace Erdman (1898–1976) was a well-established writer long before she published *The Edge of Time* in 1950. Nevertheless the novel marked a turning point in her career: no longer would she be a writer *from* Texas; now she was a major contributor to the growing library of books *about* Texas. Her earlier achievements had included a collection, *A Wonderful Thing and Other Stories* (1940), and two novels about career teaching, *Separate Star* (1944) and *Fair Is the Morning* (1945), which Eleanor Roosevelt praised for their positive view. "Write, write, write," Erdman advised ambitious students in her workshops at West Texas State University in Canyon. It was the pathway to success that she herself had followed, for she published five books in the 1940s, eight in the 1950s—seventeen novels in all during the thirty-five years of her career, three collections of stories and short pieces, a literary autobiography, and numerous uncollected stories, articles, and essays.

Erdman lamented that if she had not had to teach for steady income, she could have been a much better writer. Nevertheless, *The Years of the Locust* (1947) demonstrated that she had extraordinary abilities for structuring plot, characterizing her people, and providing details of time and place whose accuracy inspired her readers' confidence. This novel, meritorious for the flashback technique that allowed her to develop separate viewpoints for five different women attending the funeral of the family's patriarch, won the $10,000 Dodd, Mead–*Redbook* award. Another reward for her personally was that in *The Years of the Locust* she had come of age, so to speak. The tenets she formulated and advanced in this book would recur in all her writing: acceptance of challenge, faith in one's individuality, the pertinacity to endure, the courage to hold on to dreams, and the hard core of integrity that brings rewards in family ties and in the community.

Erdman spoke of herself as a "personal" writer, admitting that all her fiction is in a way autobiographical. Certainly the tenets she referred to are the essence of her own personality. Having acquired these, her characters must come to terms with their own solitude. Erdman considered her 1948 novel, *Lonely Passage,* one of her finest, if not *the* finest, believing that in it she at last had achieved a universal truth that reached beyond character or place in revealing the dimensions of loneliness:

> All our life is a seeking, a great quest for something we will never know—release from loneliness. And that is as it should be, for loneliness is a hunger of the spirit. It is our badge for immortality, the part of us that can never know a human being completely, or be known by him.

This belief, that only in confrontation with loneliness can one's individuality, uniqueness, and essence be realized, is as close as Erdman comes to a philosophical concept.

In view of her guidelines (both for herself in pursuit of her craft and for her characters in the tangled web of life) and her philosophy of solitude, Erdman was qualified to write about the Texas Panhandle homesteaders "sitting right smack dab on the edge of time."

Up to this point in her career, Erdman had drawn on her own experiences for her stories. Her successes came when she discovered that she must write about what she knew. What she knew was farm life and small-town life. Her people had been farmers, her father a storekeeper in Blackburn, Missouri. No violence, no tragedy, no passion to draw on. With uncommon straightforwardness she used her own storehouse of details about ordinary people living ordinary lives. Not scorning the woman's point of view ("I'm a woman; why should I not write like a woman?"), she gave to a popular audience a corpus of work whose realistic depiction of middle-class people deserves a place on the shelves. *Life Was Simpler Then* (1963) is a classic of such nostalgia, told with good humor.

After the success of *The Years of the Locust,* Erdman assumed she would continue writing in the same mood and manner, drawing on the same subject matter, but her editor, Edward Bond at Dodd, Mead turned her in another direction with his request that she write a novel about West Texas. Her first reaction was negative. Teaching school in Amarillo and Canyon had in no way familiarized her with cowboys and Indians. But the editor pressed her. "You can read, can't you? . . . You can do research. You can look around. You can ask questions." Erdman knew that to undertake this book was to cross a new frontier. It was a fearsome step for her because it meant turning away from the familiar materials that had brought her success—a happy childhood growing up with a brother and a sister in an extended family (she was a favored grandchild), going to college first at Central Missouri State and later at the University of Wisconsin, and coming to Amarillo with her sister in tow, the two of them to teach. She was not likely to run out of ideas for stories so long as rural Americana had its readers, but she had never run from a challenge before. She would write the novel.

When she undertook the book, early settlers in and around Amarillo could tell her stories of coming to the Panhandle in covered wagons, living in dugouts, their hardships and their triumphs. When she met old Colonel Goodnight, "It was like being given a door to the past." Now she was passing through that door to discover "what life was really like" in those early days. Students in her writing courses brought her tales from family lore. She went out on the plains and built a fire of cow chips to know the smell of them. She stood in wheat fields and looked out on endless space, and she felt small and a little frightened. Another time she watched as men fought a prairie fire. She knew storms, blizzards. The resources of the Panhandle Plains Historical Museum at Canyon were available to her, a vast treasure hoard of primary materials—diaries, records, memoirs, photographs, and artifacts—as well as secondary sources. Erdman did her homework. And the more she read and studied, the more intrigued she became with the "nesters," the homesteaders who endured drought, crop failures, the severity and freakishness of Texas weather, and, worst of all, the emptiness of the land. The ordeals of the nesters, then, became her focus. She explains in the dedication of *The Edge of Time*:

> Two groups of people have helped to build the Texas Panhandle.
>
> The rancher came with the horse and his rope and his gun and built the cattle empire.
>
> The nester came, too, with his wagon and his woman and a plow and built another kind of empire.
>
> Much has been written about the romance of the range. It is of the homesteader that I choose to write, believing that the story of his stubborn courage has been overlooked in the greater glamour that is the ranch legend.

It is no surprise that Erdman chose a woman's point of view for her story. Her grandmother had told her many times that the story of a new country is written not so much in a man's heroic struggle against changes as it is in a woman's struggle against nature's ravages.

The manuscript was rejected. Her editor struck her self-esteem a severe blow when he told her it read like a master's thesis in history. Even her sister said all it needed was footnotes. Not one to give up, Erdman put aside anger and hurt and began to rewrite. She returned to her field notes and this time concerned herself with the people rather than historical facts. "But most of all," Erdman recalled, "I wrote about Bethany Cameron, the little bride who had come to the Panhandle from Missouri and had known loneliness for a neighbor—Bethany who planted the rosebush beside their dugout and guarded it against drought and blizzard and wind and animals, feeling instinctively that if it died, their dream died with it."

The revised manuscript was accepted enthusiastically. She had endowed her characters with life and a certain tension, placing them a little too late for ranching and little too early for farming. Bethany's new home is a dugout with dirt floor, dirt walls, dirt roof. She must use cow chips for fuel and haul water from a neighbor's spring. She and Wade plant a crop and endure a wet spell. They plant crops again and a drought hits. Their stock dies from exposure to a blizzard. Desperate, they pick up bones to sell for fertilizer. There is some relief from ordeals when the pioneer doctor from Mobeetie drops by or the preacher with his black horse, Devil. Infrequently there is a party and dancing. Cowboys—Erdman's romanticized knights of the prairie—come by for her buttermilk and fresh bread. All this is told with the conscience of an ethnographer, so true to reality that some pioneer families who read the novel thought she was recording their own experiences.

Erdman's fictional artistry comes into play when Bethany and Lizzie Dillon outrace a prairie fire, and again when Bethany goes out into the vast "whiteness of a snow-filled world . . . stark terror in her heart" to fetch wood to warm Wade as he lies delirious with fever, but especially when Wade leaves Bethany alone in the dugout while he seeks work on the railroad. Early on, Bethany had recognized the stillness of the prairie as an adversary—powerful, constant, waiting. Now "loneliness was a strong taste in her mouth, a swirling surge in her heart." The stillness "came in waves, more terrifying than any noise could be. She braced herself to meet it, restrained herself to keep from running out into the night to meet it. . . . Whatever she saw wore the face of fear. And finally she knew fear for what it was, saw grinning sadness peering through its eyes." It is as Erdman claims: loneliness is universal and readers identify with Bethany, their own emotions evoked by the terror of her experience. (Likewise, West Texas winds were the enemy and destroyer of Letty in Dorothy Scarborough's novel *The Wind*.) Whatever experience Erdman had that gave her such intimate understanding of loneliness we shall never know, for she was a very private person. But we do know she is at her best artistically when one of her characters faces aloneness.

Another strong point of *The Edge of Time* is Erdman's depiction of the types of women who came to the Panhandle Plains. We are reminded of *The Years of the Locust,* in which Erdman works with five different women's points of view. This time the types are seen from Bethany's point of view, while she awaits the arrival of homesteaders who, like Wade, have come to conquer the prairie. These are her neighbors, though distant: Lizzie Dillon, who waits patiently for her man to move her and her ragged brood to some new promised land, robbed of her own will by the poverty of her situation; frail, childlike, Milly, who succumbs to the land, lacking the fortitude to survive the demands the land placed upon her; Mrs. Newsome, who wears white kid gloves when she comes calling, attempting to recreate a civilized East Texas lifestyle, and finally convincing her husband to give up; and, of course, Bethany herself, exemplifying those criteria Erdman adheres to unfailingly in her work.

Erdman produced five more novels from her research on the Panhandle homesteaders. In *The Wind Blows Free* (1952) a family leaves the comforts of East Texas for a new life on the prairie. The reader sees five children through the same ordeals as in *The Edge of Time*, the oldest girl, Melinda, being the focal character. *The Wide Horizon: A Story of the Texas Panhandle* (1956) restructures the same experiences with Katie as protagonist. Katie is a younger version of Bethany: sensitive, vulnerable to hurt, feminine in every respect, yet tough as a pioneer woman should be. Erdman uses Katie to tell readers that the frontier experience does not necessarily grind a woman into a coarse, withered, ageless being, accepting her fate and smothering her emotional being. *The Good Land* (1959) features Carolyn, the youngest girl in the family, who befriends newcomers from Chicago and helps them through the ordeals that had become Erdman's stock in trade. *Room to Grow* (1962), which completed her series of Panhandle novels for children, was inspired by her research into a French community in West Texas. Finally, *The Far Journey,* written in 1955, follows Catherine Montgomery in her covered wagon as she drives her team of oxen from the comforts of her Old South upbringing to join her husband on the plains. She proves to be of indomitable will, taking to heart her husband's words: "You have to push West if you want to keep growing. Go East and you'll die—within yourself."

By turning west, Erdman discovered new directions for her writing and established herself as the voice for women who made history in the Texas Panhandle. As a creative writing teacher and lecturer, she encouraged beginning writers to use materials at hand and write about their own experiences, lending their imagination to the facts. Participation in successful writers' conferences brought her the respect and support of J. Frank Dobie, William A. Owens, Fred Gipson, and the entire coterie of Texas men writers. They would be the first to applaud when she insisted one need not go to New York for something to write about. Fertile fields lie within oneself and in the relation of the self by imaginative embroidering to a time and a place.

JEWEL GIBSON

MELVIN ROSSER MASON

When Jewel Gibson's[1] mother received an advance copy of *Joshua Beene and God*, published by Random House in 1946, she wrote to her daughter: "I hate that I can't congratulate you on your first book; but I can't and ever face myself again. You have strayed from your rearing. You are not a good Baptist or you couldn't have written about them as you did. In fact, you sound more like a Campbellite."[2] Although the book was condemned in more than one Texas community, it received positive reviews. Mrs. Gibson (1904–89) lived to publish a second novel, *Black Gold* (1950) and to write nine plays, a book and lyrics for a musical, and innumerable feature stories for newspapers. She was a teacher for forty-three years, earned bachelor's and master's degrees, raised a family, and enjoyed sixty years of marriage with the same man. Interviewed by a reporter in 1971, she said, "I feel that God and I understand each other."[3]

When Thomas Sugrue reviewed *Black Gold* for the *New York Herald Tribune,* he observed that "Jewel Gibson is a writer with two tongues, one for each cheek."[4] Her sense of humor was clearly revealed in a "Chronology" she wrote for the book jacket for *Joshua Beene and God*. In part, it read:

1904   Born Bald Prairie, near Franklin, Texas.
1909   Chopped first row of cotton on father's farm.

	Best dressed girl in neighborhood. Always wore *new* cotton sack with shoulder straps that fit.
1914	Chopped cotton with blue-handled light hoe. Wanted to be tight rope walker in circus.
1916	More cotton-chopping. Wanted to ride wild broncos and bulldog steers.
1918	Met handsome preacher. Dedicated life to heathens in Africa.
1922	Married Felix Gibson, oil-well driller with solid-gold watch, tailor-made suit, and clean finger nails.

Although Felix Gibson had limited formal schooling, he appreciated his wife's talent, and he assisted her in continuing her education. Their first son was born before she was graduated from high school. After some work at Westminster Junior College in Tehuacana, she began teaching school in the surrounding communities while Felix worked in the Texas oil fields. Eventually she would earn two degrees from what is now Sam Houston State University, and she would give her husband public credit for doing the research for some of her major work, including *Black Gold* and the dramas *Miss Ney* and *Rachel, Woman of Masada*.

During World War II, while her sons were in the military, Jewel turned to writing as therapy, to ease her anxiety. One result was the novel *Joshua Beene and God,* published by Random House and promoted by Bennett Cerf.

Joshua Ebenezer Beene is the chief elder of the Church of Christ of Spring Creek Community, where he has carried on a fifty-year battle with the Baptists and where he serves as president of the school board, justice of the peace, and self-appointed game warden. *Joshua Beene and God* is the story of his last year on earth. At the age of sixty-nine, aware of the Biblical admonition that "The days of our years are three score years and ten," Uncle Josh knows that his time is short, for he is one man who has never borrowed anything, and why should he ask the Lord for a loan of years? Fifty years ago, after a personal conversation with God on the banks of Spring Creek, he had offered himself for membership in the Baptist Church, quoting the Lord as saying, "I want you to drive the money changers out of my temple. My house has become a den of thieves and hypocrites, and I'm a-leavin' it up to you to use the scourge." Meeting with less than enthusiastic acceptance, Joshua had stalked out of the meeting house. "I come unto my own, and my own received me not. Dadburn 'em. I'll fix 'em."

Through the years, Joshua has returned to the banks of Spring Creek for his interviews with the Lord, where they are on familiar terms.

> "Ain't You a-goin' to talk to me Lord?" asked Uncle Josh, growing impatient. "I don't ask You to come down here often, and I ain't a-wantin' You to be cantankerous with me, 'cause I'm a-doin' my best to be humble with You."

When referring to himself and the Lord, Joshua habitually places himself first. For his last year on earth he predicts that "ever thing will work for the glory of me and God," and he considers his mule, Elijah, his talking raven, Noah, and other creatures of Spring Creek to be "mine and God's pets."

Thomas Sugrue, one of the more perceptive readers of the novel, called it "a first-class piece of Americana, a superb satire on the ultimate degeneration of anthropomorphism."[5] An amazing quality of the novel is that it manages to be hilariously satirical without blaspheming. As Jesse E. Cross described the book for *Library Journal:* "Humorous—but surprisingly reverent."[6]

A key to much of the humor created by Mrs. Gibson is her anachronistic combination of King James English and rural Texas talk. As the Lord says to Joshua Beene, "Hit's been quite a spell since thou hast called Me down." The author obviously knew her Bible, and had a keen ear for the rural idiom. Uncle Josh, conscious of his role as prophet, writes original psalms, prophecies, and parables. In one of his major utterances, "The Psalm of Joshua Ebenezer Beene," he gives vent to his wrath for the Holy Rollers and the Baptists:

> Incline Thine ear unto me, Lord, and harken to my voice. Wickedness have I hated, and the wicked have persecuted. How is it there still be those who think they can out-do me? The Holiness shall I cut down in their unholiness. And the Baptists will I shatter with their baptism.

In his last year on earth, Joshua manages to buy up the notes on the Baptist Church house, gain complete control of the local school board, and discredit the Holy Roller preacher, a competitor for the souls of Spring Creek. And he courts and takes unto himself a fourth wife, the widow Phoebe Goolsby, who makes a great apple pie and wears purple petticoats.

Jewel Gibson's inspiration for Joshua Beene dated back to her girlhood in the Bald Prairie Community in Robertson County when Joshua Raines, the local chief elder of the Church of Christ, from the pulpit warned the boys in his congregation that they should stay away from young Jewel Henson, who was leading the boys of the community "to hell and damnation astraddle the horse." He had earlier criticized her disregard for the niceties of the side-saddle, but the real cause for his alarm was her taking the boys to the Baptist church. "But the Baptists really appreciated Uncle Josh," she said. "Once when my father sold a cow to one of the Church of Christ members, and he didn't pay, Papa reported him and Uncle Josh made him pay his debts." If any expected the author to get her revenge on Uncle Josh through fictional portrayal, they probably were disappointed. She makes Joshua the hero of her novel, and she obviously loves him. She satirizes him, but this is loving satire. She loves Josh Beene even as he has loved his own people. For years they had feared him, for they thought he was keeping track of their sins in a set of little black books, but he reveals on his last day on earth that the books are blank, that "for fifty years he had tried to bluff the people into the Kingdom of God, because he loved them—loved them with every minute of his waking and every hour of his sleeping. He had tried on every corner to block the road to hell."

J. Frank Dobie, reviewing *Joshua Beene and God* for *Book Week*, said, "Mrs. Gibson has skill in the art of writing, above all she has that vitality that makes the writing easy and delightful reading."[7] Unfortunately, some did not appreciate the work. One book jobber, amazed at the evident demand for the book, a popularity he had not foreseen, said, "I can sell a funny book, and I can sell a religious book—but I'll be damned if I can sell a funny, religious book!"

Pamela Hansford Johnson praised the British edition of *Joshua Beene and God*, published by Eyre and Spottiswoode in 1948: "This is something unique in American fiction, right out of the rut, a novel upon an original theme by a writer with a distinctive and authoritative voice."[8]

In 1948, when George Fuerman reviewed the manuscript in his

Houston Post column, *Black Gold* was tentatively titled *Rainbows in the Mud.* When it was published, in 1950, it was dedicated to Felix Adair Gibson, the author's husband. And justifiably so, for much of the background comes from his own recollections of the Texas boomtowns and oil fields in the early decades of this century.

The copyright page of *Black Gold* carries the conventional safeguard: "The persons, places and events in this novel are entirely fictional and any identification they may have with actual persons, places or events is coincidental and without deliberate intention." Even so, it should be obvious to many that the fictional setting of Watson, described as a 1904 boomtown, has much in common with Batson, an oil-field community near Beaumont, where Felix Gibson spent his early childhood and worked later as a driller. Shortly before the novel went to press, a Random House editor wrote to Mrs. Gibson suggesting that it would be better to give the town an imaginary name. "I suppose the people on which you base the characters in the book must all or nearly all be dead, but we certainly don't want to take a chance on one of them popping up and bringing suit."[9] It was a simple matter to change the *B*s in the manuscript to *W*s; thus the fictional "Watson" was formed.

"Watson, Texas, that year of 1904," the novel begins, "was a wild town, whose breath reeked with alcohol and sulphurous gas." *Black Gold* is a story of oil speculators, drillers, wildcat deals and shady deals, prostitutes and shyster lawyers, saints and sinners—in short, the works. Lon Tinkle, writing for *Saturday Review,* called it "one of the thickest brews of local color since Bret Harte."[10] Tinkle, calling the book "crude oil rather than refined," recognized, along with other reviewers, certain inadequacies of plotting and characterization, but no one questioned the authenticity of the oil-field background.

In addition to her two novels, Mrs. Gibson wrote, after her retirement from teaching, as many as three hundred "profiles" or feature stories, most of them published in the *Corsicana Daily Sun,* but her creative work after *Black Gold* was mainly drama, frequently written in collaboration with others, to whom she always gave full credit. She once told a reporter, "Writing novels is hard, but writing plays is fun." Her plays include dramatizations of *Joshua Beene and God* and *Black Gold,* and although her plays were never published, most were produced in Texas theaters, including Trinity University, Dallas Theater Center, and Houston's Alley Theater.

Hal Lewis, the Dallas journalist, and Clifford Sage adapted *Joshua Beene and God* for the stage, and Jewel Gibson herself played Phoebe Goolsby in the Alley Theater production that opened November 1, 1950. The show was directed by Nina Vance, with professional actor Jerome Jordan in the title role.

For years, Lewis and Sage worked unsuccessfully to achieve a Broadway production of *Joshua Beene and God*. Burl Ives held an option for a time. Correspondence between the playwrights and Ives's wife, Helen, who also was his manager, indicates that she planned to stage it in New York, but the dream never materialized. Burl Ives did star in Paul Baker's Dallas Theater Center production, opening October 20, 1961, breaking attendance records by playing to standing room only for thirty nights.

As early as 1950, Mrs. Gibson had produced a manuscript that would become the drama *Creep Past the Mountain Lion,* written in collaboration with Hal Lewis and Clifford Sage and produced in 1965 at the Dallas Theater Center. Heading a predominantly black cast was a native of Corsicana, Rex Ingram, a veteran professional actor known primarily for his portrayal of "De Lawd" in *Green Pastures.* Although the production was advertised as a "reading," the actors had memorized their lines, and the effect was that of drama without stage sets.

Once more Mrs. Gibson had chosen a preacher as her protagonist, but this time she made him African-American: Brother Amos Abraham Wess, who learns too late that he can't live his life as an imitation white man. He has looked on the white man as a big brother who will help lead the colored race out of the wilderness of ignorance and sin. All his life, Brother Wess has attempted to follow the white man's way, and he has been particularly impressed with the "unwritten law"—a man's right to kill to protect the sanctity of his home. When he learns that his unmarried daughter Elvira is pregnant and that she has been carrying on an affair with his son-in-law, he executes the younger man with a shotgun. Brother Wess is dismayed when his friend, a white lawyer, advises him to plead self-defense. Both his daughters are willing to lie on the witness stand in his behalf, but in court he insists on telling the truth and basing his defense on the "unwritten law." He is disillusioned by the white jury's reaction to his explanation that he killed to protect the virtue of his daughter. They find him guilty but give him a suspended sentence.

Convinced now that he is guilty in the eyes of God, he concludes that the white man may not be all the way out of the wilderness himself:

> Maybe we're all in the wilderness together. And the only way out is for the black man and the white man to take each other by the hand and together ease past that panther, and creep past the mountain lion.

Having worked with Paul Baker on *Mountain Lion* and *Joshua Beene,* Jewel Gibson was receptive to his suggestions that she write a play based on Charles Carver's book *Brann and the Iconoclast.* Baker, who had established a reputation at Baylor University and had founded Dallas Theater Center before going to Trinity University in San Antonio, produced the show with a large student cast at Trinity in December, 1971. William Cowper Brann, controversial Waco newspaperman, was editor of *The Iconoclast.* At cross purposes with Baptists, Baylor University officials, and others, Brann was gunned down on the streets of Waco April 12, 1898. Performances of both *Brann and The Iconoclast* and *Creep Past the Mountain Lion* received positive reviews in local newspapers, but neither play was performed again in its entirety.

Different circumstances prevailed with Mrs. Gibson's dramatization of the life of Elisabet Ney, the sculptress who came to Texas from Germany in 1873 and is remembered for her statues of Texas heroes in the rotunda of the state capitol. Before moving to Austin and establishing her studio there, Ney lived with her husband, Dr. Edmund Montgomery, at Liendo, their plantation home near Hempstead. Although Montgomery and Ney were legally married and had children, she did not publicly acknowledge their legitimacy. When her second child died in infancy, she personally cremated the body to protect Lorne, an older son, from contagion. Miss Ney's dress was eccentric, and she forced Lorne to keep his hair long and to wear clothing that provoked harassment by other children in the rural community, who questioned his gender. Upon one occasion, Lorne exposed himself publicly to prove that he was, indeed, a boy. Conflict between mother and son is a main element in the drama *Miss Ney.* During the 1960s, while she was assistant professor of English at Sam Houston State, Mrs. Gibson wrote the play with the supervision of Dr. Charles A. Schmidt, chairman of the Department of Drama. In the final scene, Lorne is being complimented for carrying out his mother's final wishes. He had brought in the massive, rough-hewn marble slab to cover her grave. His curtain line is "I just hope it keeps the old bitch down." After other characters make their exit, he begins to cry.

A "premiere" production of *Miss Ney* received critical acclaim, opening at Trinity University February 6, 1974. Later, Corsicana Community Players presented the drama with Nancy Roberts in the title role. (After Jewel Gibson retired from teaching in 1971, the Gibsons moved to Corsicana, where one of their sons is a surgeon.) Another production by the Georgetown Area Community Theater was staged in the Jonah Community Center in May–June, 1986.

In 1984, Jewel Gibson renewed friendship with Reba Rushing Robertson of Waco, with whom she had taught school years earlier. They began a collaboration that would continue for the remainder of Mrs. Gibson's life. Sensing encouragement from Houston-based actress/producer Jeannette Clift George, Mrs. Gibson and Mrs. Robertson went to work to rewrite *Miss Ney* as a one-woman show, hoping Mrs. George would make the role her own, as she had done with Gibson's *Rachel, Woman of Masada*. She had seen the script but had not performed the role. J. E. Masters of Lon Morris College, Jacksonville, working from the revised script, produced the show in October, 1987, as *Elizabet Ney: A Heart of Stone* (a title he devised), but he used several actors. A production announced for Navarro college, Corsicana, in 1986 did not materialize.

Jeannette Clift George did perform *Rachel, Woman of Masada* after it had been rewritten as a one-act play for one actress. Rachel, a grandmother, is one of few survivors of a mass suicide at Masada, an ancient fortress in Israel. After a prolonged siege in A.D. 72–73, the Jewish defenders killed themselves to avoid capture by the Romans. Drawing on the writings of the Jewish historian Josephus, Mrs. Gibson wrote the original three-act drama *Zealots of Masada* in collaboration with Jay Silverberg of Corsicana. Mrs. Gibson has been quoted as saying that she wrote with Silverberg so "it would read like a Jewish play instead of a Baptist play." This script, which called for a cast of more than thirty, was never performed. With some assistance from Pat Rice of Corsicana, Mrs. Gibson rewrote the drama as a one-woman show, and Mrs. Rice appeared as Rachel in a performance at the Warehouse Living Arts Center in Corsicana, March 13–14, 1980. In Houston, Jeannette Clift George performed the part of

Rachel at After Dinner Playhouse in May that same year and at Grace Theater, June 14–15. She repeated her performance at Laity Lodge near Leakey, June 18–21, 1980, and at the Globe Theater in Odessa, October 24–31. Four years later, at the Baylor Theater in Waco, she gave a one-night performance following an annual dinner of the Waco Conference of Christians and Jews.

A different Rachel, the wife of Andrew Jackson, was the subject of an earlier play that Jewel Gibson wrote with the help of Pat Rice. Pat Rice has said, "She had a typewriter, but was not a very good typist. . . . She would hack something out and then pencil in rewrites, add dialogue and at times scratch out whole paragraphs. Then I'd take it home and try to type it all together, take it back to her and she would mess it up again with that powerful pencil." The result was *Rachel Jackson,* a play in eight scenes for one actress. Pat Rice performed the piece at the Corsicana Community Playhouse February 13, 1976.

After retirement from teaching in her mid-sixties, Mrs. Gibson was constantly involved in research and writing, but she never thought of herself as a professional writer. At age eighty, still producing feature stories for *The Corsicana Daily Sun,* she told a reporter, "I have never considered writing a profession—it's a hobby. Teaching was my profession. The gratitude I've had from my students is what every teacher lives for—it's what makes $80 a month worthwhile."

Even so, Mrs. Gibson basked in the public acclaim she received. She was proud of being voted into the Texas Institute of Letters. Whenever she was physically able she attended performances of her plays, and all over the state she made public appearances with the traveling photographic exhibit *Literary East Texas* launched by Fred Tarpley in 1980. She was speaker for the opening exhibition in Texarkana and was co-billed with Leon Hale at the Conroe Public Library, where *Joshua Beene and God* had been banned in earlier years. With Nancy Roberts's music, she wrote book and lyrics for "Tuckertown USA" as a Bicentennial production for Corsicana. Before she died, she was honored by Corsicana with "Jewel Gibson Day," featuring short scenes from her dramatic works, performed at Warehouse Theater October 15, 1987.

Jewel Gibson remained active to the end. In her eighties, she learned to use a word processor to write her "profiles" for *The Corsicana*

Daily Sun, and she continued to work with Reba Robertson on a dramatization of *Black Gold.*

Over forty years ago, George Fuerman, writing on Jewel Gibson for his "Bookman" column for the *Houston Post,* said, "She has an earthy charm which is rural, direct, and metropolitan all at once. She is modest, of course, and this modesty is neither assumed nor artificial. The considerable kudos of being one of the state's . . . writers of unusual merit gets an altogether invisible ride from Mrs. Gibson."

NOTES

1. Although her name originally was "Jewell," Mrs. Gibson used the spelling "Jewel" for her published work. She was assistant professor of English at Sam Houston State when I joined the faculty in 1962, and we worked together on several projects until her retirement in 1971. I taped interviews with her and her husband Felix, drawing upon the material for public presentations and published articles. Before her death in 1989 she assembled a collection of manuscripts for deposit in the archives of Peabody Memorial Library, Sam Houston State University. To this collection I am adding my own materials, including a manuscript of the play *Rachel Jackson,* furnished by Pat Rice. This collection in the Peabody Memorial Library is a valuable source for anyone doing further study. It includes manuscripts of all the unpublished drama and the tape recordings I made with Jewel and Felix. I am very grateful for the help given me, through telephone conversations, by Reba Rushing Robertson, Pat Rice, Hal Lewis, Jeannette Clift George, Jay Silverberg, and others.

2. Quoted in a review of *Joshua Beene and God* published in *Texas Week,* September 28, 1946. Probably written by Cliff Sage. Clipping is signed in handwriting, "With Love, Cliff."

3. See article in *The Huntsville Item,* May 17, 1971, on Jewel Gibson's retirement. For subsequent references to "reporter," see Jody Cox, "Talented and well-acclaimed author enjoys writing about citizens of Corsicana," *Corsicana Daily Sun,* September 9, 1984.

4. Thomas Sugrue, "In the Wild Texas Bible Belt," *New York Herald Tribune,* April 2, 1950.

5. Thomas Sugrue, "Center of the Universe," in "Weekly Book Review," *New York Herald Tribune,* October 13, 1946, p. 6.

6. Jesse E. Cross, *Library Journal,* September 15, 1946, p. 1206.

7. J. Frank Dobie, "Book Week," *Chicago Daily Sun,* October 13, 1946, p. 4.

8. Pamela Hansford Johnson, *John O'London Weekly,* October 15, 1949.

9. Robert N. Linscott to Jewel Gibson, November 9, 1949.

10. Lon Tinkle, *Saturday Review,* August 19, 1950, p. 37.

ELITHE HAMILTON KIRKLAND

ERNESTINE SEWELL

Elithe Hamilton Kirkland (1907–92) was the only child of a West Texas farm and ranch family in Coleman County. She enjoyed a Wordsworthian childhood, roaming the land and absorbing nature's lore. Even as she matured, she ran free, riding her horse four or so miles to school and racing alongside the boys. She recalls that her aunts and uncles said she would never live to "courtin' age," but Elithe had dreams beyond their imagining, dreams that did not necessarily conform to the pattern for life that West Texans considered appropriate for their daughters. Neighbors opened their library to her, and she read voraciously: fairy tales, Scott's Waverley series, great poetry, historical novels, whatever was available. Often she was in trouble because she would lie in the grass, fashioning her own tales while the sheep she had been left to tend got into a neighbor's newly sprouted fields. Or she would leave her cotton sack to sit in the shade of a mesquite, shaping words into verse.

Because of her literary bent, her parents wanted her to attend college. When the time came, she chose North Texas State Teachers College, where she "corralled her interests" in astronomy, archaeology, forensics, journalism, and matters of the spirit to earn a Bachelor of Arts degree with a major in English, a minor in history, and a permanent teaching certificate. The excellence and breadth of her achievements in the years following graduation were recognized by the University in 1985, when she was named Distinguished Alumna.

Elithe held teaching assignments at various times in Mineral Wells, Crane, and Iraan, but her love for the printed word always superseded teaching. Back home, she edited the local newspaper, the *Coleman Democrat-Voice,* and became a respected newspaperwoman—this in the Depression, when journalism was man's work. Meanwhile she experienced an unsuccessful marriage, had a son (James Benjamin Beal, now an aeronautical research engineer), and traveled to New York. In the big city she had the friendship of writers Stanley Walker and Owen White, who gave her entree into literary circles, and she was offered an editorial position at *Collier's.* However she returned to Texas because her mother could help with her child and because she could help them, particularly her father, whose health was failing.

She moved to Austin, where she undertook postgraduate work. Named director of school publicity for the Texas centennial in Dallas in 1936, Elithe oversaw publication of *Songs Texas Sings* and brought fifty thousand school children to the Cotton Bowl, where NBC broadcast their singing. (She later said she did not know where she got the courage for that feat.) After the centennial she had nowhere to go, until Mr. Stamps of Stamps-Baxter Quartet fame arrived on the scene and created a job for her with the quartet. As their publicity agent she became a radio personality in her own right. One of her favorite memories is arranging a Mother's Day program broadcast from the roof garden of the Adolphus Hotel in Dallas. Fifteen thousand people crowded into downtown Dallas to hear the program.

Two years later she returned to Austin, worked in the State Lab School and eventually settled into a position with the University of Texas Radio House. She stayed there eight years, during which she wrote more than five hundred radio scripts. She took special pride in *Straight Texas,* in which she created Old Man Texas, a folksy narrator. For this series, she enjoyed the help and encouragement of her friend and former mentor, J. Frank Dobie. Also during this time the Rockefeller Foundation sent her into Mexico to investigate Nazi activities and planned to extend her work into South America, but war broke out. Still, her indefatigable energy and her reputation for excellence brought another creative outlet. She was asked to be Special Correspondent for the Business Section of the *Dallas Times Herald,* a position she held from 1944 until 1950, signing the articles L. F.

Hamilton. Having a seat at the press table in the capitol gave her an enviable place in both the political and the social life of Austin. But she relinquished all to marry Dr. Roy Defore Kirkland, an osteopathic physician and surgeon (d. 1985) and embark upon another career: writing.

Elithe Hamilton Kirkland's life had peculiarly outfitted her for the fiction she would produce. She was to write a regional epic: *Divine Average* (1952), *Love Is a Wild Assault* (1959), and *The Edge of Disrepute* (1984). As it turned out, the books all focus on a woman who understands the trauma of betrayal, who lives for one reason or another on the fringes of respectability (or acceptance), and who is "more inclined to conform to the voice of conscience than to dictates of social structures of time and place." Read in this order: *Love Is a Wild Assault*, *The Edge of Disrepute*, and *Divine Average*, the volumes come together as a thematic trilogy. Kirkland places the events and actions chronologically during the years immediately preceding the formation of the Texas Republic and running into the late 1850s—a period she had studied extensively. Her meticulous research coupled with her talent for romanticizing makes her the foremost woman writer of Texas historical fiction.

Divine Average, her first novel, covers the years 1838 to 1858 in Texas and has for its theme the hostility of the Anglo-Americans for dark-skinned people. Luvisa Templeton, the protagonist, supports the theme with her "unfaltering faith in the divine origin and goal of man and a holy conviction that the time must come when man's inhumanity to man will altogether cease," that someday racism will disappear, and a "divine average" of mutual respect be attained. Using a memoir as a structural device, Kirkland places Luvisa in San Antonio dying of consumption and writing an account of her life. The story that unfolds shows Kirkland at her best as she takes the young Range Templeton—a most admirable fellow from Tennessee, given to intense feelings, confident of himself, ambitious, and brave—and creates situations in which he degenerates into a demon, insensitive to everything that does not lend itself to his ambitious schemes and consumed with hatred for all except the fair-skinned.

Life in San Antonio in 1838, where the lovely Luvisa lives with her grandparents, is uneasy at best. Neither Texan nor Mexican is clear about boundaries. The Mexicans hold valid Spanish land grants, and the Texans look upon South Texas with visions of their own empires. Having witnessed the brutality of Indian depredations, Range Templeton is so filled with hatred that he will take any chance to kill an Indian. After his marriage to Luvisa he makes cattle drives that bring him into conflict with Mexicans, and he unleashes the cruelty and brutality that lie in the dark recesses of his being. Range leaves his family for months, sometimes years, to make drives east and west; he is lured to the gold fields of California; he endures hardship to amass a fortune and create an empire. Meanwhile his children, Luke and Lasca, grow to maturity. Inevitably these two become the instruments of retribution visited upon Range for his crimes against the dark-skinned. Luke marries a Mexican woman whose father holds land that Range covets. Lasca joins the bandit son of El Gavilan, whose sole purpose in life has been to avenge the death of his father at the hands of Range. But none of these eventualities demonstrates the extent to which hatred drives him as does Luvisa's revelation that she is of Mexican descent. When she attempts lovemaking to allay the anger of this man to whom she has been devoted faithfully and passionately for twenty years, he expends all his brutality on her, leaving her broken and pregnant.

Divine Average was published by Little, Brown in 1952. It was reprinted by Avon in paperback in 1978 and by Shearer Publishing in 1984. It has been widely acclaimed. In *Southwest Review*, Frank Goodwin wrote: "Its implications are for all races and all times." The nationally syndicated "Parade of Books" columnist compared its movement to that of *Gone with the Wind*. In the *Boston Traveler* it was pronounced "of tremendous proportions . . . as dramatic and full-blooded a novel as has been written this year. It is splendid history." Louise Putcamp, book editor for the *Dallas Times Herald*, described it as "written with a fierce fidelity to fact and overwhelming sense of history. . . . No mere résumé can do justice to *Divine Average*—its harrowing scenes of hatred, its respites of love and its precision of detail." *New York Times* book reviewer Lewis Nordyke wrote, "Elithe Kirkland has not written a bang, bang, shoot-'em up romance of a wavy-haired cowhand hero, but a serious and powerful historical novel on the tragic side." The *Austin-American* said, "An examination of prejudice's power to destroy . . . documented in solid scholarly research." The *New York Herald Tribune* commented, "*Divine Average* is no rehash of history spaded up by research; it is a story of conflict in terms of character . . . uncompromising, yet filled with compassion." The *Omaha World-Herald* said of Kirkland: "Whether she is writing of love or of Indian fights there is truth and power in every line. . . . I don't think the worth of the novel can be over-estimated. It has range and depth and vision."

Kirkland's second major work, *Love Is a Wild Assault,* is the fictionalized story of Harriet Potter, whose reputation as the bravest woman of the Texas Republic owes much to this novelization of the legend. Harriet suffered betrayal, fraud, and dispossession at the hands of the men she had loved and trusted. Her story is played out against the backdrop of the Texas war for independence from Mexico and the turbulence that marked the early days of the fledgling republic. Harriet wrote her own story when, in her eighties, she resided with a son in New Orleans, but it had been protected from public eye by a handful of lawyers. In 1953 Kirkland was approached by friends in the Texas State Historical Association to take the manuscript and write a novel about Harriet and her liaison with the historically ambivalent Robert Potter, who was active in politics in Texas despite the rumors that he once had committed murder.

Harriet had married an inveterate gambler, Solomon Page, in Tennessee and drifted with him to Texas, where he joined Sam Houston's forces in the war against Mexico. Harriet, desperate and with two children to care for, went with Robert Potter, Secretary of the Texas Navy, to the shores of Caddo Lake. There she lived as in Paradise while Potter pursued a political career until 1842, when he was killed by William P. Rose during the Regulator-Moderator War. In his will, Potter left his land mainly to two women friends in Austin, referring to Harriet as Mrs. Page, thus depriving her of legal rights to his property.

Kirkland took the manuscript, retained the romantic and ornate style, embellished it with lush descriptions, laced it with symbolism, and characterized Harriet as an Earth Mother whose story takes on mythological overtones. And, as in *Divine Average,* Kirkland is true to the history of the period. Harriet Moore at seventeen, working as receptionist for her father, a Nashville physician, is enamored of Solomon Page—"a young man with heroic face and hungry hands . . . the look of lost dreams in his eyes and a great need." Page is a gambler, and marital bliss fades all too soon. Leaving Nashville under duress, Solomon settles her and their children in New Orleans, where she opens a dress shop. One day he bursts into the shop with the news that they are going to Texas. There is land to be had for free! The scene shifts to a desolate, abandoned cabin in the bayous of Brazoria County. Saying, "You'll have to do the best you can," Solomon goes off to enlist in Sam Houston's army. Harriet keeps her children from starvation by feeding them possum-haws. Wolves howl, panthers scream, Harriet tries to ward off despair. When the Mexicans march across South Texas in pursuit of Sam Houston, she is caught in the Runaway Scrape. After rescuing her, Colonel Robert Potter takes her to the shores of Caddo Lake to homestead land he expects to be awarded him for services to the Republic. Harriet believes she has found true and enduring happiness, but again her joy is short-lived. She is apprised of Potter's unconscionable crimes in North Carolina that his flight to Texas had failed to expunge. Moreover, she has only his word that their marriage is legal, and she is aware that vicious gossips consider her still married to Solomon Page. Inevitably Potter is pulled into conflict with the Moderator, Old Rose, and killed. Harriet finds herself disinherited. But her life is not over; the trader Charles Ames marries her. His unswerving devotion and their thirteen children (she had eighteen in all) are compensation for the tragedies to which brave Harriet was heir.

Love Is a Wild Assault was first published by Doubleday in 1959 and was republished by Avon in 1978; Shearer Publishing brought out a second edition in 1984. The novel has been translated into both German and Spanish and serialized in Canada and Germany as well as in three newspaper syndicates in the United States. It has had three foreign book-club editions: in Stuttgart, Salzburg, and Zurich. When it was published in a prestigious *Omnibus Collection* of novels, the Barcelona press cited it as "[among] the best in contemporary novels over the world." In the *Southwest Law Review*, Associate Justice James R. Novell wrote that "Mrs. Kirkland had given the most valid interpretation to date on controversial Bob Potter—questionable servant to the Congresses of both the United States and the Republic of Texas." Lewis Nordyke in the *New York Times* called it a big bustling novel that "rings of fact and authenticity. It is a vivid and exciting account of living conditions, politics and chicanery in early day Texas." The *Boston Sunday Herald* called it "truly a brilliant biographical novel." The *Austin American-Statesman* wrote: "We have here a novel standing so foursquare on fact from Texas history and penned by a writer so versed in her subject and so able with her pen, that no reader will be released until the end." And the *Southwestern*

Historical Quarterly reviewer stated: "Mrs. Kirkland's fictional embellishments of the original, along with her timely interpolations, show good taste and sound craftsmanship. Even a seasoned old varmint hunter is not likely to be too annoyed over Big Tom, the panther, who saves Harriet from a deadly snakebite." Most recently, A. C. Greene listed it in *The 50 Best Books on Texas*.

The Edge of Disrepute, her third novel, begins in the 1840s in New Orleans. Sarah Belle Locke keeps a House of Recovery for men suffering from betrayal by, or separation from, their lovers. No place other than New Orleans would have afforded Kirkland the heterogeneous gathering of characters she needed for her story. Sarah Belle Locke is a Southern plantation beauty doing penance for her errancies in an early marriage; she has formed a kind of partnership with Hudson, one of the *gens de couleur libres* who quotes the Greek philosophers and drives her carriage; within their purview come a classical pianist, a voodoo queen, a merchant prince, an adventurer/explorer, and a saddle maker, among others. Not the least unforgettable is a voluptuous primitive with blue eyes and flaming pomegranate red hair ("Shades of Scheherazade!" a character exclaims). One could hazard a guess that Kirkland used this book as a clearing-house for the deep well of her mind, drawing out the accumulated interests and weaving them nicely into the threads of Sarah Belle and John's love story. There are bits of Texas history (General Somervell's expedition into Mexico in 1842, and Sam Houston's life among the Cherokee—recast as Mr. Defender among the Choctaw); her love of music and poetry; her enthusiasm for adventure tales; her curiosity about Maya archaeological sites in the Yucatan; her penchant for the elegant nineteenth-century lifestyle; and, finally, her interest in parapsychology. *The Edge of Disrepute* moves toward a realization that love is the vehicle for attaining cosmic consciousness.

Because *The Edge of Disrepute* was issued with the intent of completing the trilogy, it was given little critical attention on its own. A reviewer for *Western American Literature* praises it for capturing "the essence of romanticism," saying that the reader "is left with a sense that Sarah Belle will find whatever it is that she has always been seeking—something vague but wonderful."

The Texas Sesquicentennial marked another high point in Kirkland's later career. Her musical "Precious Memories" was produced as a sesquicentennial event jointly by the Salt Lick Group and the Hip Pocket Theatre in Fort Worth. It was enthusiastically received. Elithe Hamilton Kirkland died January 4, 1992, in Wimberley.[1]

NOTES

1. The biographical material in this paper is taken from the papers of Elithe Hamilton Kirkland, Archives, Gee Library, East Texas State University, Commerce, and from conversations between the author and Mrs. Kirkland.

KATHERINE ANNE PORTER

JANIS P. STOUT

Katherine Anne Porter (1890–1980), sometimes called Texas's greatest woman writer, might reasonably be designated Texas's greatest writer. She did not produce the volume of work published by other candidates for that honor; nor, until *Ship of Fools,* did she achieve great popular acclaim. Nevertheless, both during her lifetime and since her death she has been recognized as a consummate artist, a writer's writer.

Porter sometimes said she was born in Louisiana and educated in New Orleans at a convent school, after having been taken to live in Texas at an early age. In fact she was Texan by birth, born in a two-room log house in Indian Creek (near Brownwood) on May 15, 1890 (not 1894, as she sometimes claimed). Her childhood was not happy. That early unhappiness and especially her conflicted feelings toward her father had profound effects on her colorful life and on her fiction. Her mother died in 1892, when Callie (Porter's actual name) was not quite two years old and a younger sister was only two months old. After his wife's death, Harrison Porter took their four children, a boy and three girls, to live with his mother in Kyle, thirteen miles southwest of Austin.

Porter's strong, devout grandmother was the central presence of her early life. Born to a prosperous slaveholding Kentucky family,

"Aunt Cat," as she came to be known, had moved to Texas in 1857 and lived in steadily declining prosperity. By the time her widowed son brought his four children to live with her, she had sold all of her farm except a small strip of land with a shack on it and was living in a small house in town.

The family's life in Kyle was not only cramped but near enough to poverty-stricken that the children sometimes wore neighbor families' cast-off clothes. Harrison Porter could never bring himself to work regularly, and even the measure of stability that his mother provided was lost when, in Callie's twelfth year, she died. After her death, the family moved about the state, living variously in San Antonio, Lufkin, and Victoria. Porter's father never rallied himself to the point of providing a steady income, but he did, for whatever motive, begin purposefully to uproot the religious ideas inculcated in the children by their grandmother. The effect must have been an exacerbation of their sense of loss and insecurity.

Information on Porter's adolescence and early adulthood is scanty. One bright spot, however, was a year of good schooling in San Antonio, where she studied music and drama as well as more traditional academic subjects (in which she did not do well). Although she did not acknowledge the Thomas School in later life, there she gained the acquaintance with the arts and literature upon which she would build so richly. After a brief period spent in teaching "music, physical culture, and dramatic reading," she married a son of a prosperous ranching family from the Victoria area. She was barely sixteen years old.

Porter's marriage to John Koontz lasted for nine years, but it was troubled from the beginning. Indeed, this first marriage set the pattern for Porter's relations with men throughout her life: excesses of romantic enthusiasm followed by deep disillusion and recrimination. Koontz may have deserved a large measure of the opprobrium she heaped on him; there is some evidence he may have beaten her. But in his family's eyes, at least, she was partly to blame, creating friction by flirting with other men and going on extravagant shopping sprees.

During the seven years of her marriage when she actually lived with John Koontz, two very important events occurred: Porter's conversion to Catholicism, which she followed sporadically for the rest of her life, and her first known efforts to write fiction.

After leaving her husband, Porter was on her own with no home, an inadequate education, and no profession. Her first effort was to try to become a movie actress in Chicago. It was not an unreasonable hope; she was, all her life, extraordinarily beautiful. But she got only bit parts and found the work physically wearing on her frail constitution. After six months she went back to Texas and spent a winter caring for her two sisters, both in difficult straits, and earning a living by singing and dancing on the Lyceum circuit in Louisiana. She seems to have done well, but she abruptly threw it over, in part because she was angry at her sister Gay. Soon she was in Dallas trying to find office work. There she filed for divorce, which was granted June 21, 1915. In the same judgment her legal name was established as Katherine Porter.

Besides a new name, the year 1915 brought Porter her first serious illness, a bout with tuberculosis. During her recovery, in a sanitarium in Carlsbad, Texas, she met a young newspaperwoman—a rarity at the time—and, as a result, went into newspaper work herself, first in Fort Worth and later in Denver. There in 1918 she suffered the near-fatal bout of flu that would become the central episode of "Pale Horse, Pale Rider." Later she claimed that she was in love with a young soldier represented by Adam in her story, but apparently this is one more instance of her habit of fictionalizing her life story to make it more romantic and beautiful—and certainly more prosperous—than it actually was.

Nineteen nineteen, the year following her recovery from influenza, was momentous for Porter. First, her newspaper writing became more serious, more morally stringent; her standards for art, as evidenced in her drama reviews, rose dramatically. Second, her adored little niece Mary Alice, daughter of her older sister, Gay, died. Porter was distraught but did not return to Texas, and her absence at that time may have contributed to a prolonged estrangement between the two sisters. Third, near the end of the summer, she went to New York, determined to be a great writer.

Porter later said that her first story was published in 1923. Apparently, however, her literary career may be said to have begun with the publication of three children's stories and one story for adult readers in 1920. These works she never acknowledged. In the same year, still supporting herself with publicity work and journalism, she worked on the story for a Mexican ballet featuring Pavlova, the great star of the Diaghilev ballet. As a result she was offered a job writing about Mexico for a promotional magazine.

Sent to gather material, she arrived in Mexico City in time for the presidential inauguration on December 1, 1920. (It was not the only time she would be present for historic events.) There, while working on several journalistic projects as well as ghost-writing a novel, she immersed herself in Mexican political intrigues and made notes for the fiction she would write later. Although she projected a novel based on her experience during this trip, the publications that actually resulted were several short stories, including the celebrated "Flowering Judas." At the time, however, she produced, not fiction, but a number of articles. She was living a life of political turmoil and intrigue; many of her friends were involved in illegal and subversive activities, and for a while she herself feared arrest.

By mid-1921 she was ready to go home. Kitty Crawford, of the Carlsbad sanitarium, and her husband provided a train ticket and refuge in their Fort Worth home. Porter spent six months there, still not writing successfully but doing journalism and acting in local theater. At the start of 1922, however, with the Crawfords' help, she went back to New York. There she quickly sold an essay to *Century* magazine and settled in to work on the story "María Concepción," which she sold to *Century* for $600.

Even after this auspicious beginning, Porter faltered in the actual production of the fiction she was now so well prepared to write. It is a pattern that persisted throughout her career. Devoted to her art and demonstrably well qualified to pursue it, she let herself be incessantly distracted by social activities, by travels and changes of residence, by love affairs, by the need to earn money, and by self-doubt. Her personal life was forever uprooted and disrupted. Had she resolved these problems, there can be little doubt that she would have produced significantly more of the finely crafted work for which she is noted.

As it was, she did not publish her first volume, *Flowering Judas*, until 1930, and then in a small edition. In 1935, however, it was expanded and republished in a commercial run, and in 1937 the expanded volume, *Flowering Judas and Other Stories*, won an award from the Book of the Month Club. The volume *Pale Horse, Pale Rider: Three Short Novels* was published in 1939, and *The Leaning Tower and Other Stories* in 1944. In 1962 her long-awaited novel, *Ship of Fools*, was published and became an immediate success, though most critics do not number it among her best works. In 1965, Porter won the Pulitzer Prize for her *Collected Stories of Katherine Anne Porter*.

It is a remarkably small, though remarkably fine, output for so long and active a career.

Many of Porter's works draw on her early childhood years in Texas, but she was a long time coming to the realization that her artistic imagination was rooted in that material. Her apprentice stories, not included among her collected works, incline toward exotic places and events. She seems to have learned the importance of making art out of native materials when, in 1922, she worked on an abortive exhibition of Mexican Indian art. But instead of recognizing her need to deal with her Texas roots, she justified her use of Mexican materials on the basis that they were not exotic to her because she had grown up in Texas towns, where there was a large Mexican population. The argument is not convincing; she might simply have been avoiding emotionally troubling materials. On the other hand, her stories of Mexico *are* excellent. They must be accounted her second most important group of works.

First in importance to an understanding of Katherine Anne Porter, as they are first in achievement, are those stories in which she turns back to the South, to Texas, and to her own family and early experiences. Some of these stories, which appear in the so-called Old Order group, were being written by 1927. But it was not until 1932 that she began to work seriously with the autobiographical materials from her Texas years. In that year she wrote her recollections of a childhood stay on a Texas farm and some three-part sketches related to the theme of family tradition and personal identity, centering on a character named Amy. Then, in Switzerland, she began to develop her memories of her time in Denver. The materials would become what probably are her three finest works: "Noon Wine," "Old Mortality," and "Pale Horse, Pale Rider." The period of the mid-thirties, then, was the most productive period of Porter's life.

In 1936 Porter visited her family in Texas for the first time in many years. As a part of the reunion, they drove to Indian Creek, where Porter had been born, and visited her mother's grave. Shortly after this trip, despite the breakup of her third marriage, she began writing the final versions of the three stories. At the Water Wheel Tavern in Doylestown, Pennsylvania, which reminded her of the hotel in Basel where she had begun part of the work, she completed two of the stories, each in seven days, she claimed. She finished "Noon Wine" by November 7 and "Old Mortality" by Thanksgiving. At this time she also tried to complete "Pale Horse, Pale Rider" (which she actually did not finish until December, 1937) and started her work on the material that, after twenty-five years, would become *Ship of Fools*.

In "Old Mortality," first published in the *Southern Review* in 1937, Porter transforms her own family into the fictional Rhea family, who appear as well in "The Old Order" and, at a distance, in "Pale Horse, Pale Rider." Porter herself is represented by the character Miranda, who regards life with much of the wondering imagination and responsiveness and the mingled affection and detachment we see in her creator. The fictional grandmother comes directly from Porter's paternal grandmother, Aunt Cat, and the beautiful Aunt Amy of the story is a recreation of Porter's aunt Annie Gay. The combined romanticizing of the family past, rebellion against it, and entrapment in one's own romanticizing illusions is a delicate and intriguing projection of Porter's equally complex inner life, in which family rootedness and alienation were inextricably entwined.

"Noon Wine," often mentioned as Porter's greatest single work, depicts life in central Texas on a relatively poor farm owned by the Thompsons. Until the publication of the first reliable biography of Porter, in 1965, it was believed that the story constituted a venture into the world of a Southern social class much lower than her own. In fact, Porter lived temporarily with the Gene Thompson family on precisely such a farm shortly after the death of her grandmother. The story is noted for its wonderfully precise details, combined with an evocative dreamlike state triggered by the haunting harmonica playing of the doomed hired man, Mr. Helton. It is notable as well for the theme of strangeness within familiarity, a theme which emerges as perhaps the single unifying motif in all Porter's work, as well as in her life.

The third of the three great stories completed, or nearly completed, in the fall of 1936, "Pale Horse, Pale Rider," also appeared first in *Southern Review*. Here Porter draws on her experiences in Denver as a newspaper reporter and theater reviewer during World War I and her brush with death during the terrible influenza epidemic of 1918. The family and Texas are not as central here as they are in "Old Mortality" and "Noon Wine" but provide a backdrop of a lost and somewhat ambiguous Eden against which the wartime madness plays out its horror. The intense yet restrained poignance of the end of the story, as Miranda hears herself call out to the dead Adam and knows she must shut away the memory and her yearning for him if she is to cope sanely with the dreary future, is powerfully moving. Apparently it was powerfully moving to Porter as well. In later years, speaking of the experience from which the story grew and her loss of the love of her life, she would gallantly hold herself back from dissolving into tears, as Miranda steels herself against surrendering to her grief. Yet the evidence is strong that there was in fact no lost lover, only a kindly acquaintance whom Porter elaborated upon in response to the convincing emotion of her own fiction. The story itself and the author's elaboration of a fantasy of perfect love are among the many evidences of that yearning for a perfect lover which seems to have sprung from her early yearning for the adequate father she never had.

The other story, or group of stories, in which Porter draws upon and embellishes her childhood is the set collectively known as "The Old Order." These pieces, written over a long period and published separately, together give the clearest idea of the family Porter wanted to be able to remember. Even though it is clearly stated that the family is in reduced circumstances, they are still far better off financially than the Porters in fact were. Moreover, there are only three motherless children rather than the actual four. Here and in "Old Mortality" the infant sister whose birth was the final and fatal blow to Porter's mother's health is quietly eliminated from the picture. The faithful ex-slaves so well depicted in "The Old Order" reflect wish, not fact. Aunt Cat's household included no servants, faithful or otherwise. The scene of the grandmother's death recorded at the end of "The Journey," second of the seven sketches or stories, is, however, an accurate rendering of Aunt Cat's death, which Porter witnessed.

Besides the four works just described, "Holiday" is also set in Texas and based on personal experience, though not the familial past. The story was begun in 1924 but not completed and published until 1959. In addition, two other stories, both consummately crafted and frequently anthologized, are set in the rural South, not explicitly but implicitly Texas. These are "He" and "The Jilting of Granny Weatherall," both of which use Porter's childhood memories in much less direct ways than do "Old Mortality," "The Old Order," and "Noon Wine." The depiction of the matriarch in last decline, in "The Jilting of Granny Weatherall," is derived from Porter's grandmother though the circumstances of the death are not.

A second body of work, some of it equally fine, is the material

Porter produced out of her periods of living in Mexico. The most famous of these, "Flowering Judas," established her literary reputation upon its publication in *Hound and Horn* in 1930. The story has been the subject of extensive symbolic interpretation. Its central character, Laura, bears strong resemblance to the autobiographical Miranda (who is placed in Mexico at the end of "The Grave," last of the "Old Order" stories) but is only partly a projection of Porter herself. More directly she represents Mary Doherty, a woman Porter knew while in Mexico in 1921. Additional stories of Mexico include "María Concepción," the first of Porter's acknowledged stories to be published, "Virgin Violeta," "The Martyr," "That Tree," and the long story or short novel (Porter did not like the term novelette) "Hacienda." Of these "The Martyr" generally is judged the weakest.

Beyond the Texas and Old South stories and the stories of Mexico, Porter wrote only a few. These cannot be grouped by setting, though in almost all of them setting remains a powerful element. They are "Magic," a story of New Orleans; "Rope," based on Porter's months in Connecticut with her second husband; "Theft," an account of an emotionally desiccated woman writer in New York; "The Cracked Looking Glass," about an Irish immigrant woman in Connecticut and Boston; "The Downward Path to Wisdom," of indeterminate setting; "A Day's Work," another story of Irish-Americans in New York; and "The Leaning Tower," set in Berlin in the 1930s. "The Downward Path to Wisdom" is of particular interest in its representation of a small child disaffected from his unloving parents. We may well relate this story to Porter's motherlessness and her ambivalent feelings toward her weak, unreliable father. "The Leaning Tower," though not usually numbered among her finest works, is of interest for its depiction of Germany in the years preceding World War II. The story bears abundant evidence of Porter's dislike of the German people, a dislike also evident in *Ship of Fools*. Drawing heavily on details of Porter's months in Berlin in 1932, the story also draws on memories of one of Porter's childhood friends, Emma Schlemmer, recast in the story as a male, and some aspects of a lover she had in Mexico in 1921, Joseph Retinger.

Porter's one full-length novel, *Ship of Fools*, was already a legend when it finally appeared in 1962. The entire literary world, it seems, had known Katherine Anne Porter was working on a novel and had been anticipating its appearance for years as, time after time, its completion was promised and then postponed. The manuscript had started life as a short story in 1936. Then, when it became clear that the work would be a novel, advances were paid on it, and as early as 1942 the publisher was seriously expecting to receive the completed draft. At various times, Porter went into retreat at quiet places to complete the work but emerged without having done so. When she did finish the book, in June, 1961, at a hotel on Cape Ann, Massachusetts, located for her by her publisher, her real interest in the material had long since dried up, and many reviewers could tell it.

If the critical reception was mixed, however, the popular reception was gratifyingly enthusiastic. The book went into its ninth printing before the year was out. Movie rights were sold for $400,000 a month after publication. For the first time in her life, Porter's income was ample; she was freed of financial worries.

Ship of Fools is a microcosmic criticism of twentieth-century society in the years verging on World War II. Its characters are of various nationalities and sorts, though preponderantly middle-class Germans. Few Americans appear, and of these only one is Texan—and a very disagreeable character at that. Indeed, most of the characters are disagreeable. They are presented meanly. The almost unrelieved acerbity of the narrative point of view has often been noted. In structure the book is episodic, reflecting Porter's orientation toward the short story. Moreover, the presentation is relatively static, so that although the book is very long and provides ample dissection of individuals and groups, it offers little dramatic development. In these various ways, it has often been judged inferior to most of Porter's other work.

The action grew out of her own voyage to Germany in 1931 aboard a vessel named the *Werra* (in the book, the *Vera*) sailing, as it does in the book, from Veracruz. The various characters are based on people Porter had known. However, the book does not draw significantly on her early memories.

The latter decades of her life, from about age 44, Porter spent as the grande dame of American letters. She did reviews and occasional pieces whenever she wanted; she taught at various campuses; she was a regular on the lecture circuit; she received honorary degrees; she attended public events of all sorts, including the Kennedy inauguration festivities. Her friends included the personages of the literary world generally—Robert Penn Warren, Allen Tate and Caroline Gordon, Eudora Welty, Andrew Lytle, Glenway Wescott, Wallace Stegner, William Humphrey, William Goyen, and Flannery O'Connor. Friendship with Porter could be a stormy business, however, as many of these people, like Hart Crane years before, found out.

The entire Texas literary establishment dropped out of Porter's favor early, as her estrangement from her home state persisted. The rift first came in 1939, when *Pale Horse, Pale Rider* was passed over for the first Texas Institute of Letters prize in favor of J. Frank Dobie's *Apache Gold and Yaqui Silver*. It deepened following the dashing of her hope that a library at the University of Texas would be named in her honor. This incident, however, is difficult to assess. In 1958, while serving as guest lecturer at the University of Texas, Porter understood that Harry Ransom meant to name the Humanities Research Center building or some part of it for her and to set up a Katherine Anne Porter room as a repository for her papers. It is unclear whether she simply misunderstood, but at any rate she was deeply offended when the honor did not come to pass. She was further offended several years later when the author of a book about J. Frank Dobie obtained her routine praise in response to a gift copy, then asked permission to use her words for advertising purposes. Her angry reaction fanned the flames of mutual resentment.

The nature of Porter's relation to her home and her regional roots remains something of a puzzle. The extent to which she can be considered a regionalist is itself far from clear. In part, the problem is an outgrowth of Porter's own propensity for misrepresentation, which resulted in very false ideas, often in print, about her origins and early life. In general she created an image of herself as Southern belle, the daughter of a gracious, cultured slaveholding class. That image bore very little resemblance to fact. Given her habitual urge to recreate the past, it is easy to suppose she had deeply ambivalent feelings about returning to her home state or being closely identified with it in later years.

DOROTHY SCARBOROUGH

SYLVIA ANN GRIDER

Dorothy Scarborough (1878–1935) was a distinguished folklorist, novelist, and teacher whose professional writing career spanned only seventeen years. While working as a teacher of creative writing at Columbia University in New York City, she wrote five novels, including *The Wind* (1925), which is regarded today as a minor classic, and published two major folksong collections, *On the Trail of Negro Folksong* (1925) and *A Song Catcher in Southern Mountains: American Folksongs of British Ancestry* (1937). She also wrote and edited various other books, poems, short stories, reviews, and essays.

Scarborough was the role model for a whole generation of struggling and ambitious young writers and scholars. Nevertheless, after her sudden death in the depths of the depression, her name quickly faded into undeserved obscurity, in part because she had trained no graduate students to carry on her work. In spite of such obstacles to immortality, her publications remain as a testament to her remarkable wit, creativity, and intellectual depth.

Born January 27, 1878, near Tyler, just after the close of Reconstruction in Texas, Scarborough always maintained her personal identification as: first a native Texan, and second a southerner. She never fancied herself as a pioneer westerner.[1]

Because her health was frail, in the 1880s the family moved to Sweetwater, in the heart of the arid West Texas ranching country.

There being few educated people in this raw frontier village, the Scarboroughs quickly formed what would be a lifelong friendship with J. T. Harrington, a local physician, and his family.

John Scarborough was a Civil War veteran from Louisiana who had read law before moving west. He was immediately successful in Sweetwater, where he practiced law, served as a judge, dealt in surveying and real estate, and helped found the local Baptist church.

In spite of their civic and financial success in Sweetwater, in 1887 the Scarboroughs decided to move to Waco so that the children could be educated at Baylor University, which had just moved to Waco from Independence, where it had been chartered in 1846. Scarborough immediately was elected to the Board of Trustees of Baylor, on which he served until his death.

There were three Scarborough children: George (or Buddie) the eldest, who became a lawyer, secret-service detective, and Broadway playwright; Mattie Douglass, who married George McDaniel, later the powerful pastor of the largest Protestant congregation in the South, the First Baptist Church of Richmond, Virginia; and Emily Dorothy, the youngest, affectionately known by friends and family as "Miss Dottie" or "Dot." All three Scarborough children attended Baylor. Douglass went on to receive an M.A. at Vassar, and George attended law school at the University of Texas. Dottie completed both the B.A. and the M.A. at Baylor.

The Scarborough children grew up literally on the Baylor campus. Before it was razed, the house served as student housing, and today a women's dormitory occupies the site of the home. Dottie is remembered as a gentle and attractive but somewhat withdrawn child who preferred reading above all else. She was fond of climbing up into a large oak tree on campus and reading while the undergraduates strolled past, unaware she was perched above them.

She majored in English at Baylor, graduating in 1896. She was a popular but studious co-ed whose interests were distinctly literary. She quickly blossomed into a creative literary talent with self-discipline and a sense of purpose that lasted her a lifetime. She published poems, essays, and short stories in the school paper as well as the campus literary magazine. As secretary of the Calliopean Literary Society she wrote to authors whom the club was studying requesting from them copies of their work or personal greetings to be read at club meetings.

After she graduated, she taught for a year in the public schools of Marlin and then returned to Baylor to pursue an M.A. in English, which she completed in 1899.

After completion of the M.A., Miss Dottie became a member of the Baylor faculty, along with her sister, who taught foreign languages for a few years before marrying her classmate, the dynamic and ambitious George McDaniel.

By all accounts, Dottie was an entertaining but impartial teacher who made students work hard to earn their grades. In 1912 she developed the first journalism course taught in the state and used it as an outlet for the creative writing talents of her students.

She became increasingly bored with teaching undergraduates and more interested in becoming a professional writer. She attended summer school at the University of Chicago, where she studied writing with Robert Morss Lovett and published a book of poetry, *Fugitive Verses* (1912). In 1910 she took a leave of absence from Baylor and spent the year studying literature at Oxford University, which had just begun allowing women to attend classes on a limited basis. Her autobiographical serialized novel, *The Unfair Sex* (1925–26), describes this year in some detail, but whether or not she, like the heroine in the novel, fell in love with a classmate who was killed in the early days of World War I is a matter of conjecture.

During her absence from Baylor, the Texas Folklore Society was founded, and upon her return, Dorothy Scarborough joined and eventually became a life member. In 1914 she was elected president of the Texas Folklore Society, and her presidential address, "Negro Ballads and Reels," was the first public statement of her interest and expertise in folklore. As a child, Scarborough often had accompanied her father when he went to inspect the cotton fields, and some of her fondest early memories were of listening to the Negro field hands sing as they worked. She never lost her fascination with these songs. Nearly all the material for the TFS presidential address she collected from Negroes in Waco. She published an article, "Traditions of the Waco Indians," in the first volume of the *Publications of Texas Folklore Society* (1916) and "The 'Blues' as Folksongs" in the second volume (1923), but she did not publicly return to folklore until she published her famous collection, *On the Trail of Negro Folksong.*

After the death of her parents, Scarborough moved to New York

City to get a Ph.D. from Columbia and become a novelist. Although she was thirty-eight years old and unmarried, the move to New York City was the beginning of a new life. Upon receiving her Ph.D. in 1917, she was hired to teach creative writing in the Extension Division of Columbia, a job she held until her death in 1935. Her dissertation, *The Supernatural in Modern English Fiction* (1917), was published and received favorable reviews; today it is still a standard reference in the field, although considerably outdated. She progressed through the academic ranks at Columbia and at the time of her death was an Associate Professor, a high achievement for a woman at that time. The only woman who outranked her was Dean Virginia Gildersleeve of Barnard College.

During her early years at Columbia, Dorothy Scarborough was much more interested in writing fiction than in folklore. In 1919 she published *From a Southern Porch,* a whimsical extended personal essay recounting her adventures as a house guest in the summers at her sister's elegant home in Richmond, Virginia. Because her dissertation on the supernatural was so popular, she began editing and contributing to ghost-story anthologies. She also reviewed books for the *New York Sun* and began publishing short stories and poems. As her literary horizons broadened, she founded the Columbia Writing Club for her creative writing students and began holding popular "at homes" where the nation's literati mingled with an assortment of Columbia students and homesick Texans and Southerners who were visiting or studying in New York. Among those whom she befriended in New York were her fellow Texas folklorists J. Frank Dobie and John Lomax.

Her first novel, *In the Land of Cotton* (1923), was based on extensive fieldwork and research into the sharecropping system in Texas. Set in and around Waco, the novel was the first in a projected trilogy dealing with cotton farming. In recognition of this novel, Baylor awarded her an honorary Doctor of Letters degree.

The high point of her life and career was 1925, when she published three major works: *The Wind, On the Trail of Negro Folksong,* and *The Unfair Sex. The Wind,* a highly controversial novel, was made into a stunning silent movie starring Lillian Gish and Lars Hansen and directed by the Swedish master Victor Seastrom. Scarborough took a deep interest in the technical production of the movie and enjoyed a lasting friendship with Lillian Gish. A special screening of the movie for her friends in New York City was one of Scarborough's most thrilling experiences.

The Wind, set in frontier Sweetwater during the devastating drought of the mid-1880s, depicted the harsh environment of the West and its impact on a delicate and sensitive heroine from Virginia. The heroine, Letty, is ultimately driven to madness, murder, and suicide by the combined elemental and demonic forces of the wind and sand. Scarborough fully utilized her training and background as a folklorist in this dramatic novel, weaving snatches of folksong, regional legends, and the ballad image of the Demon Lover. As a publicity stunt, the novel was first published anonymously. The ploy backfired, however, because Texans were outraged by their assumption that a Yankee had written this scathing attack on their beloved state. After an acrimonious exchange of letters to the editor in the *Dallas Morning News,* her authorship was revealed and public opinion in Texas softened. The novel created a public-relations sensation for Scarborough and was financially successful.

On the Trail of Negro Folksong, which she wrote in collaboration with a Baylor colleague, the ethnomusicologist Ola Mae Gulledge, clearly established her scholarly reputation as a folklorist and authority on Negro folksong. The book was based on research conducted continuously since her Texas Folklore Society presidential address. The research had involved extensive correspondence, questionnaires, and on-site fieldwork combined with literary research and documentation. George Lyman Kittredge, whom she met when he came to lecture at Baylor, helped her conceptualize the book and encouraged Harvard University Press to publish it.

Both *The Wind* and *On the Trail of Negro Folksong* were incredibly successful, and she had to choose between being a novelist or a folklorist. In spite of her love of folklore, she chose writing novels. In quick succession, she published *Impatient Griselda* (1927), *Can't Get a Redbird* (1929), and *The Stretch-Berry Smile* (1932). *Impatient Griselda* enjoyed moderate success as a Book of the Month Club alternate, but the other two were mediocre at best. Unfortunately the publication of *Can't Get a Redbird* coincided with the collapse of the stock market which, combined with the novel's weak artistic merit, resulted in heavy financial losses for all concerned. Because she badly needed the money, she quickly compiled a nonfiction book for children based on her extensive research, *The Story of Cotton* (1933).

The Depression, family responsibilities, and some bad business decisions extinguished her creative spark.

During this creative lull, she turned away from fiction and undertook instead another folksong collection. This time she decided to focus on Anglo ballads in Virginia and North Carolina instead of Negro secular folksongs. In 1930 she was awarded a research grant from Columbia University. Equipped with a specially made Dictaphone, she put all her time and energy into hunting down Appalachian informants who knew and would sing the beloved old ballads brought over from the British Isles. She became a true "song catcher," a term used by her informants.

Granted a sabbatical research leave by Columbia in 1932, she went with her widowed sister to Europe, where she worked on the manuscript of this new folksong collection. She also spent a summer working at Yaddo, the writers' retreat in Saratoga Springs, New York. After completing the manuscript, she convinced Columbia University Press to publish it, an expensive undertaking because of all of the musical transcriptions. She hired a professional musician to transcribe the songs from the wax Dictaphone cylinders and an ethnomusicologist to write an essay explaining the modal aspects of the tunes. Then, unexpectedly, she died in her sleep from a heart attack on November 7, 1935.

Her death created a dilemma for the university press because the book was set in type but had not been proofread or corrected. Two of her colleagues from Columbia were drafted to help, as was her sister Douglass. To further complicate matters, one of the informants and the ethnomusicologist filed suit against the press for what they regarded as slanderous inaccuracies in the text and transcriptions. Since Scarborough had left no record of her agreements with the litigants, the publication of the book was delayed for two years until an out-of-court settlement could be reached and some changes made in the book. *A Song Catcher in Southern Mountains* was published posthumously in 1937.

Even though her professional scholarly folklore career was short, spanning the publication of *On the Trail of Negro Folksong* in 1925 to *A Song Catcher in Southern Mountains* in 1937, Dorothy Scarborough established a reputation as an authority on secular folksong in the United States. After the publication of *On the Trail of Negro Folksong*, she was eagerly sought out by African-American performers and scholars. She wrote the entry "Negro Folklore" for the *Encyclopedia Britannica* (1937) and made numerous public presentations on the radio, at scholarly gatherings such as the Modern Language Association, and to smaller interested groups, both popular and scholarly.

Scarborough was squarely in the tradition of the literary approach to folklore materials, but she was not an "armchair scholar." She collected both the texts and the tunes of folksongs directly from the informants through rigorous fieldwork and then undertook extensive scholarly research and correspondence to explicate her materials thoroughly and place them in the context of other scholarly findings. She was well known by all leading ballad and folksong scholars of her generation, both in America and abroad. Her collections are exceptional not only for the extensive contextual data she provided about her informants but also for her descriptions of her collecting methods and experiences. Both folksong collections have been republished, but currently they are out of print. Nevertheless they are regarded as standard reference texts for anyone dealing with the topic of secular folksong in America. She had planned to publish at least two more volumes based on her collected materials, but she died before she could accomplish that goal.

In spite of her expertise in folklore, her reputation today rests almost entirely on her controversial and somewhat experimental novel, *The Wind*. Her negative depiction of the Texas landscape and her tragic characters set this novel apart from those of her contemporary Texas authors, especially the men, who preferred a more heroic, positive approach consistent with the rapidly developing Texas Mystique. Scarborough's other novels follow conventional literary formulas, and today they strike readers as stilted, outdated, and saccharine. *The Wind,* however, still conveys intense conflict and memorable emotional impact. Because of the enduring appeal of this novel, Scarborough's place is secure as one of Texas's leading women authors.

NOTES

1. Biographical data in this essay are drawn from the Dorothy Scarborough Collection, Texas Collection, Baylor University.

THE PROFESSIONALS,
1960–95

In her preface to *Texas Writers of Today* (1935), Florence Barns vowed to produce an updated edition every three years. However, no second edition of this voluminous collection of Texas writers' biographies appeared. Barns apologizes for omissions from her first edition, declaring, "Texas is an enormous empire, and I am not omniscient." Acceleration of writing in Texas already had begun when this useful volume appeared. Quite possibly Barns found the prospect of preparing a second edition too daunting.

Sixty years later, with the support of university presses and recognition by national publishing houses, Texas women writers have created an even greater challenge for the would-be chronicler of their activities. Analysis of trends in the fiction, creative nonfiction, drama, and poetry that Texas women writers are producing at great rate is no easier now than in 1935 when, in her introduction, Florence Barns declared, "Looking once more at the present Texas writing pattern as a whole, we interpret it as cultural pattern in the making." Unfortunately no tidy pattern has yet emerged from critical attempts to categorize what women write in the state. Texas women writers still exhibit independence and individualism. A few dare to experiment with form; most reflect their strong belief that realistic re-creation of Texas experience is essential. Some write of urban life; others explore rural history and settings. Nevertheless, almost all contemporary women writers do manifest an exceptional sense of place and time.

A careful reading of works by contemporary Texas women writers supports two generalizations. First, although most of the state's women writers still divide their time between writing on the one hand and home and children on the other, they regard their writing as a profession and are producing critically appraised books every two or three years. Shelby Hearon, Jane Gilmore Rushing, Beverly Lowry, Elizabeth Forsythe Hailey, Laura Furman, and Carolyn Osborn have managed to retreat to that "room of one's own" that the British writer Virginia Woolf longed for and to write on a regular schedule. Others, such as Sarah Bird and Elizabeth Crook, who have launched their careers within the last decade, are following the seasoned professionals' example.

One other trend in Texas women's writing is obvious: many gain their initial recognition as writers by publishing short stories. Some, such as Carolyn Osborn and Annette Sanford, have found the genre offers the most compatible form for conveying their view of humankind. Others, including Sandra Scofield and Beverly Lowry, write graceful short fiction but focus most of their energies on shaping experience into novels. Many younger writers are honing their writing skills on short fiction.

Among the numerous nonfiction writers publishing at present, several women have excelled in a genre now designated as creative nonfiction. Beginning as journalists, Liz Carpenter, Molly Ivins, and Prudence Mackintosh have since published well-received books about their lives and times. A number of contemporary women writers in Texas have provided insight into women's lives on ranches in memoirs and autobiographies. They have shown too what life was for Texas women during the Great Depression and in oil boomtowns. Others have shaped their early Texas experiences into books for young readers.

Uninhibited by current fads, negative critical opinions, or occasional invisibility, Texas women writers approach the twenty-first century with a living tradition in place. From its beginnings, the tradition has been developed by independent women of talent who rarely conformed to current literary fads in their choice of either subject or genre. In the last two decades, Tejana and African-American women writers in the state have come into their own. Their work enriches a literary tradition now rapidly approaching maturity.

ELIZABETH FORSYTHE HAILEY

JOYCE THOMPSON

Born August 31, 1938, in Dallas and reared in Highland Park as the oldest of four children of attorney Earl Andrew and socialite-homemaker Janet (Kendall) Forsythe, Elizabeth received the B.A. from Hollins College in Virginia in 1960 and married Oliver D. Hailey, June 25, 1960. They have two daughters, Elizabeth Kendall and Melinda Brooke, both born in California. The Haileys have homes in Studio City (North Hollywood), California, and in Sussex, England.

While in college (1956–60) Elizabeth Hailey was a summer reporter for the *Dallas Morning News*. She worked as editorial assistant for the Yale University Press (1961–62) during the time her husband was earning the MFA in drama at Yale. Hailey never pursued her anticipated career in journalism. She went instead with her dramatist husband to New York, where he had several plays produced, then moved with him to Los Angeles where he wrote for film and television. Hailey helped her husband anonymously and without pay on freelance writing assignments, including television scripts for *McMillan and Wife*. She became an acknowledged collaborator with him on the Columbia Broadcasting System (CBS) soap opera *Love of Life* in 1970 and worked with him on two television series: as a creative consultant for Tandem Productions's *Mary Hartman, Mary Hartman* (1976) and as co-producer for CBS's *Another Day* (1977).

When their younger daughter entered nursery school, Hailey began work on a contemporary novel, *Letters from a Runaway Wife*. Besides her script writing, her previous work had been limited to a half-dozen unpublished short stories. With the encouragement of her husband, she abandoned her novel, deciding instead to explore the life of her maternal grandmother, Bess Kendall Jones. Hailey had a firm model for her protagonist and a strong form in mind when she drew on her grandmother's travel diaries and her own imagination to create the popular epistolary novel, *A Woman of Independent Means* (1978). In the year of its publication, the novel, which has sold more than a million copies, received the Silver Medal from the Commonwealth Club of California for best first novel and was nominated for the Texas Institute of Arts and Letters award for best work of fiction. Adapted for the theater as a one-woman play starring Barbara Rush, *A Woman of Independent Means* was produced in Los Angeles (at the Back Alley Theatre in Van Nuys) before opening at the Biltmore Theater on Broadway in May, 1984. The Los Angeles Drama Critics Circle recognized it as best play, and Rush received "best actress" honors. The play pleased New York audiences more than critics, and it was subsequently performed in Dallas to appreciative audiences and critics. In 1995, Sally Field starred in a television movie version of the novel.

Hailey's second novel *Life Sentences* (1982), a narrative, began with an idea for a situation—a crisis that would make middle-aged women of the 1980s reevaluate and renew their friendship, which had flourished two decades earlier in college. The book received mixed reviews from critics but was another popular success, remaining fourteen weeks on the *New York Times* best-seller list. Drawing on incidents and piecing together fragments of people she had known, Hailey explored the complexities of various kinds of marriage and friendship in a contemporary world. Criticism of the novel focused on the improbability of its plot; praise centered on Hailey's handling of difficult material and her creation of sympathetic characters.

Joanna's Husband and David's Wife (1986), Hailey's third novel, drew again on the resources that were the strengths of her first. It received more favorable reviews than *Life Sentences* and, like its predecessors, achieved best-seller status. In the form of journal entries by Joanna with editorial comments by David, the novel explores Hailey's continuing interest in marriage as a powerful shaping force, both oppressing and invigorating each partner at times. Sympathetic to both Joanna and David, the book parallels Hailey's marriage and her development as a writer in many ways. Hailey adapted the novel for the theater, and it had a one-night tryout at the Pasadena Playhouse in Los Angeles in 1988 with daughter Kendall Hailey playing Joanna. A sunnier nonfictional account of Hailey family life from another perspective appears in Kendall's book, *The Day I Became an Autodidact* (Dell, 1988).

All three novels have been published in British and Spanish editions. In addition, *Life Sentences* and *Joanna's Husband and David's Wife* have been translated and published in China and Brazil, respectively. Hailey has discussed her works and the practice of her art candidly in interviews and articles. An avowed feminist with a strong sense of tradition and optimism about human relationships, she presents her characters in both traditional and nontraditional families. Her advice to other writers (advice she has followed in her own best works) is to write from life and to write what they themselves want to read.

A Woman of Independent Means tells the story of Elizabeth (Bess) Alcott Steed Garner of Honey Grove and then Dallas through her letters and telegrams to family, friends, and business associates. From her first letter to her fourth-grade sweetheart, written on December 10, 1899, through her last letter to her granddaughter, almost seventy years later, her correspondence records the triumphs, the conflicts, and the occasional despondence of a woman accustomed to arranging things to her satisfaction. Always conscious of the power of her purse and her social standing, she sometimes issues orders with a regal air, a practice that creates tensions within her family and, less conspicuously, with acquaintances. Her well-intentioned manipulations lead to strained relations with her adult children. Her ambitions for them and for herself are never fully realized, but she transfers her hopes to her grandchildren and great-grandchildren.

Ultimately one both likes and dislikes Bess. Giving and demanding, she is both lavish and frugal with her independent means—financial, social, and emotional. One admires her courage even while conscious of her dependence on so many.

Life Sentences focuses on forty-two-year-old Lindsay Howard Hawkins, who is forced to review her choices and the judgments she has made of friends and family when she is confined to bed during a precarious pregnancy following her rape by a stranger in her apparently secure Manhattan apartment. A successful editor for a women's magazine, Lindsay has compartmentalized her life into days of work, evenings of visiting her paralyzed and speechless husband of nineteen years, and weekends for time alone or with Todd Newman, a man who befriended her following the death of her parents in a plane crash twelve years before the novel begins.

Determined to have the child (she had an illegal abortion following her husband's accident), she rejects Todd's repeated attempts to help her. Her apparent independence and self-sufficiency fail her, however, and she comes to depend on two college friends, the widowed Cissy and the childless Meg, both of whom have arrived at an unhappy middle age. Cissy feels inadequate and unneeded as a mother to her three children. Meg has married a lawyer instead of being one, and her numerous miscarriages have driven a wedge between her and her husband. Assisted by two doctors and, finally, by Todd as well as by her college friends, Lindsay finally gives birth to a daughter Claire, whom they declare to be "the daughter of us all."

Joanna's Husband and David's Wife, which has a contemporary setting, begins with Joanna's journal entry on the day she meets David and concludes twenty-five years later when, pregnant with a third child (a son), Joanna returns to Dallas to make peace with her parents and to begin taking active control of her life. She leaves her journal behind for whatever help it may provide her seventeen-year-old daughter Julia, who wants to live with Toby, a friend of many years, whom she has come to love. Finding the journal before Julia does, David writes a note to Julia insisting that he will not let Joanna's version of their life together be presented as the definitive view and proceeds to read the journal and add his comments.

The reader never learns Julia's reaction to her mother's revelations, but David's clear and pointed challenges to Joanna's observations reveal a growing perplexity and frustration about the woman he has loved and thought he knew. Taken together, Joanna and David's soul-searchings show the complex nature of marriage, the fears and self-doubts of husbands and wives (doubts to which mates often are oblivious), the compromises and sacrifices, and most importantly the mutual support and life-shaping influences spouses provide for each other.

In addition to David and Joanna's marriage, the novel explores the unsuccessful marriage of David's mother and father, the loving remarriage of his mother late in her life, the traditional marriage of Joanna's parents which results in divorce after their children are grown but which does not end emotionally with the divorce. Among friends of their own generation, Joanna observes a variety of unfulfilling marriages and liaisons as well as fulfilling unions outside marriage. In contemporary fashion, David and Joanna's ties to friends extend their family beyond blood relationships and sometimes prove stronger than their blood ties.

LAURA FURMAN, BEVERLY LOWRY, AND SHELBY HEARON

PATRICK BENNETT

Shelby Hearon, Beverly Lowry, and Laura Furman have a high place among current Texas writers who examine contemporary society through the microscope of fiction. Sophisticated, experimental, intellectual—these terms apply to all three writers, but one of these characteristics seems to predominate in each. Furman is the New York sophisticate, Lowry the experimenter, Hearon the intellectual.

They share certain other characteristics. All three came to Texas when they were past childhood, which allowed them to view Texas through alien eyes. Although years have passed since all three arrivals, this trio has continued to see the state with the sharpened awareness that only an alien, a person who first possessed another place, can possess. Such alienation, otherness, has a long history in western literature, going back to Montesquieu's *Lettres Persanes,* or Goldsmith's *Citizen of the World.* The outsider's perspective is seldom overt and simple in the Texans' work, the only notable exception being Furman's *The Shadow Line,* in which the protagonist's alien view of Texas runs beneath the mystery like the sound of the bass viols beneath the allegro movement in a symphony. More complex use of alien perspective is found in Hearon's *Group Therapy* and Lowry's *The Perfect Sonya;* in each a Texas woman moves to New York, adapts, then returns to look at Texas with new eyes.

Hearon, Lowry, and Furman generally write fiction centering around spunky women. A man holds center stage in a few of Furman's short stories, but a spunky woman holds it or, occasionally, shares it in novels by the three. Protagonists range in age from about eighteen to that shadowy time when women admit they are middle-aged or worse; all are capable of making a bold decision or taking a new lover; and most come equipped with families and frequently with ex-husbands.

Residence in Texas has affected all their novels, but the reader should beware of making too close an identification between a fictional work and the life of the writer who created it. A complex problem! The relationship is like that of an old crazy quilt to the housewife who pieced it together: some settings, events, and moods come directly from an author's life, some scraps of reality are borrowed from people the writer knows, and still others are reworked from items in *Time* magazine or on television's *Sixty Minutes*. As with Dr. Freud's dreams, the scraps of reality must come from somewhere. But the reader, and sometimes even the writer, can no more say with certainty where the author acquired them than I can say where grandmother acquired the colorful patches that make up her crazy quilt.

LAURA FURMAN

The youngest of the three writers and the most recent transplant, Laura Furman came to Texas in 1978 to help edit the *Houston Magazine*. By the time she arrived in Houston, a number of her short stories had already been accepted by *The New Yorker, Mademoiselle, Redbook,* and other periodicals. In her first book, *The Glass House: A Novella and Stories* (1980), are a novella bearing the book's title and five stories (only one of which, "Eldorado," is set in Houston). In 1982 she followed with *The Shadow Line*, an intellectual mystery set in Houston, and the next year with *Watch Time Fly*, a collection of ten stories set in the Eastern United States and England. In 1986 came Furman's second novel, *Tuxedo Park*, which is set in New York.

On November 19, 1945, Furman was born into a New York City household "where books were revered and writing was an honorable pursuit." After she had earned her B.A. in English at Bennington, Furman worked for Grove, Random House, Scribners, and other publishers. Finally she moved to Cambridge, New York, to begin writing seriously. She recalls her first two years of apprenticeship as "really horrible" while she "lived on nothing."

Furman has lived in Lockhart since the early 1980s, commuting to Austin to teach writing at the University of Texas. She and her husband, journalist Joel Barna, have a son. Texas writers welcomed the talented New Yorker, and by 1990 she was serving as president of the Texas Institute of Letters.

Furman writes in a style perfectly suited to the sophisticated tone of *The New Yorker,* where she made her major publishing debut. The voice of the narrator is never raised, equal emphasis is given to spreading butter on toast and a passionate embrace on the sofa, to a misplaced car key and a lost soul. Her dialogue is civilized, her characters the kind who seldom raise their voice.

A man is the central figure in a few short stories, but a Furman protagonist usually is a young woman, educated and sexually liberated but perhaps not quite understanding the situation in which she finds herself. A young New York woman is protagonist in all Furman's long fiction.

Another characteristic of Furman's fiction is her interest in apartments and houses, which she describes in loving detail. Such living quarters often play a major role in the narrative as with Arla's preoccupation with her mother's house in *The Glass House,* and Sadie's unyielding attachment to her husband's residence in *Tuxedo Park.*

That said, I hasten to add that Furman's stories examine a wide variety of situations and that her three longer fictions are very different from one another. In the novella that gives its title to Furman's first book, *The Glass House,* Arla, the protagonist, buys the upstate New York house in which her mother died. She finds work at a nearby private museum, and when the owners decide to expand it, Arla becomes involved in an affair with the young architect overseeing the construction. To further complicate her life, one of the museum owners pressures Arla to finagle the loan of a legendary glass house for display with a collection in the museum. Her mother's house, her house designer, the house of art, and the glass house—Arla becomes more and more encumbered until fate and her own initiative show her a way out.

Liz Gold in *The Shadow Line,* Furman's first full-length novel, is much like Furman: a young Jewish woman writer who comes to Houston to work on a magazine. (Furman found to her surprise that she liked Houston, and she profiles the city with skill and understanding.) Gold drives the wild Houston freeways with zest, falls in love, and seems happily settled until her editor, Cal Dayton, assigns her to write a feature on an old, almost forgotten, unsolved murder. A second complication arises when the silent partner in Cal's magazine returns and begins making decisions, but the novel is primarily a sophisticated mystery concerned with Liz's peeling away the layers of deception in the old murder.

Viking produced a beautifully designed volume to hold the ten short stories of *Watch Time Fly*. Although seven of the stories originally appeared in *The New Yorker*, the longest and best, the title story, appeared first in *Mademoiselle*. The same Furman story also appears in an anthology I used for a time in teaching college undergraduates, and they generally found this contemporary story of Anna making the final split with her ex-husband more to their liking than other stories in the textbook by such skilled hands as Chekhov and Maupassant. All the *Watch Time Fly* stories are subtly pointed and superbly done.

Tuxedo Park concerns a mismatched marriage between a nest-building woman and a wandering, dilettante husband. Sadie Ash, a twenty-year-old, middle-class, Jewish woman becomes pregnant by and marries Willard Weaver, a now-and-then art critic who has money and aristocratic East Coast roots. Willard inherits the family home in New York's Tuxedo Park, ritzy and restricted, a place that gives its name to a type of formal dinner attire for men. After they move into Tuxedo Park, Willard is restive, and eventually he disappears with his longtime mistress, Cherry Wilde. Sadie adores her home in Tuxedo Park, likes her friends there, likes raising their two daughters there, and stubbornly refuses to leave, or even to grant Willard a divorce, until the curious climax.

BEVERLY LOWRY

Beverly Lowry is far and away the most experimental of the trio. In her first two books she employs a swirl of Faulknerian eloquence to etch the grotesques who inhabit the little southern town of Eunola; in her third she switches to a kaleidoscopic style for examining her protagonist's radically split character. For a closer examination of the individual heart, she returns to classic style in her fourth and fifth. In all her work she tinkers with time, sometimes leapfrogging forward, sometimes dipping into the past, sometimes arresting time for a leisurely examination of the many details surrounding an event. Time seems almost frozen in her sixth novel. And in her nonfiction book, *Crossed Over: A Murder, A Memoir,* she combines memoir and biography.

Born August 10, 1938, in Memphis, Tennessee, Lowry is the daughter of David L. and Dora Fey. She studied two years at the University of Mississippi, then earned her B.A. in 1960 at Memphis State University, where she majored in speech and drama, "heavy on the latter," she comments. She has worked as a professional actress. She married Glenn Lowry, a stockbroker, in 1960; two sons.

Lowry drifted into Texas by way of Houston, teaching in the English Department at the University of Houston from 1976 through 1984. Her first three novels were published during those years: *Come Back, Lolly Ray* in 1977, *Emma Blue* in 1978, and *Daddy's Girl* in 1981. Lowry had moved to San Marcos by the time *The Perfect Sonya* and *Breaking Gentle* appeared, in 1987 and 1988, respectively. Most recently, Lowry published the experimental nonfiction *Crossed Over* (1992) and a single-day novel, *The Track of Real Desires* (1994). She has also published frequently in periodicals. *Lolly Ray,* in shortened form, appeared in *Redbook* before it got between hard covers. Her short stories have appeared in *Viva, Playgirl, Mississippi Review, Southwest Review,* and elsewhere. Her essays, reviews, and journalism have appeared in the *New York Times Book Review, Rolling Stone, Vanity Fair, Texas Monthly, Southern Magazine,* and so on.

In her first book, *Come Back, Lolly Ray,* Lowry explores the hidden life of Eunola, one of those small, rural towns that Gustave Flaubert, Sherwood Anderson, Jack Milburn, and William Faulkner have shown to be such imperfect Edens. Lolly Ray Lasswell is a teenager—and not a particularly brainy specimen—whose youth, beauty, and muscular coordination combine for a golden moment to make her the Anna Pavlova of baton twirlers. Because fellow Eunola residents sense the twirler embodies some ideal spirit, town leaders pool funds to send her to college. While Lolly Ray shines at the center of the novel, the author spends much of her time turning over Eunola rocks to reveal the wormy little secrets of the town's citizens, who are every bit as grotesque as anything inscribed in the book of *Winesburg's* old man with a white mustache: a secret drinker, an abortionist, several illicit lovers, a crazy old woman, a feeble-minded boy. Lolly herself falls into the passionate embrace of Lt. James Blue, who is careful not to mention his wife and child back in Chicago. In the *New York Times Book Review,* J. D. Bellamy labeled Eunola "a raging, gurgling gene-pool not very far from Yoknapatawpha." *Emma Blue* chronicles the career of the daughter who was the fruit of Lolly Ray's nights of passion with Lieutenant Blue. Many characters in the little southern town recur, but somehow the canvas does not seem as broad, nor the characters as grotesque. Emma matures, experiences sex, graduates from high school, sees her stylish, now-married mother. The writing again is graceful and probing, but Emma lacks Lolly's charisma.

By the time she published *Daddy's Girl,* three years later, Lowry felt sufficiently rooted in Texas to make her heroine a Houston resident, but the change in scene is minor in comparison to Lowry's departure from southern gothic style and subject. Sue Shannon Stovall Muffaleta is a big-city woman yanked in three directions by her family, her talent, and her craving for romance. She pours oceans of energy into working with little league for her children and acting the good daughter to her Rabelaisian father; into her career as a country-western singer and song writer; and into her affair with the owner of a honky-tonk where she performs. All this is spewed out in a stream of choppy clauses, sentence fragments, and isolated words that reflect Sue's own mental processes. Time too is fragmented, the present often sliding into the past, or the past suddenly thrusting its hairy paw into the present. When the reader is thoroughly acquainted with Sue's selves and with her father, her children, her mother, her dead husband, and her live lover, the story sends the adults bowling off to Daddy's old home, where the whole screwy clan gathers for a funeral. The best part of the novel is the first—in the second the characters are very nearly caricatures—but *Daddy's Girl* is a fascinating experiment.

Returning to conventional syntax and putting grotesques behind her, Lowry probes less outré psyches in her next two novels. In *The Perfect Sonya* a sexually promiscuous young actress named Pauline is summoned back from New York to Texas because of her father's fatal illness. When she goes to ask an autograph from her aunt's divorced husband, a writer and professor, they talk philosophically and wind up in bed together. (Some Texans judged the book a *roman à clef,* perceiving that the writer-professor walked and talked like John Graves, author of the classic *Goodbye to a River.*) The night of love in the professor's cabin is life-shattering for Pauline, who must re-make herself afterwards. *Breaking Gentle* continues Lowry's psycho-logical probing, but she widens her scope to take in the four members of a modern family. Hale and his wife, Diana, raise race horses, ani-mals Hale believes in training by gentle methods. The same system has produced mixed results with their children: grown son Roger has become a chef and lives a bohemian life in California; teen daughter Bethany has been placed in a psychiatric institution in lieu of jail after a crime spree with her thuggy beau. Lowry explores the present situation of each of her quartet thoroughly, often peeping into the past to explain how one of them got that way.

Combining reportage with autobiography, Lowry is again experi-menting radically with *Crossed Over: A Murder, A Memoir.* Lowry's rebellious son, Peter, was killed near San Marcos by a hit-and-run driver in September, 1984. Two years later, while she was trying to come to terms with her personal tragedy, Lowry read a *Houston Chronicle* story about a young murderess, Karla Faye Tucker, who had found a new life on death row. Lowry began visiting Tucker in prison, and her book combines the stories of Peter and Karla Faye. Lowry's search for understanding is powerful writing.

With her novel, *The Track of Real Desires* (1994), Lowry returns to *Lolly Ray* territory. Leland Standard has returned to Eunola, Mis-sissippi, with her son, Toby, for a dinner party with old friends, and in the course of the evening, the reader gets an engrossing view of everyone's relationship and past.

SHELBY HEARON

Often styled the "Queen of American intellectuals," Mary McCarthy in a self-deprecating mood late in life, defined "intellectuals" as little people playing with big ideas. That definition is too modest. It does, however, distinguish them from formal philosophers, those methodi-cal bricklayers of intellectual skyscrapers who spend vast quantities of thought on such esoteric questions as, "How do I know that I know I am in Texas?" Shelby Hearon, the most intellectual of Texas novelists, is content to weave an abstract idea such as *identity* into her fiction, dramatizing it, showing rather than telling it to her readers. The wide span of Hearon's intellectual interests may be gathered from the names of authors who lend epigraphs to her books: Jorge Luis Borges, R. D. Laing, Anne Sexton, Martin Heidegger, Stéphane Mallarmé, Friedrich Engels, Miguel de Cervantes.

Evelyn Shelby Reed (the somewhat androgynous "Shelby" for a Kentucky governor who was a forebear) was born January 18, 1931, in Marion, Kentucky. Her family moved to Texas while she was in high school. Graduating with honors from the University of Texas Plan II humanities program in 1953, she married Robert J. Hearon, Jr., the same year. The writer and her Austin attorney husband were divorced in 1977. She married Dr. Billy Joe Lucas in 1981 and shortly after moved with him to North White Plains, New York. After their divorce, she moved to Vermont and remarried. Her husband, William Halpern, is a cardiovascular physiologist. She returns to Texas fairly frequently, however, to visit her grown son and daughter by her first marriage.

Older than Lowry and Furman, Hearon began publishing before they did and has published more books of fiction than both put together. She also has published much nonfiction and fiction in periodicals. The biographical element in Shelby Hearon's fiction has often been remarked, but here again the crazy-quilt principle applies. Her first four novels, *Armadillo in the Grass* (1968), *The Second Dune* (1973), *Hannah's House* (1975), *Now and Another Time* (1976), deal with either divorce or the restiveness of a woman under the marital yoke. Hearon's tone grows more pessimistic with each successive book in this quartet; she once told me that she found *Now and Another Time* so depressing that she could hardly stand creating it. Her next book, *A Prince of a Fellow* (1978), a light, intellectual comedy that draws its images from fairy tales, was published the year following her divorce. The three subsequent novels are quite complex in form and thought: *Painted Dresses* (1981), *Afternoon of a Faun* (1983), and *Group Therapy* (1984). Of this trio, the first is dedicated to philosopher Bill Lucas (whom she would marry the year of its publication) and has an epigraph by Heidegger. Following this trio were two marital comedies, *A Small Town* (1985) and *Five Hundred Scorpions* (1987). *Owning Jolene* (1989) is another joyous farce that can only be paired with *Prince of a Fellow*. Next was *Hug Dancing* (1991), a less extravagant comedy dealing with a wife who turns from a stale marriage to a love affair. She returned to more somber themes in *Life Estates* (1994).

Hearon's first two books seem closely linked in style and subject. She once said that she welcomed classification as "a woman's novelist" because she believed that a woman's viewpoint had been poorly represented by male writers. Her first two novels, both from the perspective of young matrons with small children, realize the woman's viewpoint with artful subtlety. Clara Blue of *Armadillo in the Grass* is an Austin housewife whose professor husband hardly understands her longing to escape the sweet captivity of her household and small children. Clara wants to sculpt small wild animals, female animals who seem akin to her in motherhood, and she begins lessons with a handsome young sculptor to whom she is obviously attracted. Her relationship with her teacher is what Hollywood used to call "a love that can never be," but Clara does sculpt a respectable armadillo.

Before the title page is turned in Hearon's time-haunted *The Second Dune*, Ellen Marshall has divorced her first husband, Franklin, a dull and overly organized banker, so she can wed John, an outgoing attorney with whom she had slept behind Franklin's back. In Ellen's keeping are an alienated son, Frank Jr., from her first marriage, and a preschool daughter, Ellen (Jr.), from her second. Mrs. Marshall is understandably obsessed with the past and the way phases of her life overlie one another like geological strata: the years before her marriages when she was Ellen Maitland, the years with the banker, the present. Her own infidelity is again painfully forced into her consciousness when John's sister-in-law decamps with another man.

The arrangements for, and execution of, a wedding provide a frame for *Hannah's House,* in which Hearon examines convention and rebellion. The book's twist is that the mother, who must make the arrangements, is the rebel, while her daughter, the bride, is militantly conventional. Narrator is the mom, Beverly "Bananas" Foster, who has chosen to be a misfit much of her life. As the novel begins, Beverly is buying a house—the house of the title—so daughter Hannah will have a proper place for her announcement party and related events. It ends with Hannah's wedding to Eugene—and with Ben, Foster's sleep-in beau, on the road to making an honest woman of Hannah's mother. In between, the fun of the book is listening to the mother's wry shots at her CPA ex-husband and various other personages and events, a black-comedy monologue as human and shrewdly amusing as those found in Saul Bellow, Philip Roth, or Gunter Grass.

The fourth of this group, *Now and Another Time,* goes back to

Jasper County in 1927, where we see Harry Chambers fail to win a judgeship. Then around Houston in 1934, Tom Henderson and Mary Allen, both married to others, woo each other but cannot consummate their affair. In the 1970s, their children achieve the goals of the parents with a dark hint of determinism. Julia, Mary's daughter, is married to Hardin Chambers, Harry's son. Harry becomes judge; Mary sleeps with Jimmie, Tom Henderson's son.

Hearon said she felt she had to break out of the predestinating clutches of the past, and she did so with *Prince of a Fellow*. Avery Krause, "a frizzy-haired, washed-out princess," is running a small-town radio station and sleeping with the mayor of San Antonio while awaiting her prince. As in other fairy tales, nothing is what it seems in this light comedy of illusion, including Avery's prince when he appears.

Next came three of Hearon's knottier novels. *Painted Dresses* again weighs the question of fate, of determinism. One of the principals is a slew-footed, jug-eared geneticist named Nicolas Clark who early begins wrestling with the Calvinist doctrine of predestination; Clark toys with Lamarck's ideas on transmission of acquired characteristics. Nell Woodard, the other central character, seizes her destiny by leaving a dull marriage to devote herself to painting. She specializes in painting dresses, with no one in them. Clark is tricked into a loveless marriage with his sociopath brother's discarded mistress and eventually divorces her. When Nick and Nell finally meet, they discover they are in perfect harmony. Fated for one another? Well, anyway, a happy ending.

Motherhood, personal fulfillment, time, rebellion, determinism and illusion—all these themes seem strong in *Afternoon of a Faun*, the knottiest of this knotty trio. The novel begins in Paducah, Kentucky, with Mr. and Mrs. Mayfield shocking their daughter, Jeanetta, on her fifteenth birthday by telling her she is adopted. The story then loops back to June, 1955, in Aspen, Colorado, where a young violinist named Harry James from Austin meets physicist Dan Wister and his wife, Ebie. Ebie is pregnant, but in a curious sequence of events, she gives up her baby for adoption and dies in a house fire. Harry, who meantime realizes he is gay, meets Jeanetta fifteen years later at a summer camp and guesses her identity—but even he does not know the full story. Since Harry is the viewpoint character in much of the novel, *Faun* strains the generalization that a woman is always protagonist, but the novel centers on Jeanetta and her origins. Perhaps the term "protagonist" does not apply to this book's highly original structure.

While Hearon seems much interested in contrasting southern culture with northern in *Group Therapy*, she also toys with many examples of illusions stripped away from reality. Divorcee Lutie Sayre wriggles free of Austin by taking a teaching job at the State University of New York. She works at adjusting; she falls in love and bed with her group-therapist, Dr. Joe Donaldson, a divorced man himself having trouble with two teen sons. On trips back to Austin and to Savannah, Georgia, Lutie discovers that her family is capable of lying not only to outsiders but to itself. Eventually she escapes to New York again to help her therapist straighten out his life.

After this knotty trio, Hearon turned to a looser form. *A Small Town* presents the fictional autobiography of Alma Van der Linden in a small Missouri town named Venice. Alma's father and grandfather are rural physicians, and at the beginning Alma is a shrewd, adventurous little girl. Annoyed by the town librarian's refusal to lend her adult books, she later seduces the high school principal, husband of the librarian. Alma finishes college before she wrongheadedly weds the principal, Louis LeCroix, who is a bore and a half. When their son and daughter are in their teens and the second Mrs. LeCroix in her forties, Alma finds passionate love in an affair with a visiting scientist named Dyer Tanner. Such a synopsis omits the book's many, quirky characters and wealth of situations—including a murder.

Five Hundred Scorpions followed. It is the story of Paul Sinclair, who runs off from his wife and two sons in Virginia to join an anthropological team composed of a Japanese-American man and two attractive women in Mexico. Back in Charlottesville, Paul's wife, Peggy, flirts with the idea of an affair with Todd Stedman, Paul's old college classmate and enemy. In this marital comedy, Hearon switches back and forth between Virginia and Mexico with the skill of a Restoration dramatist and brings off a surprisingly satisfying solution.

After detouring through Missouri, Mexico, and Virginia, Hearon comes home to Texas in *Owning Jolene*, another lighthearted farce looking back to *Prince of a Fellow*. Young Jolene Jackson, whose divorced parents steal her back and forth from one another during her growing-up years, is mistress and model for a painter named Henry Wozencrantz. Jolene is mildly attracted to a young man her own age.

Also wanting Jolene to stay with them are an uncle and aunt, real estate promoters. For purposes of comedy, Hearon sketches Texas, and the Texans who inhabit it, in bold black-and-white cartoon lines. Father, mother, painter, beau, aunt and uncle—who will own Jolene? When Wozencrantz publicly exhibits his paintings of her, Jolene is forced to decide.

In *Hug Dancing,* again set in Texas, Hearon also returns to the theme of a housewife who climbs over the fences of law and morality surrounding her rather dull marriage to be with a man she really loves. Cile is the wife of Eben Tait, a Presbyterian minister, who becomes pastor of a church in Waco. Cile gets her first major surprise when she finds the local population includes Drew Williams, her high school beau and favorite dance partner. Drew and Cile soon tumble into a smokey love affair, and when they decide to untie their previous marriage knots, some of the expected snags prove illusory. Other surprises come, however, before they are free to trot off to wed.

Life Estates contains many of Hearon's longtime preoccupations, such as family, the status of women, sexual politics, and time (here measured by the life spans of the narrator's pet dogs). Specifically, it concerns the relationship of two friends, Sarah and Harriet, both recently widowed at the beginning of the novel. Sarah, the narrator, lives in South Carolina, Harriet in Texas. Sarah becomes romantically involved with an elderly doctor, Harriet with a man younger than she is. Sarah soon comes to realize that Harriet, a smoker, suffers from terminal lung cancer. Ultimately the book is about confronting death, and the heightened life-awareness such confrontation brings.

JANE GILMORE RUSHING

CHERYL KEY AND PEGGY SKAGGS

Jane Gilmore Rushing interprets life as it has been lived in West Texas from the time the first Anglo-American settlers arrived during the nineteenth century until the present. Although she has written a few short stories, her best genre is the novel. In historical order of settings, her Texas novels are *Mary Dove: A Love Story* (1974), set in the mid-nineteenth century; *Tamzen* (1972), in the 1880s; *Walnut Grove* (1964), near the turn of the century; *Winds of Blame* (1983), early in the twentieth century; *Against the Moon* (1968), in the 1960s; and *The Raincrow* (1977), in the 1970s. Together the novels constitute a social history of rural West Texas, as the residents strive to control, first the land and then each other. In 1982, Rushing published *Covenant of Grace,* which reflects life in colonial New England, a setting outside her usual social milieu.

Rushing comments that she creates her characters before she develops the plot, and she believes her West Texans are deeply shaped by their climate and topography. "West Texas," she writes, "encompasses more than climate and landscape; it's a breed of people, a style of life, a way of freeing and extending the mind." She feels as deeply rooted in West Texas soil as a mesquite tree: "I think of mesquite because it is stubborn, deep-rooted, hard to eradicate. . . . My intimate relationship to the country I was born and raised in, and still go back to when I can, seems that tenacious." After her literary foray into New England with *Covenant of Grace,* she did indeed hurry back to her familiar Texas landscape with *Winds of Blame,* published the next year.

Besides being a writer of fine fiction, this native West Texan has been a newspaper reporter, high school teacher, and college professor since she graduated from Texas Tech University (B.A. 1944, M.A. 1945, Ph.D. 1957). From 1957 to 1959 she was an instructor at the University of Tennessee, but the rest of her life has been spent in West Texas. She was born in Pyron, between Sweetwater and Snyder— some one hundred miles from Lubbock, where she lives today. She has been married to James Arthur Rushing since 1956, and they have one son, James Arthur, Jr. She worked as a reporter on a newspaper in Abilene for a year and taught at Texas Tech University intermittently for nine years. Since 1960 she has devoted most of her professional time to writing fiction. In 1961 her short-story version of "Against the Moon" won the Emily Clark Balch prize for best short story, awarded by the *Virginia Quarterly Review. Mary Dove* received Doubleday's award for the most promising novel of the year in 1974, and *Winds of Blame* won the Texas Literature Award given by the *Dallas Times Herald* and the Southwestern Booksellers Association in 1983.

Such awards validate Jane Gilmore Rushing's secure place among the best writers Texas has produced. Her honest but empathetic portraits give us realistic West Texans instead of the stereotypical characters who too often have been exploited, insulted, or romanticized by some writers of fiction set in that distinctive region.

Other than Rushing's own articles, few detailed analyses of her novels have been published. Cheryl Key wrote a thesis that analyzes the Texas novels in detail. A monograph-length study of Rushing's work by Lou H. Rodenberger was published in 1995 as Number 118 in the *Western Writers Series.* Rushing herself has published three articles about her books and her writing process in *Writer* and another article in *Texas Women: The Myth, the Reality,* the published proceedings of a 1984 conference sponsored by the Texas Committee for the Humanities at Texas Woman's University. In her own analyses, Rushing discusses the importance of the relationship between place and character, saying, "You have to see landscape the way it is, and you have to see people . . . you have to see them both together.

. . . Place is made up of landscape, climate, manners and morals, culture and customs; and characters are largely made up of their responses to all of these."

In "Roots of a Novel" (1975), Rushing acknowledges how strongly she identifies with the land and the characters she creates. She recognizes how deeply rooted she is in West Texas and that some of her characters reflect aspects of her own personality. She says one of her characters, John Carlile in *Walnut Grove*, resembles her own father, and she has written an essay, "The Grandmother of West Texas," about the influence of her grandmother in her fiction.

Few critics have written about Rushing's fiction, but those who have note the influence of the physical environment on her characters. Micky Sadoff, for example, says that in Rushing's stories the environment is "an integral part of the characters' personalities." Daryl Jones writes, "By dramatizing archetypal phases of human experience against the larger cycles of history and of nature, the novels assume individually and collectively the scope and resonance of myth." Rushing sets her Texas stories in that part of West Texas known as "the breaks," between Sweetwater and Snyder, which she describes as "a wonderful, lonely understated sort of country," where the severity of the climate and the land force the people to adapt and become strong or be defeated. Only the courageous, the strong, and the determined could settle such a country. Rushing creates memorable characters, including a number of brilliantly drawn women, who grow even stronger and more determined through their experiences on the Texas frontier.

Unfortunately the determination to conquer and to control becomes displaced even before the frontier is settled, and some descendants of those settlers develop an outright "zeal for righteousness," which expresses itself in attempts to control the behavior of everyone in the community. Not only must the physical environment be tamed but, especially in the novels set later, the inhabitants must be made to conform to arbitrary standards established by these self-appointed guardians of righteousness, or at least of respectability.

Mary Dove is set in the mid-nineteenth century, when Anglo-Americans were beginning to settle in West Texas. Rushing describes this novel as "almost a fantasy." Mary and Red meet, fall in love, and believe they are married in the sight of God. But racism and bigotry apparently arrived with the first wagon in the West, and they cause problems for the young interracial couple. The novel idealizes nature and contrasts Mary's natural purity with the ugliness of a judgmental society. Rushing does not wave a magic wand to provide a live-happily-ever-after conclusion; rather, she offers an ambiguous ending. As Jones says, it is "a mixed scene of sadness and promise, a scene at once suggestive of *Paradise Lost* and the New Testament Christmas story."

The next novel in her West Texas saga, *Tamzen,* is based on an actual conflict over ownership of land originally part of a railroad right-of-way, a common source of tension in that time and place. This squatters-versus-ranchers story features a strong woman (Tamzen) who experiences great satisfaction in overcoming hardships but feels little compassion for those less able to prevail. In *Tamzen,* Rushing herself seems to speak through Arthur Field, who mourns the end of the West Texas wilderness: "He had seen a wild land tamed— more abruptly than he had ever dreamed that nature would allow." West Texas in this novel "ain't no soft and pretty country," as Mrs. Hawkins, another settler, explains, and Arthur reminds another character that "the land will be here when you're gone. . . . I never thought it was for me—any more than it ever belonged to the buffalo and Indians."

Although *Walnut Grove,* the next novel in historical sequence, was the first to be written, it moves away from preoccupation with the land to focus on the evolving community that gives the novel its name. The settlers establish a school and church, but the protagonist, John, mourns that the virgin soil must be plowed and tamed for people's convenience. While the town goes all out to attract a railroad, John begs the people to remember that the land is the true source of their sustenance.

Set early in the twentieth century, *Winds of Blame* is Rushing's most strongly plotted novel. It is a tale of abuse, murder, and intrigue, but its thematic continuity with the other Texas novels is nevertheless clear. Greenfields, the town where the events take place, reflects as much hypocrisy in its name as does Walnut Grove, which has only one walnut tree—until the townspeople chop it down to make a sidewalk. In this novel, hypocrisy becomes such a dominant theme that all other motifs pale by comparison. As an epigraph, Rushing has quoted appropriately from *Hamlet*: "And for his death no wind of blame shall breathe, / And even his mother shall uncharge the practice. / And call it accident." Like *Hamlet, Winds of Blame* examines the ugly hypocrisy of a community involved in covering up a crime.

Against the Moon, which began as a short story, leaps forward in time to a summer in the early 1960s, when three generations of women in the Albright family are brought together in the small West Texas town where all grew up. Granny, the oldest, is dying. Maureen, Granny's granddaughter, comes into a belated maturity. And Linda Kay, Granny's granddaughter-in-law, moves from adolescence into adulthood. Granny, through her powerful example in life but also through her dying, teaches each of the younger women what she needs to know at her present stage of life. Granny loves the members of the community without succumbing to the tyranny of their self-righteous, small-minded code, that respectability is the equivalent of morality.

Patrick Bennett labeled *The Raincrow* "the most subtle and psychologically complex" of Rushing's works—"an iceberg novel." The time is the 1970s; the place is again Walnut Grove. But the little West Texas town that boomed in the earlier novel is now dying. As in *Against the Moon,* three generations constitute the primary cast, and the chief antagonist again is the community. In *The Raincrow* also, the oldest of the main characters, Laura, is the wisest, and she helps the younger characters mature in their acceptance of others' shortcomings. Laura's daughter, Gail, cannot forgive the people of Walnut Grove for the hurt they have dealt her mother, but she comes to realize that she too is fallible and sometimes foolish. Laura's grandson, Paul, "comes home" to Walnut Grove emotionally as well as physically.

Together, Rushing's six Texas novels reveal her keen insight into the region and its people. Clearly she feels deep kinship with and love for the land and people, but these emotions do not blind her to the determination of some small West Texas towns to impose their brand of "respectability" on one and all.

Her New England novel, *Covenant of Grace,* is a fictionalized but historically accurate account of Anne Hutchinson and the antinomian controversy that shook the Massachusetts colony. The novel begins when the Hutchinson family arrives in Boston and ends when they follow Roger Williams to Rhode Island. Anne Hutchinson tries to combat hypocrisy and judgmental attitudes in New England, as some of Rushing's other characters fight against the same kinds of human behavior in West Texas. Although Boston is far from Pyron, both settings involve authentic characters in the settling of a new place and the coming of civilization to a raw frontier. A recurrent motif in Rushing's novels is the vicious power of the organized church, which for Anne Hutchinson led to excommunication and banishment from the colony. Mary Dove suffered a similar fate at the hands of the conservative and fanatic religious settlers in West Texas.

Jane Gilmore Rushing's themes are universal. She sets most of her stories in the world that she knows best, West Texas, and her characters are authentic West Texans. But their concerns are universal concerns, and they would behave similarly no matter where they were—even as far away in time, place, and culture as colonial New England.

CAROLYN OSBORN

TANYA LONG BENNETT
AND LOU HALSELL RODENBERGER

Carolyn Osborn, one of Texas's most anthologized short-fiction writers, has often said that her stories, particularly those involving "a family's collective memory," originate in her desire to explore "the mystery of reality." Osborn's short story "The Grands," which was inspired by anecdotes she had heard her senior relatives tell, won a place in the collection *Prize Stories 1990: The O. Henry Awards*. In the "Biographies and Comments" section of the volume, Osborn explains the origin of this and many of her short stories: "The need to tell the stories, the variety of kinship, the necessity of mythology, the mystery of reality are all entwined here." Among the first contemporary Texas women short-fiction writers to publish in major literary journals, Osborn, the author of three collections of short stories, began her career as a writer in the 1960s. From the beginning she has probed "the mystery of reality" in her stories.

Carolyn Osborn was born July 11, 1934, in Nashville, Tennessee, where she spent her early years. After her parents divorced, she lived with her grandmother and two aunts until her father remarried. Then she and her brother moved to Texas to live with her father and his wife, who owned a ranch near Gatesville. Graduating from Gatesville High School in 1951, Carolyn entered the University of Texas as a journalism major. After one summer as a student intern on the *Marshall News Messenger* and graduation from college, Carolyn married Joe A. Osborn, a law student at the university.

During Joe Osborn's tour in the army, which he joined soon after marriage, the Osborns lived in El Paso, where Carolyn wrote continuity for Radio Station KEPO. After almost a year the couple was transferred to Germany, where they traveled widely in Italy, Spain, and England. Carolyn continued to write, sending travel features back to the *Friona Star,* in which Joe had part ownership. In Germany, Carolyn gained the knowledge of European culture and values that is the background for several of her more successful short stories.

Both Osborns returned to the University of Texas after Joe's tour. Joe finished his law degree in 1958, one year before Carolyn received her master's degree in English. Carolyn completed her graduate work with a creative thesis, which included six stories. "Eunice B.," the title work, was published as second-place winner of the Co-op Short Story Contest for Graduate Students in the English Department publication, *The Corral* (1963).

Since 1962, Osborn's stories have appeared in such journals as *Georgia Review, Paris Review, Antioch Review, Ascent,* and *Texas Quarterly.* She has also written two plays, both performed in Austin in 1971. *Confetti in the Bathtub* was produced by Theatre Unlimited. The Bijuberti Players performed *The Somebodies* for puppets. Since the early 1970s, however, she has concentrated on telling stories.

By 1977 the University of Illinois Press had published Osborn's first collection of short stories, *A Horse of Another Color.* Co-winner of the Best Book-Length Fiction by a Southwestern Writer award presented by *Texas Books in Review* in 1977, the collection included two stories for which Osborn received much attention. "The Accidental Trip to Jamaica" was not only co-winner of the Texas Institute of Letters Best Short Story Award in 1978; it also was translated into Spanish and included in Luis A. Ramos-Garcia's anthology, *Cuentos de Austin/Tales from Austin* (1980). It appears as well in Marshall Terry's *Prize Stories: Texas Institute of Letters* (1978). Osborn's wry humor mingles with an intense sense of the tragic in this tale of the impulsive Jamaican fling of an Austin dentist and a literature teacher, married but not to each other. In a haunting flashback the teacher remembers the affair as almost farcical while she copes with horrifying images of her paramour's drowning.

Osborn's first collection also includes the story that has most often appeared in anthologies. "My Brother Is a Cowboy" introduces Kenyon, a modern-day Texas cowboy. From her ringside seat, Kenyon's sister, Celia, conveys his actions, attitudes, and reactions in the role of bona fide Texas cowpoke as he sees it. Probably her funniest story, this characterization of the die-hard cowboy is also one of her most perceptive. Perhaps the best story in *The Fields of Memory* (1984), Osborn's second collection, is "House of the Blue Woman," in which Celia looks back at what she perceives were the realities of Kenyon's life as she clears out his ranch house after his premature death.

An epigraph attributed to St. Augustine's *Confessions* makes clear the genesis of the title, *The Fields of Memory:* "The fields, the caves, the dens of Memory cannot be counted; their fullness cannot be counted nor the kinds of things counted that fill them." In another story in this volume, "Ancient History," Celia, recognizable as the author's alter ego, and her friend encounter the reclusive old rancher Miss Agnes Doyle, who calls herself "crazy cussing old woman" and who reminds the girls on horseback that she is part of the town's "ancient history," a past that Celia up to now has valued very little. Osborn writes sensitively from a male narrator's point of view in "The Circuit Rider" in this collection. Here, Osborn examines the reasons for living that a disillusioned preacher who comes home to rural Leon creates for himself and how fragile that construct is after all. "Reversals" features Celia and her father, who must deal this time with twin cousins who arrive on their Harleys for a prolonged stay. This story appears in *South by Southwest: 24 Stories from Modern Texas* (1986), an anthology edited by Don Graham.

In 1991, Texas Christian University Press published *Warriors and Maidens,* a third gathering of Osborn's stories, including "Wildflowers I Have Known," which appeared first in *Paris Review* and later in *Her Work: Stories by Texas Women* (1982). Here Osborn introduces Margaret, a refugee from the sixties in Austin who gets caught up in the plan of her happy-go-lucky friends to return a stuffed bear they have stolen from a neighborhood shop owner.

In "Cowboy Movie," perhaps the most significant story in this collection, Osborn explores her knowledge of a modern ranch operation as well as her understanding of human nature. The narrator is a sophisticated young woman, back in her home territory and working as a bookkeeper for an old rancher friend, Charlie. When Rafe, both cowboy and employee of the film company, offers her a role in a movie to be made on the ranch, she refuses even though she is attracted to him. When Charlie agrees to let the company film *The Working Cowboy,* the narrator moves on, knowing that life on the ranch will be a long time returning to normal. After seeing the movie, she says, "You would never have known that any of those men gambled, got drunk, had fist fights, ate ice-cream, bought new pickups, went to movies, or fell in love." She is upset that the cowboys appear to be "unreal automatons" but adds, "Eventually I got out of the humor. It was only Rafe's earnest movie that changed them for an hour or so. You can't really lose cowboys." "Cowboy Movie" is also included in *New Growth: Contemporary Short Stories by Texas Writers,* edited by Lyman Grant.

Osborn's stories have been selected for inclusion in more than a dozen anthologies: "The Apex Man" in *Common Bonds: Stories by and about Modern Texas Women* (1990), edited by Suzanne Comer; "Overlappings" in *North of the Rio Grande: The Mexican-American Experience in Short Fiction,* edited by Edward Simmen and dedicated to Osborn; and "Mexicans and Gringos" in *New Growth/2,* edited by Mark Busby. Busby says he approached his task of short-story selection by searching for three qualities in short fiction: "originality, supple language, and humanity." He adds, "I looked for stories with regional elements and also for ones that . . . treat subjects central to good literature—the old verities of the human heart such as honor and courage and pity and suffering, fear and humor, love and sorrow." Osborn's stories exhibit those qualities.

When Osborn spoke at McMurry University in 1988, she shared her memories of family stories with her audience of students and professors interested in writing, and she made clear that those materials begged to be included in her fiction. "The Greats" and "The Grands," concluding works in *Warriors and Maidens,* shape those materials into moving, often humorous, accounts of old-timers back in Tennessee, where Osborn's relatives settled. In "The Greats" the eccentric Great Uncle Ambrose, probably drunk, paints the yard fence blue one Sunday although no one remembers why. As one of many individualistic ancestors, he is accepted as the family does "the other greats, their eccentric, willful, and finally, mysterious kin."

In "The Grands," a prudish Victorian grandmother copes with a fiddle-playing, drinking grandfather, whose escapades fuel family imaginations long after his death in an accident that forever would be a subject of family speculation. In 1990 the Book Club of Texas selected "The Grands" to inaugurate its New Texas Fiction series. Custom-bound in elegant red, the volume is designed and illustrated by Barbara Whitehead in two-color woodcuts. Barbara Whitehead and her late husband, Fred, known for their prize-winning book designs, worked in a studio for many years in the same West Austin house where Osborn's workplace is located. In November, 1990, at the annual meeting of the Book Club of Texas, Osborn spoke on "One Writer's Uses of the Past." She concludes her talk, printed in the Book Club's December, 1990, newsletter, speaking once again of the "unsolvable mystery of reality," and adds that this mystery as well as "the impossibility of totally capturing a whole person on paper is what most intrigued me in trying to tell this story."

Osborn's settings are most often in Texas, but her themes are universal, which accounts largely for her significant contribution to literature created by Texas women writers. Her themes encompass the search for meanings in the past, the function of illusion and myth, and the complexity of human relationships. Novelist Marshall Terry, who writes the afterword to *Warriors and Maidens,* defines Osborn's strengths as she explores these themes. He comments, "A world of contemporary consciousness, with strong roots in the past has been created here, and it stays true to itself story by story, line by line."

Reviews of Osborn's books have appeared in numerous Texas journals, but she has been recognized as well in *The Washington Post,* the *New York Times,* the *Chicago Tribune,* and the *Bloomsbury Review.* Michael King's "A Landscape to Live In," a critical review of *The Fields of Memory* in the *Texas Observer* (August 16, 1985), describes Osborn's talents as a creator of significant short fiction this way:

> These various figures do more than provide local color or bookish Texas quaintness to their narratives of realistic detail. They establish a tangible world within which the moral and emotional

discoveries can take occasion and place, and . . . they build a sense of place that takes in a wide and spacious American landscape, a landscape that Osborn knows not only how to visit, but how to live in.

Osborn lives in Austin with her husband, Joe, now an attorney. They have two grown children. They often spend their weekends on their ranch between Lampasas and Hamilton, but during the week, Osborn keeps regular office hours, writing in her studio near the University of Texas.

A REFLECTION OF PLACE AND HISTORY

The Short Story

LOU HALSELL RODENBERGER

When Mrs. E. Spann founded *The Texian Monthly Magazine* in Galveston in 1858, she had high hopes of creating a literary magazine that would showcase works by southern writers, particularly Texans because, as she made clear in her first issue, she felt the "mails were burdened with Northern publications." According to historian Imogene Bentley Dickey, the editor foresaw that the journal would be "devoted to Literature, Historical Romance, Original Tales, Incidents in the History of Texas, and Selections from the Most approved and popular Authors." If the birth of a Texas literary tradition can be dated, it began with Mrs. Spann's ambitious project, although the journal survived only a few months. Nevertheless, other Texas women found the courage to launch literary periodicals, and in turn their efforts fostered great interest in short-story writing. Women edited at least eight of the eighteen extant literary periodicals established in Texas before 1900.[1]

Short stories, more often sketches than structured fiction, appeared regularly in these periodicals. When Bella French brought her *American Sketch Book* from Wisconsin to Austin in 1878, she explained that the aim of the journal was to collect histories and reminiscences as well as "sketches and incidents of later days." A few years later, one of the most cosmopolitan of these nineteenth-century literary journals, *The Gulf Messenger,* began in Houston as the official publication of the Women's Exchange. Established by prominent Houston women in 1888, the Women's Exchange flourished under the leadership of Laura E. Foute, recently widowed, who saw promise of a livelihood in publishing the exchange's monthly journal. By 1891, Laura Foute assumed proprietorship of the journal and severed its connections with the Women's Exchange. She formed a partnership with Sara Hartman and moved her headquarters to San Antonio, where the *Messenger,* widely circulated, soon gained respect nationally. In *Early Literary Magazines in Texas* (1970), Imogene Bentley Dickey quotes a press notice in a Canadian periodical which praises the editorial "bravery and courage" of "two women, alone and unaided," for publishing such a magazine "out west."

In December, 1896, after Laura Foute's death, Sara Hartman, now editor, combined her journal with *Current Topics* and announced a new editorial policy. The magazine would become "representative of the literary and artistic merit of Texas and Louisiana." The journal, still under the editorship of a woman, Fannie Reese Pugh, was cited in 1898 as the "oldest literary magazine in the South" when it merged with *The Texas Magazine* that year and moved operations to Dallas.

If the short story that Professor Davis Foute Eagleton reprinted in his 1913 collection *Writers and Writings of Texas* is typical, the editors of *The Gulf Messenger* recognized literary quality.[2] "A Thanksgiving Story" by Belle Hunt Shortridge appeared first in *The Messenger* in November, 1892. Although almost plotless, the story captures place and persons of early-day Wise County with clarity and wit. When a young Yankee seeking adventure crashes a country family's Thanksgiving dinner, he finds hospitality and his true love. He is running away from having to read law back home. As he rides toward his destiny, he thinks:

> He *couldn't* settle down to his profession; it took too much office work and lying. (It was the law.) Life was so broad and sweet outside of offices, and it was such a blessed privilege to tell the truth, and invite a man to go to the other place if he didn't like it.

Furthermore, he has little regard for the girls back home because "he knew what they were going to say before they got the gum out of the way of their tongues to say it."

The first white child born in Wise County, Belle Shortridge caught the attention of editors of national periodicals with her wit and her realistic character portrayal. Her short stories appeared in *Frank Leslie's Illustrated Weekly, North American Review,* and the *New York World.*

Eagleton also includes a story by Olive Huck of Austin in his *Writers and Writings of Texas* (1913). First published in March, 1901, in *Century,* "The Last Hunt of Dorax," the story of a rancher's faithful dog turned sheep killer, reveals the writer's knowledge of folklore in the region and of life on an early-day Texas sheep ranch.

The best-known of the nineteenth-century women short-story writers with Texas connections was Mollie E. Moore Davis. Although chiefly a poet and novelist, Davis published short stories regularly during her career. Her stories appeared in *Atlantic Monthly, Smart Set,* and *Saturday Evening Post,* one of the most widely circulated magazines of the time. *In War Times at La Rose Blanche* (1888) included Davis's plantation-life stories. Like Katherine Anne Porter, the writer used autobiographical sketches to create the impression that she had an aristocratic southern background when in fact her early life had been spent on the San Marcos River as the child of a country doctor who also farmed to make ends meet. Her best stories, however, recapture Texas frontier life, and three tales collected in *An Elephant's Track and Other Stories* (1897) doubtless were Davis's retelling of events that already were community lore in Central Texas. In her Jim-Ned Creek stories, Davis describes the frontier practical joke, the snipe hunt. She narrates the tragicomic adventures of a backwoods family traveling from Jim-Ned Creek in Coleman County to Comanche to see the circus in "An Elephant's Track." The family has to be satisfied with having seen only the elephant's track after a card shark cons the father out of the ticket money. In these short stories, Davis realistically explores the narrative possibilities to be found in early Texas experience. Traces of the Jim-Ned community survive today southeast of Abilene on Jim-Ned Creek, or James-Edward Creek as the prim schoolmaster in Davis's "The Grovelling of Jinny Trimble" insists it should be called.

DEVELOPMENT OF THE GENRE, 1920–60

By the 1920s the short story had become popular among writers and readers. Women short-story writers in Texas began to think of their writing as a profession. Among the most successful large-circulation magazine writers were: Norma Patterson, who later teamed with her husband Crate Dalton to write serials; Anna Brand, who wrote stories based on her observations of Mexican life in El Paso; and Claudia Cranston, who served as an editor at both *Vogue* and *Good Housekeeping* during her career. Other successful short-fiction authors included Ruth Cross, whose reputation as a novelist had been established with publication of *The Golden Cocoon* (1924); Helen Topping Miller, who also published several novels; and Grace Sothcote Leake, whose novel *House of Refuge* was filmed by Fox Studios as the movie *Bondage*. Norma Patterson's "The Boy Who Couldn't Be Saved," became a Ford Theater television production starring Ann Sothern.[3]

Publishing in popular magazines proved lucrative for these writers, but southwestern short-fiction writers who valued literary quality over popular acclaim were given the opportunity to publish in a distinctive regional journal. In 1924, *Southwest Review,* founded originally in Austin in 1915 as *The Texas Review,* moved to Southern Methodist University in Dallas under the competent editorship of Jay B. Hubbell. Hilton Ross Greer, poet and editorial writer for the *Dallas Morning News* and one of first *Southwest Review* board members, soon recognized that short fiction had become a favorite genre among many southwestern writers. In 1928 he published the first of two anthologies of *Best Short Stories of the Southwest*. Stories by five Texas women writers are featured among the sixteen published. Dorothy Scarborough, well-known already for her popular, though controversial, novel *The Wind* (1925), appears in the collection. Scarborough had published several stories in New York magazines, but she was more significant as a teacher of short-story writing at Columbia University than as a writer of short stories. Other women writers included in Greer's collection are Winifred Sanford, competent recorder of life in Texas oil boomtowns; Norma Patterson, already a professional who would publish hundreds of short stories in national magazines in her lifetime; Margaret Bell Houston, granddaughter of Sam Houston and prolific author of periodical stories and sentimental novels; and Olive McClintic Johnson, creator of the Deep Ellum stories popular with *Collier's* readers in the twenties. Patterson's and Houston's stories had previously been published in *Pictorial Review*. Scarborough's appeared first in *Century Magazine*,

Johnson's in *Collier's,* and Sanford's in *American Mercury,* then edited by H. L. Mencken.

Norma Patterson and Margaret Belle Houston again appear in Hilton Greer's second series of *Best Short Stories* (1931). Karle Wilson Baker, respected poet and novelist, is also included. By contemporary standards, most of these stories fall under the classification of popular fiction, but Sanford's "Windfall" has been recognized for its literary excellence and included in at least three other anthologies.

Texas's most outstanding writer to date, Katherine Anne Porter, began her career as short-story writer during the twenties. Her first published story, "María Concepción," appeared in *Century Magazine* in 1922. In 1929 "The Jilting of Granny Weatherall" first appeared in *Transition,* and by early 1931, Porter's art as short-fiction writer won her a Guggenheim Fellowship.

Porter's carefully constructed stories established a standard for serious writers with literary aspirations. If writers followed her lead, their work probably appeared in little magazines. For many, however, the popular market proved too lucrative to ignore. One of the most successful in this field is Margaret Cousins, who was inducted into the Texas Women's Hall of Fame in 1986 for her lifetime devotion to the arts and, in the same year, received the Women in Communications Lifetime Achievement Award. In 1992, at age eighty-seven, Cousins, who died in 1996, received the Lon Tinkle Award from the Texas Institute of Letters for sustained excellence throughout a career. Cousins combined writing and editing during her long career. As managing editor of *Good Housekeeping* for seventeen years, senior editor at Doubleday for ten years, and managing editor of *McCall's,* Cousins insisted on quality in popular fiction. Her own short stories illustrate her belief that character portrayal and sense of place cannot be ignored, even in magazine fiction. *Best American Short Stories of 1948* included Cousins's "A Letter to Mr. Priest," which the year before had made Martha Foley's Roll of Honor.

In 1954, Professor William Peery included Margaret Cousins's "Uncle Edgar and the Reluctant Saint" in the often reprinted anthology *21 Texas Short Stories.* Winifred Sanford's "Windfall" reappears here, as do Katherine Anne Porter's "The Grave" and Mary King O'Donnell's "Chicken on the Wind." With the goal of including regional writing that he sees as "transcending the regional" to express the universal, Peery perhaps unwittingly reveals his reason for including so few women's stories in his collection when he observes: "We are not necessarily undergoing any great cultural awakening. Texas is in its cultural young manhood, and that makes its short stories exciting." Earlier he concludes his summary of characters in the stories with this statement: "The men are men and the women are memorable."

Recognition of women short-story writers as part of a vital literary tradition came finally in 1975 with the publication of *Fiction and Poetry by Texas Women*, edited by Janice L. White and sponsored by the Texas Center for Writers. Twenty-three short stories are featured in the collection. In 1982, Shearer Publishing launched its publication of original works by southwestern writers with *Her Work: Stories by Texas Women*, edited by Lou Halsell Rodenberger. Rodenberger's introduction makes clear that recovering the work of earlier short-fiction writers takes precedence over literary excellence in the selection of entries. Only living writers at the time contributed to the anthology, but inclusion of stories by Winifred Sanford, Anne Pence Davis, Norma Patterson, Ellen Garwood, and Elithe Hamilton Kirkland gives the reader a sense of how Texas women writers have developed the genre over the past seventy years.

In 1986, Suzanne Comer, then senior editor at Southern Methodist University Press, began her search for stories by contemporary women short-story writers in Texas. As she says in her introduction, she was "eager to gather stories that explored a variety of experiences common to women." What she discovered is that women of this era wrote mostly about urban and suburban experiences and that they "wrote most often about relationships." Because "the stories focused on relationships and spoke of shared female experience," Comer chose *Common Bonds: Stories by and about Modern Texas Women* as title of her compilation, which was published in 1990, shortly before her untimely death.

Since the award for best short story was created by the Texas Institute of Letters in 1972, seven women have received the annual prize. Marshall Terry collected the first fourteen winners in *Prize Stories: Texas Institute of Letters* (1986), which includes works by Pat Carr, Laura Furman, Beverly Lowry, Carolyn Osborn, and Catherine Petroski. Honored with the prize since this publication have been

Gail Galloway Adams, who received the award in 1986, and Lee Merrill Byrd, chosen in 1991.

Byrd is one of the more gifted short-story writers recently published. Her story "Major Six Pockets" won the TIL award for best short fiction in 1991, and in 1993 her collection of short fiction, *My Sister Disappears,* received another TIL award. In *Texas Books in Review* (Summer, 1994), Mallory Young praises Byrd's stories as products of "seeming artlessness, a simplicity that belies the skillful crafting actually required." Byrd, who with her husband, founded Cinco Puntos Press in El Paso, has stories in *Common Bonds* and *Texas Bound.* Her stories also have appeared in such journals as *North American Review.*

Two other anthologies published in the 1980s include short stories by women. Don Graham includes seven in *South by Southwest: 24 Stories from Modern Texas* (1986), and among the twenty-three stories Lyman Grant selected for *New Growth: Contemporary Short Stories by Texas Writers* (1989) are eight by women.

In 1993, Mark Busby edited a second volume, *New Growth/2,* and in the introduction he contradicts Grant's belief that stories by Texas writers no longer reflect sense of place and history so intensely as earlier fiction. Aware of the growing diversity among Texas writers, Busby includes seven stories by Texas women. Among those are works by Sunny Nash, a promising young African-American writer, and Carmen Tafolla, talented representative of the many Tejana women fiction writers now drawing national attention. Busby argues that elements of Texas mythology—journeying, ambivalence, primitivism, racism, sexism, and violence—still provide themes for modern Texas short fiction, including the stories by Texas women.

In 1993, Billy Bob Hill and Mike Hennech edited a book of short fiction, the first in a series of collections that will give beginning Texas writers with talent, as well as those with experience, an opportunity to publish their work. Among the twenty-one stories collected in *Texas Short Fiction: A World in Itself* are eight by women. *Texas Bound* (1994), an anthology of nineteen short stories edited by Kay Cattarulla, includes short fiction by Annette Sanford, Lynna Williams, Lee Merrill Byrd, Diane DeSanders, Mary K. Flatten, and Shelby Hearon. The editor selected these stories from those first read as part of the Dallas Museum of Arts series, "Arts and Letters Live."

In retrospect the publication within fifteen years of three anthologies devoted to Texas women's short fiction manifests the rapid development of the genre. Janice L. White includes twenty-three stories in *Fiction and Poetry by Texas Women* (1975). In 1982, some forty stories were submitted for publication in *Her Work;* thirty are included. Only five years later, Suzanne Comer began the difficult task of winnowing 356 manuscripts to choose finally the thirty-two stories included in *Common Bonds.* Even more revealing of the success Texas women have had as short-fiction writers is the publication of at least thirty books of short stories by individual authors since 1975. Two collections have been published as winners of the Iowa Short Fiction Award. Two are included in the University of Illinois Short Fiction Series. One book received the Flannery O'Connor Award for Short Fiction, and another introduces the New Texas Fiction Series initiated by the prestigious Book Club of Texas in 1990. Individual stories have appeared in many of the better-known literary journals. Several have been designated best stories by the annuals *Best American Short Stories* and *Prize Stories 1990: The O. Henry Awards.* As the following biographical sketches reveal, several of the more prolific writers have published more than one gathering of their short fiction in this period.[4]

CONTEMPORARY SHORT STORY WRITERS

With Carolyn Osborn leading the way, contemporary short-story writers have continued to publish prize-winning collections of their work since the late sixties. Their contributions to Texas letters are made clear in the following biographical sketches.

Gail Galloway Adams

Gail Galloway Adams won the Flannery O'Connor Award for Short Fiction for her stories collected in *The Purchase of Order* (1988). One of the stories, "Inside Dope," was one of the 100 Distinguished Stories in *Best American Short Stories of 1987.* That same year the Texas Institute of Letters chose the story as best short fiction by a Texan, and *Editor's Choice: Volume IV* anthologized the story. Adams, who was a Helen Weiselberg Scholar in fiction at Bread Loaf Writers' Conference in 1987, is a native of Graham.

Adams's stories explore the extraordinariness of ordinary people:

Bisher, the no-account brother-in-law who always knows the "inside dope" and who charms with his vitality and inexhaustible supply of pop trivia; Marva Jean, the flaky waitress who turns herself in for murdering Chuckie the prize bull and finds true love at the jailhouse; Jean Dillon, mother of a transient family who makes the best of life during hard times in an ancient tourist court and becomes an unforgettable memory for her friend Lou Maxey. Adams's strong sense of kinship with her characters, whom she often portrays with humor, draws upon her own experience as member of a colorful extended Texas family. Adams now lives in West Virginia.

Dianne Benedict

In an interview published in *The Pawn Review* in 1984, Dianne Benedict told Bettye Givens that she found her own voice for her writing through reading Flannery O'Connor, Eudora Welty, and Katherine Anne Porter. Her stories reflect particularly her admiration of O'Connor, although her vision of humankind is less dark. She adds, "I love to work in the style of the grotesque. Folk tales have always been very important to me." She says then that if she is influenced by a writer directly that would be John Cheever.

Raised on the Texas-Mexican border and in East Texas, Benedict has lived in New England a number of years, but her stories still reflect her Texas past. "Unknown Feathers," in which a middle-aged hardscrabble farmer has to face death alone, was selected by John Updike as one of the *Best American Short Stories of 1984*. Published first in *Atlantic Monthly* (February, 1982), the story appears again in *Shiny Objects*, which won the Iowa Short Fiction Award in 1982. The title story, "Shiny Objects," reveals Benedict's insight into the human heart as a lonely, harsh old woman finally accepts the boy who moves into her isolated home and into her heart without her permission. Benedict has taught in the Graduate Writing Program at Syracuse University, the Writers' Workshop at the University of Iowa, the MFA Writing Program at Vermont College, and the University of Southern Maine.

Pat Carr

Pat Carr, whose stories have appeared in two collections of Texas women's stories, was born in Wyoming but grew up in south Houston, where she earned a B.A. summa cum laude and an M.A. from

Rice University. She has a Ph.D. from Tulane University and has taught at several Texas universities. Her stories have appeared in a number of periodicals, including *Southern Review* and *Yale Review,* and in *Best American Short Stories of 1974.*

Her first short-story collection (published under the name Pat M. Esslinger) *From beneath the Hill of the Three Crosses* (1969), received the South and West Fiction Award and the Library of Congress Marc IV Award. Since that time, Carr has been awarded a National Endowment for the Humanities grant, the Green Mountain Short Fiction Award, and the Texas Institute of Letters Short Story Prize. In 1977 her collection of short fiction, *The Women in the Mirror,* was awarded the Iowa School of Letters Award for Short Fiction. Since that time she has published *Night of the Luminarias* (1986). Currently she is teaching at Western Kentucky University.

Carr's fiction explores the tenuous relationships of women with men often unworthy of attention. In her prize-winning "Indian Burial," the narrator, owner of a down-at-the-heels motel in Arizona, escapes the drudgery of her life by retreating to her private dig in the desert. Finding the skeleton of an Indian child unexpectedly makes her aware of passing time and the futility of her own life. A migration of butterflies reminds her of what might have been. In "An El Paso Idyll," Carr examines love and politics in the academic world, where a woman professor discovers that her lover can also be traitor.

Sandra Cisneros

Sandra Cisneros, who lives in San Antonio, established her reputation as a short-fiction writer in 1984 when her first version of *The House on Mango Street* appeared. Revised in 1989, this collection of short sketches, which reveal with poignancy the life of a child growing up in a Chicago Hispanic ghetto, was published as a Vintage Book by Random House in 1991. Highly praised by critics, her second collection of stories, *Woman Hollering Creek and Other Stories* (1991), examines the lives of Hispanic women on both sides of the Texas-Mexico border. In the title story, Cisneros contrasts the lifestyle of the traditional Mexican wife with that of Felice, who owns her own pickup and hollers when she crosses Woman Hollering Creek because she says, "Did you ever notice how nothing around here is named after a woman? . . . Unless she's the Virgin?"

Cisneros has received two National Endowment for the Arts grants for fiction and poetry and the Lannan Literary Prize for 1991. She has been writer-in-residence at several universities. Her work has been translated into five languages.

Laverne Harrell Clark

LaVerne Harrell Clark, now a resident of Tucson, Arizona, grew up in Smithville. A folklorist and photographer as well as a fiction writer, Clark received the University of Chicago Folklore Prize for her collection of Navajo and Apache folklore, *They Sang for Horses: The Impact of the Horse on the Folklore of the Navajo and Apache* (1966). Her short stories have appeared in several anthologies and in such literary journals as *Pawn Review* and *Vanderbilt Street Review.* Four of her stories are collected in *The Deadly Swarm and Other Stories* (1985), which won first place for fiction in the National Biennial Letters Competition of the National League of American Pen Women, was a finalist for the Western Writers Association Spur Award, and received the 1984 Julian Ocean Literature Prize. She also received an American Philosophical Society research grant. Clark has conducted numerous fiction workshops and served in the Arizona Artist-in-Schools Program.

In a 1987 interview in *Cross Timbers Review,* Clark says she was an eager listener when in the presence of Smithville's many storytellers. From them she learned the art of storytelling well. Frank Waters has called her stories the best of "grass roots writing."

Laura Furman

Laura Furman, a native of New York, has been a resident of Texas since 1978. (Her work as novelist is discussed elsewhere in this volume.) Her first major book was *The Glass House: Novella and Stories* (1980), the novella having been published previously in *The New Yorker, Fiction,* and *Houston City Magazine.* In 1983 came *Watch Time Fly,* a second collection of stories, from *The New Yorker, Mademoiselle, Vanity Fair,* and *Vision.* The title story, anthologized in an American-literature textbook, is a popular assignment in university classes. A resident of Lockhart, Furman teaches at the University of Texas, where she served for several years as editor of the literary journal, *American Short Fiction.* A recipient of the Dobie-Paisano grant awarded by the Texas Institute of Letters, Furman served as president of TIL in 1989. She received a Guggenheim Fellowship in 1982 and has been granted residency at Yaddo Writers Colony several times.

Many of Furman's most successful short stories trace the narrator's odyssey through painful experiences to acceptance of the true nature of a relationship. In "Watch Time Fly," a young woman not yet ready for independence finally takes control of her destiny when she perceives she has been more convenience than partner in a failed marriage. In "Eldorada," a middle-aged mother faces up to her solitariness when she sells the car her dead husband had cherished.

Mary Gray Hughes

Mary Gray Hughes, whose story "The Thousand Springs" has been compared to Tillie Olsen's "I Stand Here Ironing" as an expression of a busy mother's suppressed creativity, was reared in Brownsville. Daughter of novelist Hart Stilwell, Hughes was educated at Barnard College and Oxford University, where she earned a M. Litt. on a Fulbright Scholarship. Her short stories have appeared in a number of national publications, including *Redbook, Esquire, The Atlantic, Southwest Review,* and *Antioch Review.* She has published two collections of short stories: *The Thousand Springs* (1971) and *The Calling* (1980). Her stories also appear in several anthologies, including *Her Work, Common Bonds, South by Southwest, Images of Women in Literature* (1986), and *North of the Rio Grande: The Mexican-American Experience in Short Fiction* (1992). In 1978, Hughes received a National Endowment for the Arts Creative Writing Fellowship. Poet and author of children's books as well as short fiction, she has been an Illinois Writer-in-Residence. Hughes lives in Evanston, Illinois.

Two of Hughes's stories have appeared in *Best American Short Stories.* "The Foreigner in the Blood," selected in 1968, develops with gentle irony the plight of a psychiatrist's daughter who, obliged to commit her senile father to institutional care, uses techniques of persuasion she learned from him as an expert analyst in his own time. "The Judge," selected in 1972, characterizes a border judge who thinks he understands the Mexican but is actually both patronizing and naive. Hughes's themes vary widely, but her narratives exemplify the author's keen understanding of human motivation.

Annette Sanford

In 1990, Southwestern Booksellers honored Annette Sanford for her collection of short stories, *Lasting Attachments* (1989), presenting her a $1500 prize for best fiction at the seventh annual Texas Literary Festival in Dallas. As early as 1979, when "Trip in a Summer Dress" was selected for *Best American Short Stories,* Sanford's work was recognized as exceptional. Her work also was listed among this series's 100 Other Distinguished Stories in 1988 and 1989. Sanford's work has been published in *Redbook, McCall's, Prairie Schooner, American Short Fiction, Story,* and other periodicals. Her stories appear in the 1988 and 1989 *New Stories from the South* series. Sanford has received two National Endowment for the Arts Fellowships and the 1981 Texas Commission on the Arts Writer Recognition Award.

A native of Cuero, Sanford received her B.A. degree from the University of Texas. Author of twenty-five contemporary romances under pseudonyms, Sanford lives in Ganado, where she now writes short fiction full time. In 1989, Symphony Space Theater, in New York, honored her when "Six White Horses" from *Lasting Attachments* was read at a program featuring four southern writers: Sanford, Anne Tyler, Max Steele, and Larry Brown. The theater included "Limited Access" on a 1990 program. Her short-story collection has been presented as well on Texarkana educational radio station KTXK as one of the series *Writers at Work in Arkansas and Texas.* Sanford's "Trip in a Summer Dress" appears in *Texas Bound* (1994).

Anthologized in at least four other collections, Sanford's stories often explore the lives of small-town or rural Texans. The author has said that Eils Lotozo, reviewer for *New York Times Book Review* (May 14, 1989), "sums up succinctly" her major themes. Lotozo's review concludes: "In this fictional world of patient spouses, dutiful relatives and good neighbors, it is friendship, marriage, family ties—the enduring links between people—that really matter. Love is a promise for life, Ms. Sanford's stories tell us, a continuing, courageous act of will." As journalist Michael Berryhill points out in a feature story about Sanford in the January 28, 1990, issue of *Texas* (the *Houston Chronicle* Sunday supplement), "There is more than a little judgment in her work about the contemporary generation," but if this is so, they are judgments handed down with humor and sympathy for the judged.

Jan Epton Seale

Jan Epton Seale, one of Texas's most versatile writers, is known for her poetry and creative nonfiction as well as her short fiction. *Airlift,* a collection of her short stories, was published in 1992. Several of these stories have appeared nationally in newspapers as part of the PEN Syndicated Fiction Project. Others have been published in literary journals, including *The Yale Review* and *New Mexico Humanities Review.* Four anthologies include Seale's stories.

The author, an Artist-in-the-Schools for the Texas Commission on the Arts, is a native Texan now living in McAllen. She has taught at the University of North Texas and the University of Texas–Pan American, and has received a National Endowment for the Arts writing fellowship.

Writer Roland Sodowsky, in his highly readable afterword to *Airlift,* praises Seale for the intimacy of small-town southwestern life that her stories share with the reader, and he adds, "some of her stories reveal human nature, some mirror reality, some teach, depict social ills, entertain." Sodowsky's assessment of the writer's work is exemplified in the title story, a tragicomic narrative of a septuagenarian taking her first airplane trip. Seale's most recent publication is *Homeland: Essays beside and beyond the Rio Grande* (1995).

Pat Ellis Taylor

Pat Ellis Taylor, who now writes under the name of Pat LittleDog, won the Southwest Book Award for her first book, *Border Healing Woman: The Story of Jewell Babb,* about a West Texan known for her healing powers. Published by the University of Texas Press in 1981, the book introduced one of Texas's most eccentric and experimental writers. Taylor, an avowed individualist, writes autobiographical short fiction about hippies, "Baptists and seminarians and winos, racist landlords, and black tenants" living in rundown efficiency apartments in East Dallas or in Austin's seedy neighborhoods. Her major accomplishment as a short-story writer is the publication of *Afoot in a Field of Men* by Atlantic Monthly Press in 1988. A revision and combination of stories that appeared in her first collections, *Afoot in a Field of Men* (1983) and *The God Chaser: A Spirited Assortment of Tales* (1986), this edition was one of the first in a prestigious paperback series launched by Atlantic Monthly Press.

A recent collection, published with the intriguing title *In Search of the Holy Mother of Jobs* (1991), illuminates the life of a determined hippie in post-hippie Austin. Reviewer Judyth Rigler says, "The author shakes up the reader with tales of fighting the good fight, LittleDog style."

Taylor now teaches at Austin Community College. Her essays and reviews appear often in the *Texas Observer*. She has been a recipient of a National Endowment for the Arts grant, the Dobie-Paisano Fellowship, and Pen Syndicated Fiction Awards. Her stories are anthologized in *Her Work, Common Bonds, South by Southwest,* and *New Growth*.

Estela Portillo Trambley

Estela Portillo Trambley, best-known as a playwright, also has the distinction of being the first Mexican-American woman writer to have a short-story collection published. *Rain of Scorpions and Other Writings* first appeared in 1975. (A revised edition was published in 1991.) Born in El Paso, Trambley reflects her intimate knowledge of border bilingual culture in her fiction. She also explores the life of the Hispanic woman dealing with the oppressive patriarchal structure of Mexican society. In "The Paris Gown," a young woman devises a singular solution to avoid marrying the old man her wealthy father has chosen for her. Exiled to Paris for life, she tells the story many years later to an admiring granddaughter. Trambley's stories have appeared in several anthologies, including *Her Work*. "The Pilgrim" and "Village" are included in *North of the Rio Grande: The Mexican-American Experience in Short Fiction*.

Trambley, who has hosted radio and TV talk shows, won the Quinto Sol Award for literature in 1972. Honored in 1981 with a Writer Recognition Award by the Texas Commission on the Arts, she has been a drama instructor, director of community theater, and guest lecturer at several universities. She earned a master's degree in English and American literature from the University of Texas at El Paso. A groundbreaker for Mexican-American women, Trambley edited and wrote the introduction to a special 1973 issue of *El Grito,* a literary journal devoted to Mexican-American writing. This edition featured "Chicanas en la Literatura and el Arte," the first collection of literature by Mexican-American women.

Nationally recognized for their excellence in short-story creation, Texas women writers continue to publish collections of their fiction regularly. In 1985, journalist and novelist Joanne Leedom-Ackerman, who was raised in Dallas and is the daughter of former state senator Bill Leedom, published her short fiction in *No Marble Angels*. Leedom's stories explore life in the 1960s South. Anne Leaton, who has returned to her native Fort Worth after living abroad many years, was praised critically for her short-story collection, *Mayakovsky, My Love* (1984). Winifred Sanford's *Windfall and Other Stories,* privately printed by her daughters in 1980, was reprinted in a handsomely designed edition by Southern Methodist University Press in 1988.

Lynna Williams, who grew up in Abilene and Fort Worth, recently published to critical acclaim *Things Not Seen and Other Stories* (1992). A *New York Times* reviewer calls the work an "impressive first collection." Williams, now a professor at Emory University, shares her Texas experiences in such comic stories as "Personal Testimony," in which a preacher's daughter makes bible camp bearable by starting her own testimony-writing business for other campers. Elizabeth Harris's *The Ant Generator* (1991) won the John Simmons Short Fiction Award, which is presented annually by the Iowa Writers' Workshop. An Austin teacher and writer, Harris has also been honored for her story "The World Record Holder," which was chosen to appear in the 1986 edition of *New Stories from the South: The Year's Best.* Lisa Sandlin, a Texan now living in Santa Fe, chooses a variety of narrators to tell her stories in *The Famous Thing About Death* (1991).

Many Texas women writers have discovered their metier in short-story writing. The biographical notes in the collections of Texas short stories reveal that the writing of short fiction is a major choice among contemporary Texas women writers. As in no other genre, the literary tradition which began with writers of short fiction a century ago approaches maturity with national recognition of its excellence.

NOTES

1. In *Early Magazines of Texas* (1970), Imogene Bentley Dickey includes a brief history of forty periodicals published in Texas between 1858 and 1929. Description of general content of each magazine provides valuable background for research into the activities of nineteenth-century Texas women journalists.
2. *Writers and Writing of Texas* (1913), edited by Davis Foute Eagleton, includes Eagleton's "Survey of the Field," in which he classifies Texas literature as reflecting, first, "the period of exploration and settlement" and then a formative period between 1836 and 1869. Eagleton argues that between 1870 and 1913 the literature mirrors the state's "political easement and social unrest." In this anthology of both prose and poetry by Texans, the editor includes the works of a dozen women writers prominent during his time, including Mollie E.

Moore Davis and Karle Wilson Baker. In his concluding "Supplement," he lists more than one hundred other women writers, often including titles of their published works.

3. See the Texas State Historical Association's *The New Handbook of Texas* (1996) for biographical information on Norma Patterson, Margaret Belle Houston, Katherine Anne Porter, Dorothy Scarborough, and Winifred Sanford. Florence Barnes's *Texas Writers of Today* (1935) includes biographical sketches of other short story writers of this period. A chapter titled "Literature: Voices of the Southwest," pp. 211–21 in *The WPA Dallas Guide and History,* compiled in the 1930s and published by the University of North Texas Press in 1992, includes information on a number of Dallas women writers producing short stories during this period.

4. Iowa Short Fiction Award winners are Dianne Benedict for *Shiny Objects* (1982) and Pat Carr for *The Women in the Mirror* (1977). The University of Illinois Short Fiction Series includes Mary Gray Hughes's *The Calling* (1980) and Carolyn Osborn's *A Horse of Another Color* (1987). Gail Galloway Adams's *The Purchase of Order* (1987) received the Flannery O'Connor Award for Short Fiction, and Carolyn Osborn's *The Grands* was chosen in 1990 by The Book Club of Texas as the first volume to be published in its New Texas Fiction Series.

LET THE WORKS DEFINE THE FIELD:

Contemporary Creative Nonfiction

MALLORY YOUNG

Any discussion of creative nonfiction offers a few special challenges. There is no universally agreed upon definition, or even recognition, of this genre. What exactly constitutes creative nonfiction? Where is the line between nonfiction narrative on the one side and journalism or political commentary or academic essay or autobiography on the other? In selecting writers to consider, how inclusive should one be? Many writers devoted primarily to other genres—novelists, poets, short-fiction writers—have engaged in nonfiction writing. Are they to be included in a treatise of this kind?

I have decided, for the purposes of this discussion, to confront the first issue indirectly: I will let the works define the field. I have subdivided the area into three main types of nonfiction writing: the political commentary, the chronicle, and the personal essay. Admittedly these divisions are slippery; each slides over into the other. But the distinctions are convenient, and each area is well represented by the work of one or two major writers among the women currently writing in Texas. The second issue I have confronted more directly: This essay considers only Texas women writers who write primarily nonfiction—nonfiction that in some way or other qualifies as "creative."

MOLLY IVINS:
POLITICS AND THE ENGLISH LANGUAGE

For the May, 1989, issue of *Texas Monthly* magazine, Molly Ivins, along with other Texas notables, was invited to contribute an essay on her favorite state locale. Ivins's choice of Lubbock—"It's hard to be pretentious or affected if you're from Lubbock. Damned hard"—characterizes her perfectly. The reader will find no pretension but plenty of toughness, wit, and irony in the writing and person of Molly Ivins. Her political writing shines with gritty brilliance.

Ivins has been a political columnist for major newspapers both in and out of Texas. From 1970 to 1976 she honed her sharp, direct, frontal-attack style as coeditor (with fellow Texas journalist Kaye Northcott) of the *Texas Observer*, a proudly muckraking Austin bimonthly. The *Observer* has long been the nemesis of unscrupulous Texas politicians and the training ground of uncompromising Texas journalists.

Ivins is most clearly a journalist, a political commentator. Neither her columns nor her articles, however, read like straight journalistic writing. There is nothing impersonal or objective about Ivins's work. In her columns she leaps quickly, often without transition, from target to target dispensing sharp satire, keen wit, and straightforward condemnation. She says what she thinks and knows—and a surprising variety of publications, from the three-piece-suit respectable to the downright subversive, have allowed her the opportunity. Ivins's articles on such subjects as the daytime soaps, the KGB (Kinder, Gentler Bush), the romance of football, and of course, the ins and far-outs of Texas politics appear with frequency in more than a dozen newspapers and in numerous national magazines, including *Esquire, The Atlantic, Harper's, The Nation, Ms.,* and *TV Guide.* She also has been an occasional commentator on National Public Radio and the *McNeil/Lehrer NewsHour.*

Recently, Ivins's political writings have been collected in book form. Random House published the best-selling *Molly Ivins Can't Say That, Can She?* in 1991. Organized by subject rather than time—Texas politics, the Reagan and Bush administrations, women, "words and heroes"—the collection draws on some twenty years of previously published short pieces. Ivins followed with *Nothin' but Good Times Ahead,* also from Random House in 1993 with a paperback appearing in 1994. The collections offer an ideal opportunity to dip into

Ivins's biting satire whenever the urge strikes, but they also provide a significant, and hilarious, commentary on late twentieth century American culture and politics.

Ivins has not limited her journalistic and political activity to the popular media. She has long been active in several journalists' and writers' organizations, including Amnesty International's Journalism Network and the Reporters Committee for Freedom of the Press. She has served on the National News council board and written about press issues for the ACLU as well as for various journalism reviews. Ivins has received numerous journalism awards, and in 1976 she was named an Outstanding Alumna of the Columbia School of Journalism. More recently she received the 1991 Carey McWilliams Award from the American Political Science Association. As far as Ivins herself is concerned, however, her two greatest honors came when the Minneapolis police force named its mascot pig after her and when she was banned from the Texas A&M University campus.

Ivins's relationship to Texas has always been something of a love/hate affair. Born in 1944 she grew up in Houston but headed north to Smith College for a B.A. and then to Columbia for a master's in journalism. Between her stints with Texas newspapers she spent years working for the *Minneapolis Tribune* and the *New York Times*. In 1982 she returned to her home state, a homecoming that, she quips, may well be indicative of a masochistic streak. If her current popularity is an indication, Molly Ivins has come home to stay.

LIZ CARPENTER:
CHRONICLE OF WELL-SPENT TIME

Although Liz Carpenter was not one of those asked to write about her special Texas place for the *Texas Monthly* feature, one can guess what her answer would have been. For Carpenter two places in Texas require mention: the historic town of Salado, her actual and spiritual point of departure, and Grass Roots, the home in Austin which she has chosen as her point of return. In between those two quiet Texas poles come the whirlwind decades of the nineteen forties, fifties, and sixties spent in her adopted home, Washington, D.C.

Liz Carpenter is best known for her Washington career. Still, her Texas roots have always been proudly proclaimed. Born in Salado in 1920, Mary Elizabeth was the child of two leading pioneer families, the Sutherlands on her father's side and the Robertsons on her mother's. She received a degree in journalism from the University of Texas and, with her new husband Leslie Carpenter, landed in Washington. The two became prominent political journalists, eventually founding their own Carpenter News Bureau. Liz Carpenter's nationwide prominence came, however, when she became part of the Lyndon Johnson retinue, first as a Johnson vice-presidential aide and later in the White House as Lady Bird's press secretary and chief of staff. Perhaps Carpenter's best-known piece of writing is one for which she received no byline: the fifty-eight-word speech in which then Vice President Johnson expressed his sorrow at President Kennedy's death and his readiness to take on the role that had fallen to him.

Other political appointments for Liz Carpenter have included service on the International Women's Year Commission under President Ford and the position of assistant secretary of education for public affairs under President Carter. Carpenter also took on leadership roles as a founder of the National Women's Political Caucus and in the movement for passage of the Equal Rights Amendment, causes to which she is still dedicated.

Since her return to Texas in 1976, Carpenter has devoted much of her time to writing. Her articles on such subjects as White House women, Salado family reunions, surviving widowhood, and aging with style have appeared in *Redbook, Ladies Home Journal, Ms., Good Housekeeping, Family Circle,* and numerous other national publications. Her books, autobiographical in nature, are more than memoirs—they are true chronicles of our time.

Ruffles and Flourishes: The Warm and Tender Story of a Simple Girl Who Found Adventure in the White House, first published by Doubleday in 1970, is a personal account of the Lyndon Johnson years and the Lady Bird White House. The book reached third place on the best-seller list and came out as a Pocket Books paperback the following year. In 1993 it was reprinted by Texas A&M University Press with a new preface by the author. Carpenter provides her readers with inside information, from the memos that crisscrossed various White House offices to the details and disasters of White House weddings, from menu-planning for a Pakistani camel driver to managing hundreds of traveling reporters on the First Lady's whistle-stop campaign.

Carpenter's next book, *Getting Better All the Time,* was published by Simon and Schuster in 1987, with the Pocket Book paperback appearing in 1988. This book also was reprinted by Texas A&M University Press, in 1993. On its initial publication, the book received widespread attention and acclaim from reviewers across the country. *Getting Better* is a chatty, personal autobiography, a loosely organized, sometimes random collection of memoirs and reminiscences, family history and grandmotherly advice, party recipes and seasoned political wisdom. Most interesting is the book's revelation, not always intentional, of the character of its remarkable writer.

Most recently, Carpenter has contributed her personal account of foster parenting, *Unplanned Parenthood: The Confessions of a Seventysomething Surrogate Mother.* The book, with an introduction by Erma Bombeck, was published by Random House in 1994 and followed by a Fawcett Books paperback in 1995. Focusing on Carpenter's experience as parent to three teens orphaned by her brother's death, *Parenthood* clearly demonstrates what Liz Carpenter told her readers in *Getting Better:* that her life is far from finished.

Liz Carpenter is not a great writer—for her, the living is clearly more important than the telling. But her robust, ebullient nature and her fascinating experiences make her books eminently readable.

PRUDENCE MACKINTOSH: LIFE AS A PROCESS

Prudence Mackintosh is one of a circle of writers closely associated with *Texas Monthly* magazine. She is not the only woman writer in this group—others include Anne Dingus and, formerly, Barbara Rodriguez—but she is perhaps the most prominent and longstanding. A contributing editor to the publication from its modest 1973 beginnings, Mackintosh continued for nearly two decades to make *Texas Monthly* the major outlet for her work.

Initially Prudence Mackintosh focused her witty, clear-eyed essays on the rites and rituals of Texas womanhood. Early on, however, she took a different tack, focusing instead on the terrors and triumphs of Texas motherhood. Regular readers became well acquainted with the Mackintosh household: first two and then three rambunctious sons, their quietly puzzled, only-child, attorney father, and of course Mom herself, writing about it as she lived it. Mackintosh made the rearing of children her career in more than one sense.

Mackintosh's concoctions are light but never fluffy. There is real substance here: a sharp, clear eye, especially for the humor of incongruous juxtaposition, a fine-tuned ear always sensitive to the powers and possibilities of language. Equally important, Mackintosh steadfastly refuses to sentimentalize family life, the good or the bad. Her unwavering focus directs itself to the wondrous and troublesome birth of a third child or the dangers and honest reliefs of the television as baby-sitter; the ambivalent ground of pre-adolescent masculinity and femininity or the doomed attempt to instill a sense of Christmastide wonder into four- and six-year-old boys with a burning desire for an Evel Knievel Stunt Cycle. As Mackintosh makes clear, there is no fictionalizing in her writing: everything she writes is real. Still, her essays, far from being simple journalism, are as considered and finely crafted as first-rate fiction.

In addition to *Texas Monthly*, several other popular magazines have featured Mackintosh's work: *McCall's, Ladies Home Journal, Redbook,* and *D Magazine*. Her articles have appeared as well in the *Dallas Morning News* and the *Houston Post*. A number of the family essays achieved more permanent form in two book-length collections. The first, *Thundering Sneakers,* solicited and published by Doubleday in 1981 and later released as a Bantam paperback, brings together selections from six years of essays beginning in 1974. In 1985, Doubleday brought out the second collection, *Retreads*. Although *Thundering Sneakers* was reprinted in 1987 by Texas Monthly Press, neither collection is currently in print.

Mackintosh's work has garnered well-deserved recognition at both the state and national levels. In her home state she is a member of the Texas Institute of Letters, and in 1981 she became the first woman to receive the Young Texas Ex Achievement Award. The essay "Tube or Not Tube" (collected in *Thundering Sneakers*) was awarded the J. C. Penney–University of Missouri Journalism Award for Excellence in Lifestyle Journalism in 1976.

Prudence Mackintosh is a native, lifelong Texan. Born in Texarkana, she attended the University of Texas, graduating in 1966, and today lives with her family in Dallas. Mackintosh was reared in a newspaper family. She counts among her early influences the crusty reporters of the *Texarkana Gazette and Daily News* and the cadences of the King James Bible, courtesy of the nearby First Baptist Church.

It is in fact that very combination of the solidly journalistic with the highly literary that distinguishes Mackintosh's writing.

Prudence Mackintosh has said about her own writing, "I still feel that I haven't entirely lived something until I've written about it. The living and the writing are enhanced in the process." In the preface to *Thundering Sneakers* she acknowledges that "life, at least life with children, must be appreciated in the process." The process, of course, goes on. Prudence Mackintosh was another of those asked to contribute a favorite place essay to the May, 1989, issue of *Texas Monthly*. The result, an admiring, reflective, nostalgic look at an old-fashioned fishing camp, demonstrates her ability to take on new subjects. Clearly we can look forward to Prudence Mackintosh's future work no matter what direction it takes.

MARION WINIK: THE CUTTING EDGE

Unlike the other writers discussed here, Marion Winik is a relative newcomer to Texas literature. She also differs from the previously discussed writers as the only one born outside Texas. Winik, a New Jersey native, moved to Austin as an adult. Like the others, however, she made Texas her home, and in Texas she received her initial recognition as a writer. She got her start writing personal essays for a Texas-based alternative weekly, the *Austin Chronicle*. Since then her work has appeared in *Texas Monthly* and numerous national publications, including *American Way, Glamour,* and the *Utne Reader.* In 1991, Winik gained prominence as a regular contributor to National Public Radio's *All Things Considered.* Before publishing her first book of essays, she published two works with small presses: *Nonstop* (1980), a volume of poems from Cedar Rock Press, and *Boy Crazy and Other Stories* (1986), a collection of poems and short stories issued by Slough Press. It is as an essayist, however, that she has made her mark. Winik's *Telling: Confessions, Concessions, and Other Flashes of Light* received considerable attention on its publication by Villard Books in 1994. As Louis Black, the *Austin Chronicle* editor, writes in a February, 1994, article in *Texas Monthly:* "Winik may well be one of the next big writers to come out of Texas. Certainly she will be one of the more controversial."

Marion Winik might be described as a cross between Molly Ivins's character and Prudence Mackintosh's style and subjects. Winik is brash, loud, funny, earthy, sensitive, wild, impulsive, self-absorbed, and good-hearted. While Molly Ivins and Liz Carpenter are as renowned for what they have seen and done as for the words they have written, Winik has done just what many, or perhaps most, suburban kids of her generation did. Winik's circuitous path led from a family in the suburbs of the seventies through college campuses, New York streets, and New Orleans bars, back to a family in the suburbs of the nineties.

Winik's mode is confessional, and she tells all: the easy abortions, the hard drugs, the sexually ambiguous roommates, the shoplifting, the suicide attempts, the sundry and sordid affairs. At the end of the road is the eventual attainment of tranquility; like the rest of her generation, Marion and her fellow travellers have settled down now to quiet suburban lives, grown-up careers, stable marriages, kids and dogs and station wagons.

The short personal essays in *Telling* cover familiar territory: marital spats, houseguests, chores, children, car trips, lost purses, broken families. Here are all the details of middle-class life that you always thought were too dull to write about, and yet there is not a dull paragraph in the book. Marion Winik has an uncanny ability to ridicule herself without becoming ridiculous, to wallow in self-indulgence without a trace of sentimentality. She talks about no one but herself, and yet we end up knowing all the inhabitants of her inner circle—her sexually ambivalent hairdresser husband, her rambunctious small sons, her troubled younger sister, her AIDS-infected ex-brother-in-law, her workaholic father and socialite mother, even the childhood pets and untrustworthy tenants—as well as we know our own—or better.

In 1993 the National Endowment for the Arts awarded Marion Winik a Fellowship in Literature for creative nonfiction. Winik may indeed be the most authentic practitioner of creative nonfiction among contemporary Texas women writers. And the enthusiastic national response to her work might well indicate the coming-of-age of both a writer and a genre.

As I have already suggested, the writers discussed here are by no means the only Texas women engaged in the craft of creative nonfiction. Others include Austin writer Sarah Bird, former *Dallas Morning News* columnist Ann Melvin, Dallas free-lancer Karen Ray, and biographer and essayist Celia Morris. Although these writers have made a strong start, more remains to be done. Texas women have yet, I think, to produce a truly outstanding work of creative nonfiction, on the order of, say, John Graves's *Goodbye to a River* or Maxine Hong Kingston's *The Woman Warrior*. But that just gives us more to look forward to.

WELL-TOLD TALES:
Children's Book Writers

LAURIE DUDLEY

Beginning with Frances Baylor, whose *Juan and Juanita*, a story of Mexican-American children captured by Comanches, was published in 1886, Texas women have been writing for children for more than a century. After Baylor, however, many decades passed before Texas women wrote fiction for young readers again.

Several titles stand out among those published in the 1930s. Bessie Rowland James, wife of Marquis James, adapted her husband's life of Sam Houston, *The Raven*, for children. *Six Feet Six: The Heroic Story of Sam Houston* (1931) was one of the few good biographies for children at that time. The thirties also saw first books by three authors who continued to write for children.

Frances Clarke Sayers was a notable children's librarian, story-teller, and children's literature specialist. She set a high standard for Texas picture story books with *Bluebonnets for Lucinda* (1934), which has distinguished illustrations by Helen Sewell. Her later books, for slightly older children, are set on Galveston Island.

Camilla Campbell's work raised the level of nonfiction for children and young people. Her works include *Galleons Sail Westward* (1939), which narrates Cabeza de Vaca's adventures—or misadventures—in Texas; *Star Mountain and Other Legends of Mexico* (1946), which retells Mexican folk tales; and *Coronado and His Captains* (1958), which tells of Spanish exploration in West Texas.

Janette Sebring Lowrey's charming *Annunciata and the Shepherds* (1938) is set in San Antonio at Christmas time, when the folk drama "Los Pastores" is presented. *The Lavender Cat* (1944) is a memorable picture of the life of charcoal burners in the Texas Hill Country. *The Silver Dollar* (1940), for younger children, is a good story for telling or reading aloud, with handsome illustrations by Barbara Latham. Lowery's books for older girls, set in East Texas, include *Rings on Her Fingers* (1941), *Margaret* (1950), and *Love, Bid Me Welcome* (1964).

Siddie Joe Johnson, children's librarian, poet, and storyteller, wrote a number of fine books for children, stories recreating a Texas Coast childhood that becomes real even to a reader who has never seen the ocean, or presenting a pioneer girl so vividly that one experiences her delight in becoming a Texan. In addition to *Debby* (1940) and *New Town in Texas* (1942), Johnson wrote an important work of nonfiction. *Texas, the Land of the Tejas* (1943) includes much state history in a fairly brief book, with lively illustrations by Texan Fanita Lanier. *Rabbit Fires* (1951) and *A Month of Christmases* (1952) grew out of her love of the Hill Country and the ways of German Texans.

Charlotte Baker Montgomery, daughter of poet Karle Wilson Baker, began writing children's books in the mid-forties: *Necessary Nellie* (1945) and *Nellie and the Mayor's Hat* (1947) are stories of Mexican-American children in San Antonio. *Magic for Mary M* (1953) is set in Texas oil country. The later books, about East Texas children and their pets, are her own favorites.

Carol Hoff's books appeal especially to boys, though girls enjoy them too. In several she included some of her pioneer grandparents' experiences after coming to Texas. *Johnny Texas* (1950) and *Johnny Texas on the San Antonio Road* (1953) tell of a German Texan boy and his family. Another Texas biography for juveniles is *Wilderness Pioneer: Stephen F. Austin of Texas* (1955).

Loula Grace Erdman was a Missourian who came to the Texas Panhandle, fell in love with it, and spent the rest of her life there, teaching as well as writing for adults, young people, and children. Her stories present a strong picture of pioneer life in this region. Her Panhandle Trilogy is unsurpassed in its realistic presentation of the early life of Panhandle settlers. *The Wind Blows Free* (1952), *The Wide Horizon: A Story of the Texas Panhandle* (1956), and *The Good Land* (1959) are stories of a homesteading family, each told from the point of view of one of the daughters.

Lee McGiffin wrote books of special interest to older boys. *The Fifer of San Jacinto* (1956), *Ride for Texas* (1960), *Pony Soldier* (1961), and others are exciting tales that place fictional heroes in historically accurate settings. Another title, *Ten Tall Texans: Tales of the Texas Rangers* (1956) deserves special mention as well-written Texas non-fiction for children.

Jeanne Williams, who often wrote as J. R. Williams, has written many books that appeal especially to older boys and girls. *Tame the Wild Stallion* (1957), *The Horse Talker* (1960), and *Coyote Winter* (1965) are good historical fiction, notable for presenting people of different ethnic backgrounds with understanding and respect.

Wanda Campbell is a fifth-generation Texan whose love for the Panhandle and its historic places is evident in her books. Their strong feeling for atmosphere and place raises them above the average mystery story. *The Museum Mystery* (1957), *The Mystery of McClellan Creek* (1958), *The Mystery of Old Mobeetie* (1960), and *Ten Cousins* (1960) are all worthwhile.

In the late fifties and following years, Texas women began to write quality poetry for children. Myra Cohn Livingston, a young Dallasite, led the way with *Whispers* (1958) and *Wide Awake* (1959) as well as with poetic picture books, such as *I'm Hiding* (1965), and excellent poetry anthologies. Siddie Joe Johnson's *Feather in My Hand* (1967) is another fine book of poems. The work of these two writers is childlike, but never childish, and has helped introduce poetry to many children.

Byrd Baylor's picture books convey her love for the Southwest, including its people and archeology. They are well written and have distinguished illustrations by various artists. Ms. Baylor has received awards from the Texas Institute of Letters for three works: *The Desert Is Theirs* (1975), *Guess Who My Favorite Person Is* (1977), and *When Clay Sings* (1972).

The seventies and eighties saw an upsurge in the number of children's books by Texas women, but many were written as curriculum supplements, and most suffer from inadequate editing. In fiction there is a noticeable tendency toward fairly brief, popular wish-fulfillment stories that often are melodramatic and crowded with too many events.

Nevertheless, some good children's books are being published. One of the best is *Muddy Banks* (1987), by Ruby C. Tolliver, a moving, involving tale of an escaped slave who is given shelter by a white woman. Set on the Texas Coast during the Civil War, it includes a description of Dick Dowling's battle at Sabine Pass.

Janice Jordan Shefelman has contributed to literature for young Texans with a trio of books about a German Texas girl and her family. *A Paradise Called Texas* (1987), *Willow Creek Home* (1985), and *Spirit of Iron* (1937) are based on the author's grandmother's experiences. Shefelman comes from a writing family, and readers hope she will continue her good work. In *Letters to Oma: A Young Girl's Account of Her First Year in Texas, 1847* (1989) Marj Gurasich also reflects the life of German Texans through a fifteen-year-old's letters to her grandmother in Germany.

Judy Alter's *Luke and the Van Zandt County War* (1984) is an interesting story of two young East Texans in earlier times. It includes a little-known incident from Texas history, the "war" mentioned in the title. *Maggie and a Horse Named Devildust* (1989) is a fast-paced tale, fun to read, the first in a series.

Joan Lowery Nixon has a long list of titles for various ages. *If You Say So, Claude* (1980) and its sequels are brief, humorous stories for children just past early reading. Her popular "Orphan Train" books tell of the adventures of a family of children who are sent west to be placed in new homes.

In the nineties, three authors stand tall. Peni Griffin's *The Switching Well* (1993) is a fantasy with a strong feeling for time and place, well above the average. Sherry Garland has published well-written young-adult novels about Vietnamese young people. Two delightful picture books, particularly worthy of notice both for the stories and for the pictures, are Sherry Garland's *Lotus Seed* (1993) and *Why Ducks Sleep on One Leg* (1993). Carolyn Meyer's books are chiefly young adult, but her *White Lilacs* (1993), based on an actual situation, is a well-told tale for older children.

Part 2
TEJANA AND AFRICAN–AMERICAN WRITERS

INTRODUCTION

For the last two decades, Tejana and African-American women writers in Texas have enriched the state's mainstream literary production with their short stories, plays, poetry, and novels. Their success, however, was not an overnight triumph. These remarkable women achieved their present-day status as authors, often nationally published and reviewed, on the shoulders of pioneers—Tejana and African-American women writers who demonstrated what tenacity of purpose can accomplish.

At least three recent major publications testify to the strength of Tejana writers' influence on the contemporary Texas literary scene. In 1995, Roberta Fernandez, University of Houston professor, novelist, and editor published *In Other Words: Literature by Latinas of the United States,* the first anthology of Latina authors living in the United States. Fernandez includes thirteen Tejana writers among the poets, essayists, dramatists, and fiction writers. In April, 1995, inspired by the publication of this work, "Celebrating Women's Voices," an evening of literary readings in Austin, featured six of these Texas writers, Teresa Paloma Acosta, Rosemary Catacalos, Lorna Dee Cervantes, Alicia Gaspar de Alba, Carmen Tafolla, and Fernandez. Fernandez's *Intaglio: A Novel in Six Stories,* set on the Texas border, won the Best Book of Fiction Award from the Multicultural Publishers Exchange in 1990.

Fernandez, who holds a Ph.D. in Romance languages and literatures from the University of California, Berkeley, demonstrates her expertise as scholar in her editorship of *In Other Words*. Several other scholars in Texas also have been examining the development of Tejana literature in the state. The most recent evidence of their diligence is the recovery and publication of *Caballero: A Historical Novel* (1996), by Jovita González and Eve Raleigh. Written in the 1930s and 1940s, the manuscript of the novel was discovered several years ago in the archives of Texas A&M University, Corpus Christi. Edited by Professor José E. Limón and María Cotera, the novel narrates the life of a Mexican family in Texas in the crucial years 1846–48. In 1996, Bryce Milligan with coeditors Angela De Hoyos and Mary Guerrero Milligan published the anthology *Daughters of the Fifth Sun: A Collection of Latin Fiction and Poetry*.

Such careful and persistent scholarship as has inspired these two recent publications continues to recapture details of the development of Tejana writers' unique tradition. For the complete story of the African-American women writers' heritage to be told, much work must yet be accomplished. Rita Shelton Deverell, now an actress and writer living in Canada, was born in Houston's Fifth Ward in 1945. In the special edition of *The Texas Observer* featuring "Women's Voices" (September 25, 1987), Deverell writes of her early life in segregated Houston. Her essay, "Black Antigone," concludes that a Renaissance for Black achievers is at hand. She might have been speaking of African-American women writers in Texas. Increasingly visible because of their exemplary short stories, poems, plays, essays, and novels, at least a dozen successful Texas African-American women writers are providing what has long been needed—inspiration for fledgling Black women writers across the state. African-American women playwrights likewise have contributed greatly to the recent canon. The state's African-American women writers have much to look forward to in the twenty-first century as, with singular ability and hard work, they gain the acknowledgment of the Texas literary establishment and help shape the Texas literary tradition in the twenty-first century.

EVER RADICAL

A Survey of Tejana Writers

BRYCE MILLIGAN

Twentieth-century academic literary criticism often describes ethnic American literature as parochial and only a generation or two removed from a living oral tradition—as if this somehow negates the validity of such writing. During the past three decades, Hispanic women writers have suffered far more from invisibility than from censure, yet even a cursory look at this growing body of poetry and fiction reveals many works of energy and imagination. This literature is regional—these are women closely tied to the land by history and language—yet regionalism can hardly be construed as a negative criticism when applied to Texas authors of any ethnic derivation, male or female. Regional, yes; politically driven, yes; parochial or otherwise inferior, only slightly more often than Anglo writers of the same period. This latter admission must be qualified: It applies more to works produced during the Chicano Movement of the 1960s and 1970s than to subsequent work. It was brought about as much by amateur editing as by the quality of the writing itself. Chicano critics were as liable to be biased as Anglo critics were to be culturally unqualified to issue opinions of any real significance.

With several notable exceptions, American minority writers during most of this century and the last attempted to write in a manner indistinguishable from the mainstream style of American letters, a reasonable tendency because it was the only avenue to a viable market. Those few writers who maintained an ethnic identity in their work often had political or anthropological motives, writing either to improve the social and political future of their people or to preserve their folkways, culture, and/or language, which were thought to be in danger of imminent demise.

This generalization is especially true of Mexican-American women in Texas prior to the political and literary *movimientos* of the 1960s, which renamed them variously "Tejanas," "Chicanas," and "Latinas"[1] because they endured both Anglo suppression of their culture and the ills of living with machismo as a historical and daily reality. However, when la Raza ran headlong into the feminist movement in the late 1960s and early 1970s, Chicanas' cultural and career restrictions dissolved. Liberated, politically skilled, well-educated Chicana writers began exploring new directions in poetry, drama, and fiction, and scholars undertook a substantial reevaluation of the historical and contemporary sociological position of Chicanas.[2]

A body of literature and criticism began to emerge and, with it, a concern over the apparent lack of Chicana literary, political, and social role models. The search was on, and the result was the rediscovery of numerous Hispanic women who had helped shape the American West. Yet, as Texas critic María Herrera-Sobek writes in *Beyond Stereotypes: The Critical Analysis of Chicana Literature* (1985), the recovery of a truer history does not mean that popular misconceptions about American history will be corrected easily:

> The contributions of . . . early pioneer women have laid [sic] dormant in the pages of history (when not omitted altogether) and it is only recently, stimulated by the revisionist impetus of the Women's Movement and the Chicano Movement, that we have begun to accord them the proper historical respect and acknowledge women's role in the founding of the United States' colonies. Stereotypes are hard to exterminate once they have taken root in people's minds. And so it will take a long time to eradicate stereotypical images of [Hispanic] women that in no way conform to reality. (p. 17)

COLONIAL PERIOD TO 1848

In Texas, at least, a tradition of strong women did exist, going back to the earliest Hispanic settlers, though literary endeavors were hardly their strong suit. Prior to 1836 the vibrant Hispanic culture of South Texas was characterized by many strong women, of whom a few examples must suffice. To begin at the beginning, the founding settler of San Antonio was María Betancour (1703–79), one of the leaders of the thirty-one Canary Islanders who arrived in 1731. Known as *La Pobladora,* the "foundress," Betancour helped lay out and name several sites in the village, including the Plaza de las Islas. By the late 1780s the largest general store in San Antonio (and thus the entire region) belonged to María Josefa Granados. In 1790, Doña María Hinojosa de Balli inherited her husband's estates and began expanding them. Ultimately she owned nearly one-third of the Lower Rio Grande Valley, to which her son, Padre Nicolás Balli, added the whole of Padre Island, which he purchased from the Spanish crown around 1800.[3]

In all, some sixty Hispanic women held Texas lands granted directly to them by Spain or Mexico, and many others held lands inherited from male grantees. Some of these grants were dissolved by the Mexican government after the revolution of 1810–11 as punishment for royalist sympathies; others were denied for various (generally fraudulent) reasons under the Republic of Texas. Most were simply abandoned owing to the rise of virulent anti-Mexican sentiment following 1836.

Given this economic and political oppression, it is not surprising that there are few literary vestiges from the colonial period. In fact, beyond María Betancour's will, preserved in the Bexar County Archives, and a few scattered letters, virtually no documents exist whereby one might accurately gauge the type and amount of writing by Hispanic women. Spanish and English advertisements in mid-nineteenth-century newspapers indicate that books were available at stationers and general stores, but the nature of these books is debatable. Thus the literary culture of early Texas remains almost as mysterious as is the one female Hispanic writer whom we actually can connect, in a manner of speaking, with Texas—the Spanish nun and mystical writer María Jesús de Agreda, who claimed to have visited Texas in out-of-body experiences between 1620 and 1631. Sor María's visionary sermons to the Amerindian population must have been powerful: Padre Alonso de Benevides encountered reports of a "Lady in Blue" who had catechized the Jumanos tribe in far West Texas before he visited them in the late 1620s. Comparing notes with Sor María during a return visit to Spain in 1631 apparently convinced him that the

Jumanos' Lady in Blue was present before him in a Spanish convent. Regardless of who or what the Lady in Blue was, she provided Texas with one of its earliest and most enduring folk legends.

1848 TO THE
MID-TWENTIETH CENTURY

Chicano scholars generally date the establishment of Mexican-American self-identification from the 1848 Treaty of Guadalupe-Hidalgo, which effectively robbed Mexico of much of what is now the southwestern United States, overturned long-established social, religious, and cultural conventions, and replaced Spanish with English as the language of government and business. In Texas the date was less important than 1836 as a demarcation point between dominant cultures, but it did force Mexican-Americans to realize that Mexico was, after all, powerless against the manifest destiny of the North. Rather than exiles, the Spanish and mestizo peoples of what had been northern Mexico now had to accept that they were U.S. citizens—second class to be sure, but citizens nevertheless. Thus the hope of empowerment turned from the South to the North, from the glories of old conquests and ancient cultures to the daily grit and grind of survival coupled with a new political awakening.

It is not surprising that the first Tejana to achieve national recognition did so outside the state. In 1871, Lucía Eldine Gonzáles (1853–1942) of Johnson County married the radical Republican journalist Albert Parsons, who became secretary to the Texas senate the same year. This radical "mixed" marriage was symptomatic of the couple's political views in general. Neither their marriage nor their politics having gained them much popularity in Texas, in 1873 the couple moved to Chicago, where for thirteen years they led various labor, Marxist/socialist, and anarchist organizations. In 1886, Albert was charged as one of the instigators of Chicago's Haymarket Riot. Speaking in his own defense, he was convicted and hanged. But the fight went on. Writing as Lucy Parsons, this Tejana crusader was first published in the *Socialist*. Thereafter, for a half-century, Parsons published a stream of poems, articles, pamphlets, and books championing one cause after another—thereby chronicling her rise as a labor reformer/organizer. She became one of the most prominent nineteenth-

and early twentieth-century leaders, originating the drive for an eight-hour workday and helping to found, among other things, the Industrial Workers of the World (IWW).[4]

Like many other Chicanas with non-Hispanic surnames, Lucy Parsons was hardly ever recognized as either a Texan or a Mexican-American during her own life, and, as well known as she was among labor activists, only in the 1970s did she come to the attention of Chicana scholars actively searching for their cultural and intellectual forebears. As Alfredo Mirandé and Evangelina Enríquez state in their 1979 book, *La Chicana: The Mexican-American Woman:* "The importance of Lucía Gonzáles Parsons to contemporary Chicanas cannot be overstated. With a lifetime that spans from just after the American takeover [of the American Southwest] until well into the twentieth century, she is a transitional figure linking the nineteenth-century woman and the contemporary Chicana" (p. 95).

Parsons's impact as a role model for Tejana labor, civil-rights, and political activists was more immediate. Among the women she inspired was political writer and organizer María Hernández. In the 1920s, Hernández founded both the Liga Pro-Defensa Escolar and the civic and civil-rights organization Orden Caballeros de America. Half a century later she helped found La Raza Unida and was actively involved in the crucial 1972 political events in Crystal City, where today a bilingual media center is named in her honor.

Other, equally revolutionary Mexican women with Texas connections are being proclaimed proto-Chicanas as quickly as scholars rediscover them. One of the best known is feminist poet and journalist Sara Estela Ramírez (1881–1910), teacher, editor, political and labor activist, and a founder of the Partido Liberal Mexicano (PLM). In 1901, Ramírez founded the Laredo newspaper *La Corregidora,* which she saw as a news link for Mexicans on both sides of the Rio Grande and as a more or less official voice of the PLM. In 1910, just prior to her untimely death and the birth of the revolution, she founded the literary magazine *Aurora.* According to Inés Hernández, no copy of either publication now exists, and the "extant body of her poetry appears in the Texas-Mexican newspapers *La Crónica* and *El Democrata Fronterizo.*" Her personal connection with Texas began when she moved from Villa de Progreso, Coahuila, her birthplace, to Laredo around 1897. As an organizer, Ramírez traveled often to Mexico

City and throughout the northern state of Coahuila, but she based her literary, journalistic, and political activities in Laredo.[5]

Ramírez's work has reached across the twentieth century to affect some contemporary Chicana writers, most especially poet Inés Hernández, whose dissertation, at the University of Houston, focuses on Ramírez and who has translated many of her poems. Ramírez's influence, however, is surely limited to the example of her life and to the force of her political rhetoric rather than to any stylistic aspect of her poetry, which is typical turn-of-the-century Mexican verse, ornate and passionate. But politics and literature have always gone hand in hand in Latin America, which tends also to blur geographic and national boundaries. Ramírez is a good example of a writer who worked both sides of the U.S.–Mexico border in the service of oppressed peoples. As Hernández states, her life and work show "how the border often becomes erased when considering the experience of the Mexican people and in their response to domination and oppression" (p. 112). The fact that there is not a single contemporary Chicana writer whose literary work is devoid of political themes is a good indication that such precursors as Sara Ramírez reflect an enduring *conciencia de la raza* rather than a revolutionary fervor limited to any one particular period or conflict.

Ramírez also is an excellent example of the many Tejana poets who published almost exclusively in newspapers. Juanita Luna Lawhn summarizes the situation:

> Recent historical literary studies are documenting and illustrating the influence of Spanish-language newspapers on contemporary Chicano literature. These studies illustrate that Chicano literature is a natural outgrowth and a continuation of an on-going Hispanic literary tradition that has always been present in the United States, especially in the Southwest and in the greater Chicago area. Consequently, the theory often vocalized that today's Chicano literary as well as non-literary community has evolved strictly from an oral tradition is no longer viable. Instead, a new theory which states that the literary, social, and moral development of the Chicano community has been strongly influenced by the written word can and should modify and redefine the old theory of orality. (p. 134)

Lawhn's work with *La Prensa, El Regidor,* and the other two dozen or so Spanish-language newspapers printed in South Texas during the early years of this century has unearthed a number of Tejana writers of substance and power,[6] yet her argument for the existence of a "literary tradition" stretches the definition of tradition. Most contemporary Latina writers, in Texas and elsewhere, will cite any number of non-Latina writers as early influences and admit that they became aware of intellectual forebears such as Ramírez only when they were well into the development of their writing careers. On the other hand, early twentieth-century Mexican and Mexican-American women writers may have had a substantial impact on the grandmothers of contemporary Chicana writers. It is interesting to observe that virtually all Chicana writers who came of age in the 1960s or shortly thereafter have described their female role models as belonging to the generation prior to that of their parents. Numerous *abuelita* poems and stories depict strong-willed survivors, women who somehow had acquired a yearning for independence long before the women's movement of the 1960s.[7]

This awareness might stem from growing up with the strident feminist rhetoric of various short-lived publications such as El Paso's *La voz de la mujer* (July–October, 1907) or from witnessing the 1920s editorial debate that raged in *La Prensa*, a paper that reached almost all Spanish-language readers from Texas to California. This debate pitted the traditional views held by the paper's male editors against the emerging feminism of its many female editorial writers (notably Antonieta Rivas), short-fiction writers, and poets. The community of intellectual Mexican exiles in San Antonio, known as *El México de Afuera*, became a microcosm of the larger implications of this debate. As Lawhn points out, "By the second half of the 1920s, the selection of feminist essays . . . published in the '*Sección del Hogar y La Sociedad*' [of *La Prensa*] broke the silence of the women of *El México de Afuera*." Similarly, the "*crónicas femeninas*" of María Luisa Garza (writing under the pseudonym Loreley), published in the Texas-Mexican newspaper *El Imparcial de Texas*, and her feminist novels, published by Quiroga Company of San Antonio, were very popular among Hispanic women on both sides of the border.

Writers of the same period and status as Sara Ramírez, Loreley, and Antonieta Rivas but who are "undiscovered," whose major works have yet to be translated or published, probably will become major influences as scholarship continues to delve into this period. One such writer is journalist and activist Leonor Villegas de Magnon (1876–

1955), the author of *La Rebelde* (*The Woman Rebel*), an autobiographical novel set during the Mexican Revolution. This work was discovered by Clara Lomas, who translated a portion of it for inclusion in the *Longman Anthology of World Literature by Women, 1875–1975*. Lomas's complete translation was published by Arte Público Press as *The Rebel* in 1994.

Villegas de Magnon was born in Nuevo Laredo, Mexico, but she was educated in San Antonio and New York, and she married a U.S. citizen and conducted much of her political work from Laredo, where she ran a bilingual kindergarten. She was a co-founder (with Jovíta Idar, another Laredo Mexican-American) of *La Cruz Blanca,* an auxiliary unit of nurses who accompanied the revolutionary Carrancistas from Coahuila to Mexico City. She was a member of Laredo's Junto Revolucionaria (Revolutionary Council) and wrote editorials and dispatches for the Texas-Mexican newspapers *La Crónica* and *El Progreso.*

The radical inclinations of Chicana scholars searching for intellectual forebears have, to some extent, blinded these scholars to the obvious, namely the few Chicana writers who achieved statewide and even national recognition for work that sometimes confirms mainstream Anglo stereotypes about Mexico, the Southwest, or Hispanics in general. Thus the works of Jovíta Guerra González de Mireles (1899–1983), and the woman herself, are just beginning to catch the attention of contemporary Chicana scholars.

Born in Roma, González obtained a teacher's certificate and taught for several years at the exclusive San Antonio girls' school, Saint Mary's Hall. She went on to obtain a master's degree at the University of Texas, where she met J. Frank Dobie in 1925. Five years later, González became the first Tejana president of the Texas Folklore Society—a startling feat when one realizes that the year she joined the society, there were only two other Hispanic names on the membership roster, Adina de Zavala and University of Texas Spanish professor E. J. Villavaso. Publishing articles regularly in *Southwest Review* and elsewhere, González probably exerted more long-term influence on both Dobie and the society than many would admit. Her own studies in folklore led her to collect and edit "Folk-Lore of the Texas-Mexican Vaquero" in the 1927 Texas Folklore Society annual publication, *Texas and Southwestern Lore,* and to write a collection of her own memories of life along the Rio Grande, "Among My People," which she did as a series of gently humorous tales focusing on individual characters. Originally published in *Tone the Bell Easy*, volume 10 of *Publications of the Texas Folklore Society* (1932), edited by J. Frank Dobie, these stories surfaced again in Charles Tatum's 1990 *Mexican American Literature*. Other studies by González appeared in Dobie's *Puro Mexicano* (*Publications of the Texas Folklore Society*, volume 12, 1935). Two novels by González were published posthumously in 1996: *Caballero: A Historical Novel* (Texas A&M University Press), coauthored with Eve Raleigh; and *Dew on the Thorn* (Arte Público Press), edited by José Limón and including a brief autobiographical sketch.

González and her husband, Edmundo E. Mireles, established the state's first major bilingual grade-school program in the 1940s in Corpus Christi, for which they wrote *El Español Elemental* and, with R. B. Fisher, a three-volume series, *Mi Libro Español*. According to Tatum, the books "have been used to promote bilingual education throughout the southwestern United States." A minor writer at best, a high school Spanish teacher in Corpus Christi for twenty-seven years, Jovíta González was a quiet revolutionary who broke ethnic barriers and overturned systems.

An even more startling omission on the part of contemporary Chicana scholars, at least upon initial inquiry, is the novelist, short-story writer, poet, and dramatist Josefina Niggli (1910–83). As Chester Seltzer ("Amado Muro") was to Chicano writers, so Niggli was, and remains, to Chicanas—an Anglo with a deceptive name and the "correct" geographical background and topical inclinations. Niggli was born in 1910 on an old Mexican estate, La Quinta del Carmen, near Hidalgo, Nuevo Leon, where her parents had lived since 1893. Niggli's father's Swiss/Alsatian forebears had arrived in Texas around 1836, and her Virginian mother's people were of Irish, French, and German extraction. Thus she fails to pass the *prueba de sangre* to be classified a Chicana.

The blood test is, however, a delicate matter, and it has caused real consternation among Chicano critics when applied to male writers. In a seminal essay, Raymond Paredes offered the following definition: "Chicano literature is that body of works produced by United States citizens and residents of Mexican descent for whom a sense of ethnicity is a critical part of their literary sensibilities and for whom the portrayal of their ethnic experience is a major concern." Claiming life-long dual citizenship, and setting all her best work in Mexico among indigenous residents, Niggli seems to fit the technical requirements of this definition, if not the blood test. Even a purist Chicano critic such as Juan Bruce-Novoa has admitted that it would be "difficult" to "justify the exclusion" of Niggli from the canon, though this is virtually all he has to say of her or her work.[8] Carmen Salazar Parr and Genevieve M. Ramírez, in a short essay entitled "The Female Hero in Chicano Literature" in *Beyond Stereotypes,* discuss several characters from Niggli's plays and apparently accept Niggli as a Chicana without question. But isolated references and a single essay do not constitute critical acceptance, especially given Niggli's notable absence from other Chicana critical works. The inclusion of Niggli in Charles Tatum's groundbreaking high-school textbook, *Mexican American Literature,* the only textbook of its kind to be issued by a major U.S. publishing company, likely will render the question of Niggli's bloodline moot by establishing a canon with or without the approbation of purist critics.

Niggli's Texas credentials, however, are impeccable. Beyond her father's Texas background, Niggli herself spent a good deal of time in the state. After the assassination of Madero, the Niggli family fled to the United States, eventually settling in San Antonio. Niggli returned to Mexico at the age of ten in 1920, remained for five years, and returned to San Antonio to attend Incarnate Word College. Her first book of poems, *Mexican Silhouettes,* was published in Hidalgo, Nuevo Leon, in 1928; a larger edition was published on King William Street in San Antonio in 1931. After studying playwriting for a short time under Coates Gwynne, director of the San Antonio Little Theater, Niggli went on to do graduate work in drama at the University of North Carolina, where she became associated with the Carolina Playwrights group—which included Paul Green and, occasionally, Thomas Wolfe. From Chapel Hill she moved to Western Carolina College, where she completed most of her important work and taught drama and radio production until her retirement.

Niggli's reputation was assured upon the publication of several one-act plays, especially "The Red Velvet Goat" (1938) and "Sunday Costs Five Pesos" (1939). According to the publisher, Samuel French, as of the mid-1970s the latter work was the "most produced one-act play in English," and Niggli herself said she could have "managed" on the royalties from that play alone. Of more interest to contemporary Chicanas are her two plays "Soldadera" (1936) and "The Ring of General Macías" (1943), which show Niggli's revolutionary sympathies through her depiction of female heroes on both sides of the political struggle. A less strident and much more popular work was *Mexican Village* (1945), a collection of ten novelettes set in Hidalgo, the author's hometown. When the book became a best seller, MGM Studios hired Niggli to help script *Mexican Village* into the movie *Sombrero,* which starred Pier Angeli and Ricardo Montalban.

Two popular textbooks followed, *Pointers on Playwriting* (1945) and *Pointers on Radio Writing* (1946). Niggli's *Step Down, Elder Brother: A Novel* (1947), her first novel, received only middling reviews, and the author lapsed into silence. Perhaps her finest prose work, though it is seldom so recognized, was her novel *A Miracle for Mexico* (1964). This thoughtful retelling of the story of the apparition of the Virgin of Guadalupe to the Aztec peasant Juan Diego, published as a finely crafted illustrated book, is much sought after by collectors.[9]

According to John Igo, a long-time friend of the author, in the late 1930s and 1940s Niggli experimented with "narrator, point of view, a double sense of reality, in short, some of the techniques popularized by others, such as Carlos Fuentes, Camus, even Beckett." To back up this assertion, Igo published three short pieces of surreal fiction, part of a manuscript collection bequeathed to him following Niggli's death.[10]

CONTEMPORARY TEJANA WRITERS

In September, 1973, *El Grito,* with Estela Portillo Trambley, a Tejana from El Paso, as contributing editor and guiding light, became the first U.S. journal to dedicate an issue exclusively to Chicana literature. Within a short time, most Chicano publications had addressed the topic in some manner, and new, often short-lived journals devoted exclusively to Hispanic feminist perspectives appeared. Yet a decade later, mainstream critical acceptance remained an elusive goal. As Evangelina Vigil noted in her introduction to the 1983 "Woman of Her Word" issue of *Revista Chicano-Riqueña,* "Removed from the mainstream of American literature and barely emerging on the Hispanic literary scene, the creativity of Latina writers exists autonomously" (p. 7). Or, as Vigil put it more succinctly in a poem, "It is damn hard making it as a Chicana in the U.S.A."

Tomás Rivera once described three stages of development in Chicano literature: first, conversational records of the culture itself; second, political rhetoric combined with cultural identification; and third, pure invention. From this viewpoint, most contemporary Chicana literature is a fusion of the second and third stages. This is understandable: the fusion of the feminist liberation of the *nietas* with the cultural strengths of the *abuelitas* had to be explosive, and as long as economic exploitation, cultural suppression, and political repression remain facts of life, Chicana writers probably will feel ill at ease with "pure invention," which lacks a political rhetorical point. All this roiling creativity has produced some truly remarkable literature. To get a glimpse of the state of Tejana literature, we will examine the careers and works of five major poets, each of whom played a significant role in the literary *movimiento* and has continued to produce substantial work.

Angela De Hoyos

Without doubt the writer with whom one must begin a discussion of Tejana poetry is Angela De Hoyos. In fact, any broad-minded discussion of Texas poetry could begin here as well. What other Texas writer, much less Texas poet, is the subject of two book-length critical studies and numerous dissertations, articles, and reviews on four continents and has had her work published in the United States, Argentina, Australia, Brazil, Colombia, England, Germany, Italy, Mexico, Peru, Spain, and Switzerland? Besides being a well-known, well-regarded poet, she played an important role in the development of Tejana writing as a "discovery" editor, publishing the first books of Inéz Hernández, Carmen Tafolla, and Evangelina Vigil, among others, through her M&A Editions. A painter, graphic artist, a coeditor of the important journal *Caracol* and editor/designer of the small literary journal *Huehuetitlan,* this renaissance woman is deeply committed to the social causes that first inspired her to write in the late 1960s.

Born in 1940 in Coahuila, Mexico, De Hoyos soon moved with her family to San Antonio. "Greatly influenced" by the poetry her mother read to her—ranging from Sor Juana Inés de la Cruz to García Lorca and Octavio Paz—De Hoyos became "a child bookworm, spending days and days reading at the public library." Because she was moved by the struggle of Texas migrant workers and by the plight of the urban poor, her poetry turned increasingly political. Soon she was publishing in literary magazines and giving readings whenever the just-awakening Texas *movimiento Chicano* had need of a poet. By the mid-1970s, De Hoyos had established a wider audience: her poem "The Final Laugh" won the 1972 Diploma de Benemerenza of the Academia Leonardo da Vinci in Rome; in 1974 she took second place at the International Poetry Competition, also in Rome, with "The Missing Ingredient."

These two poems and a few others made up her first slim book, *Arise, Chicano!* (1975), a collection of overtly political poems centered on the twin issues of poverty and social injustice. Curiously, all of these poems are in English, with Spanish translations by poet, novelist, and scholar Mireya Robles. "Curiously" since in her next book, *Chicano Poems: For the Barrio,* also published in 1975 but containing newer poems, De Hoyos exhibited one of her most distinctive talents—"code switching" between English and Spanish phrases within the same sentences. Anglo critics have occasionally dismissed code switching as indicative of an incomplete command of either language (forcing one to wonder what they have to say of the multilingualism of Ezra Pound or T. S. Eliot), but De Hoyos's use of the technique is far too effective to be anything but well designed.[11] In *Third Woman,* Naomi Lindstrom says of De Hoyos's poem "Chicanita Flor del Campo" that the "lines conveying the artificial values of mainstream U.S. society stand out in English; those representative of the more coherent Hispanic-rooted values have Spanish as their natural medium" (p. 65). In *The Multi-faceted Poetic World of Angela De Hoyos* (1985), Marcella Aguilar-Henson discusses how De Hoyos's code switching plays against English cliches (of both word and thought) to criticize the dominant culture. Cuban poet and critic Maya Islas agrees, stating that De Hoyos's bilingual lines occasionally display substandard English "romper el concepto de superioridad lingüística en términos del idioma inglés que tiene el anglo contra . . . el chicano" ("to destroy the notion of linguistic superiority regarding the English language that the Anglo holds against . . . the Chicano").[12]

> *Y la pregunta que ofende:*
> *Ain't you Meskin?*
> *How come you speak*
> *such good English?*
> *Y yo le contesto:*
> *Because I'm Spanglo, that's why.*

Ramón Saldivar claims that the poet "deliberately switches linguistic codes, to establish a deeper semantic rapport with fellow Chicanos" but also to reflect more accurately the mood of particular images or statements. With the obvious exception of Alurista, few other Chicano or Chicana poets exhibit such conscious intent, or such insight, in code switching.

While *Arise, Chicano!* took a rhetorical hammer to the most obvious social and political ills besetting Chicanos, to their "migrant world of hand-to-mouth days" and "festering barrios of poverty," *Chicano Poems* employs a less strident tone, addressing what De Hoyos sees as an essentially rural, family-oriented, culture-rich community in danger of becoming dysfunctional when brought into conflict with urban American reality, where "every day the price of hope goes up." Here she also takes on the ironic tone that will become so characteristic of her work, chiding, for example, a Chicano male:

> but wasn't it you
> I saw
>
> > yesterday
> coming out of that motel
> con una gringuita
> > all smiles. . . ?
> No te apenes, amigo:
> Homogenization
> > is one good way
> to dissolve differences.

Of course the problem is not to be solved in a motel bed. Another kind of love is essential writes De Hoyos in the poem "Hermano": "Born too late / in a land / that no longer belongs to me," she must "wait for the conquering barbarian / to learn the Spanish word for love: / Hermano." But love here implies understanding, specifically an understanding of history. Just as Americans tend to forget that "their" land was taken by force from its indigenous inhabitants, so Anglo Texans tend to think of 1836 as the year the region was "liberated" from an oppressive government—forgetting that much of it was stolen from Tejanos who, in general, had supported the war against the Mexican tyrant. Thus De Hoyos's opening epigraph to the poem, "Hermano": "'Remember the Alamo' . . . and my Spanish ancestors / who had the sense to build it."

Luis Arturo Ramos, who explicated these two books in his study, *Angela De Hoyos: A Critical Look* (1979), found that the "we" of the earlier book speaks in a heroic voice while "la naturaleza intimista que predomina en la segunda vertiente . . . podría calificarse de anti-heroica" ("the natural intimacy pervading the second work . . . should be called antiheroic"). Calling for Anglos to learn the meaning of *hermano*, however, probably was more heroic on the part of the poet than crying out "*Levantate!*"

The poet's third book was published first as *Selecciones* (1976) and then, in a facing-page bilingual edition, as *Selected Poems/ Selecciones* (1979). This book established a dialectic between personal poems and narrative ones, between past and present, between, as Spanish critic Chazarra Montiel put it, "the instinctual desires for life and death."

De Hoyos's latest book, *Woman, Woman* (1985), is also her largest and most complex. Rolando Hinojosa warns us in his introduction: "Beware! You are in the hands of a poet. You're meant to read slowly, to ponder, to reread." Certainly *Woman, Woman* is worth multiple readings, but it is a difficult book to read slowly because many of the poems are short epigrammatic pieces. In earlier works the poet's predilection for distilling larger issues into these pithy statements functioned as a form of semantic punctuation within longer poems, but here she lets them stand on their own. Because epigrammatic poetry has not been a "hot" literary form in English for a number of centuries, this is a daring step on De Hoyos's part. But she has the nerve, and the wit, to carry it off, as in "A Lesson in Semantics":

> *Men, she said*
> > *sometimes*
> > > *in order to*
> > > > *say it*
> *it is*
> > *necessary*
> > > *to spit*
> > > > *the word.*

In a narrative context, De Hoyos can carry off the same sort of punch. "Fairy-Tale: Cuento de Hadas," for example, finds a young girl's romantic dreams dashed when she finds that her Prince Charming has more than one princess on the side. "Never never never again" will she "blindly believe / in deities, or / in men." But De Hoyos's criticism of machismo can be more subtle, systematically inlaying symbolism and literary/historical references. In "Where the Wound Lies," she brings together Christian iconography, Pygmalion and Galatea, and Eros—and makes these diverse images function as an organic whole.

Throughout *Woman, Woman* an erotic tension is poised against political awareness, specifically in the battle between the sexes. Occasionally De Hoyos must "spit" the word "man" or, as in the poem "You Will Grow Old," "go about / grinding my teeth / on the thankless endless / daily task: / dusting your (male) wings," but she is not unfair in her treatment of men. Her vision of feminism was severely criticized by Sandra Cisneros in an essay in *Third Woman*, pointing to this poem in particular and to another, "Words Unspoken," in which De Hoyos declares: "Perhaps / underneath all that bravado / quakes a hopeless desperado / who longs to win a battle / now and then." Cisneros says, "Feminism as defined by this Tejana, is one of solidarity with your man even if it means growing old doing 'thankless tasks like dusting his wings' because 'under all the bravado / quakes a hopeless desperado / who longs to win a battle / now and then." Evangelina Enríquez, on the other hand, calls "Words Unspoken" a "remarkable piece":

> She is able to peel back the abstract roles of dominance and bravery that govern machos, revealing a human being beneath the mask who must wrestle with life's battles. Surprisingly, neither man nor woman suffers from this revelation. It is rare that machismo is handled with such insight and understanding as it is in this poem. "Words Unspoken" should stand as an exemplar of machismo as it touches the sympathies of the Chicana rather than as it victimizes her. (p. 184)

Perhaps the most important poem in *Woman, Woman* is a dramatic dialogue entitled "La Malinche a Cortez y Vice Versa." La Malinche (or Doña Marina) is the concubine-translator-guide of Cortez, whom Chicano and Mexican writers have both celebrated as the mother of all mestizos and reviled as a whore and traitor. The voice De Hoyos gives to Marina is that of a bright survivor, a sensitive and intelligent but conquered woman speaking boldly to her conqueror.

Marina suggests to Cortez that they carve their names in the sand, an image that plays the temporary against the timeless, the ever-changing seashore and the eternal sands of time. But Cortez, a male-chauvinist pig if ever there was one, rejects the idea out of hand. The whole world, he says, knows you are "mi querida Marina. / No necesitas / adornos superfluos." Love is enough, he concludes. Of course the fact is that Cortez couldn't bear the idea of actually marrying a barefoot Indian, no matter how great her charms might be— "Es cierto, / es una hembra / olé! a todo dar." Marina, of course, was no fool. Her anger rises as she names Cortez a "gringo desabrido," bringing to mind the poem's present-day parallels.

In *Woman, Woman,* De Hoyos gave us numerous depictions of how it is to be a Chicana in the mid-1980s, envisioning the more remote past with a clear eye, finding humor in the contemporary middle-class predicament, and expressing outrage at finding the Chicana a doubly oppressed minority. The call for political solidarity remains unequivocal. "*Levántate!*" she seems to shout again, "Arise!" Only this time it is "Arise, Chicana!"

In her more recent writing, De Hoyos has refined her ironic tone, balancing humor against caustic wit. She has been working on more complicated collections, in which she buries meaning beneath silk-smooth narrative surfaces, or beneath humor. Her *"Gata"* ("Cat") poems are dedicated to the proposition that we cannot be civilized until we learn to laugh at ourselves. A more recent work, "The Minuscule Araña," ostensibly a "parable" told by a "bilingual beetle," is a poetic sequence dealing with the tenuous nature of existence, of life lived on a thread, so to speak, held up by hope and weighted with despair. Yet the poet is determined to survive; as she writes in this collection, "I'm a cannibal lady, / I want 8-legged poems / or none at all."

Pat Mora

Pat Mora's first book, *Chants* (1984), opens with an invocation to the Chihuahuan desert, in imitation of the "Indian women" whom she saw "long ago bribing / the desert with turquoise threads." The poet intones a similar prayer: "Guide my hands, Mother, / to weave singing birds," while secretly, she buries a "ballpoint pen / and lined yellowing paper," asking the land "to smile" on her as she composes these poems, to help her "catch her music with words." The desert thus forms a second persona early in the book, a mother-muse figure whose wild wisdom teaches the poet endurance. This theme has pervaded all of Mora's subsequent work.

Chants chronicles the development of a Tejana consciousness that can bridge the gap between mythic antiquity and the more immediate past—a past riddled with superstition and with rules for both social and physical survival in hostile environments. Mental health, not to mention humanity, depends less on the poet's crossing the bridge than on her *being* the bridge. The position is a poetic necessity but, Mora says, is uncomfortable:

> *an American to Mexicans*
> *a Mexican to Americans*
> *a handy token*
> *sliding back and forth*
> *between the fringes of both worlds*
> *by smiling*
> *by masking the discomfort*
> *of being pre-judged*
> *Bi-laterally.*

Uncomfortable perhaps, but survivable, the will to survive supplied by both the solitude of the desert and the bustling responsibilities of the poet's Anglo-dominated workplace. By intoning these chants, lyrics describing situations and persons caught "between the fringes of both worlds," the poet ritualizes her duality. Mexican, Anglo, and Mestizo worlds, past and present, village superstitions and paneled office realities, all collide here in a tumult of images. Ultimately, Mora concludes, one must live with the scar of this ambivalence. The conclusion is valid wherever the American melting pot has failed to assimilate and homogenize independent cultures.

Mora was born and reared in El Paso, in sight of the Rio Grande, constantly in contact with residents of La Ciudad de Juarez who crossed the river to work as day laborers. Every day of her life, Mora said in an interview once, she was "aware of the differences between my life and theirs, and of the role of chance in one's life. I could have been born on the other side of the river." After taking undergraduate and graduate degrees in English and speech from the University of Texas at El Paso, Mora worked as assistant to the president at UTEP and as director of the university museum—lending considerable weight to her repeated references to committees, paneled boardrooms, and other office imagery. Yet she remains acutely aware of her position: "I function day-to-day in an Anglo culture and yet just a mile or two away are people caught up in a different world."[13]

Mora's dilemma is described from various perspectives in a number of her poems, but perhaps nowhere so clearly as in "Aztec Princess." In this poem a young woman on the edge of independence is taken by her mother to the spot in the house where her own umbilical cord was buried—a sign, her mother tells her, that she would "nest inside." That night the girl digs in the spot but finds nothing but "earth, rich earth." Placing it in a jar, she takes it out into the moonlight and whispers, "Breathe." This is a perfect reflection of the ambivalence in *Chants*: wishing to break free of the mystical implications of the buried umbilical cord but needing a ritual act in order to achieve that freedom.

That such a ritual must be a logical necessity is supported in *Chants* by several poems describing the both the ceremonial magic of *brujas* and the herbal cures of *curanderas*. In "Bruja: Witch," Mora gives a first person account of shape-shifting from an old woman into the body of an owl, then back again. "Chuparrosa: Hummingbird," a more complex poem, begins "I buy magic meat / of a chuparrosa from a toothless witch." The killing of the hummingbird is part of a love-potion ritual to make her lover "see me, only me." It is painfully effective:

> You hover,
> Your eyes never wander.
> More and more
> on hot afternoons
> I sleep
> to escape your gaze.

The abrupt juxtaposition of these different worlds, different sensibilities, and different fates is crystal clear in El Paso, where one can shed a good deal of the twentieth century simply by crossing a river. Thus her second book, *Borders* (1986), attempts to refine the notion of the border as a metaphor for the no-man's zone separating cultures, languages, sexes, realities. As the poet puts it, "I live in a doorway."

Even when she was a child, Mora writes, she knew precisely who held the power, yet the road to such success remained a mystery. Like generations of aspiring young Chicanas, Mora grew up under the influence of female Anglo teachers. She recalls this in "Withdrawal Symptoms":

> We were hooked early,
> brown-eyed, round-faced girls
> licked our lips
> tasting secret pleasures
> even in first grade
> rushed to school to push
> tacks into bulletin boards
> until our thumbs were sore
> craving
> smiles, smiles
> pounded erasers, our cymbals
> hiding us in white dust,
> re-copied grammar drills
> until abuilita worried
> into our blood-shot eyes
> all for gold stars, secret
> winks from pale teachers.

But Mora is more than just a survivor of the Texas education system. She is a living witness to the Chicano-Anglo cultural collision. The addiction to "sticky sweet smiles" is endemic, so that when the little girl grows up and encounters an Anglo world of "bitter frowns / in committees and board rooms," she must ask herself, "Why am I the only Mexican American here?" Over and over the poet describes crossing, as a successful Chicana in a superficial Anglo world, back into a world that is safer, somehow more real. From a boardroom inhabited by "careful women in crisp beige / suits, quick beige smiles" she crosses into "the other room" where "señoras / in faded dresses stir sweet / milk coffee, laughter whirls." In "Bilingual Christmas," Mora juxtaposes the images of an eggnog-and-rum-balls office party, with the poverty outside the windows where "Not carols we hear / whimpering / children too cold / to sing / on Christmas eve." "Echoes" is a vignette of the poet at a birthday party, where she witnesses the simplest sort of blind cruelty—"just drop the cups and plates / on the grass" her host says, "My maid / will pick them up." But for Mora, both the host's attitude and her own silence are disgusting.

"Again and again I feel / my silence, the party whirring round me. / I longed to hear this earth / roar, to taste thunder, / to see proper smiles twist." But it does not; instead, Mora writes, "my desert land waits / to hear me roar, waits to hear / me flash: NO." Critic Robin Fast describes the dilemma: "She is fluent in two languages and two worlds but not entirely accepted by either, and thus ill at ease in both, and in herself."

In *Chants,* Mora developed a sense of cultural identity; in *Borders,* a longer work, she moves through a series of life experiences that define her as a woman and, ultimately, as a writer. In the fourth and final section of the book, Sandra Cisneros points out, Mora "finally abandons the mask of mother, wife, professional woman, and begins to explore her inner self, her poetic 'I'." She is away from the boardrooms now, on her own, where "motels are my convents," where "I wake early / mumbling phrases, / litanies / holding a pencil / rather than beads."

Both *Chants* and *Borders* won Southwest Book Awards, and Mora's work has received other recognition as well. With these successes, Mora left her beloved El Paso in 1989 to go with her husband (an archeologist) to Cincinnati, where she has been free to write without bearing the "bureaucratic weight" of her university jobs.

Her latest collections of poetry, *Communion* (1991) and *Agua Santa: Holy Water* (1995), show an even more refined poetics. Gone are the thunder and flash of righteous indignation that punctuate the first two books. In their place are reflective and diverse collections of powerful, imaginative, and well-crafted poems. Divided into three sections, *Communion* is full of place-specific poems, ranging from "Divisadero Street, San Francisco" to "The Taj Mahal" by way of Peru, Cuba, Pakistan, New York, and elsewhere. Some of her favorite theses reappear in portraits of various *brujas* and *curanderos* and of "The Young Sor Juana." A couple of potent protest poems address domestic violence. In "Emergency Room," for example, a young wife can stand naked and say:

> so I don't cover my breasts
> with my hands or a white sheet
> no
> you can look and touch
> i m blue neck to knee
> he clothed me in bruises

Here Mora is clearly experimenting with punctuation and capitalization, something she rarely did in previous work. And there are explorations into traditional forms—a well-crafted villanelle, for example ("Strong Women"). On the other hand, she has provided bottom-of-page translations for all Spanish words and phrases used in the book. This is unusual in Chicano literature, the general assumption in the past having been that if the reader did not know enough Spanish to get through the text, then forcing him or her to resort to a dictionary was a form of linguistic activism. Mora has never used much code switching in her poetry, however, and has more than once expressed a fear of being unintelligible to half her audience.

Still, this substantial book was transitional, and it is clear that the poet was giving birth to a new voice. As she says in the final poem of *Communion,* she is "gathering from within, / a light safe to follow." In *Nepantla: Essays from the Land in the Middle* (1993), her power is expressed in another format—the essay. For readers interested in the characters who inhabit Mora's poetic landscape, *Nepantla* is required reading.

Evangelina Vigil-Piñón

The covers of Evangelina Vigil-Piñón's books tell too much to ignore. Her first, a substantial chapbook, *nade y nade* (1978), announces the radical nature of her bilingualism in the title itself. The "swimming" of the title implies both a survivalist intent—keeping one's head above the water—and the joy of plunging headlong into the richly idiosyncratic linguistic pools that are the barrios of west-side San Antonio. Fresh from winning the 1977 Coordinating Council of Literary Magazines (CCLM) national poetry contest with her strident feminist poem "Ay qué ritmo," Vigil has a what-am-I-doing-here expression in the snapshot on the back of her first collection, and we can believe that these poems are, as she says in her introductory monologue, "little pieces" that "fall off me every day. Like hilo strands of my long, black hair."

The cover of her second book, *Thirty an' Seen a Lot* (1982), which received an American Book Award, shows the survivor who kept her head above water and her eyes open standing defiantly in front of a cracked bar window beneath a neon "ladies welcome" sign, her thumb cocked in invitation. On the back cover, Vigil sits at the bar inside, nursing a beer next to a bleary-eyed *borracho.* Independent, this cover screams, and proud. Five years later, Vigil has become Vigil-Piñón and we find her in a business suit and a perm on the back of *The Computer Is Down* (1987).

This evolution is reflected in the poetry. For Vigil, code switching never meant conscious movement from one language to another, reflecting shifts of perspective or intent; what she used to such effect in *nade y nade* was in fact a single language—that spoken in her home barrio in west-side San Antonio. Ramón Saldívar described its Spanish half as being "correct according to its own logical and rigorous grammatical rules, lacking no inherent suitability for ordinary or poetic expression. In fact, under Evangelina Vigil's control, this idiom exhibits a rich and varied simplicity." The same can be said of the English component. Neither language functions well on its own here, but together they form a distinct and expressive bilingual dialect. Vigil's ear for conversational rhythms makes this dialect come alive as a poetic idiom. With admirable skill she records for us the cultural expression of an isolated community.

Besides recording the expression of the community, however, Vigil records an interior dialogue of considerable interest. She is *la Chicana* coming to grips with her vocation, her role as a spokeswoman, though it goes against the traditional roles assigned women in her culture:

> *I spill my whole life on you*
> *and don't even know who you are.*
> *I don't understand it.*
> *I've always been taught*
> *to be very careful who you trust.*
> *Qué confianza, verdad?*

The water theme of the title of *nade y nade* may have come from the crucial poem "lo hondo," in which the paradox of Vigil's role as a radical poet in a tradition-bound culture is reflected in the equally perplexing questions posed by love:

> *entre más nos acercamos*
> *más distante te me haces*
> *guess that's what happens*
> *when two people discover*
> *each other's depths*
> *y hijo*
> *no sé cuál es más peligroso:*

lo hondo
o la corriente

(The closer we come together / the farther apart we grow . . . and man, I can't tell which is more dangerous / the depths / or the current.)

By the time she published this poem, Vigil was accustomed to living with the question of "the depths or the current." Born in 1949 she began college with a four-year scholarship in business administration at Prairie View A&M in 1968. Eventually she switched to the University of Houston to finish as an English major, and in 1976 she was teaching in the artist-in-education program of Harlandale school district of San Antonio. A frequent contributor to San Antonio's *Caracol,* the fieriest of the Chicano journals of the era, Vigil soon accumulated a sufficient number of prizes and fellowships (an NEA writing fellowship, for example) to establish her as a major Tejana voice.

After Vigil returned to Houston in the early 1980s, she was selected by Arte Público Press to edit the important first women's issue of the *Revista Chicano-Riqueña,* entitled "Woman of Her Word."

In her introduction to "Woman of Her Word," Vigil said: "As a persona in the literature, the Latina is a woman of her word—mujer de su palabra . . . . She conveys values to her family members by way of example, and through the oral tradition, and, as such, she represents a tie to the cultural past." These notions, representing tradition and turning to the past for strength, seem at odds with her yearning for personal freedom and, in her most recent work, a futurist bent. In *nade y nade,* Vigil questioned life over and over, voicing what one critic called "the uncertainty many have felt at the twilight of the seventies. . . . [E]xpressing those doubts in the vernacular of the majority, she speaks not as a single alienated intellectual, but as a spokesperson of a community." On "that double threshold / between algo / y nada" she struggled "every day / translating vague answers to this question / into real, concrete things"; she pondered whether "I should have done this / or done that" only to realize "that should have done / is past tense / and that the catch is in the moment"; she left us with undiluted desire: "I want so much / and if you ask me what / I won't know what to answer / only that I want a lot." But beyond all the doubts, the questions, the vague desires, only one particular desire is voiced in *nade y nade*: to be an "artist" like her grandmother, a master storyteller whose "words paint masterpieces," words, Vigil says, she hung "in the galleries of my mind."

The questions did not disappear in *Thirty an' Seen a Lot,* but the doubting voice did. Her strongest poems record the essence of the barrio. Sandra Cisneros wrote: "At her best, Vigil captures with a sociolinguist's accuracy the Tex-Mex speech patterns of her San Antonio home in an unaffected kitchen-philosophical manner. Her barroom observations and anecdotes are funny and unequaled in power not for what is said, but what is left unsaid." In the atmosphere of the bars, alive with talk, with people "pensando en esas cosas reales de la vida," Vigil finds much to record, celebrating both life and language. At the same time she can pack a mean punch when machismo, "asqueroso sexismo," rears its head, attacking anyone "with brain cells / displaced / replaced / by sperm cells."

Vigil also can reach back to her own barefoot urban childhood to make points forcefully. In "was fun running 'round descalza," she juxtaposes gang wars, obscene graffiti, "chuco hieroglyphics," and other urban ills with the simple childhood joy of:

> *running 'round descalza*
> *shiny brown legs leaping with precision*
> *to avoid nido de cadillos crowned with tiny blossoms pink*
> *to tread but ever so lightly on scorching cement*
> *to cut across street glistening with freshly laid tar*
> *its steam creating a horizon of mirages . . .*
> *to land on cool dark clover carpet green*

But this book reaches beyond barroom and barrio to political concerns of the time. In "evening news" and "Para El Machete, Arturo Valdez," Vigil suggests that the political consciousness of Chicanos is informed by the means and ideologies of oppressed peoples of the Third World. One critic points out that although Vigil "celebrates revolutionary means to bring about liberal reform . . . she is silent about how the Movimiento will come to terms with what she has shown to be the source of Chicano oppression, racist capitalism."

This is one aspect that makes Vigil-Piñón's *The Computer Is Down* disconcerting. Here the work takes on a sophisticated sheen, celebrating the glittery image of the late twentieth century American city but, at the same time, bemoaning the cruel realities upon which that image rests. The images are pure Houstonian: the cars on the highway are spaceships ("it is imperative / that you own a spacecraft" the first poem begins), the population hails from every country on the map, and the realities of daily life are financial ("it is imperative that you verify the balance" begins the third poem) as the poet keeps encountering MBank, IRS, Muzak, MPACT, and pre-recorded hold messages interrupted by "a sweet melodic voice . . . 'Thank you for calling Southwest Airlines / this is Cindy, may I help you?'"

It is a world of many parts, most of which have nothing to do with the glitz of the surface image. There is the mother sitting with her toddler on a trash can, for example, "taking slow drags from a cigarette just lit / though thin lips painted frosted pink / her pallid freckled face expressionless / mascaraed blue-gray eyes / fixed in a distant gaze." Around the corner are teenagers on the "threshold to alternative success," gospel street preachers haranguing, business people rushing by blind. Yet it is a place of constant intercourse, where "the weak, the strong / the damned, the blessed / the wretched, the fortunate / the shrewd, the innocent" coexist, holding "their ground / their niche secure / in a scheme of existence / based on time that must advance." And all the while:

> *the headlines will tell*
> *of likely and unlikely victims*
> *Darwinian theory affirmed*
> *the world as it's always been*
> *wherein laws*
> *can instantly become nonfunctional*
> *like a computer, down*
> *a bankrupt bank of objective intelligence.*

Another disconcerting aspect of *The Computer Is Down* is that the culture Vigil-Piñón describes is rootless. There is no introspective questioning of the poet's role in life; in this place the poet has no role. There is no underlying bilingual *cultura* here, only doublespeak and double standards. This harsh reality affects Vigil-Piñón's ear, formerly so attuned to the music of language: she reaches a Cassandra-like screech. Her attention to the linguistic environment of Houston sometimes affects her natural voice as well, leaving us uncomfortable and dissatisfied. Vigil-Piñón's book is an experiment. Unfortunately, though, her experimentation with poetic verisimilitude to this particular reality did not produce great poetry; it did, however, "push the envelope" of poetic possibility in Texas.

Carmen Tafolla

Carmen Tafolla is another multi-talented writer whose natural poetic idiom derives from a west-side San Antonio barrio. Alex Haley once called Tafolla "a world class writer," and she is. Born in 1951, she attended substandard local public schools until she was given a four-year scholarship to Keystone, a private high school for gifted students. Here she learned that her beloved barrio was not seen by all in the same light; in fact, this encounter with fear born out of cultural ignorance probably formed the basis of Tafolla's lifelong work in support of multicultural education and understanding.

Her contribution to the 1972 Creative Arts of San Antonio Project was a compilation of folktales and folklore gathered from elderly residents of west-side San Antonio. In 1973, after receiving her M.A. in education from Austin College in Sherman, Tafolla joined the faculty of Texas Lutheran College as director of the Mexican American Studies Center, a position she held for three years. In 1976 she coordinated a program producing Multi-Media Parent Training Packages for the Southwest Educational Development Laboratory, and soon afterward she became head writer for the pioneering bilingual children's television program, *Sonrisas*, nationally recognized at the time and since as a major step forward in this area of education. She received her Ph.D. in bilingual education from the University of Texas in 1981. Tafolla taught at the University of Texas, was associate professor of women's studies at the University of California at Fresno, and served as special assistant to the president of Northern Arizona University, at Flagstaff. Since 1990, Tafolla has lived in McAllen and in Phoenix. When she is not writing or giving poetry readings, Tafolla is an educational consultant and speaker, in this country and in Europe.

Tafolla's publications are numerous and cover a broad range of genres. Besides poetry and television scripts, she has written *To Split a Human: Mitos, Machos y la Mujer Chicana* (1984), a sociological study of Chicanas, and numerous articles on bilingual education and Hispanic art and literature. *Patchwork Colcha*, a bilingual collection of poems, stories, and songs for children, was published in 1987;

several of Tafolla's children's stories and poems appear in newer editions of elementary and secondary school readers from the major textbook companies. Her most recent major publication is *Sonnets to Human Beings and Other Selected Works,* edited by Ernesto Padilla (1992). This large collection of poems, short fiction, and essays by Tafolla also contains fifteen essays about Tafolla and her work.

Like other Tejana poets, she began by publishing her first poems in *Caracol* (1975). Soon her works were included in the University of Texas Center for Mexican American Studies anthology *Hembra* and in *Travois: An Anthology of Texas Poets* (both 1976). Her poems appeared, with that of Cecilio Garcia-Camarillo and Reyes Cardenas, in *Get Your Tortillas Together* (1976), a small but important publication, and have appeared regularly in numerous anthologies and literary magazines since. Her first full-length collection of poetry was *Curandera* (1983), which Chicana scholars regard as a core document in several respects, but primarily for the skill of its code switching. The most notable poems in the book are the five in "Los Corts," each written in a distinct voice derived in part from Tafolla's 1972 research into the folklore of the west-side barrios. Her collection "La Isabela de Guadalupe y otras chucas" was published in *Five Poets of Aztlan* in 1985, which also contains several revised poems from *Curandera.* Tafolla's manuscript poem sequence, "Sonnets to Human Beings," won first place in the 1987 National Chicano Literary Competition.

Tafolla's use of code switching in her poetry is similar to that of Evangelina Vigil, which is to say she uses a particular west-side bilingual dialect rather than simply inserting Spanish words or phrases for effect or to make a point. When she uses Spanish in poems of personal statement, not evoking any particular aspect of Chicano culture, however, her Spanish is a rich and flawless Castilian. As Rolando Hinojosa wrote in his preface to *Curandera:* "Tafolla sabe quien es y de donde viene; conoce y aprecia sus raices mexico-texanas, maneja que no manipula el idioma, y lo encaja donde cabe y debe. Parece cosa facil pero no lo es." ("Tafolla knows who she is and where she comes from; she understands and appreciates her Mexico-Texan roots, she controls her dialect without manipulating it, and she uses it when it is fitting and proper. This may seem easy, but it is not.") Santiago Daydí-Tolson identified "at least three language registers, perhaps four, depending on the persona adopted as the speaker of the poem." That this is true of her English as well should give pause to critics who would make too much of any poet's use of two languages. More than being writers, true poets are listeners and observers, and Tafolla has excellent ears and eyes. As she herself has pointed out in the anthology *Common Bonds:*

> My favorite style and approach are to write in the voices of people, to let poetry or prose come in their words and thoughts, and to let it come in their language and accent, be that good-ol'-boy English or my native language, Tex-Mex. I like my works to understand, to profundizar, people—to reveal our strengths and our weaknesses, our struggles and victories and failures and flaws, and, ultimately, our beauty as human beings.

Many of Tafolla's most memorable poems in *Curandera* recount her middle-school experiences, most of which focus on her and her peers' "struggles and victories." In "and when I dream dreams . . ." the young poet witnesses the rapid demise of students who flee from the school's institutionalized subservience training (where "the lockers of our minds . . . were always jammed stuck") into whatever alleys of hope or oblivion offer themselves—into the military because "war looked easy (compared to here)," into the workplace, where a twice-pregnant fifteen-year-old works sixteen-hour days, into drugs, into "dropout droppings, prison pains, and cop car's bulleted brains." These things haunt the poet who hangs her "honorary / junior school diploma" next to her Ph.D. because it means:

> *I graduated*
> *from you*
> *and when I dream dreams,*
> *—how I wish my dreams*
> *had graduated too.*

Regarding her first encounters with "serious" education, we can hear Tafolla's blood boil in "Quality Literature," a prose-poem vignette. The student asks her professor to let her write a paper on a Chicano author, only to be told that "Chicano literature simply isn't quality," after which she is directed to read "Beckett's En Attendant Godot, which is really superb in its handling of the alienation of the individual in society." A litany of the best Chicano authors follows, all of which are deemed inappropriate until the professor erupts:

"But it hasn't even been critiqued in the *PMLA!* and until it's been critiqued in the *PMLA,* I can't say it's quality literature!

And the professor walked off into a semi-colon . . . as the face of the student became an epic poem."

This sort of bravado is capable of flights of fancy as well, as when, in "Voyage," Tafolla imagines herself as the fourth of Columbus's ships. She delights in the gulls, the sunsets, the "moonbreezes and starvision nights" while the other ships "set their charts" and "point their prows":

> *I was the fourth ship.*
> *Playfully in love with the sea,*
> *Eternally entwined with the sky,*
> *Forever vowed to my voyage,*
> *While the others shouted "Land."*

Similarly, in her "La Isabela de Guadalupe" collection, she imagines the character of Marina, la Malinche, differently from most other Chicana or Chicano writers. "Yo soy la Malinche," she declares, and she is as feisty as was the poet's fourth ship—and daringly prophetic as well. "Not as others have defined her," wrote Elizabeth Ordóñez, "but as she defines herself: daring, decisive, and visionary. In the final lines of the poem, the reborn Malinche issues a cry from gut level to replace the violated, passively silent flesh of the old Malinche with the prophetic greatness of the new":

> *But Chingada, I was not.*
> > *Not tricked, not screwed, not traitor.*
> *For I was not traitor to myself—*
> > *I saw a dream*
> > > *and I reached it.*
> > > > *Another world . . .*
> > > > > *la raza*
> > > > > > *la raaaaaaaa-zaaaaa*

Rosemary Catacalos

Another Tejana writer to emerge from the barrios of San Antonio— and in turn to celebrate them in poetry—is Rosemary Catacalos. Born in 1944 in St. Petersburg, Florida, where her father was stationed during World War II, she returned with her family to their hometown as soon as the war ended. Family is a constant theme in her work. Her poem in celebration of her Greek grandfather, "Katakalos," is one of her best known, and from it we learn a number of the things this poet holds sacred: she has a deep and abiding love for tradition, for sincere religious ritual, and, almost conversely, for the entrepreneurial spirit, all of which have played substantial roles in her own life and art.

A solitary child, Catacalos began keeping a journal at an early age and was an avid denizen of the local public library. Other than the two years when she attended San Antonio College, Catacalos is an autodidact, though this has rarely impeded her ability to function in academic circles. (She is currently director of the Poetry Center at San Francisco State University, the largest poetry archive in the United States.) During the 1960s and early 1970s she worked as a copywriter, an arts publicist, and a newspaper reporter. And, spurred on by John Igo, an English professor she encountered in college whose interest in her poetry never flagged, she became confident of her abilities as a poet. Her first poems appeared in a University of Houston literary magazine in 1970. From 1974 to 1985, while working in various arts-in-education programs in Texas, though mainly in San Antonio, Catacalos published poems in numerous magazines and anthologies around the country. Beyond a few initial poems, however, Catacalos never submitted her work to magazines or any other publisher. Believing that poetry, like all art, should stand on its own, she gave readings and published only when asked, letting her work "gradually seep into the consciousness of editors and readers." It did. After she received repeated requests for manuscripts, her books were published.

Because Catacalos had edited more than thirty chapbooks of student writing, her last job with the arts-in-education program was to write and produce a cable-television series highlighting student creativity. Selected to sit on the panels of both the National Endowment for the Arts and the Texas Commission on the Arts, Catacalos became increasingly involved with the local arts scene, until in 1984–85 she chaired the San Antonio Arts and Cultural Advisory Panel, a job requiring hundreds of volunteer hours but affecting the direction of public arts funding and promotion in the city for the ensuing decade.

In 1984, Catacalos's first two books were published, *As Long as It Takes,* a limited-edition fine press chapbook, and *Again for the*

First Time, which won the Texas Institute of Letters poetry prize. She also received the Institute's Dobie-Paisano Fellowship, which she took up in January, 1986. Catacalos returned to San Antonio later that year to begin a three-year stint as director of the literature program for the Guadalupe Cultural Arts Center, during which time she redesigned the Annual Texas Small Press Bookfair, renaming it the San Antonio Inter-American Bookfair, an event that soon gained national prominence for its multicultural focus. In 1989, awarded a Wallace Stegner Writing Fellowship, Catacalos departed Texas for Stanford University.

Whether Catacalos plans to return to her hometown or not is an open question, but it is certain that San Antonio will not stay out of her poetry. Those who visited her shady home only a block from a virtually untouched section of the San Antonio River described it as a "serene shrine"—filled with books, plants, and iconographic mementos. "Like having tea inside a poem," one fellow poet put it. This creation of intensely poetic personal space is paralleled by the sense of place in her poetry—the kind of sense that can transform into cosmic stages those mundane places we usually ignore. Thus, in *Again for the First Time,* she draws street names, churches, bars, local markets, and landmarks together into a kaleidoscopic world inhabited both by such mythic figures as Ariadne, Dionysios, and Odysseus and by Lupe of the J&A Ice House, a downtown "bum" called the Dog Man, and Mr. and Mrs. Ozdabeano Maldonado, who keep "whirling their eternal polka" across the poet's walls. Natural companions for this "East Side Meskin Greek" who grew up where:

> *. . . every day at noon*
> *black girls at Ralph Waldo Emerson Junior High School*
> *made a sacred drum of the corner mailbox, beatin'*
> *on it to raise the dead. And make them dance.*

Like a curandera of the soul, Catacalos leads her companions on a journey of healing and mourning through the twentieth century, trying to understand and comfort the dead children of Atlanta, the multitudes dying in Latin America and the Middle East, "where the oldest angels / have always known it would come to this." Drawing on her Greek and Mexican ancestry, Catacalos can witness all the midwives of Aztlán "polishing / their instrumental silver hands," while she seeks, with Odysseus, to "couple with time"—finding that "the world's

clocks and calendars / are splattered with the blood / of would-be
lovers." Then there is the matter of personal betrayal and the death
of loved ones. Early in the book she is almost overcome:

> *Ancianos, forgive me.*
> *All my life you have given me*
> *songs and lessons and hope . . . .*
> *Now because I have lost my way,*
> *lost what you taught me to celebrate,*
> *I betray you.*
> *Ancianos, forgive me this failure.*
> *You are innocent of it.*
> *I do not deserve you.*
> *It is I who have died badly.*

Yet there is a gathering of strength throughout the book, almost a
manual acquisition of faith:

> *We will all be learning the moonstruck*
> *skills of gauze and hot water*
> *again for the first time.*

Woven among the poems in *Again for the First Time* is a series of
almost narrative pieces wherein the poet assumes the character of
Ariadne, the hapless princess who aided the escape of Theseus from
the labyrinth and later was abandoned by the hero on a deserted
island. This short sequence lies close to the painful heart of the book,
exemplifying in narrative terms what is more or less implicit in other
poems. Yet here too we find the poet's realization of personal strength
tempered with the acceptance of personal limitations:

> *I am, even if a princess, a simple weaver*
> *of spells. Sometimes of faith that*
> *there will be no more mazes, no more beasts.*

Or as she puts it in the opening lines of the final poem in the book:

> *So it's not that we relearn faith every*
> *day. It's that we need to reassign it. In*
> *that sense, Penelope was right. Every day*
> *doing and undoing the whole cloth. The middle,*
> *of course, would always be more tightly woven*

than the edges. And there would always be stray
threads. One takes this sort of thing for granted.

Calling herself a "simple weaver of spells," Catacalos sees poetry and the life it demands as "the chance to pitch stars / back into the heart of everything." She may be a simple weaver, but the products of her loom draw blood from stones and force the reader to acknowledge that "any candle can be lit at both ends." These are hard poems, hard words. Not hard in Eliot's sense of having to piece together a jigsaw puzzle of meaning, but hard meaning very real. Hard the way stones are hard, yet still can be shaped—chipped and chiseled until something useful and/or beautiful results: an arrowhead or a David.

Dave Oliphant once wrote that the poems in her collection "will astound, and not merely because they manipulate myth and reality so artfully but because they are spoken with the strength of a person who has learned to lament and give thanks at once." This undertone of wisdom gives the collection a feeling of deep seriousness, yet there are moments when the poet shakes herself, and reveals:

> *I know how to carve my own heart,*
> *lean from fat, fruit from sorrow,*
> *flower from seed and vice versa.*
> *I who sing so much about being woman.*
> *I who believe in worshipping my ancestors,*
> *in the serious game of enchantment,*
> *in the ultimate triumph of memory.*
> *When I feel myself beginning to stoop*
> *too heavily, I catch my head*
> *and throw it back on the sky.*

Rosemary Catacalos is unique among Tejana poets in that she rarely addresses issues or makes political points unless they fall within the scope of the particular imagery that is hers alone. An introspective, intensely personal art form, Catacalos's poetry somehow manages to be at once cosmopolitan and regional. The painstaking craft involved here is a sort of poetic alchemy, transmuting the base elements of life—thought, sorrow, joy—into a living thing that reaches deep into our consciousness and embeds itself there. According to Coleridge's dictum, real poetry goes through one like a spear; Catacalos's poetry nearly always brings blood.[14]

. . . *and so many more*

The five contemporary poets discussed above are among those who have shaped Tejana literature. However they are only the tip of the iceberg—and hardly all of that. Gloria Anzaldúa, for example, wrote the brilliant and difficult *Borderlands/La Frontera: The New Mestiza* (1987). An amalgam of poetry, anthropology, literary and cultural criticism, and autobiography, this volume both examines the conceptual implications of being caught between two cultures and traces the mythic and historical migrations of the Aztec peoples from what is now the southwestern United States into Mexico and back—and does so with style and considerable power. Anzaldúa is also the author of two children's books.

Other poet-critics are Inés Hernández-Tovar and María Herrera-Sobek. A native of Galveston, Hernández-Tovar is one of the masters of code-switching, the author of a striking if small collection of poems, *Con razón Corazón* (1977, 1987), and one of four Texas writers included in the *Longman Anthology of World Literature by Women, 1875–1975*. Half Chicana and half Nez Perce, Hernández-Tovar is active in Native American literary, cultural, and political activities and is a professor of Native American studies at the University of California at Davis. The founding editor of the Austin feminist/literary journal, *Hembra,* she is also the authority on Sara Estela Ramírez. Herrera-Sobek, one of the most important Chicana critics, has edited three texts, *Beyond Stereotypes: The Critical Analysis of Chicana Literature* (1985); with Helena Maria Viramontes, *Chicana Creativity and Criticism* (1987); and *Reconstructing a Chicano/a Literary Heritage: Hispanic Colonial Literature in the Southwest* (1993). A native of Rio Hondo, Herrera-Sobek is a professor at the University of California, Irvine. A collection of her poetry, "Naked Moon/Luna desnuda," is included in the important three-author anthology, *Three Times a Woman* (1989).

Several other poets deserve mention, though it would be impossible to discuss them all. Rebecca Gonzales is the author of *Slow Work to the Rhythm of Cicadas* (1985). Her poetry is consistently good and occasionally outstanding, as it is in "Workers in the Watermelon Fields," from which the book's title is derived. Born and raised in Laredo, Gonzales has taught in Beaumont since 1970. Xelina R. Urista is a native of San Antonio and the author of *Ku* (1977), a collection that documents the cultural oppression afflicting Chicanas living in such ostensibly liberal places as Austin, where "psychedelic lights / blasting progressive country music / massacre dreams de abuelitas and sleeping niños." A talented political poet, Urista lives in La Jolla, California. Unfortunately she has not published much recently. Alicia Gaspar de Alba hails from El Paso, which greatly affected the subject matter of her poetry, as it did Pat Mora's. Gaspar de Alba's collection *Beggar on the Córdoba Bridge* was included in *Three Times a Woman* in 1989. Her most recent work is *The Mystery of Survival and Other Stories* (1993). She taught at the University of Massachusetts, Boston, until moving to California, where she is working on several novels.

Today's best-known Tejana writer, Sandra Cisneros was born in Chicago, but since 1984 she has been an intermittent resident of Texas. She was director of the literature program at the Guadalupe Cultural Arts Center in San Antonio (1984–1985), she has held a Dobie-Paisano fellowship, and she has received numerous major awards, including two NEA writing fellowships and a MacArthur Foundation fellowship. Though she is widely recognized for her poetry, especially *My Wicked Wicked Ways* (1987) and *Loose Woman* (1994), Cisneros is without doubt the country's premier Chicana fiction writer. Her first book, *The House on Mango Street* (1984), has become an underground classic. Having sold out several printings with Arte Público Press, it was republished in 1991 by Random House together with a new collection, *Woman Hollering Creek and Other Stories,* which received the Lannan Award for Fiction and the PEN Center West Award for Fiction. Cisneros is the first Chicana to achieve such recognition, complete with large advances, extensive advertising, international tours, and translation into a dozen languages.

Denise Chávez, a prolific playwright and accomplished actress, burst onto the fiction scene in 1986 with *The Last of the Menu Girls,* a well-crafted collection of seven interrelated existential feminist stories, one of which had won the 1985 Puerto del Sol fiction award. *The Last of the Menu Girls* won the Steele Jones Fiction award in 1986, and Chávez has received two NEA writing fellowships and a Rockefeller Foundation fellowship. Born in New Mexico, Chávez has spent much of her life in Texas, including a stint teaching at the University of Houston. Currently she lives in Las Cruces. Her lengthy novel, *Face of an Angel,* was published by Farrar, Straus and Giroux in 1994.

Until recently, fiction writers of the quality of Cisneros and Chávez were rare among Tejanas. Estela Portillo Trambley of El Paso, one of these exceptions, has been publishing short stories for more than two decades. *Rain of Scorpions and Other Writings* (1975) contains her short story "The Paris Gown," which is especially well regarded and often anthologized. *Trini,* her long-anticipated novel, came out in 1986. But Trambley is even better known as a dramatist, with several published/produced prize-winning plays to her credit, including "The Day of the Swallows" (1971), "Sun Image" (1979), "Sor Juana" (1985), and "Backlight," which took second place in the Hispanic American playwrights' competition at the 1985 New York Shakespeare Festival. Trambley won a Quinto Sol Award for literature in 1972, and in 1973 she edited the famed Chicana issue of *El Grito.* Thus for more than a decade she was one of the most visible Chicana writers in the country, and her work received considerable critical attention. She was, for example, the only woman included in Bruce-Novoa's crucial 1980 work, *Chicano Authors: Inquiry by Interview.*

Among the several Tejana fiction writers who have appeared in the last ten years are Roberta Fernández, Irene Beltrán Hernández, E. D. Santos, and Enedina Cásarez Vásquez. Roberta Fernández's *Intaglio: A Novel in Six Stories* (1990) is a magical-realist novel, each story a different character's voice. This work was awarded first prize by the Multicultural Publishers Exchange. A native of Laredo, Fernández has taught in colleges and universities from California to Massachusetts. As senior editor for Arte Público Press, in Houston, she edited the anthology *In Other Words: Literature by Latinas of the United States* (1994). She is now a professor at the University of Houston.

Irene Beltrán Hernández, a resident of Dallas, was raised in the Rio Grande Valley. Her two novels, *Across the Great River* (1989) and *Heartbeat, Drumbeat* (1992), are among the few Hispanic works for young adults. Both works show considerable promise. E. D. Santos has written the only Chicana hippie novel, *On the Road Too* (1988). Santos, who dropped out of Texas in 1966 at age seventeen to head for San Francisco, recounts the drugs/sex/rock-'n'-roll adventures of a young Tejana heroine in this often hilarious, occasionally touching, picaresque period piece. Santos lives in Hondo, where she runs La Sombra Publishing Company. Her second book, *Mesquite Sighs,* was published in 1991. San Antonio native Enedina Cásarez Vásquez is well known as a painter and illustrator. Her *nichos* (decorated box-like constructions resembling altarpieces) have been shown at the Smithsonian and in Europe and are widely collected. Vasquez is the author of *Recuerdos de una niña* (1980) and several stories in magazines, most notably "The House of Quilts." She received the Hidalgo de Bexar Prize and the Marguerite Davenport Humanities Prize. Vasquez is one of the founding members of Mujeres Grandes, a Chicana writing/performance group. Other members of the group include Angela De Hoyos, Mary Guerrero-Milligan, and Sheila Sánchez Hatch. Rocky Gámez and Adela Alonso both had stories in *Common Bonds*. Gámez, a native of Pharr, now teaches in San Francisco. Her stories appear in several Chicana anthologies. Alonso, a poet, was born and raised in Mexico but has lived in Texas for almost ten years. Her story in *Common Bonds* was her first published fiction.

New Tejana writers are appearing almost more rapidly than they can be chronicled. Sheila Sánchez Hatch, a deft and sophisticated short story writer who edited *Tierra Norte: A Collection of Works from North Texas* (1994) was included in *Daughters of the Fifth Sun*. Her first book, *Guadalupe and the Kaleidoscopic Screamer,* was published in 1996. Deborah Paredez, former editor of *Trinity Review,* now finishing her Ph.D. at Northwestern University, and Nicole Pollentier, currently studying at the University of Texas, were the two youngest contributors to the Milligan, De Hoyos, Guerrero-Milligan anthology, *Daughters of the Fifth Sun: A Collection of Latina Fiction and Poetry* (1995). Both also were included in Milligan's anthology, *This Promiscuous Light: Young Women Poets of San Antonio* (1996). Victoria Garcia Galaviz, winner of the 1995 PBS-televised San Antonio Poetry Slam, likewise appears in *This Promiscuous Light.*

There are so many others. It says a great deal that, in a book in which most authors have been discussed in their own individual chapters, Tejana writers are grouped in a single essay. When *Texas Women Writers* was first conceived, nearly a decade ago, virtually no Tejana works were taught in university literature classes anywhere in Texas. Some of these works are now considered core components of contemporary American literature. It goes without saying that there will be more.

NOTES

1. In this article the term "Tejana" will be used most often, though it is not the most frequently used term among members of the group it identifies. Although the term "Mexican-American" is current, it is objectionable to many on the grounds that it implies second-class citizenship. (Polish-Americans, for example, are rarely so identified.) "Chicana," which refers specifically to individuals of Mexican mestizo ancestry, is rapidly losing currency as the period of overt Chicano politicization recedes. "Hispanic," the term preferred by governmental and educational institutions, is generally considered objectionable because technically it refers only to individuals of Spanish extraction. "Hispana" is used by scholars only in reference to the colonial period. "Latina" is the preferred term as of this writing, allowing as it does for multiple countries of origin. Tejanas are defined as women of Hispanic lineage who either were born in Texas or spent a considerable portion of their writing careers here.

2. See *Essays on la mujer,* ed. Rosaura Sánchez and Rosa Martínez Cruz (Los Angeles: UCLA/Chicano Studies Center Publications, 1977). The breadth of topics addressed in this anthology—from "Participación de las mujeres en la sociedad prehispánica" and "The Chicana Labor Force" to "The Role of the Chicana Within the Student Movement"—indicates the scope of the scholarly explosion that occurred at this time.

3. See Marta Cotera's *Diosa y Hembra: The History and Heritage of Chicanas in the United States* for a more extensive history. See also her *Profile of the Mexican American Woman.*

4. Carolyn Ashbaugh, *Lucy Parsons: American Revolutionary.* Albert and Lucy Parsons were extremely close, and Lucy's *Life of Albert R. Parsons, with Brief History of the Labor Movement in America* contains much information on the author's life and views as well as those of her subject. Mrs. Parsons most likely was a double minority, half Hispanic and half Black, which makes her accomplishments even more remarkable.

5. Marian Arkin and Barbara Shollar, eds., *Longman Anthology of World Literature by Women, 1875–1975,* 199–202. Of the nearly three hundred women writers from more than fifty countries selected by the editors for inclusion in this major anthology, the four Texas representatives are all Hispanic: Leonor Villegas de Magnon, Sara Estela Ramírez, Angela De Hoyos, and Inés Hernández. See also Clara Lomas, "Mexican Precursors of Chicana Feminist Writing," in Candelaria, ed., *Multiethnic Literature of the United States,* 21–33.

6. Juanita Luna Lawhn, "Feminism in *La Prensa*: Women's Response to the Ideology of *El Mexico de Afuera,*" and "The Generation of *El Mexico de Afuera* in San Antonio, Texas," which introduces a bibliography of Hispanic San Antonio publications. Both papers, part of Lawhn's ongoing research into Hispanic Texas-Mexican women writers, are subject to periodic updates; they are on file in the library of San Antonio College. See also Juanita Luna Lawhn, "*El Regidor* and *La Prensa*: Impediments to Women's Self-Definition." In 1996,

Lawhn was awarded a Rockefeller Humanities Research fellowship to extend her studies in this area.

7. These general conclusions are based both on numerous interviews and discussions with Chicana writers conducted by this author over the past fifteen years and on published interviews conducted by other critics.

8. Juan Bruce-Novoa, *Retrospace: Collected Essays on Chicano Literature*. See pages 132–45 for an excellent discussion of the canonical and noncanonical texts of Chicano literature.

9. See *Current Biography 1949,* 455–56. Amy Freeman Lee, "Playmaker of Mexico," *San Antonio Express News,* June 4, 1939. "Josephina [sic] Niggli" in Spearman, ed., *The Carolina Playmakers: The First 50 Years.* Obituary [by John Igo] in *North San Antonio Times,* December 22, 1983.

10. Josefina Niggli, "Call Them Dreams."

11. Readers interested in code switching would do well to read Tino Villanueva's introduction to the first issue of *Imagine: International Chicano Poetry Journal* (Boston, 1984), pp. vii–xxxvii.

12. Unless otherwise noted, all translations from the Spanish are by the author of this essay.

13. Norma Alarcon, "Interview with Pat Mora," 121. See also Sarah Nawrocki's study of Mora, in "Asking Their Own Questions: Chicana Poets in the 1980s."

14. See Bryce Milligan, "Raising the Dead." See also one of the few interviews Catacalos has granted: "Catacalos versed in hardships of poetry 'job'," by Steve Bennett.

A DEVELOPING TRADITION

African-American Writers

LOU HALSELL RODENBERGER

In her memoir, which appears in *Growing Up in Texas* (1972), Lorece Williams recaptures her childhood in a Black community near Luling, in Caldwell County. She remembers most vividly her remarkable grandmother, midwife and comforter of grandchildren, who once held a shotgun on a white man who periodically had ridden his horse through her flower beds. Williams describes this strong woman, whom she called Mamma: "[She] may not have been a one-woman revolutionary, but she was no white man's patsy either. There was power in her the day she confronted Mr. M_____ at our gate."

Williams was in the vanguard of African-American women writers in Texas who began to gain recognition in the 1970s. At the time, Williams was a faculty member in the Graduate School of Social Work at Our Lady of the Lake College in San Antonio. A few years later another teacher, Dorothy Redus Robinson, wrote a book-length memoir of her experiences in the Black rural schools of South and East Texas and the first days of desegregation in the Palestine schools, where she finished her career. In *The Bell Rings at Four: A Black Teacher's Chronicle of Change* (1978), Robinson shares both her dedication to teaching and, perhaps unconsciously, her expertise in human relations during a difficult era in Texas education.

Setting the benchmark for writers such as Williams and Robinson was Maud Cuney-Hare, one of the first African-American women native to Texas to receive attention for her writing abilities. Born in Galveston in 1874, she was educated as a musician at the New England Conservatory, in Boston, and was best known as a music historian. A collector of Creole songs and a folklorist as well as a pianist, Cuney-Hare published several books, including an anthology of poetry and a biography of her father. Her *Negro Musicians and Their Music* (1936) provided considerable information on the development of African-American traditions in music.

Another pioneer among African-American women writers in Texas was Ada DeBlanc Simond, longtime teacher, Texas State Department of Health employee, and community leader in Austin. Simond's career as author began after her retirement when she began creating a series of books for young people. Narrated by Mae Dee Lewis, whom Simond identified as a childhood friend, the six stories explore the African-American experience in Texas during the early 1900s—weddings, Juneteenth celebrations, holidays. Simond said, "Mae Dee speaks for all of us from the generation born in the early 1900s or late 1800s."

The first of the series, *Let's Pretend: Mae Dee and Her Family Go to Town*, appeared in 1977. In 1982 the Austin City Council recognized Simond with a day-long celebration of her accomplishments and the Black Arts Alliance presented her with the Mattie B. White Award. In 1980 the Texas Historical Commission gave her series a special Texas Award as an outstanding publication on a historical subject. Ada Simond was inducted into the Texas Woman's Hall of Fame in 1986. At the time of her induction, Simond said she wrote her series for African-American children learning to cope in newly integrated public schools in the 1970s. She added, "I wanted blacks to have a strong image among others and themselves."

Early African-American women poets were recognized by folklorist and college teacher John Mason Brewer, who included poems by Texans Berniece Love Wiggins, Maurine L. Jeffrey, Birdelle Wycoff Ranson, Lauretta Holman Gooden, and Gwendolyn Bennett in his *Heralding Dawn: An Anthology of Verse* (1936). In "Gathering Like Heat: Black Writing in Texas," an essay in *The Texas Humanist* (April, 1980), the poet Lorenzo Thomas discusses African-American literary achievement in Texas. Among "the new Texas voices" receiving recognition in the 1970s, Thomas cites J. E. Franklin, Houston short-fiction author and playwright, who was acclaimed for her play *Black Girl* (1970). The women poets he names who were beginning to receive recognition include Lacy Chimney, Edith Brandon Humphrey, Glo Dean Baker, and Elaine Taylor.

Thomas's greatest praise is reserved for Harryette Mullen, "by far the most impressive of the younger black writers in Texas." Mullen, a Dobie-Paisano Fellow, is both poet and short-story writer. Her poetry has been collected in *Tree Tall Woman* (1981) and several poetry anthologies. Her stories appear in *Her Work, South by Southwest,* and *Common Bonds.* Born in Fort Worth, Mullen graduated from the University of Texas and earned a doctorate from the University of California at Santa Cruz. She has lived at various times in Houston and Galveston and in Beaumont, California. Presently she lives in Ithaca, New York, where she teaches in the English Department at Cornell University. Her short stories, including "Tenderhead" in *Common Bonds,* often chronicle the day-to-day lives of girls growing up and unable to fit into the role of lady. She once said, "I was fascinated by those black women in the community who had no interest whatsoever in ladylikeness."

Other African-American women whose short stories appear in *Common Bonds* and who are gaining recognition for their work are Njoki McElroy, Hermine Pinson, and Sunny Nash. McElroy, who teaches alternately at Northwestern University and Southern Methodist University, is also a businesswoman, head of a cosmetics firm. In "The Ninth Day of May," McElroy recaptures the horrors of the 1930 race riot in Sherman, which her grandparents experienced. Hermine Pinson, a native of Beaumont, earned her doctorate from Rice University and now teaches at William and Mary College. Most often published as a poet, she has works in a number of anthologies, including *Kentecloth: African American Voices in Texas* (1995), the first volume in a series to be issued by the Center for Texas Studies at the University of North Texas. (The Center for Texas Studies also devoted the 1994 edition of the journal *New Texas* to works by Texas African-American writers.)

In recent years, Sunny Nash has developed her considerable talents as a short-story writer, although she began her writing career as a journalist. Among the first Black women to graduate from Texas A&M University, Nash grew up in an African-American enclave called Candy Hill in Bryan, and many of her stories reflect that experience.

When Nash received Suzanne Comer's request for a contribution to the anthology *Common Bonds,* she decided to concentrate on writing fiction. Since then she has published "Too High for Birds," in *New Growth/2,* and "Amen," her story of a child's keen judgment of a fake faith healer, in the spring 1995 issue of *Southwestern American Literature.* Nash also writes a syndicated newspaper column about life in Candy Hill, and her essay "A Mission Completed for Doll," first published in the Sunday *Texas Magazine* of the *Houston Chronicle,* appears in *State Lines* (1993), a collection of *Texas Magazine* essays edited by Ken Hammond. Her story "Sanko's World" won the Houston Public Library Literary Award after publication in the *Houston Post.* Nash has also established her reputation as a photographer with the 1992 national tour of her exhibit "Shopping for Hope: A Photographic Study of Back Street Churches in America." Nash's first book, *Bigmama Didn't Shop at Woolworth's,* was published by Texas A&M University Press in 1996.

One of the best-known contemporary African-American women with Texas connections is J. California Cooper, who resides in East Texas. Although she has established a national reputation as both a short-story writer and a novelist, she also was named Best Black Playwright of 1978 for her play *Strangers,* one of seventeen she has written. Acclaimed in 1991 for her novel *Family,* the saga of a slave woman's descendants, Cooper is the author of four collections of short stories: *A Piece of Mine* (1984), *Homemade Love* (1987), which received the American Book Award in 1989, *Some Soul to Keep* (1988), and *The Matter Is Life* (1991).

Cooper's stories chronicle the lives of feisty African-American women who prevail over unfaithful husbands, hard times, and poor self-image to discover for themselves lives worth living. First-person narrators, often experienced old women wise in the ways of the world, share these stories as observers. Their philosophical asides add dimension to Cooper's fiction as they share their pithy, often humorous, commentary on life and the nature of humankind. Alice Walker, who published Cooper's first collection, calls such a woman She-Who-Listens-to-Other-Women or "sister-witness." Never precise about place and vague about the circumstances of her early life, Cooper creates narrators and situations that could occur in Nash's Candy Hill or any other deep East Texas region.

Cooper's most recent work is a novel, *In Search of Satisfaction*

(1994). In the introductory "Author's Note," Cooper advises her readers not "to depend on anyone else for your happiness." Then she concludes with an explanation of the novel's title, "I believe you can survive anything and move on . . . with the right tools. Move on to seek, to find what you need . . . in the search of satisfaction." In this novel, Cooper builds her plot around the lives of half-sisters, both daughters of a freed slave, but separated in their kinship by the fact that one sister is daughter of a white woman. An engaging speaker, Cooper has been recipient of numerous awards including the James Baldwin Award, the University of Massachusetts 1990 Woman of the Year Award, and the Literary Lion Award from the American Library Association.

Another talented contemporary writer, Rosalyn M. Story, is a violinist with the Fort Worth Symphony Orchestra. After publishing her history of African-American women opera singers, *And So I Sing: African-American Divas of Opera and Concert* in 1990, she received the 1994 Betty Greene Fiction Award for best short story published in the journal *New Texas 94*. Her story, "Quiet As It's Kept," reflects the mixed emotions of an African-American career woman who learns secrets of her past she never knew until she visits home.

A remarkable Black woman's story unfolds in *I Am Annie Mae, The Personal Story of A Black Texas Woman* (1983), the oral history of Annie Mac Hunt recorded and edited by Ruthe Winegarten. Produced later as a musical by Naomi Carrier, an African-American lyricist from Houston, Annie Mae's story went into second printing within a few months. Winegarten has since published *Black Texas Women: 150 Years of Trial and Triumph* (1995), which provides a much-needed social context for the accomplishments of African-American women in Texas.

African-American women writers in Texas continue to develop their talents as publishing outlets grow. Phyllis W. Allen of Fort Worth won the *Kentecloth* 1995 Short Fiction Award for her short story "The Shopping Trip." More than twenty African-American women writers, including poets, short-fiction writers, and essayists appear in *Kentecloth*. In her novel *Black Gold* (1994), a Houston writer, Anita Richmond Bunkley, narrates the story of two Black families who strike oil in Mexia. Bunkley's first novel, *Emily: the Yellow Rose* (1989), narrates the story of the mulatto Emily West, who in Texas legend kept the Mexican general Santa Anna occupied while Sam

Houston led the attack against the Mexican troops at San Jacinto.

Angela Shelf Medearis of Austin has written five books for children. Her first, *Picking Peas for a Penny* (1990), was published by State House Press in Austin, but national publishers produced the next four. Medearis has said that she tries to fill a gap in children's literature for African-American children. It is a gap that Ada Simond recognized when she wrote her *Let's Pretend* series in the 1970s.

At least seven San Antonio writers have published their work. Antoinette V. Franklin, author of short stories and poetry, received the Literature of Merit Award from the San Antonio Ethnic Arts Society in 1993. Her poetry has appeared in a number of journals. Olga Samples Davis, known for her storytelling, is also a playwright and poet. Her collection of poetry and prose, *A Time to Be Born,* is in its third printing. Fatimah, pseudonym of Debra F. Medows, a graduate of Incarnate Word College in San Antonio, is a poet and playwright. She is a performance artist as well. Her choreopoem, an autobiographical sketch she titled *donkey face's soliloquies have arrived / & it's not just the poet / but the poem itself,* was produced at the San Antonio Little Theatre and became a two-part television series on ART TV. Peggy L. Mott's poetry has been published in several journals, including *Concho River Review.* Local historian Susie E. Piper and poet Linda Everett Moye also are San Antonio residents. Publisher LaRita Booth Pryor has provided a compendium of information for Black writers with publication of *The African-American Writer's Digest: How and Where to Sell What You Write* (1994).

As African-American women writers in Texas develop a tradition unique in origin and history, scholarly studies of the role they have played in the literary life of Texas surely will be initiated. One African-American playwright, Elizabeth Brown-Guillory, a professor at the University of Houston, analyzes a number of plays by African-American women in *Their Place on the Stage: Black Women Playwrights in America* (1988). She includes a study of Ntozake Shange, a playwright, novelist, and poet who taught at the University of Houston several years. Much of her work is set in other regions, but Shange wrote one book she called *Ridin' the Moon in Texas* (1987). Brown-Guillory includes her own play, "Mam Phyllis," in her anthology, *Wines in the Wilderness: Plays by African American Women from the Harlem Renaissance to the Present* (1990).

LITERARY TRADITIONS IN WORKS BY AFRICAN-AMERICAN PLAYWRIGHTS

PATRICIA R. WILLIAMS

From the early musicals and dramatic creations of Maude Cuney-Hare to the more recent theatrical productions of J. E. Franklin, Celeste Colson-Walker, Cheryl Hawkins, and Dianne Tucker, who writes under the penname of diannetucker, the voices of gifted African-American women in Texas have emerged in their creation of drama. In 1936 a Galveston native named Maud Cuney-Hare began a little-theater movement among the Negroes of Boston with the production of her original drama, *Antar*. Not until the 1950s, however, did the little-theater movement for Texas African-Americans begin to develop.

Poet and playwright Vivian Ayers, a South Carolinian by birth, initiated Houston little-theater activity for African-Americans in the 1950s with her play *Bow Boly*. Another of her plays, *The Marriage Ceremony,* which could be called a pageant, is penned in poetic style and written for presentation "in an open field," as the playwright recommended. The play emphasizes the communal or "tribal" involvement in the ceremony, reflecting the shared experience of African-Americans.

In the 1970s, Alma Carrier wrote *Coming to a Head*, a tragicomedy, but not until the 1980s did African-American women playwrights in Texas begin to depict broader social themes in more intimately domestic subjects. What African-American women wrote at this time might be classified as contributing to the School for Domestic Drama. In particular, Celeste Colson-Walker's plays reflect features of domesticity. Walker, a native Houstonian, has become one of the rising stars among Texas playwrights over the past two decades. Her plays include *Sister, Sister; Once in a Wife Time; The Wreckin' Ball; Smokes Bayou; Spirit; Adam and Eve, Revisited; Camp Logan; Reunion in Bartersville;* and *Over Forty.* She has also written one teleplay, *A Christmas Gift.*

Walker's first play, *Sister, Sister,* was produced initially in Houston but later was performed, starring Esther Rolle, at the Wilshire Ebell Theatre in Beverly Hills, California. One of Walker's better-known plays, *Reunion in Bartersville,* explores class conflicts among Blacks. The play's action revolves around a class reunion that turns into a detective-like search to solve a murder committed in the distant past. *Reunion* received five NAACP Award nominations and four of New York's Audelco Award nominations, winning in the category of best supporting actor.

Walker excels as a playwright of social commentary, developing both problem and domestic drama. In *Camp Logan,* however, she experiments with the presentation of social injustice in a historical play. This drama recounts the story of the 24th U.S. Infantry, an all-Black regiment whose members mutinied in Houston in August, 1917. Maintaining careful control of tone, Walker delivers a forceful social commentary in this tragedy.

Among her many dramas, Walker also has produced musicals or symphonic dramas. *Over Forty* succeeded as a musical before audiences in San Francisco's Egypt Theatre and in New York.

Walker, whose versatility is evident in the wide range of themes and modes she has developed in her plays, established a tradition that continues in the work of two younger playwrights, J. E. Franklin and Cheryl Hawkins. Franklin, a Houston writer, and Hawkins, a native of New Orleans, have in common their training in creative writing at the University of Texas in Austin. Hawkins first majored in communications at Texas Southern University.

Franklin has garnered praise for her most famed work, *Black Girl,* an imaginative recreation of experiences from her own childhood. The play captures such realities as living as a stepchild, struggling with economic depression, and coping with the unrealized aspirations that befall the disadvantaged. Franklin's treatment is believable because of her realistic depiction of African-American folk culture. The screenplay of *Black Girl,* also primarily created by Franklin, was not nearly so successful.

The reflection of African-American folk culture contributes to the success of a musical created by Naomi Carrier of Houston from the autobiography, *I Am Annie Mae,* originally recorded and transcribed by Ruthe Winegarten for Annie Mae Hunt. A combination of history, domestic commentary, and social realism, the musical foreshadows development of a new genre in African-American drama.

Two of Cheryl Hawkins's plays demonstrate the versatility found in the African-American literary tradition. *Shattered Home,* a one-act play that is domestic drama, won the $5,000 Joseph Kesselring Award in 1984 and later was produced in New York. On the other hand *A Visit to the Earth* is a comedy that explores incongruities in the human condition. In a satire on planetary displacement of humankind, Hawkins defies an aesthetic tradition of African-American literature by placing the action of this play in real, rather than cyclic, time. The protagonist is an allegorized figure developing the theme of good and evil. A unique element of this play is the interplay of dialogue in Creole French, Vulgate Spanish, and Pidgin English. Hawkins's place in the literary tradition of African-American women writers in Texas is noteworthy.

The most recent approach to drama by African-American women playwrights, as diannetucker of Dallas demonstrates, is allegorized storytelling. Writing specifically for the Dallas Drama Company, Tucker points to a new direction in play production with drama that reflects the author's philosophical turn-of-thought. Among her plays performed in Dallas and Fort Worth are *Cat Cross, The Gamesmen, Profiles in Faith, Shoes, The Christmas Secret,* and *Mahalia Speaks . . . Remembering Martin.* Tucker shares her messages for action and her stories of wisdom and truth through poetic narration. The dramatist often employs the reversal techniques of tragedy to present her powerful didactic themes. In this sense she is loyal to the perspective of tragicomedy established by her sister forerunners.

Part 3
POETS

INTRODUCTION

Sam H. Dixon began work on *The Poets and Poetry of Texas: Biographical Sketches of the Poets of Texas, with Selections from Their Writings Containing Reviews Both Personal and Critical* in 1878 as a university student, but he reports in his preface that yellow fever "made sad havoc" of his ambitions. When his publisher fell victim to the disease, he asked that his manuscript be returned, but most of it never reached him. Determined, Dixon rewrote the work. He describes the difficulty of his task:

> When I first conceived the idea of writing this book, it was my object to collect the scattered gems of the Texas writers, and present them in a small volume. But when I began to investigate the subject of Texas authorship thoroughly, I found it impossible to encompass them in so small a space, and the book has grown to its present dimensions because I could not avoid it.

Dixon's collection of biographies and selected works of major poets, which finally appeared in 1885, was more than three hundred fifty pages.

Dixon's discovery that dozens of Texas writers had found, as early as the 1870s, that their metier was poetry writing is no surprise for those who have examined literary activity in nineteenth-century Texas.

From early girlhood, Texas's first woman writer, Mary Austin Holley, responded to each major event in her life by going to her desk and writing a poem. Two years before Holley's untimely death from yellow fever in 1846, her poem, "The Plea of Texas," was published in the New Orleans *Republican*. The poem, urging acceptance of Texas as a state in the Union, was reprinted in a number of Texas newspapers as its citizens pondered annexation.

Often Texas women poets in the nineteenth century were invited to read poems at special events. In 1878, Florence M. Gerald read "The Lays of the Republic" to an Austin audience at a benefit for yellow-fever victims. In Houston, Mrs. Lee C. Harby read a poem of welcome to open the 1880 annual meeting of the Texas Press Association and in so doing launched her career as a journalist, fiction writer, and poet. In 1891, Mrs. Mary Hunt McCaleb, who had been invited to read her poetry to the Texas Press Association several times, was elected official poet of that organization.

By 1921, Therese Kayser Lindsey, influential in Texas literary circles, visited in New York with Edwin Markham, then president of the Poetry Society of America, and learned of the success of the Poetry Society of South Carolina. She stopped in Charleston on her way home to learn more about organizing a state poetry society. In November of that year, after Lindsey enlisted the help of Hilton Ross Greer, Dallas journalist and poet, the Poetry Society of Texas was organized. In 1922, when the society had begun to grow, Lindsey established the "Old South Prize" to be awarded annually for best poem of any style by a member of the society. Lindsey's influence on the Texas literary scene still persists. In 1978 her daughter, Louise Lindsey Merrick, endowed a Therese Kayser Lindsey Chair at Southwest Texas State University in memory of her mother. The endowment made possible the Therese Kayser Lindsey Lecture Series, initiated that year by John Graves, R. G. Vliet, Larry McMurtry, and Lon Tinkle. The title of the 1978 lecture series was "The American Southwest: Cradle of Literary Art."

In 1925 the poetry society Lindsey had worked so diligently to initiate began a book-publication contest. Books by Grace Noll Crowell, Margaret Bell Houston, Jan Isbelle Fortune, Hazel Harper Harris, and Lexie Dean Robertson were among the first published.

Vaida Stewart Montgomery and her husband, Whitney, began one of the most durable poetry journals published in Texas in May, 1929, when the first issue of *Kaleidograph, A National Magazine of Poetry* came off the press. The Montgomerys established The Kaleidograph Press in Dallas, publishing collections of poetry exclusively, including many by Texas women. In 1934, Vaida Montgomery published *A Century with Texas Poets and Poetry,* which includes the history of the Poetry Society of Texas, biographies of contemporary poets and works by each. In 1932 the Texas legislature noticed the work of Texas poets and began selecting a state poet laureate, to be appointed every two years.

During the 1930s, women poets often in the news included Fay Yauger, Grace Noll Crowell, Karle Wilson Baker, Goldie Capers Smith, Siddie Joe Johnson, Ruth Averitte, and Albany poet Berta Hart Nance. Because Nance took three years extension work in English from the University of Texas with J. Frank Dobie's guidance, she claimed him as her mentor. He in turn quotes her well-known "Cattle" at the beginning of chapter 2 ("The Texas Breed") of *The Longhorns* (1941).

The following essays trace extensively the history of women poets in Texas. Among the many contemporary Texas women poets recognized for their art is Teresa Palomo Acosta, a teacher, short-story writer, and poet who has published in numerous journals and who received the Voertman Award for best poetry in *New Texas 93.* Susan Bright of Austin, editor and publisher of Plain View Press, has published several collections of her poems and is a recipient of two Austin Book Awards. Wendy Barker, a San Antonio resident and winner of a 1986 Creative Writing Fellowship from the National Endowment for the Arts, is author of *Winter Chickens and Other Poems* (1990). The poetry of Janet McCann, a Texas A&M English professor, appears often in national periodicals, as does the poetry of Carol Coffee Reposa, Violette Newton, Brenda Black White, Betty Adcock, Cynthia Macdonald, and Del Marie Rogers. Carol Cullar, editor of The Maverick Press, is publisher of the Southwest Poet Series as well as author of a number of poetry chapbooks. Works by several of these poets were selected for *Texas in Poetry: A 150 Year Anthology,* edited by Billy Bob Hill and published in 1994 by the Center for Texas Studies.

Laura Ballard Kennelly, teacher at the University of North Texas, editor of *Grasslands Review,* and poet has published her work in numerous literary journals. In 1989 her work was collected in *The Passage of Mrs. Jung: Collected Poetry.* More recently her anthology

A Certain Attitude: Poems by Seven Texas Women (1995) establishes for readers the themes and subjects that Texas women poets approaching the twenty-first century have begun to choose. Arranged in seven sections, the anthology includes works by SuAnne Doak, Lynn Hoggard, Vicky Lee Santiesteban, Sheryl St. Germain, Guili Coniglio, Frances M. Trevino, and Kennelly. Charlotte Wright, Denton writer and editor, introduces the collection. Betsy Colquitt, who reviews the book for *Texas Books in Review* (Fall, 1995), observes that "these seven native daughters," as Wright has designated them, "most holding degrees from Texas universities and now connected to in-state educational institutions, rarely turn to the rural, though Texas setting and culture are important in many of these poems, most of which are revelatory about the persona's internal world." Here, it seems clear, Colquitt perceives the state of Texas women's poetic art and foresees as well the nature of Texas experience that Texas women poets will explore in the future.

FROM LADY TO LAUREATE

Texas Women Poets, 1836–1936

BETTY SUE FLOWERS

What does it mean to be a "Texas woman poet"? The use of such a term assumes that Texas women writing poetry have common characteristics worth exploring. Writers often object in principle to any such classification, arguing that they are poets first and that where they happen to live and what gender they happen to be are incidental to their art. No one wants to be a mere regional writer, they complain, or, worse yet, a "poetess."

In spite of these legitimate protests, we can learn a great deal about Texas, about Texas women, and about the conditions of writing for Texas women from a historical study of poetry written by Texas women from 1836 to 1936. I have limited my subject to published poems by Anglo poets. (During this period, not surprisingly, other ethnic groups did not have the access to publication resources that Anglos did.) Throughout this early period, women wrote about their surroundings, both geographical and personal. Two important themes appear and reappear in the poetry: the motif of the landscape, with its harshness as well as its wild freedom; and the burden and joys of domesticity. Only toward the end of this period does a new theme emerge: the woman poet consciously coming to terms with her art and its relation to her life as a woman.

From 1836 to 1936, when much published poetry by Texas women dealt with the founding of Texas, life in Texas, and the landscape, "Texas" also was a central theme for male poets. Following the European tradition, they described the land in female terms.[1] Perhaps because Texas was a young land to the settlers, pre-Independence poets spoke of it not as a "mother" but as a fair maiden held captive by barbarians (Mexicans and Indians). Narrators of such poems were likely to cast themselves as crusading knights, destined to win the hand of lady Texas because they were brave, Anglo-Saxon, and favored by God.

However useful the convention representing Texas as fair damsel in distress was to male poets, it posed a special problem for women writing of Texas. Many chose not to personify Texas but pictured it as an alien, inhospitable land. Margaret Lea Houston epitomizes this approach. Although her husband, Sam Houston, the first president of the Republic of Texas, had as good a claim as any to the title of "savior" of the fair damsel, his wife ("Mrs. Gen. Sam Houston," as she was called in a popular poetry anthology) wrote of Texas as a "foreign land":

> *Alone I roam upon the earth*
> > *Without one friend or kindred tie,*
> *Far from the spot that gave me birth,*
> > *In a foreign land I sigh.*
> > *(from "An Evening Ramble"[2])*

The theme of Texas as inhospitable wilderness is seldom found in male poetry of the period. Much of this early poetry is the nineteenth-century equivalent of Captain John Smith's diaries—descriptions of strange geography and heroic tales of adventure. Hugh Kerr published one of the earliest literary works produced about the state, a book-length poem called *A Poetical Description of Texas, and Narrative of Many Interesting Events in that Country, Embracing a Period of Several Years, Interspersed with Moral and Political Impressions: Also, an Appeal to Those Who Oppose the Union of Texas with the United States, and the Anticipation of that Event. To Which is Added The Texas Heroes, No. 1 & 2.*[3] In Kerr's poem the poetry often takes second place to the geography:

> *Gonzales and Victoria*
> > *Are towns upon the Guadalupe;*

> *The first is distant from the bay,*
> > *The latter, some thirty miles up. (p. 83)*

Lines such as these prompted a contemporary critic to remark, "O Kerr, Kerr, Kerr / What did you write these poems fur?"[4]

Kerr praises the beauty of Texas with great extravagance ("Few spots on earth can this excel"), yet even he admits:

> *In these remarks we do not mean*
> > *The whole of Texas to include:*
> *Some parts of Texas, we have seen,*
> > *Which, from this praise, we must exclude. (p. 11)*

A few early women described Texas as if it could hardly be distinguished from Sherwood Forest. For example, Mrs. Anna Word Spragins in "Farewell to Texas" [ca. 1869] speaks of "River blue and vale of cashmere, / Emerald land-."[5] However, most Texas women poets spoke of desert landscapes and of drought and dust:

> *Here is the land*
> *Where roots have long decayed*
> *From the mouths of bitter seeds:*
> *Dust and the red earth*
> *And the thick dead grass bending for miles:*
> *Here no shadow has ever fallen,*
> *And the birds go over all day*
> *Screaming.*
> > *(from Kathleen Tankersley Young, "Three Poems*
> > *of the Southwest"[6])*

For others the landscape was barbaric and threatening:

> *This was the land that God forgot,*
> > *That evolution scorned,*
> *Every tree and bush and flower*
> > *Was spiked or barbed or thorned.*
> > *(from Vaida Stewart Montgomery, "Desert"[7])*

Even the shape of Texas—not an orderly rectangle or square like so many other Western states—seemed raw and violent:

> *Other states are long or wide,*
> *Texas is a shaggy hide,*
> *Dripping blood and crumpled hair;*
> > *(from Berta Hart Nance, "Cattle")*[8]

Those women poets who did describe Texas as a woman often did so by assuming a male persona, or at the least they praised Texas with a male lover's praise. The nineteenth-century poet Lizzie Hamlett in "Shall We Divide the State?" scoffed at exchanging the "goddess" Texas for a "puny sisterhood":

> *Divide the State! Who dare suggest*
> > *Such act of sacrilege?*
> > *
>
> *Divide the State for which they bled!*
> > *A goddess grand and good,*
> *And rear upon its base instead*
> > *A puny sisterhood?*
> *No!*[9]

By 1936, the year of the centennial, the personification of the state by women poets had shifted in a psychologically significant way. In poems by Leola Barnes and Grace Noll Crowell, for example, Texas is not a goddess but a mother or sweetheart, not a "free" lady but a "wilful" one. In Barnes's "A Texas Century," Texas takes on the characteristics of an unappreciated mother:

> *And you, who have not loved her,*
> *This wilful, this lavish land,*
> *Cannot know the depths of her caring,*
> *Nor the grip of her friendly hand;*
>
> *But He, who made the centuries,*
> *Made home, and will understand.*[10]

In Grace Noll Crowell's "Texas, the Woman" (1936), only the image of the star reminds us of the lady's former glory as goddess of freedom. In these lines, Crowell speaks of Texas as a woman but attributes this personification to "men":[11]

> *As if she were a woman, men have loved*
> *Their Texas through the years:*
> *

And men are men, and love is what it is:
Impelling each to grapple with his hands
For his beloved, possessing what is his:
Texas, the woman, soft-eyed, gracious, fair,
Her head held high, a star caught in her hair.[12]

Of course any state can be personified as a lady, but what makes this analogy so pervasive in Texas poetry is that Texas, unlike most other states, was pictured as independent from its beginning. The 1836 struggle was seen not as a civil war, one section of Mexico rebelling against another, but as the war of Liberty against Tyranny, with Texas as Liberty, "a star caught in her hair."

Early in the history of Texas women's poetry, an image emerged that united the theme of Texas as "free" with the landscape poetry depicting Texas as inhospitable desert or wilderness. Women used the mediating image of a native Texas wildflower, the bluebonnet, to tame the inhospitable wilderness without losing the value attached to "free" or "wild." The name itself connotes both wildness (*wild*-flower) and domesticity (blue*bonnet*). Like Barnes's personification of Texas as "lavish," the vast fields of bluebonnets, stretching to the horizon in some places, suggest a richness and depth that go beyond the image of roses or cultivated gardens. Even a half-century after the bluebonnet motif reached its peak in Texas poetry (during the Centennial), many Texas women joined the former first lady, Lady Bird Johnson, in a project involving the propagation of Texas wildflowers.

A survey of the vast bluebonnet poetic literature reveals three major motifs: bluebonnets as a gift to Texas, a mark of God's chosen land; bluebonnets as a psychological substitute for water; and bluebonnets as the union between land (female) and sky (God).

One of the clearest statements of the bluebonnet as a special gift from God is found in Annabel Parks's "The Queen of Texas." Here the bluebonnets are personified as "Queen," tended not by an earthly gardener but by God:

But Texas is the only State where God
Made prairies blue to bless our weary eyes.
Bluebonnets never cross the boundary—
No traitors they, to smile on foreign lands—
Content are they to bloom on hill and lea,
Queen of the prairie, tended by God's hands.[13]

The speaker in Margaret Bell Houston's "Song from the Traffic" walks along the streets of Manhattan conjuring up the image of Texas as a field of bluebonnets. Here the dual image of bluebonnets as "crowds" and "clouds" reflects the tendency to treat bluebonnets both as the personification of Texas and as a natural phenomenon, like sea or sky:

> (Manhattan-Manhattan-I walk your streets today,
> But I see the Texas prairies bloom a thousand
>   miles away!)
>
> *
>
> *Bluebonnets fold the windy ways—*
> *Is any blue so blue?*
> (Clouds of them, crowds of them, shining
>   through the gray.
> Bluebonnets blossoming a thousand miles away!)[14]

In an inhospitable land, far from the maternal sea, the fields of bluebonnets also serve as a psychological substitute for water. Lexie Dean Robertson's "Mesa Miracle" dramatically stages the special relationship between Texas women and the Texas wildflower:

> I'll run till I die! This barren land
> Is more than a woman can take!
> *She was out of breath when she topped the rise,*
> *And there lay a beautiful lake!*
>
> *Dappled and bright, bloom spread in the sun.*
> *As lovely as water could be;*
> *And her mind found peace while she laved her heart*
> *With bluebonnets, blue as the sea.*[15]

The bluebonnets thus turn dry prairie into blue sea and are then seen to reflect the sky, uniting heaven with earth through a kind of lavish, optical miracle—as in Hallie Whittaker's "When Texas skies reflect the hue / Of her carpeted plains of heavenly blue."[16] In "Texas Bluebonnets," Annabel Parks extends this image of union by empowering the bluebonnet to recreate not only the water missing from Texas, but also the snow:

> *Their blue is a part of the afternoon sky,*
> *Their white is the purest of wind-driven snow:*
> *Still mothered by nature and God, great and high,*[17]

These lines contain an implicit image of the wildflower as pure ("as the driven snow") and free maiden, mothered by the land/nature and fathered by the sky/God. Structurally, a family of father, mother, and daughter is set up in which the son image is missing. As in the centennial poems, in which Texas is the woman whom only God can understand, the female—whether mother or maiden—is described in relation to God but not in relation to a male peer.

The absent male—in the form of an East Coast skeptic—sometimes appears to be the implied audience to whom much early Texas writing is addressed. The first book published in English on Texas, Mary Austin Holley's *Texas: Observations, Historical, Geographical and Descriptive. In a Series of Letters, Written during a Visit to Austin's Colony, with a view to a permanent Settlement in that country, in the Autumn of 1831* (1833), was written as a collection of letters to a reader back East. Although Holley herself sometimes describes Texas as a kind of Eden, she criticizes the extravagance with which other admirers of Texas speak—"as if enchantment had, indeed, thrown its spell over their minds."[18]

Even poems asserting that "to know her is to love her" often carry a tone of special pleading. In "The Plea of Texas," published in Texas newspapers a decade after her *Texas Observations* appeared, Holley continues to address an audience presumed to be unsympathetic to Texas. Here the convention of Texas as lady shifts. Texas is the child, addressing a plea to the much more powerful mother, the United States:

> *Admit us—we would deem it shame,*
> *Of other lands such boon to claim,*
>   *For we are free and proud.*
> *But we a mother's love may seek,*
> *And feel no blush upon our cheek,*
>   *Before her to have bowed.*
>   *
> *They call us poor! 'Tis false—the Sun,*
> *A fairer land never shone upon,*
>   *Than this we offer you.*[19]

Holley's "Plea" was published anonymously and reprinted by newspapers all over the state. This was common practice in the 1840s. Most newspapers printed from one to four poems each issue, many of them anonymous reprints from other newspapers. Anonymous publication makes it difficult to trace which of the earliest Texas poems were written by women. Some anonymous newspaper poems on the cholera epidemic of 1846 (in which Mary Austin Holley died) appear to be written by women. Others, such as the "Address to Slander" (a response to the notorious gossips who had "wronged both President Houston and President Lamar," according to the anthologist) were signed "By a lady."[20] And others of the anonymous poems, such as the 1839 poem called "Squeezing," are spoken by female narrators:

> How diffident the beaux have grown,
>   In fact, they're perfect churls;
> Such shameful coldness now is shown,
>   They never squeeze the girls.
> But the girls have devised a plan:
>
>   In lieu of these cold elves,
> They now—Oh, shame upon you men—
>   With corsets, squeeze themselves.[21]

Perhaps this anonymity was a form of freedom; for example, it allowed Mary Hunt McCaleb to print "Just So!"—a poem that, according to anthologist Sam H. Dixon, created a "*furor.*"[22]

> Engaged to a girl and not kiss her,
>   Is something I don't understand;
> Why, I never can sit by my darling
>   Without slyly squeezing her hand.[23]

"Just So!" and many other anonymously published poems appeared in Dixon's *The Poets and Poetry of Texas: Biographical Sketches of the Poets of Texas, with Selections from Their Writings Containing Reviews Both Personal and Critical* (1885). Like most early Texas poetry anthologies, Dixon's collection lists more female than male poets. It seems likely, then, that many anonymous newspaper poems that were not anthologized were written by women, and that of these (if the poems in Dixon's anthology are any indication), poems with domestic subject matter almost certainly were written by women.

In Dixon's anthology, most poems by men are on military themes and those by women on domestic or religious themes. Whether this is attributable to the poets themselves or to Dixon's principles of selection is hard to tell. Dixon felt that there was "more heart and less brain in Southern literature,"[24] and his selections from female poets appear to bear this out:

> *And I love to think, when he looks so wise*
> *From the thoughtful depths of his earnest eyes,*
> *Of the future greatness that waiting lies*
> *For baby, Grandmother's Baby.*[25]

"Grandmother's Baby" was written by Fannie Darden, who in the same year that Dixon's anthology appeared, published a far more interesting poem in a collection called, *Gems from a Texas Quarry; or Literary Offerings by and Selections from Leading Writers and Prominent Characters of Texas: Being a Texas Contribution to the World's Industrial Exposition at New Orleans, La., 1884–5.* Compiled by Ella Hutchins Steuart, the material in this anthology contains, in addition to poetry, addresses by officials and miscellaneous items such as a letter from Sam Houston "To Flaco, Chief of the Lipans," essays by women on "Laces," "Theosophy," "Poetry," "Sappho," and "Tasso," and a particularly remarkable essay on Mary Austin Holley's cousin, Stephen F. Austin, which begins, "Perhaps none more than the historian feels the deep and sad significance of the Lama prayer, '*Om mani padme haun . . .*' ('O God, consider the jewel in the Lotos!')." (p. 225)

Gems even contains a tract with some early feminist themes. Mrs. C. M. Winkler of Corsicana argues against suffrage on the grounds of its relative unimportance when compared with the issue of "equal wages for equal work." Near the conclusion of her essay, in a passage remarkable both for its feminism and its unconscious racism, Winkler says, "to the women of to-day, clamor not for female suffrage":

> Talk about slavery, talk about oppression, but I was a slave-owner, and I unhesitatingly say that the blacks under the old regime never knew anything to compare with the burdens the educated, refined working women of the South have to endure, the women whose lives are poems, rhyming musically in supplying the wants of helpless childhood, broken-down manhood and decrepit age. (p. 203)

The essay closes with the advice to "Get closer to your sisters . . . remembering that united we stand, divided we fall." (p. 204)

In such a context, perhaps it is not surprising that Fannie Darden's contribution to *Gems* is far more interesting than her contribution to Dixon's anthology. "The Whispering of the Sea"[26] is a composite poem written by three women: Darden, Mrs. M. J. Young, and the early Texas novelist, Mollie E. Moore (known as "The Texas Mockingbird"). Each woman calls her section "What the Sea Said" and dedicates it to the other two women.

Darden begins the poem with an introduction ("We were three sisters of one mystic tie") describing the personality of each sister: one is like a queen, one (the youngest) is called "little Sister," and the author herself is the one whom night and day both claim "for their own." Following the introduction, Darden's section of the poem is a first-person narration of the ocean as a woman waiting for the sun, her lover ("For the sun hath looked down with his magnetic eyes").

Young responds with "The sea hath many voices, sister mine":

> *This mighty basin, called by you the sea,*
> *Is simply earth's great treasure-house for things*
> *Too sad for Heaven, too pure for dark Hades,*
> *Which to the human heart doth memories bring*
> *As sweet as David's harp, or mad as Israel's king. (p. 99)*

The third poet, Moore, ends with a section exploring the relation of the ocean to time and suggesting an alternative to the ocean-sun love imagery of Darden:

> *If a storm*
> *Wooes her with lightning and with thunder, she*
> *Hath care within her deeps for things that be*
> *Of worth to outlive time. The lovely form*
> *Lies waiting somewhere safe in coral caves,*
> *As under waving grass! (p. 101)*

Moore, known as Mollie E. Moore Davis after marriage to Thomas E. Davis in 1874, later emigrated to New Orleans, where she wrote novels and poetry and became, by 1893, "perhaps the most thoroughly written up southern literary woman of the day."[27]

Less fortunate than Moore was her contemporary, Florence M. Gerald. Gerald's first major poem, "The Lays of the Republic" (1878) was read to an Austin audience for the benefit of yellow-fever suffer-ers. Then, in 1880, she published *Adenheim, and Other Poems* and "won her way at one bound into the society of the rich and refined; while many others who wrote quite as well were on the outskirts and little noticed," as Dixon reports. (p. 81)

But two years later, Gerald's *Adenheim* was harshly criticized on the grounds that its ideas were taken directly from "Story of a Faith-ful Soul" by the popular English poet Adelaide Proctor. Gerald left almost immediately for New York, returning a few months later with *A Friend,* a drama she had written and in which she starred. The drama failed, bankrupting both Gerald and her manager—which fail-ure, it was reported by a friend, "seemed but the prelude to a giving away of her mind."[28]

Perhaps to avoid such criticism, or to avoid notoriety of any kind, many women still were publishing anonymously as late as 1893. In that year the *Galveston Daily News* ran a two-part series, "The Women Writers of Texas," by Bride Neill Taylor (June 18 and June 25). In part one, Taylor explains that one reason such an article is neces-sary is that "specially pleasing productions appearing in journals outside the state have after a time—and often quite by accident—been discovered to be from the pens of Texas women."[29] Even when the author's name was known, it was sometimes impossible to trace her if her husband had died.

Throughout Taylor's brief biographies of Texas women writers is a common theme, easily gleaned from even a single column of news-print:

[About Mrs. George] Domestic duties have for many years absorbed all her time, but recently she has resumed the pen.

[About Mrs. Armstrong] She is the wife of a minister with all the duties which that position implies.

[About Mrs. Billings] . . . probably the only woman in the state who follows the calling of a regular preacher. She is likewise the wife of a minister. The arduous duties of her double vocation have not pre-vented her from being also an industrious writer.

[About Mrs. Hill] . . . began to write for publication while she was still a girl, but before she could be said to have fairly launched her-self upon the career of her choice she married Dr. A. M. Hill of Bastrop county and abandoned the pen for the sake of the domestic duties she had assumed. After years of silence, however. . . .[30]

The single most vivid impression emerging from Taylor's sketches is that of industrious women who wrote while fulfilling heavy family responsibilities. Lydia Starr McPherson, for example, who owned and edited the *Sherman Democrat*, was twice widowed, raising her children alone. In addition to publishing a book of poems and a novel, she established the *Whitesboro Democrat* (1877)—the first newspaper in Texas, Taylor points out, to have been published by a woman. In 1879 she moved the paper to Sherman and, in addition to her other responsibilities, was for four years postmistress at Sherman.[31]

Even Dixon's anthology contains a poem complaining about the difficulty of combining domestic duties with the vocation of writing:

> *So, though I've lost a week from sleep,*
> *And often bitter tears do weep,*
> *Still I must try to imitate*
> *These pictures in the fashion plate.*
> *Ye gods! was ever a task so hard,*
> *Or ever rhymed a truer bard?*
> *
> *Still I must sweep, and churn and brew,*
> *And make my dresses nice to view;*
> *And nurse the baby, read the news,*
> *Darn socks, keep buttons on the shoes,*
> *Play the piano, beat the steak,*
> *Then last, not least, this undertake.*
> *Not Euclid's problems intricate,*
> *Have half so puzzled my poor pate.*
> *If men to such a task were set,*
> *They'd lock their doors, and swear and fret,*
> *And send for all their counselors.*
>
> *And say an age were time too short*
> *To learn this trade, perfect this art*
> *But we must learn a hundred trades*
> *Without apprenticeship or aids,*
> *And practice all with equal skill,*
> *'Tis their good pleasure, our good will.*
> *I knelt and prayed me, for a time*
> *When women frail should learn a trade*

And buy their dresses ready made.
(from Helena Gillespie, "A Dress to Make")[32]

Taylor concludes her biographies with a statement that women writers of Texas "work almost without exception in hopeless bitterness of spirit, recognizing that their only chance lies in the forlorn hope of gaining the notice of the far away critics and readers of the eastern and northern centers of thought." She goes on to say that "this noble body of talented women is one of the richest treasures of the state. . . . Each one is a fortunate antidote for several dozen frivolous women and hundred or so of vicious men."[33]

Following Taylor's article, the editors add a biographical paragraph on Taylor herself in which they point out that her essays frequently appear over the initials "B.N.T."—"evidence of that peculiar timidity which, inconsistently enough, she preaches against in the foregoing sketches."[34]

Taylor's article clearly points out how difficult it was to combine the demands of wifely duties with a vocation as writer. Women could not justify spending time alone writing poetry, but they could justify establishing societies for self-improvement and cultural "uplift." Even though a sense of duty might prevent a woman from allowing herself the time necessary for writing, membership in a literary society could claim her time because it qualified as a civic duty. Some of these societies were closely associated with the growth of public libraries. In the 1890s, for example, the Houston library rooms were shared with the Shakespeare Club and the Ladies Reading Club,[35] the "oldest women's club in Texas";[36] and in 1898, when the library moved to a new building, the Ladies Reading Club helped pay expenses.[37]

By the first decade of the twentieth century, the equivalent of Ladies Reading Clubs began springing up even in the small towns. In Clarksville, for example, a Shakespeare Society was founded in 1905 (and lasted until the early 1960s). Membership at first consisted of seven or eight women, many of whom were sisters or cousins. Later the group expanded to twenty, with new members being voted on— prospective members who were not "serious enough" being "blackballed." The women were expected to read and "interpret" a play for each meeting.[38]

During this same period, similar clubs began to form for purposes of writing as well as reading. The stated object of the Houston Pen Women, organized in 1906, was to "encourage young writers and to improve each other's technique and style by holding literary Contests."[39]

These literary contests became a major feature of the Poetry Society of Texas, which was organized in 1921, "coincident" with "the renaissance of poetry in Texas."[40] Unlike many smaller literary societies, the Poetry Society was advertised as being "open to any lover of poetry."[41] The formation of a Poetry Society probably did encourage many young writers, but its contests and those of the poetry magazines that sprang up in the 1920s and 1930s resulted in an emphasis on certain highly conventional forms of verse.

For example, the *Kaleidoscope* magazine (later called *Kaleidograph*), founded in 1929 by a charter member of the Poetry Society, offered prizes in each issue for the best cinquain, couplet, and quatrain. Not surprisingly, in a era in which major poets were experimenting with free verse, the *Kaleidograph* was dominated by poems written in cinquain, couplet, or quatrain form.

But in spite of its generally conservative cast, the *Kaleidograph* offered many women poets access to publication for the first time. When the magazine was discontinued, thirty years later, its Kaleidograph Press had published "more first volumes for poets than any other poetry press in the nation"[42]—and most were by Texas women. Probably one reason the Kaleidograph Press offered such encouragement to Texas women poets is that the coeditor of the magazine, Vaida Stewart Montgomery, was herself a poet.

While Montgomery's own book, *Locoed and Other Poems*, contains its share of Texas poems, it also exhibits a number of interesting poems about the relationship of a woman poet to her writing:

> *I am not satisfied to spend my days*
> *Juggling trite words into a hackneyed rhyme,*
> *Competing with other scribblers of my time*
> *To win a few ephemeral crumbs of praise.*
> *
>
> *Rather, I would keep silence, crush desire,*
> *And leave its white-hot flame a mass of scars,*
> *What need to sing, if song can rise no higher*
> *Than any goal beneath the tallest stars?*
> *I am not satisfied, nor shall I be*

Till I have conquered mediocrity.
                    (from "Intransigeant"[43])

The ambition to write, and to write well, is a theme of several of Montgomery's poems. But connected with ambition is the sense of loneliness, of being an outsider in those very literary societies that had generated what Montgomery, in other contexts, referred to as a poetic "renaissance."

Rows of stout women,
Rows of anaemic women,
Rows of other women—
All looking important.

One has written a play,
One has written a pageant,
One has written a poem—
All still unpublished.

Why cannot I
Sit so importantly
Upon the soft pillow
Of utter complacency?

Because some rude joker
Has placed in the cushion
With the point turned upward
The tack of Ambition.
                    ("At a Literary Tea"[44])

Aspiration, the curse of ambition, and fear of failure—these three themes are central to Montgomery's *Locoed*:

I do my little dance in life, and do it well,
I hear the plaudits of the crowd, and bow and smile,
And yet within my heart I realize the while,
Their cheers would change to hisses, if I tripped
                    and fell.
                    ("Vicissitude"[45])

A poet afraid of failing is likely to avoid experimentation and to write, instead, in forms that win contests and other public assurances of success. Eighteen years after *Locoed*, Kaleidograph Press published

Montgomery's second book, *Hail for Rain*. The themes are those of disappointment and old age: "Counting the World Well-Lost," "Psalm to Adversity," "Hail for Rain," "The Unborn," "The Years that the Locust Hath Eaten," "I Would Not Be Forever Young," "End of Summer," "Dark Day," "Admonition in Autumn." The forms are, for the most part, quatrains and couplets. But even though the acknowledgments page begins with a list of the prizes the poems have won from the Poetry Society of Texas, the poems themselves still exhibit an intense concern with the opinions of others:

> *Yet ever mindful of the critics' frowns*
> *And thinking, without hope, of pleasing them . . .*
> *(from "For Contemporary Poets"*[46]*)*

In the eighteen-year gap between her first book and her last, Montgomery, in addition to coediting and publishing the monthly *Kaleidograph,* and directing Kaleidograph Press, edited *A Century with Texas Poets and Poetry* (1934). In the introduction she says, "I personally know of approximately three thousand persons in Texas who are devoting some time to the writing of verse."[47] At this time she also wrote a series called *Help Yourself Handbooks,* designed to help young poets find publishing markets. The prime market was, of course, the Kaleidograph Press itself: Kaleidograph books listed in the December, 1939, issue of *Kaleidograph* included six by Texas women poets advertised as "recent" and thirty more by women in the "General List."

That Montgomery was sensitive to proportional representation by women is indicated in her review of Dixon's poetry anthology, in which she remarks, "Of the 74 poets treated in this volume, 41 were women, or 'female poets,' as they were generally termed."[48]

Montgomery's own output of poetry was relatively small, but probably more Texas women published poetry under Montgomery's stewardship than at any time before or since. When she became ill in 1954, *Kaleidograph* appeared quarterly rather than monthly, and when she died in 1959, *Kaleidograph* also died, after "thirty years of continuous publication."[49]

Joining the formation of the Poetry Society and the establishment of the Kaleidograph Press as factors in the "poetry renaissance" of the 1920s and 1930s was the creation of the Poet Laureateship of Texas in 1931. House Committee Resolution No. 33, "Relative to naming poet laureate," declared:

Whereas, there is a close connection between the growth of civilization and the development of literature; and Whereas, it has been
customary in all ages for governments to recognize this relation by
elevating the poet to the same plane as statesmen and military leaders; Whereas, the recognition of outstanding poets in this state and
their elevation to places of honor will have a wholesome and beneficial effect on literature in this state; now, therefore, be it Resolved
by the House of Representatives, the Senate concurring, that at each
Regular Session of the Legislature the Speaker of the House and two
members of the House to be named by the Speaker, together with
the Lieutenant Governor and one member of the Senate to be named
by the Lieutenant Governor, shall constitute a committee of five to
appoint and designate some outstanding and recognized poet, who
is a citizen of Texas, who shall be poet laureate of the State of Texas
for a period of two years from such appointment and designation.[50]

Soon the term of two years was shortened to one and alternates
were added so that more could share the honor. "This is a good plan,"
declared Margaret Royalty Edwards, poet laureate for 1957–59, "as
the Poetry Society of Texas alone has in excess of six hundred members, besides members of smaller groups over the state"[51]—and of
course Texas poets not affiliated with the Poetry Society.

However the Poetry Society so clearly dominated the laureateship
that by 1966 four-fifths of the laureates and alternates were members
of the society—and two-thirds of these were women. In other words,
in most years from 1932 to 1966 the Poet Laureate of Texas was a
woman member of the Poetry Society of Texas.

The most famous of these women was the Centennial Poet Laureate, Grace Noll Crowell. Although not a Texan by birth, Crowell
adopted the state as her own ("Oh, my adopted mother"—"Texas")[52]
and, like so many Texas women poets, used it as an image of struggle.
In such poems as "Texas," "Red Earth," and "Heritage," Texas, or
the South, is the Mother, misunderstood by the North, land of the
Father:

> *Always from the North a call,*
> *Through the sweet blue distance—*
> *Always from my father's land*
> *A definite insistence.*
> *But my roots have struck so deep . . .*

Deep beyond believing
In this red soil of the South . . .
I shall not be leaving.
              (from "Red Earth"[53]*)*
My mother bore me, looking toward the South
A fierce nostalgia clutching at her heart.
My father, stoic product of the North
Could never understand, nor have a part
In her wild longings for a languid South;
But hidden in my veins she left to me
A smoldering passion for white Southern moons,
And soft warm winds that sweep up from the sea.
              (from "Heritage"[54]*)*

The opposition between the languid and the stoic—values associated with beauty and those seen as belonging to duty—emerges clearly from Crowell's poetry as well as her biography. However, in neither the poetry nor the biography is this struggle ever discussed directly. In the sense that all biography makes a myth or creates a story from the facts of a life, the myth of Grace Noll Crowell, as told by her good friend Beatrice Plumb, is of a sensitive, dutiful homemaker who, through misfortune, found herself an invalid and made the best of her condition by learning how to write poems that would inspire others. Plumb presents Crowell as a wife who valued her household duties far more than her writing and who regretted the weakness that kept her from assuming the full range of household tasks she so yearned to perform: "I made the cranberry sauce for the Thanksgiving dinner," she wrote me last November, "and the dressing, and feel prouder of the job than if I had written a sonnet."[55]

Plumb describes how Crowell, with the money earned from her thousands of published poems, her eight books of poetry, the Braille translations, and lectures, buys things for the house, each thing named in her mind "for the poem that put it there":

"It has been a comfort to do this for my home. It has made up, in a way, for what I couldn't—"

One hears the catch in her nice voice, and is sorry. For although there is nothing organically wrong, poor health has sent her back to a sick bed time and again. Sometimes she runs her house by "remote control" from her bed. And there are days of greater suffering when it must be left to the devoted hands of helpers. (p. 22)

As an eight-year-old girl, Crowell wrote a poem that she read aloud to her family—who laughed at her. Crying with humiliation the little girl never wrote again until, years later, illness turned her back "reluctantly," as Plumb insists, to her pen. But during the years when, as Plumb describes her, Crowell was "[r]acing along with the joyous months, breathlessly busy" as a new wife ("How she loved transforming that new little house into a home, keeping a shining kitchen, being a smart little manager, a good wife!") and then later as a mother ("*Now* she must learn to be a perfect mother!"(p.18)), there must have been some memory of that other, "languid" part of her that once wrote poetry:

> For the sake of the young girl I was once
> I must keep faith with loveliness.
> I could not bear to see her eyes
> Darken with sudden deep distress.
> (from "For Her Sake,"(p. 51))

But keeping faith with loveliness when there was so much to do was difficult. Finally, illness allowed her the time to begin writing again, but when she did she was immediately confronted with the patronizing family attitude that so discouraged her as a girl:

> When her husband found her picking at his typewriter with two uncertain fingers he laughed affectionately, rumpled her black shining hair, and pocketed the poem. *He* was the writer in that family! Her job was to get rosy and strong again. (p. 21)

But Crowell continued her illness and her writing, and gradually her poems began to sell. As if to atone for the hours spent away from household duties, she wrote of the beauty of household work:

> A happy woman singing at her work,
> Who loves the shining things of everyday:
> White curtains, and clean dishes, and swept floors,
> Where warm lights play,
> Who finds contentment in four lifted walls—
> I think that any man can safely take

Such a woman to his heart to love
For her own lovely sake.
(from "The Home Makers," pp. 12–13)

As a sister poet laureate, Margaret R. Edwards, commented: "Her poems have done much for women around the world by turning drudgery into dreams in the performance of routine household tasks."[56] Thousands of women responded to Crowell's poetry in letters like this one:

> Let me thank you for the happiness your poems have brought me. Through them I have come to see romance and poetry in putting shining dishes on a clean shelf. I have found delight in stretching fragrant sun-pure sheets on a bed. The making of light rolls is more than the preparation of food. It is an adventure! For this beautiful thing you have done for me, you have all my life's gratitude. . . . (p. 13)

Doctors wrote to tell her that copies of her books were passed around hospital wards until they fell apart. The sick and dying slept with her poems under their pillows. Radio talk show hosts were deluged with requests to read her poems. One poem, printed on a card, sold 36,000 copies in a few months. Neighbors banded together in a "Crowell Circle" to read her poems. And eventually her husband abandoned his own career to devote himself full time to managing hers:

> "You see, it was this way," he grins, "the greatest handicap a writing-man can possibly have is another writer in the same family who can outwrite him. Here I would spend the better part of a day pounding out a thing that netted me a mere pittance—when properly revised. And she would flit into a room like a butterfly, flop onto the old machine and thump out a poem that knocks somebody for fifty dollars! There ought to be a law—." (pp. 29–30)

When asked to what he attributed her success, Mr. Crowell responded, "To having a husband like me." (p. 41)

In 1938, Texas Centennial Laureate Grace Noll Crowell was designated American Mother of the year and one of the ten outstanding women of the United States. In the same year she was declared "Outstanding Poet of the Nation" and "Honor Poet" for national poetry week (an award previously granted to Robinson, Sandburg, and Frost among others). Plumb, looking over the thousands of testimonial letters Crowell received, "dreamed and wept over them": "'What a mission she has!' I mused. 'This woman who so reluctantly turned from the making of bread to the making of poems!'" (p. 34)

But as her poems testify, Crowell never allowed herself to turn completely from bread to poetry; in this her story is that of almost all early Texas women poets—and those of other states as well.

Critics telling the story of Texas women poets from 1936 to 2036 will be telling a significantly different story. Poets from the first fifty years of this new era have already begun to treat the geography of Texas not as a personified maiden but as an expression of the artist's psyche. In a sense, even the early poets psychologized the landscape, for descriptions of its "inhospitable" wildness expressed the fears of those who felt threatened by it. However, contemporary women poets are appropriating the landscape in much more self-conscious ways. Olive Hershey's "The Grasses of Texas" begins with a botanical description of weeping lovegrass ("*Eragrostis curvula*") and ends with four lines that move from the bleached landscape to an image of a man on a horse, an image that unites the Texas landscape with the suggestion of sexuality ("veins swell") and of internal rivers of emotion (veins/rivers/weeping lovegrass):

> The fat cactus is blackened.
> Bones whiten on the sand. A man
> whips a horse on the neck with reins.
> Its veins swell like intricate river systems.[57]

In part because Helena Gillespie's dream of buying "dresses ready made" has come true, the treatment of domesticity also has changed. In most contemporary poetry by Texas women, domestic life is treated in the manner neither of Gillespie nor of Crowell—it is neither a burden nor a joy. Instead the intimacies of the private world and its effect on individuals is explored. In Sandra Lynn's "Meta Physical Pregnancy: A Conceit," the narrator takes the image of the new land as a woman and applies it to her own body:

> there's a new world rounding my belly
> over my globing sea christopher columbus sings out landfall
> a "passage to more than india" awaits me

the heartbeat below mine a mystery deeper than the vedas
to compass it, i must become more than a new geography

i enter the waters of the now inevitable discovery
enter too the circle, the eventual circumnavigation
passage to yet a farther sea
to journeys of risk into, beyond me
what was before will no longer be my boundary[58]

There is much continuity from the first hundred years of Texas women's poetry to the second. There are even contemporary bluebonnet poems, such as Hershey's "Geography," in which the narrator states that "Bluebonnets hum on the chalk hills" and adds: "There is such a thing as too much blue."[59] In spite of the continuity, however, the next hundred years of Texas women's poetry is likely to bear out the implications of Lynn's image of pregnancy: "what was before will no longer be my boundary."

NOTES

1. For an interesting discussion of the metaphor of the land as female, see Annette Kolodny, *Lay of the Land: Metaphor as Experience and History in American Life and Letters.*
2. Sam H. Dixon, *The Poets and Poetry of Texas: Biographical Sketches of the Poets of Texas, with Selections from their Writings Containing Reviews Both Personal and Critical,* 147.
3. Published by the author, New York, 1838.
4. William Ransom Hogan, *The Texas Republic: A Social and Economic History,* 172.
5. Dixon, 307.
6. D[on] Maitland Bushby, ed., *The Golden Stallion: An Anthology of Poems Concerning the Southwest and Written by Representative Southwestern Poets,* 151.
7. *Hail for Rain,* 38.
8. B[enjamin] A[lbert] Botkin, ed., *The Southwest Scene: An Anthology of Regional Verse,* 38.
9. Dixon, 114–15.
10. Leola Christie Barnes, *Silver Century,* 1.
11. I am grateful to Beverly Stoeltje for this observation.
12. Grace Noll Crowell, *Bright Destiny: A Book of Texas Verse,* 7.
13. Annabel Parks, *Big Texas: Centennial Poems,* 82.
14. Vaida Stewart Montgomery, ed., *A Century with Texas Poets and Poetry,* 53–54.
15. In Margaret Royalty Edwards, *Poets Laureate of Texas, 1932–1966,* 23.

16. "Bluebonnets," *The Kaleidoscope* 1 (March 1930): 11.
17. Parks, 84.
18. Holley, 6.
19. Philip Graham, ed., *Early Texas Verse, 1835–1850*, 23.
20. Graham, 115.
21. Graham, 62.
22. Dixon, 205.
23. Dixon, 206.
24. Dixon, 312.
25. Dixon, 52.
26. Steuart, 95–102.
27. Taylor, June 18.
28. Dixon, 84.
29. Taylor, June 18.
30. Taylor, June 25.
31. Taylor, June 18.
32. Dixon, 101–102.
33. Taylor, June 25.
34. Taylor, June 25.
35. Mrs. W. M. Baines, ed., *Historic Souvenir Dedicated to Texas Centennial, 1936*, 99.
36. Baines, 91.
37. Baines, 99.
38. Information contributed by Ruth Marable, Clarksville.
39. Baines, 1.
40. Montgomery, *A Century*, 22.
41. Montgomery, *A Century*, 23.
42. David Russell, "Editorial," *Kaleidograph* 30, no. 4 (1959): inside front cover.
43. Montgomery, *Locoed*, 41.
44. Montgomery, *Locoed*, 51.
45. Montgomery, *Locoed*, 49.
46. Montgomery, *Hail for Rain*, 64.
47. Montgomery, *A Century*, vii.
48. Montgomery, *A Century*, 17.
49. Russell, *loc. cit.*
50. Quoted in Jency Miller, comp., *Texas Poets Laureate*, n.p.
51. Edwards, xii.
52. *Bright Destiny*, 5.
53. *Bright Destiny*, 15.
54. *Bright Destiny*, 40.
55. Beatrice Plumb, *Grace Noll Crowell: The Poet and the Woman*, 30–31.
56. Edwards, 13.
57. Olive Hershey, *Floating Face Up*, 32.
58. Sandra Lynn, *I Must Hold These Strangers: Poems by Sandra Lynn*, 39.
59. Hershey, 24.

THE BURIED LIFE

Texas Women Poets, 1920–60

PAUL CHRISTENSEN

Women in Texas started writing poetry seriously in the 1920s, when elsewhere many classics of modernism were being published: in 1922 came James Joyce's *Ulysses* and T. S. Eliot's *The Waste Land*; in 1925, F. Scott Fitzgerald's *The Great Gatsby* and Ezra Pound's *A Draft of XVI Cantos*. The major plays of Eugene O'Neill were premiering in New York. It was the epoch of the Black American artist, whose examination of slavery and race relations during the Harlem Renaissance created the image of the Black intellectual in America. It was the decade of the flapper, of Dixieland jazz, prohibition, of T-men and organized crime. The nation was plunged into a sudden, new postwar prosperity, as the stock market boomed and America continued receiving war reparations from its vanquished European enemies. American artists lived abroad and enjoyed the inexpensive life of Paris, London, Venice, and Rome, writing about European Bohemian life and opening the boundaries of American experience to international art and ideas.

It was a time when the nation's consciousness expanded rapidly, in all directions, from sexual freedom to what the sociologist Thorstein Veblen called the "conspicuous consumption" of status symbols. The sense of renewal was everywhere. In the arts, such regional cultures as the South and the Midwest endured scorching reappraisals of their customs, mores, scandals, and provincial ways as writers and other artists absorbed the postwar international spirit.

But as the boundaries of regional culture melted away and a new national character emerged in business, politics, and the arts, the vast territories of Texas and the surrounding Southwest remained isolated and inward and took no part in the major self-examination sweeping the rest of the nation. Texas being the youngest settled area of the country, the most remote outpost to the south, its "history" was as yet formless and simplistic and posed no intellectual burden on the young to demand a radical reappraisal. Texas was still catching up with its more sophisticated neighbors and laboring to distinguish itself from Mexico, its troubled neighbor to the south. Soon international currents in the arts and changing world relations would impinge upon Texas, setting it off on its own ambitious artistic renaissance, but throughout the 1920s and early 1930s the state and its fledgling arts remained an enclave of older, provincial American attitudes.

The character of Texas was still unannealed by 1920, though traits were forming that would determine its voice and outlook in the ensuing decades of the century. Its soul was shaped by a pioneer ideology of self-determination, of laissez-faire capitalism, a bracing version of social Darwinism inspired in part by distrust both of immigrants from south of its border and of a rag-tag citizenry as yet unassimilated into the white Protestant mainstream. It was a masculine culture of small ranches, farms, and rural communities with few amenities or contacts with the world beyond its own meager social resources. In such communities, where livelihoods were eked out according to the vagaries of the weather, terrain, and local economy, a deeply rooted ethic of individualism nurtured distrust of the arts as modes of self-disclosure. Keeping one's own counsel in moments of failure or triumph took on a moral aspect in rural Texas society.

The place of women in Texas resembled that of women in New England communities of the eighteenth and nineteenth centuries. Agricultural life empowered females and gave them authority as highly skilled partners in the farm or ranch enterprise. The average rural woman's duties ranged from child-rearing to cooking, canning, gardening, healing, and house-cleaning, to the hard labor of fencing and herding. Many also undertook to educate their own and others' children. Bryan Barker's bronze sculpture, "The Pioneer Woman," commissioned in 1927 and reproduced in Major and Smith's celebrated anthology *The Southwest in Literature* (1929), commemorates the importance and authority of her role in prairie life. A tall, bonneted woman strides proudly forward with lunch sack on arm, young son in hand, and large book held firmly to her side—all the symbols of her skills. Even so, a Texas woman's authority was strictly circumscribed by home and garden; it did not extend into the community, the male's domain.

Though this may strike us now as a bleak world for women, it was a condition that for some nurtured their creativity and artistic skills. As crucial partners of households, women were credited with possessing certain knowledge and experience it was their right to communicate; as lesser members of the community, their exploration of self was not an offense to taste or custom so long as the result was morally affirming or uplifting. Hence the role of artist in early Texas society fell largely to women, who pursued its function within a narrowly defined range of subjects and themes that endorsed the rudimentary social vision of the community. Susan Turner Adams's "A Bibliography of Texas Poetry: 1945–1981," a master's thesis completed in 1981, indicates that a majority (nearly 60 percent) of the state's published poets were women, a pattern that persisted from the 1920s well into our own period. In general their views of nature and ranch life were brightly optimistic, partly because women writers were now city dwellers and graduates either of normal schools or female colleges. In general they pictured nature as tame, decorative, under the control of a puritanical male will.

The implications of such rudimentary art are more subtle and complex than might first be thought. The meek and orderly landscape seen though the eyes of amateur female painters, writers, and essayists characterized their own repressive lives. Things were portrayed as being in their place, performing their assigned tasks as flowers, beasts, hills, and desert—and thus supportive of a well-run, male-dominated social order where few ambiguities of life were tolerated or permitted to retain their savage aspect. The feminine perspective was limited to observing the attractive elements of the natural world and incorporating them into the domestic sphere, as in the poem "Silver Poplars" by Grace Noll Crowell:

> *God wrote his loveliest poem on the day*
> *He made the first tall silver poplar tree,*

And set it high upon a pale-gold hill
For all the new enchanted earth to see.

I think its beauty must have made Him glad
And that He smiled at it—and loved it so—
Then turned in sudden sheer delight and made
A dozen silver poplars in a row.

Mist-green and white against a turquoise sky,
A-shimmer and a-shine they stood at noon;
A misty silver loveliness at night
Breathless beneath the first small wistful moon.

And then God took the music of the winds,
And set each leaf a-flutter and a-thrill—
Today I read His poem word by word
Among the silver poplars on the hill.

Bold questions about the nature of things or their functions, as posed in Georgia O'Keeffe's erotic portrayals of the southwestern desert, in the Mexican stories of Katherine Anne Porter, and in the philosophical excursions of Gertrude Stein, were discreetly withheld from Texas women's portrayals of the world, but such doubts (dangerous in their import) were subtly insinuated in their attention to sensuous detail and in their portrayals of the vast landscape dwarfing the fragile human estate. Dorothy Callaway's "Lure," included in the Poetry Society of Texas *Yearbook* for 1938, hints broadly of a female perspective through her chafing against male certainty and logical explanations:

Perhaps we hourly flirt the fringe of light
And never know, or falter blindly near
While vast dimensions veiled to mortal sight
Accost our senses through each tender spear
of grass.

I think a million answers will not feed
My soul nor quench the quivering thin flame
Consuming me. . . .

> . . . *For even now the singing words attest*
> *To secrets that are half articulate.*

The theme of a "secret earth" runs all through the poetry of the ensuing decades, a mystery which only intuition and dreams—female powers?—can penetrate. "There is secret mystery," Lexie Dean Robertson tells us, doubling the emphasis, "In earth and sky." In her poem, "Once Edwin Markham," which won the "Old South Prize" in 1948 from the Poetry Society, she confides, "I was the witched one / Under his spell / What he would he made of me / While the words fell."

A strong thread of paganism that runs through the best women's poetry of the 1930s and 1940s reflects the efforts of some writers to construct a female tradition for their work. In Leona Hahn's poem "White Butterfly," she lightly remarks, "I worship like a pagan / This idol of my heart," but the implications seem rich enough. Another prize winner in the 1931 *Yearbook,* Ethel Mary Franklin's "Persephone" takes on Swinburne in the opening lines:

> *My soul was a high free thing*
> *Woven of fire and tears*
> *Fashioned of white sea spray,*
> *Blown dust from the feet of the years.*
>
> *And my body a white wave curled,*
> *Of singing salt and the spume*
> *Of the raging sea, for the Sisters Three,*
> *Who wove my fate on a loom.*

Some poems present the landscape as an arena between the mothering earth and the ravaging male spirit of dominance. Lois Vaughan McClain's poem "White Heron" picks up on the story, earlier told by Sarah Orne Jewett, of a hunter and the little girl Sylvia, who conceals a white heron from him. McClain makes the fable into a tragic episode in male/female relations:

> *A shot rends the air!*
> *The white heron has fallen!*
> *Wings that have soared are forever still;*
> *Blood-stained and crumpled the rare lovely creature*
> *That but a fluttering breath-space ago*

Was a wisp of white cloud
That the wind was pursuing—

In Jewett's tale the bird lives on. Here we have building slowly a theme of ravagement that, in the 1960s and 1970s—when women's writing acknowledged environmental issues and male dominance came under increasing critical scrutiny—became a major preoccupation of women in Texas and beyond. The winner of the "Alamo Prize" for 1951, a poem entitled "Oil Land" by Edna H. Vines, declares at one point that "Man has set his seal upon the land,"

> *Wherever oil—time's hoarded treasure—lies,*
> *Skeleton forests of tall derricks stand*
> *Gaunt as half-starved ground from which they rise.*

Note the sexual imagery of forced entry that closes this first stanza:

> *And far into the pallid sand's deep hold*
> *The twisting drill pierces to liquid gold.*

Male rape imagery continues into the next stanza in a vivid piece of phrasing,

> *Gas pockets flare like bivouacs at night*
> *In growing numbers, until man has rent*
> *and gashed the soil in a Titanic fight*
> *That sucks its substance bare, and leaves it spent.*

But the skeptical, sometimes pagan turns of thought in poetry from 1920 to 1960 are a few colorful threads in a mass of altogether conventional writing. The best work explored sexual roles in a variety of new voices. The regional imagination sought not to violate forms but to undermine authority by siding with its opponents and victims. However even the best poets, such as Lexie Dean Robertson, were not strong enough by themselves to produce memorable writing; they did yeoman work by anticipating the themes and characteristics of good writers, such as Vassar Miller, yet to come.

The poetry of most Texas women of this period, though wooden and often shallow in perception, tacitly sketched their emotional circumstances and depicted in formulaic imagery their borrowed philosophical bearings as regionalists. The core of their beliefs derived from eighteenth-century English doctrines on human perfectibility and the goodness of reason and from the sturdy principles of Anglo-Saxon protestantism, elements that inspired fairly pallid lyrics wrought from English prosody and that echoed many themes found in prayer books and hymnals of the day. Their image of the world included balance, proportion, divine authority, with a small, somewhat secretive respect for esthetic pleasure. Their other nature as doubting females lay hidden.

Hence, though her circumstances in Texas society in the 1920s were perhaps harsh and repressive, the Texas woman found herself characterized by her intuitive perceptions and esthetic sense, factors that encouraged and warranted her role as artist in the community. One of Vassar Miller's later poems, "The Subterfuge," which appears in *Selected and New Poems: 1950–1980* (1981), is a case in point. Her portrait of her father, a successful developer in burgeoning Houston, giving his physically handicapped daughter a present captures the precise relation of Texas fathers to their potentially artistic daughters:

> *I remember my father, slight,*
> *staggering in with his Underwood,*
> *bearing it in his arms like an awkward bouquet*
>
> *for his spastic child who sits down*
> *on the floor, one knee on the frame*
> *of the typewriter, and holding her left wrist*
> *with her right hand, in that precision known*
> *to the crippled, pecks at the keys*
> *with a sparrow's preoccupation.*

To an outsider's eye, poetry written by Texas women in the forty years following 1920 would seem the residuum of orthodoxy one might have predicted in a rough, out-of-the-way region of the country. But the poem has a therapeutic function and is the place where one confides a troubled spirit. Heaped on the poem are many social obligations that frustrate that confiding urge, and the body of Texas women's work—thousands of volumes published by such busy Texas publishers as Naylor of San Antonio and Kaleidograph of Dallas, and by some New York trade houses—attests to a Leibnitzian worldview: on the one hand, *this* Texas was the most perfect of worlds; on the other, the wind howled full of nature's torments, the ground shriveled under the spade and the diamond-bitted drills, and the wildlife shrank away into ghostly memories of the old Paradise. The maturing of the Texas female vision coincided, it turns out, with the spread of Confessional poetry elsewhere in the country. The central figure of female poetry in Texas, Vassar Miller, voiced not only the buried spirit of women in the region but by midcentury was regarded as a principal force in the nation's outpouring of feminine rage and grief.

EXPLORING THE NEW PSYCHIC GEOGRAPHY

Vassar Miller, Jan Epton Seale, and Sandra Lynn

BETSY FEAGAN COLQUITT

Texas writing since the 1930s has been variously defined and interpreted, but it is clear that prose rather than poetry dominates this literature. It is clear too that Texas poetry gained attention only about midcentury, when several notable Texas poets, including Vassar Miller, published important first collections. With *Adam's Footprint* (1956), Miller introduced herself to a national audience. Her career as poet, which now spans four decades and has brought her many awards and honors, coincides both with the development of poetry in Texas and with the heightened attention to women's literature more generally. Since the 1980s, Texas poets, many of whom are women, have enjoyed increasing prominence regionally and nationally.

In contributing to and reflecting the strength of the women's movement, women's literature invites many kinds of examination and study. An obvious value of this writing comes from the enlarged understanding of the human condition it offers. This condition—however gendered—is probably always in a state of becoming, but as Simone de Beauvoir remarks in *The Second Sex,* "becoming" is an especially apt metaphor for women: "Woman is not a completed reality, but rather a becoming, and it is in her becoming that she should be compared with man; that is to say, her *possibilities* should be defined. What gives rise to much of the debate is the tendency to reduce her to what she has been."

Since Bradstreet's *The Tenth Muse* (1650), American women as poets have given voice to this "becoming." As Adrienne Rich remarks in her 1971 essay, "When We Dead Awaken: Writing as Revision," women's literature necessarily examines and redefines "previously accepted truths, among these, the truth Rich remembers as informing her formal education: that literature to be "universal" must be "of course, nonfemale." A consequence of this "truth," Rich notes, is that for women generally and for the woman writer particularly, "[R]e-vision—the act of looking, of seeing with fresh eyes, of entering an old text from a new critical direction—is for us more than a chapter in cultural history: it is an act of survival." Through such action, women writers as well as their readers explore "a whole new psychic geography." Contemporary Texas poetry is rich in such explorations as seen in the poetry of Wendy Barker, Cynthia MacDonald, Carol Coffee Reposa, Ntozake Shange, Pat Mora, Betty Adcock, Evangelina Vigil, and others, some of whom are examined elsewhere in *Texas Women Writers*. This essay concentrates on only three poets—Vassar Miller, Jan Epton Seale, and Sandra Lynn—as explorers of this "new psychic geography."

VASSAR MILLER

Every poet knows
what the saint knows

that every new day is
to retake the frontier of one's name.
        (from "An Essay in Criticism by Way of Rebuttal")

If I Had Wheels or Love: Collected Poems of Vassar Miller (1991) confirms that Miller's "retak[ing] the frontier of one's name" requires the act of the poet as maker. Like the saint the poet repeatedly confronts the necessity of "retaking" this frontier on which the self transforms language to poetry.

Miller's success in this transformation is evident in *If I Had Wheels or Love,* in which her eight out-of-print poetry collections are re-printed together with two sections of recent poems. The first of these sections, "The Sun Has No History," reprints poems first collected in the Latitudes Press edition of her *Selected and New Poems: 1950–1980* (1981); the second, "If I had Wheels or Love" gathers uncollected poems since 1980.

Critical response to *If I Had Wheels or Love* has been consistently laudatory, but probably the most noted tribute to Miller remains Larry McMurtry's in "Ever a Bridegroom: Reflections on the Failure of Texas Literature" (1981) in which he praises her "high gift wedded to long-sustained and exceedingly rigorous application." Though this essay provoked controversy by its questioning of many iconic works in twentieth-century Texas letters, McMurtry commends "Adams's Footprint" and its successors as "among the very few Texas books to which one can, with confidence, always return. . . . To Vassar Miller, if to anyone we have, belongs the laurel."

Miller earns her laurel, at least in part, for the acuity with which her poems create a persona seeking to understand the nature of selfhood, an understanding that Miller often seeks in religion. Though several Miller poems in the 1960s and 1970s ("Age of Aquarius, Age of Assassins," for example) measure society by religious norms and find it wanting, her most constant concern is, like Augustine's in his *Confessions,* examination of the individual who would be Christian. Like the metaphysical poets, with whom she has been compared, Miller usually speaks through a persona ("I") easily equated with the poet herself. "Adam's Footprint" (1956) and "Approaching Nada" (1977), the longest of her published poems, suggest these aspects of her writing.

"Adam's Footprint" opens with the "I" recalling her childhood game of hopping "[o]n round plump bugs" to "make them stop / Before they crossed a certain crack":

> *My bantam brawn could turn them back,*
> *My crooked step wrenched straight to kill*
> *Live pods that they screwed tight and still.*

Recalling Augustine, another "small sinner" stripping boughs and "nuzzl[ing] pears from dam-sin's dugs," the "I" who "scrunched roly-poly bugs" wonders, "How could a tree [Augustine's pear tree] be so unclean?" The last of the poem's three six-line stanzas answers this question:

> No *wolf's imprint or tiger's trace*
> Does Christ hunt down to catch with grace
> In nets of love the devious preys
> Whose feet go softly all their days:
> The foot of Adam leaves the mark
> Of some child scrabbling in the dark.

Miller's thesis is traditionally Christian: through Adam's fall we all fall, and the adult "I" finds her self—past and present— in the image of the child "scrabbling in the dark."

In contrast to the closed form and concentration on a single incident in "Adam's Footprint," "Approaching Nada," first published by Wings Press, is an open-form poem of five sections of varying length in which the "I" is placed in several contexts, including the Arizona setting described in Part 1 as the place "where these white-headed trees / blanched by the cold desert sun / open upon rosy rock / nippled and cocked toward the sky / stabbing my eye with its gaze." In the third and final stanza of Part 1, the "I" senses the mystery of the divine in this harsh land. The inhospitable desert ("the air is too thin for my lungs, / the water too scant for my mouth") leads the "I," as similar settings led the early Christian ascetics, to yearn for and feel the power and immediacy of Christ: "My Lord and My Christ, dare I come / here where the sun shrieks Thy name."

Part 2 moves to a patio, where a "tortoise-shell kitten / dart[s] feather-footed / at dream prey." But here, as throughout the poem, the "I" is central. Speculating on responses to "this Aztec land," the "I" thinks, "One might become Quaker" though "Christ is mostly Catholic / (Roman, properly)." This sixteen-line section shifts quickly between allusions to the lofty—the passion and communion—and to the mundane. Sexual play in imagery ending this section is reminiscent of such writers as Donne and St. Theresa of Avila: "the sun / softly pawing my belly / parting my blouse from my trousers, so / letting my handiest fancies have all their way willy-nilly."

Part 3 opens with contrasts between words/the Word and dumbness/silence and concludes with the persona speaking of faith and doubt. The last of the section's three five-line stanzas introduces the "phoenix," an allusion to the city where the poem evidently was written, and to the pagan and Christian symbol of death and rebirth.

In Part 4 the "I" considers herself as poet. Recalling Abbé Bremond's description of the poet as "mystique manqué," the "I," seeking to translate this phrase, settles for "sorry mystic":

> *. . . since*
> *the poet like the mouse will scuttle*
> *clean to the border*
> *of the ineffable,*
> *then scurry back*
> *with tidbits of the Vision.*

In the final section of "Approaching Nada," the "I" thinks of family. The speaker, who "know[s] my name," remembers grandparents, father, an aunt—all now "skeletons, rattled / by chancy breezes, a tree rooted / but in God's chancy hand," and the persona "prowl[ing]" this past discovers freedom from it. "Approaching Nada" ends with the "I" recognizing the self as unique and thus responsible. This recognition leads the "I" to acknowledge such divine mystery as the Nada that St. John of the Cross describes. The final lines of Part 5 affirm with some irony the willingness of "I" to undertake the quest:

> *Middling-good ghost,*
> *I seek my roots of shifted waters*
> *shifting toward Nada.*

In its complex development, symbolism, and religious vision, "Approaching Nada" differs considerably from "Adam's Footprint," which speaks directly of a single incident that traditional theology can adequately if troublingly interpret. But the poems share a tone of irony and wit that contributes to the poet's truthfulness and authority, and the "I," who judges herself a "middling-good ghost" and hopes to experience the Nada, clearly is kin to the "child scrabbling in the dark." The voice in Miller's strongest poems is this knowing, ironic poet-persona who would understand the self through religion but who remains the "I who am my own dilemma," as she writes in "Paradox."

The "dilemma" of the "I" in "Paradox" is most happily fulfilled, if never quite resolved, in her work as poet. Her poetic vocation, a secondary motif in "Approaching Nada," is primary in many of her poems, including the playful and allusive "Raison d'Etre":

> *I grow from my poems*
> *In a green world.*
>
> *Outside them I suck my breath,*
> *grow pale and poor.*
>
> *For I am the toad*
> *in my imagined garden.*

Though in "Raison d'Etre" poems "grow" with seemingly little effort on the poet's part, in "Addict" the poet's labor and self-revealing create poems: "Each day I hacked out my heart / into black chips of words / until it was gone." Like the poet in "Approaching Nada," whose poems are "white pieces" of herself, the "I" of "Addict" knows the expense of creative effort.

The persona in "Prayer to My Muse" also laments the labors poetry demands and is "none too sorry" when the door closes "where ghosts hide, / where gods hide, / where even I hide." Even as the persona longs "to be back / coiled in my wombworld," she knows the poems come by the poet's labor and hopes that the door will crack "a little" to show "stepmother muse" and "a night light burning."

If I Had Wheels or Love shows Miller's attentiveness to subjects and themes she found as a young poet. The "frontier" her poems seek to claim has remained the real and illusory one of the self as understood and measured by religion and/or aesthetics, which also prove real and illusory. Though recent poems treat such subjects as the aging and death of friends, Miller's most engaging poems remain those that explore the increasingly complex terrain her early poems discovered. Her excellence in craft is such that, as Denise Levertov fittingly remarks in her "Foreword" to *Selected and New Poems,* "These are poems that seem to call for something other than print and paper—one imagines them carved in stone, engraved in metal. . . . I salute Vassar Miller's artistry and strength, and the beauty of her somber, profoundly experienced creations."

JAN EPTON SEALE

We mean;
we know it's undeveloped land,
we're pioneers,
there's thrill in adventure and all that.
But we could use a sturdy two-wheeled cart,
some voices beside us,
a prototype or two reflecting in our eyes.
              (from "Virgin [Sic] Country" [Bonds])

Like Miller, Jan Epton Seale as poet seeks self-understanding, but Seale's insight usually comes as the "I" understands herself in relation to others, as titles of her poetry collections, *Bonds* (1981) and *Sharing the House: Poems by Jan Epton Seale* (1982), suggest. Seale's persona, like Seale herself, is daughter, granddaughter, wife, mother, and artist. Her twenty poems in *A Quartet: Texas Poets in Concert* (1990) and her fiction collection *Airlift* (1992) also show women in such roles, although in these later writings the persona sometimes moves in locales and cultures removed from the world of family and the familiar. But even in a familiar setting, Seale's persona often explores "an undeveloped land," in which familiar relationships are reunderstood and "invented."

Section titles in *Bonds* ("Woman to Self," "Woman to Woman," and "Woman to Man") point to Seale's concentration on woman as subject and voice. Unusual in Seale's writings are poems in "Woman to Self" in which the solitary persona experiences self-discovery, often through her body, as in "Ovulation." "For the Duration" makes of childhood illness and "the innocent will to live" a metaphor by which the woman who "thinks she must know the enemy / to survive" is "forged." In "Runaway, with Credentials," the persona flees her "image," "niche," "encas[ing]" to "flow backward . . . to a private grotto / she will, with time, / explore." Eschewing the "credentials" for her roles, the "she" seeks the self she imagines finding by "running freely / uphill, / running to rendezvous / herself in some / dark, sweet wood." Only in the solitude of the "dark . . . wood" can the persona enjoy the freedom to know herself apart from her varied "images."

But other sections of *Bonds* show Seale's persona as enriched and enlightened through relationships. In "Pearl Bell Pittman," for example, the "I" who visits her grandmother re-creates the pioneering life of the dying woman. Despite generational and societal differences, the "I" honors the bonds between her and her grandmother by their experience as wife and mother and their ties of blood and mortality. The "I"'s farewell acknowledges:

> *A part of me lies in her eighty-eight-year-old*
> *death-ridden body.*
> *A part of her walks in my thirty-six-year-old*
> *death-ridden body.*

In "To My Unborn Daughter" (Seale is the mother of three sons), the "I," here the older generation, finds herself searching for her daughter "in the faces of nieces" and "embraced . . . in the daughters of friends."

In "Virgin (Sic) Country" the poet responds sensitively to the difficulty of woman's pursuing even two directions:

> *We intended to be mythic,*
> *prophetesses crying in the streets:*
> *a mess of pottage burns unless it's stirred.*

As "Virgin (Sic) Country" speaks of the heroism of women artists, so "Song for Obscure Women" praises the heroic in lives often dismissed as ordinary. Taking its epigraph from Virginia Woolf— "All these infinitely obscure lives remain to be recorded," the poem honors women who live "in a dailiness monumentally unspoken, / a rapture of the objects they tend." Saying "they should / refuse the menial, shun the low" is easy, but the voice in the poem knows that maintaining the seemingly predictable order of the daily requires the work and vision of the "obscure":

> *. . . who are made noble through the filigrees*
> *and labyrinths of your minds,*
> *the countless renderings of your hands upon reality*
> *which daily overlay the world with a secret order.*

Other poems in *Bonds*, especially those in the "Woman to Man" section, affirm the trust bonding man and woman. Among Seale's best poems are those on marriage, such as "Intercourse," in which the "I," after performing her evening ritual of securing "this old farmhouse," goes to bed: "you take my cold hands and fold them into

your shirt. / Naughty but thankful, my cold feet become your soles."
As the "I" lies beside her sleeping husband:

> My poems stir—the literary lizards
> mate, biting necks upon sestina,
> himself into herself, sex-duty for this house.
>
> Through spacious dark the planet slings our bed.
> I quietly lie; the avenue between us sleeps.

Sharing the House centers on the mother/son bond but also re-marks on insights this bond brings to other relationships, as in "Chew-ing," in which the daughter discovers a new bond with her father, who visits her and his new grandson. "[I]ll at ease with people into sex, / having babies," the father takes refuge in helping her with her hospital meal, "each bite . . . / paying like a nub of peyote." For the persona "chewing backward / to my father / he feeding forward / to my child," the meal is a sacrament. Her father's gift to her and her newborn is her understanding of the "genealogies / called to supper."

Several poems in *Sharing the House,* among them "To a Boy Who Lost His First Tooth Today," "Note to the Teacher," and "Public School of America the Beautiful," speak of "I"'s response to her son's experience. In one of the loveliest of such childhood poems, "Crack of Dawn," the "I" finds the boy abed with "drawing tablet, / a pen-cil, the 'L' / of the encyclopedia":

> My son,
> did anyone ever tell you
>
> eight year olds
> in America
>
> do not sketch
> from Leonardo
>
> on cold mornings?
> No one has given you
>
> instructions
> for shaping the aquiline nose,
> shading the sfumato.

You are
a sketchbook intact,

a flying machine,
a Milanese horse,
a Florentine sundial.

You are the reason
behind my enigmatic smile.

In "Lies, You Wish," the "I" describes the pubescent son whose voice ranges unpredictably between bullfrog and "a rodeo horse bucking / soprano or bass laughter." His "dirty top lip / (you'd hoped it was newspaper print)" and other "sinister signs" presage the son's adulthood and freedom from parents.

The title poem of *Sharing the House* is the longest in the collection and encapsulates its themes. "Sharing the House" traces the mother/son bond from pregnancy, when the mother's body/house "contained you and you rose / yeasted by your father," to the son's coming of age and the mother's recognition of separations. Like "To My Unborn Daughter," this poem is benedictory in tone, especially in its ending, in which the persona blesses "the simpleness / of owning each other, / of letting each other go." By "letting go," the mother can continue to create bonds with her son out of his discovery of new loves. Thinking of the "new mothers, new sons" and the ties between generations, the "I" imagines the joy this extended family will bring.

Themes of accepting and "inventing" new ways of bonding are prominent in Seale's recent writings. In her story in *Airlift,* "The Past Tense of Mom," the mother is regretful and good-humored at her son's returning to college. "Letting each other go" isn't easy, but the mother hopes that he will "continue to introduce himself every time" he comes home and that she can learn "to curb the impulse to protect him." In this visit home, the mother finds this "new thing between them. . . . this friendship, of all things, with her own son—it amazed her almost as much as his birth."

Seale's poem "Believing Is Seeing" (*A Quartet: Texas Poets in Concert* 41–42) also accepts and is hopeful about change. Here the son instructs the mother in using a telescope and leads her to see "Orion's Nebula":

> Afraid to blink, I whisper, "Yes, I see them.
> Yes." The astronomer's hand tightens on my arm.
> "The Trapezium Cluster, at fifteen-hundred light-years."
> He laughs. "I give them to you because you see them."
> "I take them," I say, and feel him near.

Seale's poetry is admirable for its authenticity in creating "woman's world" as constant in values which must find new ways of being expressed. Seale's loving, courageous personae are good at "invention," which involves reunderstanding the familiar and exploring the new in old relationships. This openness to experience, even if painful, leads to the affirmation and sense of discovery that distinguish her writing.

SANDRA LYNN

> there's a new world rounding my belly
> over my globing sea christopher columbus sings out landfall
> a "passage to more than india" awaits me
> the heartbeat below mine a mystery deeper than the vedas
> to compass it, i must more than a new geography
>
> i enter the waters of the now inevitable discovery
> enter too the circle, the eventual circumnavigation
> passage to yet a farther sea
> to journeys of risk into, beyond me
> what was before will no longer be my boundary
> > (from "Meta Physical Pregnancy: A Conceit," in I
> > Must Hold These Strangers: Poems by Sandra Lynn)

Lynn's conceit in the above poem creates the persona as an explorer who knows the risks and rewards of experience and who delights in the prospect that "what was before will no longer be my boundary." In the practice of her craft, Lynn is similarly adventurous. An open-form prosodist, she likes to experiment with the shape of her poems. Though she shares several subjects with Miller and Seale, she differs from them in that she often draws her subjects from nature. In "A Leaf from the Book of Trees," for example, trees as "mirrors," give vignettes of the persona's life. Each of the poem's eleven imagistic stanzas creates such a mirror, such as "a tall gowned spruce" in Connecticut, the rain-silvered olives along the "autostrada tunneling fiercely to Rome," and the cypress in Greece "announcing darkly / the vertical journey." In the poem's final section, the mimosa becomes the poet's muse:

> Here, spring on my hill
> under a canopy
> of mimosa
> pitched overnight
> an Arabian seductress' tent.
> She brings songs, my love
> and tales, my love
> and old praise.

Trees as inscriptors with a "system of writing" become a metaphor in "The Trees Are Burning," in which fire imagery signals the change of season:

> The trees are burning the sky this spring.
> Sap boils up trunks, and flash fires
> in tops threaten
> the sane blue boundaries.

Lynn's most extended use of nature comes in the *Where Rainbows Wait for Rain: The Big Bend Country* (1989), a collaborative volume of photographs by Richard Fenker, Jr., and poems by Lynn. Such titles as "Desert Afternoon," "Camped below Burro Mesa," and "The Chisos Mountains" suggest the emphasis on place in her forty poems. Like her other nature poems, these find nature more than only scenic.

This volume also includes "Shape to Shape" (titled "In the Big Bend" in *I Must Hold These Strangers*), in which the "we" find themselves "submerged in the absence / of an ancient sea," a mysterious "proteus" beyond the capacity of geologic and historic data to explain. In a setting in which the dark comes suddenly as "the sun goes down like a hammer / on an anvil," the "we" perceive the limits of their knowledge. Elsewhere, Lynn combines nature and art, as in "The Birth of Venus in the Gulf of Mexico," a revisionist version of the Botticelli painting that points to Old and New World distinctions.

Other poems in Lynn's poetry collection, among them "To Roberto and the Children" and "Of Toledo I Remember," evince her empathy with particular locales and their people. But the theme in her most moving poems, as in "Grandmother's Photographs Are Making Demands," is empathy across generations nearer home. The "photographic delicacies under glass cover" on the kitchen table confuse the grandmother. Seeing "these are my who are these?":

> She says the pictures over and over
> They bind her to the flickering light
> Fast, click, this bead of person is kept to be counted
> The litany of their images holds her
>
> Her bedroom walls are covered with icons of paper progeny
> No easier to live with than big brown water stains
> or roses the color of dried blood
> harder, in fact, because she says the photographs waken her
> and tell her to go to the kitchen to cook breakfast
> which she can no longer do.

Lynn draws again on the subject/theme of generational relationships in "I am a bruise," in which the "I" remembers when she and her father spread "maps on the gold carpet" to study "places and faces in National Geographic . . . so they would be familiar / when we arrived. / Our arrival was delayed many years." In fact the father's travel was limited to "our Sunday drive." Thinking of the father in age and illness, the "I" sees his confinement to the familiar world as expressing "his final fear" of the "autonomy" of those in distant places. As legatee of her father, the "I" inherits her sense of his losses by such fear. Left to "bump into what he abandoned at every turn, / making bruises like birthmarks," the "I," in existentialist mode, praises engaging what is:

> They say the world is shrinking.
>   LAST CHANCE TO WITNESS ITS WANING POWERS
> I chafe at the time lost,
> cutting unseen fences.

Lynn's persona, eager to cut "unseen fences," speaks with most love and hope in poems to her son, who in "Answer to the Often-Pondered Question of Why Bring a Child into This Cruel World" becomes her teacher. In this dialogue between the persona and her unborn child, the persona advises, "You oughta stay where you are / It's splendid out there / on the / air-conditioned / mega-jewel / cat-walks" of the solar system. Lines below show the child rejecting the advice and the woman consenting to his birth:

> *I [the son] wanta get in*
> *into that cloud traffic*
> *that cinematic world beatific*
> *that green chance*
> *of a horse race of a place*
> *So I [the mother] see that this kid has a point*
> *and I say*
> *Okay*
> *Come on in*
> *The water's fine*

Lynn's poems suggest that of all relationships, that between mother and son is the most transforming for women. "To My Son" uses "Rubens' lusty cherubs" and "a certain cupid / in one of Tiepolo's ceilings" to "illumine" the child's beauty, but because the child is "more solid / than a dab of god on canvas," the mother finds sculpture a better metaphor than painting for comparing her and her son: "you are the bronze putto / in the courtyard of the Palazzo Vecchio."

Lynn's poems present woman's relationship with man as less certainly durable and happy. In "An Afternoon Rain," for example, the "we" now encounter one another only "on dry land, matters / of money, legal tender? (no not), what / will the baby eat?" Yet a "terrain / of restraint," though "heavily cratered" and "bare and ruined even for grasses," proves "nonetheless solid / a place to stand." Separated, the "we" find again "the need for speech . . . greater than the need for footing."

A Lynn poem from 1986, "The Body Remembers an Old Grammar," suggests the promise in the persona's relationship with the man "from the Adirondacks, / down here in the kiln of Texas." As they walk, "cold wind" and rain reach them, and the man, who is "homesick for the onslaught / of mountain winter" delights. On the "long way / to shelter over rough ground," they hold one another:

> *Later I believed*
> *I had been spoken to in secret,*
> *though besides the stun of the rain*

I could recall nothing said
but his hands.

Lynn's metaphors of speech, writing, and grammar consistently praise openness to experience, a response the title poem of her collection also commends as it acknowledges the pain such openness can occasion. In the first section of "I Must Hold These Strangers," the persona finds in metaphors of touch a means to evoke her dead parents, her young son, and his father, who "has taken / touch away." In "II," the persona interprets her body as "one rung / of the ladder of genes," and the "I," who as mother connects generations, thunders "in the mother and father / echoing in the child / the plain song, the pain song / played on / every fine hair." In "III," the metaphor of the circle reinforces the persona's uniting of past, present, and future. Not "know[ing] the changes," the speaker moves—as she must—in worlds familiar and new. Though she is unable to "move smoothly," arms catching her move her "on deeper into the circle":

> *A stranger is turning me*
> *surely as a planet.*
> *If I obey the music*
> *I must hold these strangers.*
> *Whoever they are, these other dancers*
> *wait for the grasp of my hand.*

In methods, themes, and poetic voice, each poet examined here is unique and original. Differences among these poets are many, but evident too in their work are common threads, among them an emphasis on empathetic response to experience whether happy or painful or both. Seale's title for her first collection, *Bonds*, suggests a theme each writer explores. Though less prominent in Miller, the theme resonates in poems by Seale and Lynn.

Common among the three poets, too, is their concentration on the female persona (almost always "I") whose experience correlates with the poet's. Though none of the three is aggressively feminist, each finds in a female persona the voice to express meanings and values each poet holds.

Simone de Beauvoir's metaphor of "woman as becoming" is fitting for these poets, each of whom at times creates her persona through metaphors of discovery, pioneering, and exploring, metaphors that point to realities, necessities, and possibilities for women in our time. These personae find in the familiar and the mundane the means to encounter, in addition to the immediate, the unknown and unexplored, an encounter that requires daring and candor about the self. Such requirements suggest a new model for the heroic, one in which the contest is to understand and therefore respond insightfully to the self and beyond the self. Such heroics are nonviolent. No lands except imaginative ones are taken, and the battles these poets record are within the self. For such understanding as these seek, identification with that beyond the self—the metaphysical for Miller; the others, projected and real, to whom Seale's "I" responds; the natural and human worlds of Lynn's persona—is essential.

In these poets the search for meanings in and beyond the self is constant (and offers an ideal compatible with the lives most of us lead). As these poets suggest, our lives are spent in a dailiness that imposes many demands and is also the means by which our understanding of self, others, and the metaphysical—in whatever form—can be achieved.

THREE CONTEMPORARY POETS

Naomi Shihab Nye, Pattiann Rogers, and Betsy Feagan Colquitt

JAN EPTON SEALE

NAOMI SHIHAB NYE

Several years ago, in a planning meeting to consider visiting artists for classrooms in a Central Texas school district, the name of Naomi Shihab was proposed, her previous visit to the district having been a positive experience. Apparently, though, one of the planners opposed the suggestion "because she wore funny socks."

Nye's "funny socks," part of the rich-textured clothes that are her predilection, may have worried provincial Texas folks in the past, but her track record worldwide in those socks has given her an enviable national reputation as a poet, and Texans, even those in the outback, have come to accept and admire her.

Born in St. Louis, Missouri, in 1952 of an Arab father and an American mother, Nye graduated from Trinity University in 1974 and since has made her permanent home in San Antonio. She is married to the lawyer-photographer Michael Nye. They have a son, Madison Cloudfeather.

Nye has worked principally as a writer-in-residence through the arts commissions of Texas, Wyoming, and Maine. She also has held visiting lectureships at Lewis and Clark College, the University of California at Berkeley, the University of Texas at San Antonio, and Our Lady of the Lake University at San Antonio.

Nye has traveled extensively, having visited Central and South America and represented the United States in the Middle East and Asia through the Arts America program of the United States Information Agency. In 1988 she was one of three recipients of the Lavan Younger Poets Award sponsored by the Academy of American Poets.

Two chapbooks, *Tattooed Feet* (1976) and *Eye-to-Eye* (1977), both in the Texas Portfolio Chapbook Series, preceded her first book-length publication, *Different Ways to Pray,* brought out in 1980 by Breitenbush Books. *On the Edge of the Sky,* another chapbook, appeared under the Iguana Press imprint in 1981. The second major book, *Hugging the Jukebox,* was published by E. P. Dutton in 1982 as part of the National Poetry Series, judged by Josephine Miles. The publication of *Hugging the Jukebox* produced a spate of national reviews and enhanced Nye's already growing reputation outside the state.

Yellow Glove, published in 1986 by Breitenbush, was reviewed extensively in such publications as *The Georgia Review, Kenyon Review, Booklist,* and *Southwestern American Literature.* Critics acclaimed it for showing Nye's unique worldview and her subtle handling of language.

Recent publications include *The Spoken Page,* a tape/text set produced by International Poetry Forum in 1988. This work provides fifty selected and new poems in a printed text, with an hour's reading on tape by the poet. *Library Journal* calls Nye's work "vital and searching," each poem with "a power and a story."

Many of Nye's poems reveal her sharp eye and ear for skillful use of metaphor. Earlier poems tended to contain fairly uncomplicated comparisons, but in *Yellow Glove* the metaphors become bolder and more daringly juxtaposed:

> *The tune she hummed was nobody's tongue.*
> *Already she had seen the brothers go off*
> *in airplanes, she did not like the sound.*
> *Skies opened and took people in.*
> *The tune was long and had one line.*
> *(from "Her Way")*

The approach to the subject, or the story, is often indirect. It may be only after the second or third grouping of lines that the reader begins to understand the circumstances. Consider the first two stanzas of "My Uncle Mohammed at Mecca, 1981":

> This year the wheels of cars
> are stronger than the wheels of prayer.
> Where were you standing when it hit you,
> what blue dome rose up in your heart?
>
> I hold the birds you sent me,
> olive wood clumsily carved.
> The only thing I have
> that you touched.

The effect is that of a quilted poem, with one imagining Nye working as much with arrangement and rearrangement of ideas as with the initial outpouring. One of the charms of Nye's gift is her wisdom rising out of the disjointedness which—the reader comes to realize—she has taken pains to create.

Many poems are rooted in Nye's travels, sometimes for their direct subject matter but more often for observations of the human condition or the telling of an evocative story. Palestine, Pakistan, Tegucigalpa, Berkeley, Fredericksburg—all are there, seemingly with effortless juxtaposition. The poems are alive with marketplaces, bread, jasmine, tomatoes, shrimp, gaunt men, soft women. Even in San Antonio the exotica come through:

> She feeds her roses coffee
> to make them huge. When her son was in Vietnam
> the bougainvillea turned black once overnight,
> But he didn't die. She prescribes lemongrass,
> manzanilla: in her album the grandchildren
> smile like seed packets.
> (from "Where the Soft Air Lives")

Nye's use of place as metaphor and launching point makes a case against the dullness of the straight "travel" poem. Her poems might serve as a model for the novice poet tempted only to lyricize the yearly vacation.

Her lessons learned, precepts acknowledged, are still cautious. Her way is to present a scene and then ask a question or draw a measured conclusion. The poems abound with questions: "And did they like what they saw?" "How bad is it to dress in a cold room?" "Morning, shiny shoe, what do I do to deserve you?" She is always searching. Her oft-quoted question, "What will we learn today?" is followed by hope: "There should be an answer, / and it should / change" (from "Telling the Story").

Much has been made of Nye's progression as a poet. In praising her talent, critics have devoted noticeable space to questioning Nye's positive outlook and celebration of life, particularly apparent in her first two books. One critic went so far as to observe that "our reality is not contained in her book"—as if the poet's chief concern were a collective reader reality. Nye's published work, regardless of how early, has never been naive, but it has progressed toward a more complex rendering of the world around and inside her.

Nye has paid her dues to Texas literature. She edited poetry for David Yates in the now-defunct *Cedar Rock*. She published the work of school children of Texas, including an album of songs from children of the San Antonio area, and performed with Sharda Brody in children's Fine Arts Series programs across the state. She has participated in and organized many festivals of literature around the state through her work as an artist with the Texas Commission on the Arts. Nye's subject is not the wide-open prairie, barbed wire, or honky-tonks. She is, instead, a part of the greening of Texas literature.

This Same Sky: A Collection of Poems from Around the World, edited by Nye in 1992, was named "Notable Book" by the American Library Association, "Editor's Choice" by *Booklist*, and one of the "Best Books for the Teen Age" by the New York Public Library. The collection also received the Jane Addams Award for Social Justice. *Sitti's Secrets* (1994) was a "Pick of the List" of American Booksellers and named "Best Book 1994" by *School Library Journal*. *Red Suitcase* and *Words Under the Words: Selected Poems* also were published in 1994.

PATTIANN ROGERS

Pattiann Tall Rogers was born in 1940 in Joplin, Missouri. She has a B.A. in English literature from the University of Missouri-Columbia and an M.A. in creative writing from the University of Houston. In

1989 she moved with her family to Denver, Colorado, after having resided in Stafford for twenty years. At that time, she wrote of her Texas affiliation, "With the exception of maybe three or four poems, *everything* that I have ever published was written in Stafford, Texas."

Rogers's ascent as an American poet has been meteoric. In 1981, Princeton University Press chose her *The Expectations of Light* for their Series of Contemporary Poets. Book-length volumes have followed: *The Tattooed Lady in the Garden,* (1986), *Legendary Performance* (1987), and *Splitting and Binding* (1989). Two chapbooks during that time also made significant contributions: *The Ark River Review: Three Poet Issue* (1981) and *The Only Holy Window* (1984).

Her list of awards and prizes is equally impressive. *Poetry* magazine awarded her the Eunice Tietjens Prize in 1981 and the Bess Hokin Prize in 1982. The Theodore Roethke Prize from *Poetry Northwest* came also in 1981. She also has received two grants from the National Endowment for the Arts and a Guggenheim fellowship. In 1991 she was awarded a Lannan Foundation Fellowship and the Prairie Schooner Strousse Award. She also received the Pushcart Prize in 1991, as she had in 1984, 1985, and 1989.

She has held visiting lectureships in creative writing at The University of Texas, Vermont College of Norwich University, the University of Montana, the University of Houston, and Southern Methodist University. In addition she has visited numerous cities and campuses with readings and workshops.

With the publication of *The Expectations of Light,* Rogers was established in what one reviewer called "the American Adamic tradition." The poems play with nature, cataloging ("Counting What the Cactus Contains"), posing hypothetical situations ("Suppose Your Father Was a Redbird"), and using nature as a metaphor for the inner land of the spirit ("Handling Despair").

When asked about her already unique voice in this first collection, Rogers replied, "There was a point in my writing in which I learned to do something new, and it marks a point in my mind. . . : all the poems that came before I learned how to do this and all the poems that came after." What she learned was that she was disappointed. "This experience was such a pleasurable. . . feeling that I wanted it to happen over and over again, and I was willing to work hard for it; it was a disappointment when it didn't come, and the poems in which it didn't come, these I put aside."

Although she began to have poems published in prestigious magazines and to win national prizes, it was 1986 before her second major book, *The Tattooed Lady in the Garden,* was brought out, by Wesleyan University Press. In this volume, there is a less studied catalog of nature; she conducts fewer Einsteinian experiments than in *Expectations.* She moves out in imagination to wonder about "The Possible Suffering of a God during Creation," shows a flair for the personally sensual, as in "Love Song" and "The Hummingbird: A Seduction," and meditates on the meaning of death in such poems as "The Limitations of Death." In this poem her wit and penchant for paradox come into play when she observes of death:

> *No form of its own at all, less than a wraith,*
> *It is bound forever to the living.*

Also in *Tattooed Lady* are introductions to characters later featured in *Legendary Performance.* They are Kioka, a self-styled native, and a sort of latter-day Bloomsbury group composed of Gordon, Sonia, Felicia, Albert, and Cecil.

In *Legendary Performance* (1987) these people hold conversations poem after poem, often in the manner of two-year-olds who play side by side, watching each other but without direct interaction. Sometimes they are joined by blind beggars, naked boys on ponies, or Felicia's uncle. They rarely make value judgments about each other, preferring to speak tangentially by stanzas on various aspects of things such as a parlor concert, the color violet, sorrow, or a lost journal. On first encountering the quaint group, a reader may be irritated by their *non sequiturs,* seeing them only as a clever device Rogers has brought on to relieve the complexity of the lecture style critics have noted in earlier poems. But as the poems roll along, the fantastical group taking tea or running down a hill together or receiving the Gentlemen of Leisure, we gain an affection for their unlikeliness, their pretensions, their calm observations or passionate longings. Their innocence and eggheadedness are endearing.

Splitting and Binding (1989) takes a different turn, this time to things of the spirit. Without being sentimentally religious or naively pantheistic, Rogers acknowledges here in a new way an Energy in being that she wishes to explore. There are praying irises ("The Answering of Prayers)" and meditating birds ("for the Wren Trapped in a Cathedral"). There is a god puzzled over: What did he have in mind in creating an ash-colored toad? Whom could a snowshoe hare have been calling to in its cry at the moment of death? And there are poems in a style Rogers has called "just a song, just a carefree voice of praise," such as the poem "Rolling Naked in the Morning Dew" where she concludes that such an activity would provide a "healing energy," "beneficent results," and "good delights":

> *Just consider how the mere idea of it alone*
> *Has already caused me to sing and sing*
> *This whole morning long.*

Rogers's poems are conservative in form, with the daring saved for the content. Her lines tend to be long, with from four to six accents, the sense building over several lines to a periodic climax, perhaps followed by an elliptical question or answer. She seems to be most comfortable with a poem of forty or fifty lines.

An anomaly in modern poetry, her use of scientific and abstract terms has been marveled over and commented upon repeatedly. In her earliest published poems she was more inclined to direct discourse, such as in "The Rites of Passage" in *Expectations*:

> *The inner cell of each frog egg laid today*
> *In these still open waters is surrounded*
> *By melanin pigment, by a jelly capsule*
> *Acting as cushion to the falling of the surf,*
> *As buffer to the loud crow-calling*
> *Coming from the cleared forests to the north.*

Later work reflects a refinement of the didactic method with the facts of the universe worked in perhaps more playfully but with no less verve. Consider "The Family Is All There Is" from *Spitting and Binding*:

> *Remember the same hair on pygmy*
> *dormouse and yellow-necked caterpillar,*
> *covering red baboon, thistle seed*
> *and willow herb? Remember the similar*
> *snorts of warthog, walrus, male moose*
> *and sumo wrestler?*

Pattiann Rogers's poems contain a Noah's ark of animals, a garden with everything labeled, skies and forests and deserts. But lest she be categorized as a nature poet, there is also evidence of the metaphysical: "experience," "performance," "imagination," and "revelation."

Rogers continues to publish collections of her work, including *Firekeeper, New and Selected Poems* (named one of the best books of 1994 by *Publishers Weekly), Geocentric* (1993), and a chapbook entitled *Lies and Devotions* (1994).

BETSY FEAGAN COLQUITT

One of the most stable, most influential figures in Texas letters for the past five decades, Betsy Colquitt has been less well known as poet, probably in part because of her innate modesty and most certainly because of her devotion to tending the work of other writers.

Colquitt has been editor of *Descant,* a literary magazine originating from Texas Christian University, for more than thirty years. The guidance of a small magazine by a single sensitive editor for thirty years is a rarity in publishing, either in Texas or nationally. Looking over the twenty-fifth anniversary issue, (1956–81) one notes Colquitt's editorial predilection for nourishing Southwest writers: June Welch, Elroy Bode, Bryan Woolley, Carolyn Osborn, William Barney, Albert Goldbarth, and Walt McDonald, among others.

Colquitt, born in 1926 in Ft. Worth, is the author of a substantial volume of poems, *Honor Card* (1980). In addition her poems have been published in magazines such as *Quartet, New Laurel Review, New Mexico Humanities Review,* and *RiverSedge,* and anthologized in such standard works as *Southwest: A Contemporary Anthology* and *Fiction and Poetry by Texas Women.* Two notable groupings of her poems may be found in the 1982 and 1986 issues of *Latitude 30° 18'.*

In reading Colquitt's poems, one is impressed with her consistent and unique voice. She seems to have escaped the whims of each decade, and she is far too wise to write imitatively. Her style is formal, with demanding vocabulary and syntax. She is most at home with stanzas, or with near-even groupings of lines. Colquitt's poems are quiet, even philosophical, filled with wit. Her subject matter is far-ranging, from figures in Renaissance art to the complexities of long marriage, from Mexican vacations to modern Neanderthals.

Her crispness of diction, lean phrases scoured of definite articles, predilection for playing with words, and adherence to the demands of rhythmic language do not countenance a cozy armchair once-over

of her work. A poem called "the lie and truth of this land" is a thir-
teen-stanza extended metaphor comparing a long domestic coupling
with an epic war. Sometimes the couple are combatants:

> and when our armies met, war was guerrilla.
> You were good at hiding even in bare land,
> but I'd skills for ferreting your defenses,
> seeking keenly in private terrains.

Notice the quaintly arranged "war was guerrilla," the little-used con-
traction "I'd" for "I had," and the cool and formal "ferreting your
defenses" and "private terrains."

Later in the poem as children and household management appear,
the warfare continues as "skirmishes" or weekend "campaigns," and
"if compass couldn't guide, necessities did: / do:" Note the economy
here in the ellipsis.

As time goes by, the couple grows more comfortable, less combat-
ive, and even if they've not captured "south fields / bountied of gentle
flowers," still "more now other unnorthern needs avail." As the poem
closes, Colquitt observes that "If not love, it's more love than hate."
And the two are "mainly easy at armistice / and rarely foraging,
commissaried now / mostly from home." Difficult phrases alternate
with forthright, and the moderating effect of the qualifiers, "more
now," "more love than hate," "mainly," "rarely," and "mostly" seem
to bring the poet to rest as auxiliary parachutes might open before a
landing.

Colquitt's role as professor of English at Texas Christian University has given her an enviable ease with literary and mythological
subjects. She uses them either as subjects or as metaphors. In "two
on gulliver" the poet imagines Mrs. Gulliver's reaction to her husband's
various homecomings. Colquitt's wit dazzles in these imaginary scenes:

> His first trip back, he fondled her
> like a kitten, a doll, kept wanting her
> to walk on his hand, find the sheep tucked,
> he said, in his pocket. After second trip,
> he shouted each day her grossness,
> then crept to her breast like a babe.

On his final return, Mrs. Gulliver keeps to her duties as housewife
and mother, sheltering her children from their "whinnying father."

In "museum scene: an *adoration*," Colquitt addresses one of the wise men, a "magus," in a tone echoing the language in a fourteenth-century studio:

> *Let the posturing go, sir,*
> *and look to his comfort.*
> *I would you would see*
> *and word his ease at this stable,*
> *beasts breathing warm on him*
> *and arms of his mother crossing*
> *gently to sure his limber back.*

Notice the use of "word" as a verb, presumably meaning to noise abroad the Holy Child's comfort in his lowly circumstances, and "sure" for reinforce or insure. This unusual diction, popular with her throughout her poems, works best in poems such as this one, in which the reader is prepared for the quaintness by the speaker's tone and the circumstance.

Other poems in this category include "for xanthippe: praise" and "helen unloved."

Her lifetime of reading and classical training appear as second nature in her poems. In a poem called "cuptowels," she notes that a woman who has decorated dishtowels with needlework cannot eradicate pictures of chickens from the original feed sacks of which the cuptowels are made:

> *these hens beyond all lycing*
> *parade as mighty shades*
> *bloodless and real*
> *over stitched and fabulous being.*

Colquitt is at home in a number of content areas, some already indicated. Others are her beautiful and moving poems on various women in her life: her mother, wishing away her loneliness and old age in "omnibus," seeing her young and happy in her girlish smartness in the title piece "honor card"; her daughters, telling one to be still and enjoy a dragonfly in "scene," praying another learns to cope with adversity as she falls on the icy hill below their Ft. Worth home in "going with gravity"; her students in "girls in the rain"; and a companionable female friend in "bells of ireland." Her most completely drawn female is Eve, in a cycle of poems printed in *Latitude*

30° 18'. Primordial Eve figures out that work is rather fun in "basket case," helps her mate out of the miry clay in a surprising switch in "adam," allows Adam to do strange things to her in "making kind" (though "his brief act is enough / i am so nearly parthenogenetic"), learns about evil via the food chain, and finally, in Part 1, is "ungardened."

In Part 2 of "eve: the autobiography," Eve writes Cain (in exile, of course) and—true to Betsy Colquitt—meets with Dr. Freud, and placates a troubled Kafka who comes visiting to blame her for original sin.

Betsy Colquitt is wise, scholarly, constant, influential. Her poems are sculptured, filled with wit and sense, testimony of an art taken seriously and a life well-lived.

Part 4
DRAMATISTS

INTRODUCTION

Although women playwrights in Texas have not achieved national attention very often, many are promising models for future women dramatists in the state. Active in the little-theater movement in Texas, which began in the 1920s, many women associated with amateur theater also wrote skits and plays for presentation by local actors. Amateur theaters were often encouraged by women's groups, and the Dallas Woman's Forum hired a director and created a dramatic department (soon to become the respected Dallas Little Theater) in 1920.

In 1942 the *Southwest Review* published three plays written for the Dallas Little Theater by Texas playwrights. *Three Southwest Plays*, with an introduction by the then-famous Dallas drama critic, John Rosenfield, features plays by two men and a courageous and far-sighted Dallas high school English teacher, Kathleen Witherspoon. Entitled *Jute,* the play was controversial from its first production in 1929 as an entry in the Texas Little Theater Tournament in Fort Worth. Rejected for presentation by the Dallas Little Theater, the play was staged in 1930 by the Little Theatre of Oak Cliff.

The play stars Jute, the mulatto daughter of a small-town white judge in Georgia. Jute's search for true identity provides the action of the drama. Racial conflict as a theme was a bold choice for Wither-spoon in 1930, but Rosenfield says the "Dallas public remembers

Jute as perhaps the best original script that has emerged from the city's little theater activity." Ironically, although the play offered roles for both Black and white actors, when the drama played in the little theaters, white actors played the Black parts, and when the Dallas Negro Players produced the play at Booker T. Washington High School in 1931, Black actors took the roles of the white players. Rosenfield says that "four years later another Little Theatre of Oak Cliff director wanted to try the experiment of producing *Jute* with a mixed cast of whites and Negroes, and ran into a stupid but stubborn invocation of the Jim Crow law." The novelist Theodore Dreiser saw the play and asked to be presented to Kathleen Witherspoon. He praised her work and asked her what she planned to write next. Unfortunately, Witherspoon never found the time or will to create another drama.

Although contemporary Texas women playwrights may not have heard of Kathleen Witherspoon, the spirit she exemplified lives on.

EMERGING FROM THE WINGS

Texas Women Dramatists

WILLIAM B. MARTIN

That original drama, an urban literary form, has been late to develop in Texas is understandable. Why women playwrights have lagged behind their male counterparts, however, is less clear.

It is a harsh but nevertheless true observation that good drama is seldom if ever written except for professional-quality acting companies. Maybe there is an analogy between playwrights and music composers writing for symphony orchestras rather than for high school bands or even for violins rather than harmonicas. Only when the instruments of interpretation are capable of subtle and wide-ranging expression are the writers challenged to produce their best. Until after World War II, Texas had few if any resident acting companies of quality sufficient to develop discerning audiences, capable players, or serious dramatic writers. Until that time, road shows and amateur groups (either community or school based) had supplied the theater experience of most Texans. As John Rosenfield of the *Dallas Morning News* said about his beat, "The arts were nothing more than spiritual and recreational comfort until the post-World War II period."

Ramsey Yelvington and Horton Foote were the first Texas playwrights of distinction. However, because Yelvington wrote most of his plays for Paul Baker's Baylor University theater in Waco, his reputation was necessarily restricted. Living and writing on the East Coast kept Foote from being considered particularly Texan until he began making films here in the eighties. Not until the mid-1970s, first with Preston Jones and then with Jack Heifner, D. L. Coburn, and James McLure in rapid succession, did Texas playwrights receive widespread recognition.

There have been quality women dramatists in Texas, but they have not yet attained attention comparable to that of the best male playwrights. None has yet turned out a play that has won major New York success, generated regular regional productions, or been adapted into a well-received film. Without attaining at least one of these accomplishments, and without trade publication, there is little chance of national media notice or a national reputation.

One would think that the strong positions women have held in Texas theaters would have encouraged Texas women to write for the stage, but in spite of the clout wielded by Margo Jones, Nina Vance, Iris Schiff, Pat Brown, Rose Pearson, and Norma Young over the years, no major woman playwright has been nurtured in a theater under their active management. Paul Baker at the Dallas Theater Center and later Ted Swindley at Stages Theater in Houston deserve the most credit for developing new playwrights of both sexes in Texas.

Those women who have done noteworthy stage writing seem to have arrived from one of two directions. Either they were successful writers first in other genres and then branched out to dramatic forms, or they were primarily theater people whose writing grew from their interest and skill in associated aspects of stage art.

Outstanding among the first group would be Jewel Gibson, Elizabeth Forsythe Hailey, and Patricia Griffith. Gibson can be credited as the first Texas woman to achieve serious stage success as a writer, but she was celebrated for her novel *Joshua Beene and God* (1946) before her first play was written. In fact, a dramatization of *Joshua Beene and God* by collaborators Hal Lewis and Clifford Sage was Gibson's introduction to the stage. The play was produced in 1950 by the Alley Theatre of Houston and in 1961 by the Dallas Theater Center in a production that featured guest artist Burl Ives in the title role. Like many of Gibson's later plays, this adaptation dealt with controversial material. The central character was a small-town minister who both dominated and bullied his parishioners and reveled in his privileged position in God's plan while leading them into Christian understanding. Although the work was condemned from at least one Baptist pulpit and considered shocking by many, critical opinion agreed, for the most part, that the material accurately reflected small-town East Texas fundamentalism.

Gibson's next play, *Creep Past the Mountain Lion*, written with collaborators Sage and Lewis, took up the racial issue, cautioning Negroes that progress will depend upon "creeping past the mountain lion and easing by the panther." In 1966, when Preston Jones directed the play at the Dallas Theater Center, Paul Baker judged it "a penetrating dramatic episode in the evolution of American race relations." Today, though, the play's view of African Americans seems paternalistic, occasionally condescending.

The subject of Gibson's *Brann and The Iconoclast*, which premiered at Trinity University in 1971, was the nineteenth-century journalist William Cowper Brann of Waco, who so irritated portions of that community with his inflammatory newspaper, *The Iconoclast*, that he was shot to death on a public street and his funerary bust was later defaced with gunfire. The play utilized both real and fictitious characters and emphasized the clash of ideas and moral stances prevalent in the 1890s in central Texas.

Gibson's most original and most successful playwriting experience was *Miss Ney*, a work based on the life of the early Texas sculptor, Elizabet Ney, who emigrated from Bavaria in 1871. In this play, Gibson was able to depict a powerfully independent female artist in rebellion against the controversial social restraints placed on her gender, an artist from a European cultural tradition in conflict with the crudity of frontier life. Both in its conventional form and in a later monodrama version, *Heart of Stone,* which utilized Reba Robertson as collaborator, the play movingly displays the central character's courage and the price that she, her husband, and her son paid for her devotion to her ideals. It is surprising that these dramas are not presented more often today by companies desirous of appealing to the heightened public interest in pioneering feminists.

Gibson's *Rachel* is based on the life of Andrew Jackson's wife. Another play, *Rachel, Woman of Masada* is a monodrama depicting siege and martyrdom in biblical Palestine. It has been given distinguished performances by Jeannett Clift George in Houston and on tour.

Elizabeth Forsythe Hailey is a writer of autobiographical fiction who dramatized her first novel into a play in 1978. The resulting stage version of *A Woman of Independent Means* had a short New York run followed by a very successful tour that took the play to Dallas (for ten weeks) and Houston and to major cities on both coasts. The play is handicapped by its form, a single actress reading letters that cover fifty years of the life of a character, Bess Steed Garner, derived from Mrs. Hailey's own grandmother. There is no action and no shift in point of view, but the portrait of the character herself is sufficiently interesting to charm most audiences. She is a woman who learns her own strength and develops it in response to the demands of early widowhood. Through her ladylike success in meeting challenges and her practical business sense she becomes an inadvertent feminist heroine. (The television version of this play, produced in 1995, starring Sally Field, develops all the major characters introduced in the novel.) In 1990, Hailey adapted her second novel, *Joanna's Husband and David's Wife,* to the stage. After performances in California, the original cast (including daughter Kendall Hailey) brought this comic treatment of the extraordinary marriage between Hailey and playwright Oliver Hailey to Dallas's Theatre Three.

Patricia Browning Griffith, a Baylor University graduate now residing in Washington, D.C., was a widely published journalist and author of fiction before she turned her hand to drama. Her novel *Tennessee Blue* (1981) was well received, and her short stories have been anthologized both in *O. Henry Prize Stories* (1970 and 1976) and in Lou Rodenberger's *Her Work*. In fact, a film made from her *Harper's* short story "Nights at O'Rear's" and shown at the 1980 New York Film Festival led her to write her first play, *Outside Waco*. After its initial performance at Theatre Three in Dallas in 1984, *Outside Waco* had a New York production.

Featuring the relationship between three very different sisters faced with the responsibility for a newly widowed, doddering father, this richly comic play pleased audiences but suffered from critical notices emphasizing its resemblance to Beth Henley's *Crimes of the Heart* without acknowledging its singular merits. One distinction of the play is its prologue, a four-way telephone conversation (three women and one answering machine) that reaches rare levels of contemporary hilarity. It bears comparison to Wendy Wasserstein's comic use of recorded telephone messages in her play, *Isn't It Romantic?*

Her second play, *Safety* (1987), is set on the Texas Gulf Coast before and during a hurricane. Like *Outside Waco,* it premiered at

Theatre Three and included outstanding comic scenes, for which the actress Cheryl Denson deserves considerable credit. Unfortunately the play's melodramatic secondary plot strained credibility and clashed with the comic tone of the main plot. *Safety* might work better if it were pared to an intense one-act version.

In 1989, Griffith completed a third play, set in post-oil-boom Houston, tentatively titled *The Last Stand at the Pirate's Cove Motel,* and in 1991, G. P. Putnam's published her second novel, *The World Around Midnight.*

University of Texas graduate Terry Galloway made the transition from poetry to playwriting. After having given public readings from her first volume of poetry, *Buncha Crocs in Surch of Snac and Other Poems* (1980), she began writing and performing sketches for the off-the-wall Austin cabaret, Esther's Follies. Then she wrote *Heart of a Dog,* an intense, introspective play for one woman (and one artificial dog). Now titled *Out All Night and Lost My Shoes* (1993), it has been performed on more than one occasion in Austin and New York. This free-flowing stage piece deals with such autobiographical elements as Galloway's deafness and her childhood life in Germany and, at the same time, with such worldly concerns as the Cold War and Elvis Presley. The tone is sometimes flip, occasionally sardonic, often comic. Although it is far from a completely satisfying work, it displays a heady virtuosity, and it provides welcome relief from the domination of psychological realism on Texas stages.

During her six-month Dobie-Paisano Fellowship in 1984, Galloway worked on a play, *Hamlet in Berlin,* now completed as *Peg's Hamlet.* In 1988 she toured in her one-woman play *Lardo Weeping,* which features an obese recluse commenting obsessively on life between trips to the refrigerator. A University of Texas *Daily Texan* critic called Lardo "one of the most repulsively lovable and memorable characters to have rolled onto an Austin stage." Currently Galloway is working on a performance piece, about daring female performers of the 1920s and 1930s, for the P.S. 122 Group in New York.

Jan Seale, another poet who is an accomplished fiction writer and college writing teacher, has taken a different approach toward drama. Her major play, *Radical,* is a powerful didactic work that sometimes lets its upbeat messages and social observations overpower its dramatic qualities. The play's title is a shortening of "radical mastectomy," and the plot traces the life of a cancer patient from her first biopsy to her eventual death. Produced at the Back Porch Theater in Wichita Falls, the play examines the changes terminal illness makes in a very ordinary, self-effacing woman—putting her in the spotlight and leading her, for the first time, to put her own concerns ahead of those of her husband and children. A brisk work, *Radical* succeeds in avoiding sentimentality and melodrama; it conveys insight into the impact of major illness on a family.

Another play of Seale's, *Solarium*, a one-act dialogue between two women of strikingly different backgrounds, is set in a hospital social area. Seale has said that she finds the human mix and charged atmosphere of a hospital setting useful for dramatic writing and that she intends to utilize it again.

In addition to these plays, Seale also has written a collection of children's plays based on the lives of historical Texans. These are published in *Texas History Classroom Plays*, part of a classroom instructional package designed for elementary-school use.

Maybe the most direct and amusing transition of a Texas author's work from a previous form to the dramatic is illustrated by *Texas Tacky*. Martha Ebersole originally wrote this work as a *Texas Monthly* article published in April, 1984, under the title, "I Opened Mail for the I.R.S." After being urged to convert the witty article into a play, she completed a first version called *The Mail Room* and then an expanded one, *Texas Tacky*, which was produced at the Bastrop Opera House in the fall of 1984 under the direction of Paul Baker.

Mary Rohde, of San Antonio, was an actress while she was a student at Alamo Heights High School (in the 1960s), at Trinity University, in New York, and at the Dallas Theater Center. Today she is still active on stage, although her family responsibilities limit the number of roles she can accept. She wrote her major play, *Ladybug, Ladybug, Fly Away Home*, as a thesis project for her MFA degree in the collaborative atmosphere of the Dallas Theater Center. Its first interpreters were her friends and colleagues; Michael Scudday, now her husband, had a role in its early productions.

Ladybug, Ladybug expresses a strong feminine sensibility. Much of its action takes place in a distinctly female preserve, a beauty parlor, and its strongest character is a grandmother, Mama Alice Kayro, from whom her daughter and granddaughter draw strength and to whom they turn in crisis.

This play powerfully expresses the emotions of a young woman who is unwilling to accept the traditional compromises of her mother's generation but lacks any clear concept of a viable alternative. She has abandoned her husband and infant child to avoid a trap, just as earlier she had rushed into marriage to gain freedom from childhood dependency. She brings unwanted pain to all who love her, yet she is driven, like a latter-day Nora Helmer, to find herself, regardless of the cost.

First presented at the Dallas Theater Center in 1978, *Ladybug, Ladybug* had subsequent productions there in 1979 and 1980 and at the Kennedy Center in Washington, D.C., in 1980. It was nominated for the American Theater Critics Award for Best Play Produced Outside New York, which led to Rohde's receipt of a Rockefeller Foundation Playwright in Residence Fellowship. Her only other play, *Keeper of the Home Fire,* is a less successful one that deals with theatrical people. Its only full production was by the Shreveport Community Theatre in 1986.

Celeste Colson-Walker, of Houston, builds her plays on twin foundations of stage savvy and Black identity. In 1978 she played the lead in her first play, *Sister, Sister,* in Houston's Music Hall; since then her works have been performed in Los Angeles, Chicago, Detroit, and New York as well as in Texas. A native of Houston, this actress-playwright-producer-writer has won numerous awards for her works. Mayor Kathy Whitmire of Houston declared January 15, 1986, Celeste Colson-Walker Day in honor of her playwriting and singled out *Sister, Sister* and *Camp Logan,* her most powerful play, for special mention. Later that same year, Colson-Walker was nominated for a NAACP Image Award by the Beverly Hills-Hollywood Chapter for her play *Reunion in Bartersville.*

Colson-Walker's plays are characterized by sudden plot turns, exaggerated characterizations, and wild costumes as well as by tight dialogue and accurate social observation. *Sister, Sister* (later titled *Once in a Wife Time*) is structured around a wife's retaliation for her husband's foray into polygamy as a part of his new enthusiasm for his African roots. *Reunion in Bartersville,* which has been produced frequently around the country, is based on an East Texas Black high school reunion. Swerving rapidly from one genre to another, it combines clowning, dancing, social commentary, and violent melodrama in a high-spirited mix. Colson-Walker's use of ethnic material, however, is not limited to comedy.

An early play, *The Wreckin' Ball,* took a strong political stand against the demolition of an old, inner-city ward in Houston, and *Camp Logan* deals with the long-obscured events of the 1917 Houston Riot of Black soldiers and the subsequent Fort Sam Houston court-martial and execution of nineteen Black soldiers from the 24th Infantry Regiment. In *Camp Logan,* Colson-Walker makes public an important part of Black American history that has been subject to official cover-up and public rejection. By dramatizing the frustration of a small group of soldiers from the 24th whose honorable service under General Pershing had been ignored and who were subjected to a regular pattern of racial harassment and demeaning treatment in Houston, the author makes their final explosion into destructive violence not only comprehensible but inevitable. They reach their breaking point when their longing for combat duty in France is thwarted and they are relegated once more to construction-battalion duty. The play was produced widely in Texas, in Chicago, and most recently, in 1991, as a part of the Texas Festival at the Kennedy Center, in Washington, D.C.

Estela Portillo Trambley, of El Paso, is first a Chicana writer and second a dramatist. Beginning with a play for a bilingual theater at El Paso Junior College, where she taught, she has written six plays, but this solid body of work constitutes only part of her literary output. She is also the author of a collection of poetry and two novels that draw on the Mexican-American experience. In 1981 the Texas Commission on the Arts honored her with a Writer Recognition Award for her unpublished manuscript, "Woman of the Earth." In addition, she has been active in radio and television in El Paso and currently is employed in the public schools there.

She has said that she finds playwriting a difficult struggle but that her experience as an actress and involvement in the practicalities of play production have disciplined her to avoid striving to express the grand schemes and to seek, instead, the simple and honest expression that works convincingly on stage. She respects her craft and has shown herself willing to expend sustained effort to achieve her goals. Commitment and versatility are her dramatic strengths.

Portillo Trambley's plays vary so widely in subject matter and style that their only common characteristics seem to be their concern with some facet of Mexican-American experience and their adherence to traditional western dramatic structures rather than the looser forms so popular with many Chicano playwrights. Two of her most interesting plays deal sensitively and lyrically with strong but distinctly different female characters in Mexican settings. *The Day of the Swallows* depicts a strong, aristocratic lesbian in a social context that traditionally respects machismo. It shows how eager society is to credit the powerful with virtue. *Sor Juana* is a historical portrait of a famous seventeenth-century Mexican feminist intellectual who struggled against her pride while living the life of a cloistered nun.

Three other of Portillo Trambley's plays deserve attention here. *Puente Negro,* about *mojados* crossing the border illegally into the United States, blends social commentary, lyricism, and comedy. It was well received in a 1984 production at the Mary Moody Northen Theatre of St. Edward's University in Austin. *Blacklight* is a gothic play containing generous portions of passion and violence in a poverty-ridden and doom-stricken Mexican American family whose father is haunted by the Maya gods of his ancestors. In the last act he interprets a bloody catastrophe as the sacrifice demanded by Itzamna. *Morality Play* uses the medieval form to show man's struggle over a five-thousand-year period to free himself from dehumanizing institutional values.

Sallie Baker, noted director Paul Baker's older daughter, grew up in the midst of stage activity and has supplemented her family-centered experience with diverse formal education. In addition to taking her MFA at the Dallas Theater Center, she has studied in Austria and Switzerland and in Colorado, where she now lives and works. Her first two plays, which were produced at the Dallas Theater Center, illustrate her familiarity with modern experimental drama and her desire to go beyond the limits of realistic theater. *Still Song* (1976), a big play, used a large cast and the full playing space of the Kalita Humphreys stage to drive home the impact of overlapping generations of life in rural America. In it the dead "ancestors" live in the attic of a family farm house and the action of the play moves fluidly between past and present. *Door Play,* written in 1977 and revised as *Intercourse* in 1987, was planned for an intimate stage and has its roots in European symbolism. In it a husband and wife struggle with their desires and face various ramifications of "the door" in their apartment. The door serves, among its many functions, as a gate to be guarded and a passageway to worldly and frightening experience.

Baker's latest play, *Sky Giant,* was performed at the Paul Baker Second Harvest Celebration in Waco in 1990. It exhibits a mythic dimension as its main character, an aging pictorial artist, signals his dwindling interest in life by climbing a derelict windmill tower and refusing to come down. This work shows the playwright's increased interest in such traditional dramatic elements as convincing lines and moving characterization.

Barbara Gilstrap, born in Canton and educated at North Texas State University and the Dallas Theater Center, now lives in New York City. She is another playwright who made the transition from acting to writing. Although *The Alto Part,* her first play, uses a deep East Texas setting familiar to her from childhood, it received its premiere production at the WPA Theatre in New York. Set in Manhattan during the Bicentennial Fourth of July Celebration, her most recent play, *Liberty Week-End,* deals with a forty-two-year-old Texas woman writer's anxieties about both her career and her personal life, all the while taking satirical swipes at assorted recent fads. It was given a 1991 performance in Gilstrap's hometown of Canton.

That most of Gilstrap's plays include performing-artist roles, usually musicians or dancers, attests to Gilstrap's special interest in the artist's sensibilities and concerns. In fact *The Alto Part* might be more difficult than most plays to cast because it requires two singers to play the major roles, a thirtyish mother able to "sing in a voice reminiscent of Billie Holiday" and a twelve-year-old daughter whose voice must be good enough to give credence to her mother's decision to take the "alto part." The music is essential to the play. It underscores emotion, suggests a tantalizing world beyond ordinary small-town East Texas life, and serves as a metaphor for the mother's last-act decision to put her daughter's goals above her own.

Much of the material in *The Alto Part* is familiar, but the play has an authenticity that puts it in select company. It has content in common with Horton Foote's *The Traveling Woman,* which also deals with a young wife and mother who has difficulty accepting the reality of her husband's profligacy. By keeping her heroine's professional-wrestler husband, Killer King, offstage, Gilstrap keeps the focus relentlessly on the painful, romantic dreams of the woman.

Gilstrap has written three one-act plays in addition to her full-length ones, but in comparison they tend to be mere anecdotal sketches. One, *Credentials,* is set in New York. The remaining two,

Love in Sanitary Conditions, and *Miracle on Dogwood Trail,* share the East Texas small-town setting of *The Alto Part.*

Another Texas playwright who uses small-town Texas settings skillfully, Jo Vander Voort has had success in Houston and around the country. Her career has included teaching, writing, and modeling, but her acting led most directly to the writing of her plays, which have won prestigious awards, good critical notices, and considerable popularity. When The *Wisteria Bush* was produced in Nashville at a meeting of the American Theater Critics Association, Dan Sullivan of the *Los Angeles Times* called it "the richest of the new plays we saw" and complimented the playwright's knowledge of small towns—which she, a native of Thornton (pop. 473), comes by naturally.

Although Vander Voort has written eight full-length plays, *The Wisteria Bush* and *Box Church* are her best known. In spite of the success of *The Wisteria Bush,* a raucous, revealing, broadly comic evening of woman talk, the playwright herself says that it was not her best work. *Box Church,* much more ambitious and complex, was featured in the 1986 Texas Playwright's Festival at Houston's Stages Theatre. It was inspired by Vander Voort's discovery of the actual Texas hamlet of Box Church (pop. 45) south of Waco. It features the changed relationship over twenty-two years of a black girl and a white girl. Closely related to the personal circumstances of the central characters are the changed social ones of the community, also depicted in detail. The play's execution fails to match its worthy goals, but its best moments are very good indeed.

The same, unfortunately, is true of Vander Voort's *Temperature Trilogy,* made up of the one-act plays *Sweltering, Freezing,* and *Tepid.* Their best-realized elements—a memorable characterization of hard-to-hold, hair-spray sniffing, would-be killer Willie Scroggins and the continued failure of the central character's parents to accept or even comprehend her Hispanic former husband's racial otherness—are brilliantly executed. But other bizarre touches often seem strained exaggerations, and devices such as a telephone operator's intrusions into conversations are overdone. In spite of her earthiness, her manic comic sense, and her sensitive ear for dialogue, Vander Voort has yet to create the one major work that would firmly establish her reputation.

Although native Houstonian Shelley Fitze has been both an actress and an opera singer, it was her knowledge of practical stagecraft and enthusiasm for flying that made her *Daughters of Heaven* such an original play. She studied scenic carpentry during her undergraduate years at Sam Houston State University and then completed her MFA at the University of Houston with concentrations in acting and directing. Afterward she worked with properties, costumes, and set-building for several Houston theaters. Then, for her first play, she drew on stories of heroic female aviators of the 1920s and 1930s and her own flying experience for a piece about the 1929 Women's Cross Country Air Race, which was first presented at Stages Theatre in 1982. When the historic pilot-characters enacted flight scenes, they mounted small platforms, adopted stylized poses, and spoke in "overlapping yet independent monologues." The striking result was a lyric, dreamlike evocation of flight. The original two-act *Daughters of Heaven* was later adapted into a one-act version titled *The 1929 Powder Puff.*

After following *Daughters of Heaven* with a one-woman play, *Madame Scandal,* based on a private journal of Georges Sand, and writing a one-act play, *Ordinary Crime,* depicting an actress who had been a victim of child abuse struggling with a role that had similarities to her own life, Fitze quit playwriting for three years. Not satisfied with the results she had achieved in writing mainstream plays, and desiring more privacy, she began her career anew by writing specialized plays for designated audiences under a pseudonym.

Denise Chávez, formerly on the University of Houston drama faculty and now teaching at New Mexico State University in Las Cruces, is an energetic writer who defies easy classification. She writes prose fiction and poetry of distinction and has written plays and performance pieces since high school. She acts, directs, and speaks widely on Chicana issues. Although she prizes her Southwestern roots, her reputation is wide ranging and rapidly ascending after the 1994 publication of her novel, *Face of an Angel.* As with many Mexican-American writers, her life and literary subject matter transcend political boundaries. Although she was born in Las Cruces, New Mexico, and took her B.A. from New Mexico State University and her M.A. from the University of New Mexico, she also spent part of her childhood in Marfa and took her MFA degree from Trinity University and the Dallas Theater Center. Some of her plays have a specific New Mexico setting, such as *Plaza,* which depicts daily activities in the Central Plaza of Santa Fe, but she insists that the setting of her work is within the Mexican-American culture wherever it exists in the general region.

From her graduate student play, *The Novitiates,* which was produced at the Dallas Theater Center in 1973, to her latest, a dramatization of her book of prose sketches, *The Last of the Menu Girls* (1986), produced by the Main Street Theatre and Teatro Bilingue de Houston in 1990, Chávez has focused on character and its cultural context rather than on plot. Her plays use setting only to establish a cultural context for characters' lives and are so loosely constructed that characters can be added or dropped to suit the exigencies of performance. When the play *Santa Fe Charm* was revised into *Plaza* for touring to New York and Edinburgh, Scotland, several characters were cut. For a White House performance, Chávez presented only the monologue of the character Pauline from *Novena Narrativas.* Some of her works, such as *El Santero de Cordova,* which is based on the life of a New Mexico wood-carver, depict only one character. More commonly, though, as in *Hecho in Mexico,* a bilingual, multimedia performance about women who work as maids, they deal with various characters. *El Mas Pequeno de Mis Hijos* is her only play completely in Spanish, but she regularly blends Spanish words and phrases into her English dialogue just as naturally as members of Mexican-American communities do in their daily conversation.

Denise Chávez's works are often poetic in tone and frequently feminist in point of view. By connecting traditional Hispanic traditions and myth with contemporary social concerns, they remind their audiences of the richness of southwestern culture. In Chávez's writing the mystical is more readily expressed than in Anglo writing, and the struggles for economic improvement and personal respect are more basic.

In spite of their relatively late appearance on the literary scene, Texas women playwrights are making themselves known in steadily increasing numbers. Since 1978, Terri Wagener, a Midland native now living in New York, has written numerous plays of note that have been produced in Houston and Louisville and on both coasts. She was a finalist for the Susan Smith Blackburn Prize for women playwrights in 1978 for *Renascence* and again in 1983 for *Ladies in Waiting.* Sara Prejean, an anthologized Houston poet, has had three plays produced by Stages Theatre. Nancy Mercado of Houston, with *Ride in the Sun,* Chaddie Kruger of San Antonio, with *Chiarina,* and

Ann Clayton of Fort Worth, with *Tongue and Groove,* received favorable notice for their plays in 1990 and 1991. Joyce Gibson Roach has written a well-received musical folk drama, *Nancy MacIntyre: A Tale of the Prairies,* and a musical pageant, *Texanna!* as well as her prize-winning nonfiction book, *The Cowgirls* (1977).

Part 5
SYMPOSIUM

INTRODUCTION

Surveying the accomplishments of women pioneers who contributed to the Texas literary tradition in the nineteenth century and examining the rapid development of Texas women writers as professionals in the twentieth century leads logically to summation and forecast. Five women, distinguished for their activities in the Texas publishing world, were asked here to comment upon the present state of the art for writing women in Texas and to share their insights into what the twenty-first century may offer Texas women writers.

Credentials of these contributors vary. Judyth Rigler is book editor for the *San Antonio Express-News* and writes a weekly syndicated newspaper column reviewing Texas books. Judy Alter and Fran Vick are directors of university presses. Jane Tanner is a university teacher and the former editor of *Texas Books in Review,* a quarterly journal, and Nancy Baker Jones, who served several years as associate editor for the *Handbook of Texas* revision project, is also coeditor of *Women and Texas History: Selected Essays* (1993), an anthology by and about Texas women. All, however, have ample knowledge of the state's literary activities, which accelerate yearly. Their well-honed critical abilities are evident in this gathering of opinions and predictions.

JUDYTH RIGLER

Who among us is qualified to predict the future? And who would even *try,* especially in the 1990s, when readers' attention is so easily diverted to other forms of entertainment, all requiring far less participation in the work than does literature?

Predicting the future for women writers in Texas is a formidable task. The temptation is strong to say that the future for us is whatever we choose to make of it, and for the most part, that is true. Yet there is more to it.

When I was asked to write this essay, when it was still way off out there in the list of long-term projects, it seemed a delicious assignment, filled with opportunities to be the cheerleader for an emerging female "team" in Texas letters. Now that the deadline is here, it seems that being a cheerleader is not enough, that in order to raise the flag for female writers, I must lower the colors for male voices. When one goes up, the other must come down—mustn't it?

Is there indeed a difference between male and female writers? Is one sex's treasure automatically the other's trash? Can the two coexist on the literary range? I think the answer to the last question lies in the response to the second—with some qualification.

New York writer Cynthia Ozick, currently enjoying an international reputation for excellence in all kinds of literary endeavors, has perhaps addressed the male-female difference issue best: "A writer is someone born with a gift," she says. "An athlete can run. A painter can paint. A writer has the facility with words. A good writer can also think. Isn't that enough to define a writer by?"

Probably it is. But things are a bit different here in Texas. If we are to make predictions about the future for one sex or writer in one state in the union, we must decide what it is that will spell success or failure for that sex, *in relation to what has gone before.*

Male Texas writers are a pretty tough act to follow. They have told the same story, in pretty much the same way, for so long that we have begun to believe it was the real story, the only story. To borrow a female image to describe a male-dominated field, the fabric of Texas writing is so tightly woven with threads of myth and macho that many readers are unable to find the seams, to pick the material apart and discover that they are not getting the whole story.

But that opens the gates, too. Because a lot of readers, raised on a diet of horseflesh and gunsmoke, father-son rancor, drugs and guns, failed romances, and middle-class ennui are more than willing to dine on something fresh and imaginatively prepared, women are beginning to gain acceptance for telling the other side of the story.

Several years ago I participated in a symposium sponsored by the Center for Texas Studies and the Department of English at the University of North Texas. Part of Women's Fortnight, the program addressed the issue "Texas Women in the Professions: Discrimination and Opportunity." That symposium and its conclusions seem appropriate now to the subject matter of this book, particularly because four of the five panelists have published books.

On the panel with me were Shirley Chater, then president of Texas Woman's University; Mary Beth Rogers, chief of staff and former deputy treasurer for Governor Ann Richards; Judy Alter, director of Texas Christian University Press; and Evelyn Oppenheimer, literary agent, reviewer, and writer.

This symposium predated both the issue of sexual harassment and the serious man-bashing going on these days. Even so, I half-expected the five-woman panel (myself included) to spend far too much time reciting a litany of instances in which we had been prevented or slowed—by men or institutions they had set up—from realizing our potential because of our sex. There were a few amusing tales of the "There, there, little lady, don't you worry your pretty head" ilk, but the tone was mostly positive. Rather than concentrate on missed chances, most of us stressed opportunities we may have had *because* we are Texas women.

There were a number of memorable comments that afternoon. Shirley Chater said that to achieve her success, she had to "leave the comfort zone," not give in to the always-present temptation to relax, settle back, and do the "easy" thing.

That comment was repeated frequently throughout the discussion, as all of us recalled instances in which we had been tempted to take a step backward into the familiar, the necessary, the day-to-day tasks that can take up a whole life—home management, family care, those "easy" things (*sure,* they are)—because they were things that always needed doing, that we knew we *could* do, and that still carried a certain amount of approval in most circles. Anything else, anything new and challenging in which we knew we'd have to work twice as hard as the men around us, was always risky. What if we failed?

Mary Beth Rogers stressed the importance of turning obstacles into opportunities, of seeing ordinary things with a fresh eye, of showing with a story rather than dazzling with stats.

Judy Alter dismissed her considerable accomplishments as a matter of "being in the right place at the right time," of needing a job when there was one being offered. What she did with that job once she took it has become almost legend among Texas women writers; very quietly and efficiently, with little fanfare, she directs a highly respected university press, managing "in her spare moments" to turn out her own finely crafted books. Her motto seems to be "pick up the ball and run with it."

Evelyn Oppenheimer urged the women gathered to focus their goals and make the choices necessary to achieve them. "You can't have everything," she warned, describing a life and career with a double whammy, being female and Jewish, in an era dominated by male WASPs.

My comments centered on finding a gap, a worthy job no one had done before, and creating an opportunity within that gap. I also mentioned, as did others, the most dangerous kind of discrimination, the kind that comes from within, that says to us: "Don't push against the barriers. What makes you think you have something new to contribute? Make nice."

All these points seem relevant to writing in Texas, and about Texas, as a woman. We do need to leave the comfort zone created by men, to break out and say something new in a fresh way—to realize that what looks like an obstacle is really an opportunity.

The gap is there; the time is right for a new voice. The audience is ready.

As essays in this literary history show, Texas women writers are making themselves heard both within and beyond our state.

I've noticed the healthy trend myself. As a reviewer of Texas books for more than a decade, I'm seeing more books from Texas women writers than ever before. Shelby Hearon, Beverly Lowry, Carolyn Osborn, Jane Gilmore Rushing, and others have established solid reputations. A few of the many up-and-coming writers in Texas are Gail Galloway Adams, Janis Arnold, Sarah Bird, Cindy Bonner, Anita Richmond Bunkley, Sandra Cisneros, Elizabeth Crook, Carol Dawson, Margot Fraser, Sarah Glasscock, Paulette Jiles, Angela Shelf Medearis,

Harryette Mullen, Naomi Shihab Nye, Annette Sanford, Jan Seale, Carmen Tafolla, and Jane Roberts Wood.

There are lots of others, all with voices that speak not just to women, and not just about women's experiences, but to all discerning readers. They describe the rural and the urban, the past and the present, the individual and the universal experience, with a facile grace I find lacking in the work of many of their male counterparts, who often seem bound to one era, stuck in a single mood and mode of expression. Lest this begin to resemble an anti-male diatribe, I hasten to add that some of my best friends, and favorite writers, are men. And yes, male writers in Texas are beginning to experiment more, but female writers have a head start, I think.

What I find most promising among Texas women writers is their ability to get to the real heart of relationships, to give the reader that truly joyful experience of seeing something in print that he or she had known somewhere deep within, of having a basic human emotion shared and thus made more real, more valid somehow.

I also like Texas women's sense of humor, about themselves and others, and their ability to grow with each poem, each essay, each short story, each novel. It's all about taking risks, pushing against the boundaries, but it's worth it all if we create a new agenda, if we make a literature that is dynamic and forceful in its innovation.

So I *am* a cheerleader after all. What Texas women are doing in the literary arena *is* exciting; and as one who makes her living from what is written in and about Texas, it looks as if I will have plenty of material to keep me employed into my dotage—uh, better make that "until I'm sent to cover that great literary roundup in the sky."

JUDY ALTER

In 1958 the Texas Institute of Letters juvenile award went to a novel about a young Texas boy kidnapped and held prisoner on a Mexican hacienda for a year. While there, the young man goes from condescension to grudging admiration and, finally, respect and affection for many of the Mexicans at the ranch. And when he catches and then sets free a magnificent black stallion at the expense of his own liberty, he comes to understand what freedom really means. It's a wonderful and strong young-adult novel.

But when it came time to present the award, nobody could locate J. R. Williams, who had written *Tame the Wild Stallion*. Three weeks after the TIL annual meeting, someone finally tracked down Jeanne Williams, then in Bryan, and she received the prize money, but she had missed the chance to bask in the glory of the award made to her first novel.

An attempt to put together an anthology on literature by and about women in the American West—which almost did not appear, because everyone consulted had a different vision of the table of contents, and particularly whether works by men belonged in a women's anthology—has set me to musing on the differences between what men and women write about and their differing reception in the world of commercial publishing, particularly when regional—that is, western—writing is in question. Thirty years after Jeanne Williams won her award, are women still fictionally tied to romance while men are free to roam the range of action and adventure? Would B. M. Bower use her first name today?

Greg Tobin, former western editor for Doubleday/Bantam, estimated that thirty percent of his submissions came from women, and in the early 1990s he commissioned a woman to write a mountain-man series. Still, Tobin admits that most publishing houses do not promote women authors on their western lists. A first novel by long-time screenwriter Margaret Armen, titled *The Hanging of Father Miguel*, was published under the name of M. A. Armen in 1990. And in 1989, when a novel based on the life of a woman physician won a Western Writers Spur Award as Best Western Novel, WWA members found themselves in the midst of a tempest. "That's a man's action adventure category," stormed one disappointed male.

Mystery writers seem to have broken the bonds of gender. The national writers' organization Sisters in Crime boasts something like fourteen hundred members, and women write everything from Amanda Cross's intellectual puzzles to Sara Paretsky's detective stories about V. I. Warshawski. (Don't call her Vicky!) Warshawski is so hard-boiled, her adventures are little more than caricatures of men's private-investigator novels. But women so dominate the mystery field that they have almost edged out Mickey Spillane and his brothers. Surely the western can't be far behind—or can it?

In the spring of 1991, *Publishers Weekly* praised a novel called *The Four Arrows Fe-As-Ko* by Randall Beth Platt for bringing "a rare female perspective to a generally male fictional domain." Platt joins a few other women who are writing traditional westerns, but today if you are a woman and you write about the American West of the past, it is generally assumed you write historical romances, complete with panting and passionate romance. A personal anecdote illustrates the point. When I wrote *Mattie* about a woman physician on the turn-of-the-century Nebraska frontier, the manuscript went to a New York house where the westerns editor said it was a fine novel but he could not fit a romance into a western line. So he sent it to the house romance editor, who read it and said it was a fine novel—but she couldn't fit a horse opera into a romance line.

But maybe we build our own pigeonholes. After a brief and nonscientific survey of women authors, mostly Texan, who set their work in the American West, I decided Jeanne Williams's novel about a young boy was an exception. It is a broad generalization, but most women have written about women, and men about men. My selective memory calls up Dorothy Scarborough, whose classic *The Wind* is undeniably about the peculiar problems faced by women in this land; Elithe Hamilton Kirkland, whose *Love Is a Wild Assault* romanticized the life of Harriet Page Potter, wife of the secretary of the navy for the Republic of Texas; Edna Ferber, whose vision of ranch life was skewed to the ruthless romantic but nonetheless was clearly a woman's book; and Loula Grace Erdman, who wrote of pioneer settlers from the woman's point of view, nicely counterbalancing some of the masculine presentations. Maybe Katherine Anne Porter does not fit in that group, but she denied her Texas origins, too, and would never have tolerated being called a regional—let alone western—writer. If you go beyond Texas, you confront Dorothy Johnson, who well may be another exception, but also Mary Hallock Foote, Willa Cather, and Mari Sandoz, all of whom seem to bear out my generalization.

Unabashedly a writer of women's fiction myself, I began to look around at the Texas women currently writing, some regional writers, some who have broadened their horizons (and publishing opportunities): Carolyn Osborn tells stories of women that almost always involve their relationships with men; Shelby Hearon and Beverly Lowry similarly write of women and their relationships; Jane Gilmore Rushing's work focuses on family life; Fort Worth novelist Carole Nelson Douglas has moved into that most masculine of worlds, the Arthur Conan Doyle/Sherlock Holmes canon, but she has made that move with a feminine (and feminist) heroine in her Irene Adler series, which began with *Good Night, Mr. Holmes*. And Jeanne Williams? Most of the sixty-plus novels she has written since *Tame the Wild Stallion* feature feisty and independent women.

By contrast, Texas novelist Robert Flynn writes of men and, frequently, of war; Elmer Kelton writes of ranching and the world of West Texas men (and is often criticized for less-than-effective treatment of women); and David Lindsey's Houston is a graphically violent world of men—in spite of the women who appear on his pages.

Doris Meredith of Amarillo writes mysteries that feature sheriffs and lawyers, mostly masculine, and Larry McMurtry is often most sensitive in his portrayal of women. But these are exceptions.

Why does any of this matter—if it does? Certainly I am not advocating a unisex literature; nothing could be more dull. Readership crosses gender lines already. I'm a strong fan of Elmer Kelton and Bob Flynn, and Marshall Terry recently wrote that Carolyn Osborn is one of the two or three most original contemporary Texas writers. So what's the point?

Or, maybe, what's the question? Do women write about other women and about relationships because that is what comes naturally to them or because that is what publishers, and perhaps the reading public, will accept (as demonstrated by Jeanne Williams's novel)? If the former, women's western and/or regional literature in Texas and elsewhere ought to follow a fairly predictable track. But if publishing demands have dictated what women write, the twenty-first century ought to prove challenging.

FRAN VICK

When Bill Shearer, owner of Shearer Publishing, called me in the spring of 1978 to tell me that a meeting was being held in Austin to discuss forming an association of Texas publishers, I knew I wanted to be involved. The book publishing world is very small, so anytime one publisher can find another one to talk to, it is a treat indeed. I showed up for the meeting, paid my dues, and have been a member ever since, like just about everybody else who came that day. The name has since changed to Book Publishers of Texas to distinguish book publishers from other types of publisher, but the organization remains pretty much the same—changing only as publishing itself changes.

Several women involved in book publishing came to that formative meeting. I do not know how the rest of these women came to be publishers, but I came to publishing because that was where I had wanted to be all along. To give some insight as to how we became publishers, here is how I arrived at that place. My first job at fourteen years of age was with the *Lake Jackson News,* a weekly newspaper whose owner and publisher was our neighbor, Frances Lindveit. So I came early to the notion that women owning their own publishing companies was an accepted practice. Later I worked for the Humble Research Center in Houston, where we published the company publications, and then for Official Publications at the University of Texas, before the University of Texas Press had become a full-blown publishing entity under Frank Wardlaw. There I was trained by two of the best in the business—Louise Barekman and, after her untimely death, Dorothy Lay. Later I became the associate editor of the Directory of Texas Manufacturers at the Bureau of Business Research at the University of Texas. For me the joy of these jobs was in putting the publications together. Writing was, is, and apparently always will be an incredible chore for me. I do it because I have to, not from any joy.

Because jobs in publishing in Texas were not easy to come by, I spent much of my time in classrooms teaching English to students of all ages, from junior high school to college. But in 1977, when Bill Wittliff of Encino Press left active publishing (which included publishing the Texas Folklore Society Publications) for the bright lights of moviedom, I was eager to take on the task of publishing the society publications. This was a double treat for me because my interest in folklore had gone back to my undergraduate days when folklorist Mody Boatright, chairman of the English Department at the University of Texas, was my advisor, and one of my favorite professors, E. Bagby Atwood, was collecting material for *The Regional Vocabulary of Texas* when I was taking his courses. Later, while acquiring another degree at Stephen F. Austin University in Nacogdoches, I met F. E. Abernethy, English professor and secretary/editor of the Texas Folklore Society. It seemed to me the society publications had been waiting for me all along. I already had formed a typesetting company with some of my former students from Baylor University, so the timing was perfect. If all this seems a rather flimsy reason to quit a good job and start a publishing company, another thing needs to be confessed here. Publishers are Mississippi riverboat gamblers. We will take all sorts of risks to produce a book we think needs to be in print. Indeed, every book we publish is a gamble and a risk. There are absolutely no guarantees in book publishing, but the society publications came with a built-in buying audience of at least the size of the Folklore Society, so the risks were somewhat less, though not by much when you consider that the size of the society was about five hundred members. Whatever the reason, E-Heart Press was born.

When I came to book publishing via the Texas Folklore Society Publications, I did not know any women who owned book-publishing companies, in Texas or anyplace else, but that soon changed. The two women I knew early on in book publishing were, like me, publishing because they wanted to publish, not because they wandered into it as frustrated writers or because no other jobs were available. Ellen Temple, who had attended the Rice publishing school early in her publishing career, began by publishing children's books and books about women's issues. Anne Dickson had bought Pressworks and continued the publication of limited-edition books as well as adding a line of trade books to the list. Good friends long before we were publishers, Ellen Temple and I have conferred with each other since the beginning of our publishing careers and continue that practice today, including a partnership in some publications and with Ellen serving on the editorial board at the University of North Texas Press. She is one of my touchstones in publishing as well as in my life. I think this can be said of many women in publishing. I feel a special kinship with them because of the common bonds we have as women in publishing.

I do not know how other women Book Publishers of Texas members came to publishing, but many are driving forces in their companies, and I believe we all consider each other friends and confidants, even if we do not talk to each other for long stretches. When we do meet, we take up our relationships and indeed some of our conversations just where we left off at the last meeting. We all feel free to call each other to pass along information, ask for advice, or commiserate over some publishing disaster. Some women in publishing in Texas who have been friends and acquaintances in the Book Publishers of Texas over the years are JoAnn Long, Hendrick-Long Publishing; Charlotte Whaley, founder with her husband of Still Point Press; Judy Mangan, publisher of Mangan Books with her husband; Kathy

Shearer and her late husband, Bill, owners of Shearer Publishing; and Debbie Brothers and her partner, Tom Munnerlyn, co-owners of State House Press. Of more than fifty full-publisher members (as distinguished from associate and corporate members) of the Book Publishers of Texas, at least twenty-five are either led, managed, or owned by women.

When I became involved in university publishing, first as co-director and then as director of the University of North Texas Press, I found another set of women in book publishing—those in management positions in university presses, either as directors, editors, or heads of marketing. The American Association of University Presses (AAUP) has presses divided among four categories: full member, affiliate, international member, and associate. The full members are normally well-established presses in the Americas that meet certain requirements regarding scholarship, size, and staffing. To be eligible for full membership a press must publish five or more scholarly books a year, have a committee or board composed of faculty members who certify the scholarly quality of the works published, have not fewer than three full-time employees, including a director reporting to an appropriate senior university officer, and submit evidence to show that the parent institution is prepared to provide sufficient support. Affiliate members are smaller university presses with the same eligibility requirements as those for full members, except that affiliates may publish fewer than five books per year and need not conform to the requirements for full membership in regard to staffing. Associate membership is open to not-for-profit presses of non-degree-granting scholarly institutions and associations. Currently, the AAUP membership is ninety full members and twenty-three affiliate and associate members. Six of these presses are in Texas and three of the directors are women.

So what does all this mean? First it should be clear that publishing is indeed a small industry. Not every book publisher in the state of Texas belongs to the Book Publishers of Texas, but the majority do, and the ones most likely to be publishing trade books do. Further, Texas' six AAUP-member university presses and other active presses, such as Arte Público at the University of Houston, are a boon for writers in the state. In harsh economic times the university presses have stepped into the void left by struggling independent publishers who simply cannot afford to gamble as they do in more flush times.

However, as the parent institutions feel the crunch of hard times, that will be reflected in the presses housed in those institutions. Presses are having to become more self-sustaining as university budgets are tightened.

Because the industry is so small, most of us consider our fellow publishers friends rather than rivals. This is not to deny that there is healthy competition for good manuscripts, but by and large, publishers tend to share more than they compete. When a manuscript arrives at a publishing house that does not have a slot for it or that has a different editorial emphasis, that publisher usually will send it on to a fellow publisher who does have a place for the work. This camaraderie creates a better climate for writers seeking to place their work, and that is what good publishing is all about—matching the right publisher with the writer.

JANE TANNER

It is dangerous to try to predict the future—doubly so in matters of literary taste. All we can do is analyze past trends and, on the basis of our observations, make an educated guess about what to look for in the coming years. Having said that, I will plunge right in to my personal prediction for the future of Texas women's letters.

The unrelenting attempt to define "Texas" literature irritates me. Every literary conference in this hemisphere will feature at least one session on so-called regional literature, with all the participants (Texans included) doing their best to argue that the fiction coming from *their* region is not regional, but universal. All literature is regional insofar as it comes from a particular region. Everyone has to live somewhere. I think that the women who live in Texas (or who, like Shelby Hearon, Beverly Lowry, and Sandra Scofield, lived in Texas) are as observant and talented as women writers anywhere. That the setting of their fiction is often Texas does not make their work any less universal than the fiction of someone from New York or California.

I think we can expect to see more of what we like to call "serious" literature from Texas women in the coming decade. Certainly Texas is well represented by the writers of formula fiction—romance, mysteries, and westerns. For the last two, D. R. Meredith and L. J. Washburn, whose use of initials instead of names is symptomatic of the difficulty women have breaking into the mainstream, largely masculine, detective and western "club," continue to publish high-quality work.

But if the material I have seen lately is any indication, authors who can see into the woman's heart of things, whose viewpoint is not necessarily feminist but is certainly *feminine* in the sense that Scarborough's is feminine in *The Wind* (1925), are increasing in number and quality. The experiences they write about are varied, but the perspective, the voice, is consistently female. With the publication of *A Place Called Sweet Shrub* (1990) and *Dance a Little Longer* (1993), Jane Roberts Wood has completed her trilogy, the story of the young schoolteacher, wife, and mother Lucy Richards in *The Train to Estelline* (1987). Wood gives to this world, which for the most part no longer attempts to shield its girl-children, a delectable picture of a time when growing up and gaining focus still was a shock to the system for a young woman. Sandra Scofield explores the dynamics of family, particularly its women, in *Gringa* (1989), *More Than Allies* (1993), and *Opal on Dry Ground* (1994). The works of both these authors are well written and unflinching, with the promise of increasingly sharper focus and even more interesting characters in their future books.

Sandra Cisneros, whose work, representative of the growing Chicana movement, does not have padded corners and rounded edges and offers a searing perspective in *Woman Hollering Creek and Other Stories* (1991). J. California Cooper's *Family* (1991), *The Matter Is Life* (1991), and *In Search of Satisfaction* (1994) give voice to the black experience. Sarah Bird has contributed one of the most effective, original satiric voices in print with *Alamo House: Women without Men, Men without Brains* (1986), *The Mommy Club* (1991), and *Virgin of the Rodeo* (1993).

Janis Arnold has answered her first effort, *Daughters of Memory* (1991), with the biting *Excuse Me for Asking* (1994); and Carol Dawson, whose *Waking Spell* (1992) demonstrated such promise, has more than followed through with her delightful *Body of Knowledge* (1994), which resonates with literary and mythic allusion.

I see prospects in some exciting first novels: Polly Koch's sharply feminist *Invisible Borders* (1991); Mary Robinson's *Subtraction* (1991); Margot Fraser's satirical *Laying Out of Gussie Hoot* (1990); and Lane Von Herzen's *Copper Crown* (1991). Austin's Elizabeth Harris offers *The Ant Generator* (1991), a prize-winning collection of short fiction from the University of Iowa Press. Elizabeth Crook, in *The Raven's Bride* (1991), has written a well-researched historical romance that steps out of the formula restrictions. All the evidence suggests that Texas will continue to be home to a great variety of female perspectives, the best of all possible scenarios for literary development.

NANCY BAKER JONES

As a student of both history and literature, I have become familiar with their differences, but I am more intrigued by their common ground. The fictional uses of history are best exemplified in the genre of the historical novel. In my case, a childhood addiction to Thomas B. Costain's novels about English royalty was probably in part to blame for my later decision to major in both history and English. After winning an undergraduate short-story contest, I even wrote an earnest thank-you letter to my benefactor describing my ambition to become a writer of historical fiction. I enrolled in a graduate history program instead, and there was thoroughly disabused of the notion that history could ever be appropriately fictionalized. Historians, after all, pursue truth.

Or so I thought. Several years of researching, writing, and assessing the accuracy of entries for the Texas history encyclopedia, *The New Handbook of Texas,* added to even more years of reading and analyzing contemporary North American fiction by women, have only confirmed a suspicion born in that first graduate year, that the grail of historical objectivity is at best a noble ideal, that the boundaries between history and fiction are more fluid than solid.[1]

Nobody, as recently trained literary critics will tell you, stands nowhere. Or, to put it only slightly less obtusely, everyone stands somewhere. We all have viewpoints that emerge from the complexities of time, place, and experience and that change as we age. Historians follow interests as well as evidence. We want to think that the written is more reliable than the oral, but of course even documents can be inadequate or contradictory. Hence, our need for "revisionist" historical interpretations.

Historians define their field as a discipline, believe in rules of evidence, and invoke a chain of being to judge the reliability of sources (primary sources are closer to God than secondary sources). I am now enough of a historian to complain that historical fiction does bend evidence unnecessarily. Why not just tell what "really" happened? On the other hand, one wonderful outgrowth of historical fiction is that people who ordinarily would not read history will, through fiction, still come to have a sense of the past and its importance to the present. Nevertheless, in my own chain of being, the historians closest to God are those who get the facts right *and* tell a good story.

The basic elements of good history are much like those of fiction. These elements are: identifiable characters who act out of some motivation, the assemblage of events into a recognizable pattern, and a chronological framework. So it seems to me that historians, like fabulists, serve as our culture's storytellers. If I am right, the two groups do not hold separate territories called "truth" and "fiction" but share common ground.

That ground is storytelling. Storytelling, the way women were once believed to "carry" culture, emerged from oral traditions that transmitted a culture's history. Told long enough, or granted enough significance, stories become myth, and myth becomes the psyche of culture, the commonly held knowledge by which a culture defines and describes itself and its members.

Women were labeled culture carriers because they had neither the duty nor the prerogative to change stories in important ways; this was the power to create culture, and that was thought to be men's work.

Because most recorded myths, as anthropologist Marta Weigle has said, have been collected by male researchers from male informants, what some regard as a mythology with universal import is in reality a revelation of men's stories and rituals. One of these, an American creation story we all recognize, involves the confrontation of what literature scholar R. W. B. Lewis called the American Adam with an expanse of time and land ahead of him. Divorced from history and society, he finds himself born on a new continent, facing the promise of self-definition through the strength of his own power to conquer the land before him. He is the archetypal human, the father of us all, a namer, creator, and arbiter who defines himself in opposition to civilization and womanhood.

If the function of woman, in his eyes, is to domesticate, to associate, and to dominate, then his only recourse is to strike for the woods. As long as the American Adam defines unboundaried space as female, success in molding it to his purposes secures his sense of self and illuminates the extent to which he is not trapped, not civilized, not a woman. His enemy is the American Eve, the ensnarer who motivates such varied literary runaways as Rip Van Winkle, Huckleberry Finn, and Rabbit Angstrom. Jay Gatsby learns that running towards her ends in disaster. There is implicit in this view of women a fear of her supposed power, which in turn suggests a justification for subordinating her.

Eventually, and one suspects always, women told and created stories particular to their own experiences and perceptions. In doing so, women added new information to the mythic pool and transformed themselves from carriers into creators of culture. In place of passing on, unexamined, what had always been, women developed, through their own exertion, the voice to revise, reconstruct, and rewrite, using themselves as their subjects. The process has been difficult and is not complete.

An obvious prerequisite for storytelling is voice. Proscriptions against women's speaking out have existed for centuries across cultures. Writer Tillie Olsen has described the silences imposed on women who write, and historian Mary Kelley has documented the extreme difficulty with which nineteenth-century North American white women writers reconciled the public nature of their work with the private nature of their lives. To claim to be the creator of a piece of writing was a revolutionary act. Even in the twentieth century, stories in which a woman's quest for self-definition does not end in death are not commonplace.

When women write about themselves on their own terms rather than allowing themselves to be defined, they challenge centuries of such mythic accretions as the American Adam and offer replacements for him. Like the heroine of Adrienne Rich's poem "Diving into the Wreck," they understand "the book of myths in which our names do not appear." Assuming authority for and thus authorship of their own life's text, they write themselves and their experiences into the mythic memory of their culture and thereby create culture itself.

This makes some readers nervous. Such license also makes the women who take it unreliable as traditional cultural reporters. But that is their intent. Maxine Hong Kingston has called this kind of writing the production of a "truer mythology." As a result, the works of a writer like Kingston often defy categorization. She blurs the lines of both storytelling and history by invoking both in the service of what poet Alicia Ostriker calls "revisionist mythmaking."

If myth is the psyche of a culture, then the things people create, their artifacts, become what T. S. Eliot called objective correlatives, the tangible manifestations of emotions or ideas. Similarly, cultural analyst Annette Kolodny maintains that a culture's historic and economic processes are the external projections of internal patterns. If this is true, the power of myth is enormous: it not only explains the past but also shapes the future. Thus to construct or reconstruct stories (and to retell them) is indeed an act of revolution as well as of salvation.

I entered the thicket of these ruminations with an idea about the fictional uses of history. I have emerged on the other side with a question about the historical uses of fiction. If our artifacts are the tangible manifestations of our ideas, then literature is an artifact, and it can be used by historians to tell us about the state of our myths and thereby the state of our thinking. What women are saying in the stories they tell reveals some things about identities, relationships, and society at the time the stories are written. In metaphoric terms, they could be considered snapshots. At a deeper level, we may find that stories by women determine the accuracy of the prediction made by Virginia Woolf in 1931, that it would take fifty years for women to break their literary silences and tell what they know about "the world that lies submerged in our unconscious being." I look forward to finding out if that is true in Texas.

NOTES

1. My late mentor, Joan Lidoff, was at work on a manuscript tackling "fluid boundaries" when she died. I am thankful to her for stimulating my thoughts in this regard.

BIBLIOGRAPHY

The purpose of this bibliography is twofold: to provide publication data on key works cited in the text of *Texas Women Writers* and to provide a selective listing of key works by and about the writers themselves. This bibliography is not intended to be comprehensive and definitive; rather, it is a finding list to provide the springboard for further reading and research.

The alphabetized Authors section of the bibliography is broken down into two categories: the primary works, especially books, of each author, whether or not they are mentioned in *Texas Women Writers,* and selected secondary critical and/or biographical works about some of the authors. A few authors, primarily journalists, have secondary but no primary works listed. Individual short stories, poems, dramas, and book reviews generally are not listed. Selected autobiographical, scholarly, and/or critical essays are included, especially for nineteenth-century writers. Biographical sketches readily available in standard data bases and reference works, including *The New Handbook of Texas,* are not included. The non-Texas works of authors are included because they demonstrate the versatility and wide range of interests among both early and contemporary Texas women writers. No effort has been made to provide the complete publication history of the various works, although some important reprints and editions are listed. In most cases, coauthored and coedited works are cross-referenced to the primary author or editor. In cases where the primary author or editor does not have a listing due to gender or regional affiliation, the title is listed under the relevant secondary author or editor with an attribution note appearing in brackets.

The General section contains references, other than those in the Authors section, that are mentioned in *Texas Women Writers* or that contain broad background information on the field.

This bibliography is only a first gathering of the materials. The next task is to develop a definitive listing of, as well as salient criticism and biographical information about, all Texas women writers and their works. Much research is needed before a comprehensive list can be developed. For example, the current listing of contemporary writers of nonfiction about Texas is incomplete; likewise a finding list of short stories by Texas women authors needs to be compiled. The publication history of the various works, including reprints, translations, and foreign editions also needs compilation. Much research remains to be done regarding branches of Texas women's writing not covered in this book, including fantasy, mystery, romance, lesbian writing, and cookbooks with a Texas focus.

The editors and the contributors hope that readers will use the materials in this bibliography as a place to begin their own research and therefore will add to the growing body of knowledge concerning Texas women writers.

GENERAL

Abernethy, Francis E., ed. *Legendary Ladies of Texas.* Publications of the Texas Folklore Society, vol. 43. Dallas: E-Heart Press, 1981.

———. "Maria de Agreda: The Lady in Blue." In *Legendary Ladies of Texas.* Edited by Francis E. Abernethy. Dallas: E-Heart Press, 1981, pp. 9–14.

Adams, Andy. *Log of a Cowboy: A Narrative of the Old Trail Days.* New York: Houghton, Mifflin and Co., 1903.

Adams, Susan Charlotte Turner. "A Bibliography of Texas Poetry, 1945–1981." Master's thesis, Texas A&M University, 1984.

Allen, Martha Mitten. *Traveling West: Nineteenth Century Women on the Overland Routes.* Southwestern Studies, vol. 80. El Paso: University of Texas at El Paso, 1987.

Andreadis, Harriette. "True Womanhood Revisited: Women's Private Writing in Nineteenth Century Texas." *Journal of the Southwest* 31 (1989): 179–204.

Arata, Ester Spring. *More Black American Playwrights: A Bibliography.* Metuchen, N.Y.: Scarecrow, 1978.

Arkin, Marian, and Barbara Shollar, eds. *Longman Anthology of World Literature by Women, 1875–1975.* New York: Longman's, 1989.

Armen, Margaret. *The Hanging of Father Miguel.* New York: Doubleday, 1990.

Atwood, E. Bagby. *The Regional Vocabulary of Texas.* Austin: Univ. of Texas Press, 1962.

Bagnall, Norma Hayes. "Children's Literature in Texas: A History and Evaluation." Ph.D. diss.: Texas A&M University, 1984.

Beauvoir, Simone de. *The Second Sex.* New York: Knopf, 1953.

Bennett, Patrick. *Talking with Texas Writers: Twelve Interviews.* College Station: Texas A&M Univ. Press, 1980.

Botkin, B. A., ed. *The Southwest Scene: An Anthology of Regional Verse.* Oklahoma City: The Economy Co., 1931.

Bradstreet, Anne. *The Tenth Muse Lately Sprung Up in America.* London: 1650. Second edition, Boston: John Foster, 1678.

Braziel, Kay Pinckney, and Dorothy Brand Smith. *Texas in Children's Books*. Austin: University of Texas Graduate School of Library Science, 1974.

Brewer, John Mason. *Heralding Dawn: An Anthology of Verse*. Dallas: June Thomason Printing, 1936.

Brown, John Henry. *History of Texas from 1685 to 1892*. St. Louis: L. E. Daniell, 1892.

Bruce-Novoa, Juan. *Retrospace: Collected Essays on Chicano Literature*. Houston: Arte Público Press, 1990.

Busby, Mark. *New Growth/2*. San Antonio: Corona, 1993.

Bushby, Don Maitland, ed. *The Golden Stallion: An Anthology of Poems Concerning the Southwest and Written by Representative Southwestern Poets*. Dallas: The Southwest Press, 1930.

Candelaria, Cordelia, ed. *Multiethnic Literature of the United States*. Boulder: Univ. of Colorado Press, 1989.

Cattarulla, Kay, ed. *Texas Bound: 19 Texas Stories*. Dallas: Southern Methodist Univ. Press, 1994.

Christensen, Paul. "A Dark Texas of the Soul." *The Pawn Review* 8 (1984): 1–10.

———. "From Cowboys to *Curanderas*: The Cycle of Texas Literature." *Southwest Review* 73 (Spring, 1988): 10–29.

Collins, Karen Louise Sikes. "Guide to Diaries in the University of Texas Archives Produced Before 1900." Master's thesis, University of Texas, 1967.

Clifford, Craig, and Tom Pilkington, eds. *Range Wars: Heated Debates, Sober Reflections, and Other Assessments of Texas Writing*. Dallas: Southern Methodist Univ. Press, 1989.

Crowell, Norma H. "The Poetry Society of Texas." *The Woman's Viewpoint* 2, no. 12 (January, 1925): 56–58.

Croxdale, Richard, and Melissa Hield, eds. *Women in the Texas Workforce: Yesterday and Today*. Austin: People's History in Texas, 1979.

Cummins, Light, and Alvin Bailey, eds. *A Guide to the History of Texas*. New York: Greenwood Press, 1988.

Daydí-Tolson, Santiano, ed. *Five Poets of Aztlán*. Binghamton, N.Y.: Bilingual Press, 1985.

Desprez, Frank. *Lasca: The Story of a Texas Cowboy*. Houston: Rein Co., 1931.

Dewey, Annette Barrett. "The Panhandle Pen Women's Club." *The Woman's Viewpoint* 2, no. 13 (February, 1925): 19.

Dixon, Sam H. *The Poets and Poetry of Texas: Biographical Sketches of the Poets of Texas, with Selections from Their Writings Containing Reviews Both Personal and Critical*. Austin: Sam H. Dixon and Co., 1885.

Dobie, J. Frank. *Apache Gold and Yaqui Silver*. Boston: Little, Brown, 1939.

———. *Guide to Life and Literature of the Southwest*. 6th ed. Dallas: Southern Methodist Univ. Press, 1969.

———. *The Longhorns*. New York: Grosset and Dunlap, 1941.

Downs, Fane, and Nancy Baker Jones, eds. *Women and Texas History: Selected Essays*. Austin: Texas State Historical Association, 1993.

Dreer, Herman. *American Literature by Negro Authors*. New York: Macmillan, 1950.

Dunsany, Edward J. M. D. P. *Fifty-One Tales*. London: Elkin Mathews, 1915.

Duval, John C. *Adventures of Big-Foot Wallace*. Edited by Mabel Major and Rebecca W. Smith. Dallas: Tardy, 1936. Reprint, Lincoln: Univ. of Nebraska Press, 1966.

———. *Early Times in Texas; or The Adventures of Jack Dobell*. Edited by Mabel Major and Rebecca W. Smith. Dallas: Tardy, 1936. Reprint, Lincoln: Univ. of Nebraska Press, 1986.

Eagleton, Davis Foute. *Writers and Writings of Texas*. New York: Broadway Publishing Co., 1913.

Edwards, Margaret Royalty. *Poets Laureate of Texas, 1932–1966*. San Antonio: Naylor Co., 1966.

Ellet, Elizabeth F. *Pioneer Women of the West*. Philadelphia: Henry T. Coates and Co., 1852.

Ellis, Sarah. *The Mothers of England. The Prose Works*. 2 vols. New York: Langley, 1844.

Evans, Emma Cobb. "Pen Women Afield and at Home." *The Woman's Viewpoint* 2, no. 14 (March, 1925): 19.

———. "Texas League of American Pen Women." *The Woman's Viewpoint* 2, no. 13 (February, 1925): 18; 2, no. 15 (April, 1925): 19.

Fenwick, Marin B. *Who's Who Among the Women of San Antonio and the Southwest*. San Antonio: n.p., 1917.

Ferber, Edna. *Giant*. Garden City, N.Y.: Doubleday, 1952.

Ferguson, Mary Anne, ed. *Images of Women in Literature*. Boston: Houghton Mifflin Co., 1986.

Fernea, Elizabeth W., and Marilyn P. Duncan, eds. *Texas Women in Politics*. Austin: Texas Foundation for Women's Resources, 1977.

Fitzgerald, F. Scott. *The Great Gatsby*. New York: C. Scribner's Sons, 1925.

Gaston, Edwin W., Jr. *The Early Novel of the Southwest*. Albuquerque: Univ. of New Mexico Press, 1961.

Goldsmith, Oliver. *Citizen of the World*. Chiswick, England: Printed for C. Whittingham, 1819.

Graham, Don. "Literature." In *The New Handbook of Texas*. Vol. 4. Austin: Texas State Historical Association, 1996, pp. 218–26.

———, ed. *South by Southwest: 24 Stories from Modern Texas*. Austin: Univ. of Texas Press, 1986.

———, ed. *Texas: A Literary Portrait*. San Antonio: Corona Press, 1985.

———, James W. Lee, and William T. Pilkington, eds. *The Texas Literary Tradition: Fiction, Folklore, History*. Austin: College of Liberal Arts of the University of Texas and the Texas State Historical Association, 1983.

Graham, Philip, ed. *Early Texas Verse, 1835–1850*. Austin: Steck Co., 1936.

Grammer, Norma Rutledge. "Writings by Women in Texas." Master's thesis, Texas Christian University, 1937.

Grant, Lyman, ed. *New Growth: Contemporary Short Stories by Texas Writers*. San Antonio: Corona Publishing Co., 1989.

Graves, John. *Goodbye to a River: A Narrative*. New York: Knopf, 1960.

Greene, A. C. *The 50 Best Books on Texas*. Dallas: Pressworks Publishing, 1982.

Greer, Hilton Ross, ed. *Best Short Stories of the Southwest.* Dallas: The Southwest Press, 1928.

———, ed. *Best Short Stories of the Southwest.* Second Series. Dallas: The Southwest Press, 1931.

———, and Florence Elberta Barns, eds. *New Voices of the Southwest.* Dallas: Tardy Publishing Co., 1934.

Hailey, Kendall. *The Day I Became an Autodidact.* New York: Dell, 1988.

Hammond, Ken, ed. *State Lines.* College Station: Texas A&M Univ. Press, 1993.

Harrington, Mildred P. *The Southwest in Children's Books: A Bibliography.* Baton Rouge: Louisiana State Univ. Press, 1952.

Hartley, Margaret L., ed. *The Southwest Review Reader.* Dallas: Southern Methodist Univ. Press, 1974.

Healey, Jane F. "Privately Published Autobiographies by Texans: Their Significance to Scholars." *Southwestern Historical Quarterly* 95, no. 4 (April, 1992): 497–508.

Henley, Beth. *Crimes of the Heart: A Play.* New York: Viking Press, Penguin Books, 1982.

Hield, Melissa. "The Texas Women's Literary Tradition: Passing It On." *Texas Libraries* 45 (Winter, 1984): 115–18.

Hill, Billy Bob, ed. *Texas in Poetry: A 150 Year Anthology.* Denton: Center for Texas Studies and Texas Studies Association, 1994.

———, and Mike Hennech, eds. *Texas Short Fiction: A World in Itself.* Fort Worth: ALE Publishing Co., 1993.

———, and Mike Hennech, eds. *Texas Short Fiction: A World in Itself II.* Fort Worth: ALE Publishing Co., 1995.

Hogan, William Ransom. *The Texas Republic: A Social and Economic History.* Norman: Univ. of Oklahoma Press, 1946.

Holmes, Maxine and Gerald Saxon, eds. *WPA Dallas Guide and History: Written and Compiled from 1936 to 1942 by the Workers of the Writers' Program of the Work Projects Administration of the City of Dallas.* Denton: Dallas Public Library, Texas Center for the Book, Univ. of North Texas Press, 1992.

Hubbell, Jay B. *South and Southwest: Literary Essays and Reminiscences.* Durham, N.C.: Duke Univ. Press, 1965.

Hughs, Fannie Mae. *History of the Texas Woman's Press Association.* Huntsville: n.p., 1935.

Immroth, Barbara Froling. *Texas in Children's Books: An Annotated Bibliography.* Hamden, Conn.: Library Professional Publications/Shoestring Press, 1986.

James, Marquis. *The Raven.* New York: Blue Ribbon Books, 1929.

Jenkins, John H. *Basic Texas Books: An Annotated Bibliography of Selected Works for a Research Library.* Austin: Jenkins Publishing, 1983.

Jewett, Sarah Orne. *A White Heron and Other Stories.* Boston: Houghton, Mifflin, 1886.

Joyce, James. *Ulysses.* First American edition. New York: Random House, 1934.

Kennelly, Laura Ballard. *A Certain Attitude: Poems by Seven Texas Women.* San Antonio: Pecan Grove Press, 1995.

Kerr, Hugh. *A Poetical Description of Texas, and Narrative of Many Interesting Events in that Country, Embracing a Period of Several Years, Interspersed with Moral and Political Impressions: Also, an Appeal to Those Who Oppose the Union of Texas with the United States, and the Anticipation of that Event. To Which is Added The Texas Heroes, No. 1 and 2.* New York: published for the author, 1838.

Kingston, Maxine Hong. *The Woman Warrior: Memoir of a Girlhood Among Ghosts.* New York: Knopf, 1976.

Kolodny, Annette. *The Land Before Her: Fantasy and Experience of the American Frontiers, 1630–1860.* Chapel Hill: Univ. of North Carolina Press, 1984.

———. *Lay of the Land: Metaphor as Experience and History in American Life and Letters.* Chapel Hill: Univ. of North Carolina Press, 1975.

Lasher, Patricia, and Beverly Bentley. *Texas Women: Interviews and Images.* Austin: Shoal Creek Publishers, 1980.

Lawhn, Juanita Luna. "*El Regidor* and *La Prensa*: Impediments to Women's Self-Definition." *Third Woman* 4 (1989): 134–42.

Lee, James Ward, ed. *Classics of Texas Fiction.* Dallas: E-Heart Press, 1987.

Lewis, R. W. B. *The American Adam: Innocence, Tragedy, and Tradition in the Nineteenth Century.* Chicago: Univ. of Chicago Press, 1955.

Lynch, Peggy Zuleika, and Edmund C. Lynch, eds. *Behold Texas: The Poet's View.* Austin: Nortex Press, 1983.

Mainiero, Lina, ed. *American Women Writers: A Critical Reference Guide from Colonial Times to the Present.* New York: Frederick Ungar Publishing Co., 1979.

Marshall, Carol. "The Fairy Tale and the Frontier: Images of Women in Texas Fiction." In *The Texas Literary Tradition: Fiction, Folklore, History.* Edited by Don Graham, James W. Lee, and William T. Pilkington. Austin: College of Liberal Arts of the University of Texas and the Texas State Historical Association, 1983, pp. 195–208.

Martin, William B., ed. *Texas Plays.* Dallas: Southern Methodist Univ. Press, 1990.

McDonald, Walter, and James P. White. *Texas Stories and Poems.* Dallas: Texas Center for Writers Press, 1978.

McGuire, Kathryn S., and James Ward Lee, eds. *New Texas 94.* Denton: Center for Texas Studies, 1994.

McMurtry, Larry. "Ever a Bridegroom: Reflections on the Failure of Texas Literature." In *Range Wars: Heated Debates, Sober Reflections, and Other Assessments of Texas Writing.* Edited by Craig Clifford and Tom Pilkington. Dallas: Southern Methodist Univ. Press, 1989, pp. 13–41. Reprinted from *Texas Observer,* Oct. 23, 1981, pp. 1, 8–18.

———. *Horseman, Pass By.* New York: Harper and Bros., 1961.

McWilliams, Carey. *The New Regionalism in American Literature.* Seattle: University of Washington Book Store, 1930.

Miles, Elton. *Southwest Humorists.* Southwest Writers Series, no. 26. Austin: Steck-Vaughn, 1969.

Miller, Jency, comp. *Texas Poets Laureate.* N.p., [1936?].

Milligan, Bryce, ed. *Corazon del Norte: A Selection of North Texas Latino Writing.* San Antonio: Wings Press, 1996.

———. *Linking Roots: Writing by Six Women with Distinct Ethnic Heritages.* San Antonio: M&A Editions, 1993.

———, ed. *This Promiscuous Light: Young Women Poets of San Antonio.* San Antonio: Wings Press, 1996.

———. "Raising the Dead." *The Texas Observer,* September 28, 1984, 29–30.

———, Angela De Hoyos, and Mary Guerrero-Milligan, eds. *Daughters of the Fifth Sun: A Collection of Latina Fiction and Poetry.* New York: Putnam, 1995.

Mirandé, Alfredo, and Evangelina Enríquez. *La Chicana: The Mexican-American Woman.* Chicago: Univ. of Chicago Press, 1979.

Montesquieu, Charles de Secondet. *Lettres Persanes.* [1722]. Translated as *Persian Letters.* New York: Garland, 1972.

Montiel, Chazarra. "Dialoguing with Thanatos." *Vortex: A Critical Review* 4. Mansfield, Tex.: Latitudes Press, 1989, pp. 22–24. Originally published in *La Estafeta Literaria* (Madrid, Spain: February, 1971).

Moreland, Sinclair. *The Texas Women's Hall of Fame.* Austin: Biographical Press, 1917.

Nathan, Debbie. *Women and Other Aliens: Essays from the U.S. Mexico Border.* El Paso: Cinco Puntos Press, 1991.

Bruce-Novoa, Juan. *Chicano Authors: Inquiry by Interview.* Austin: Univ. of Texas Press, 1980.

———. *Retrospace: Collected Essays on Chicano Literature.* Houston: Arte Público, 1990.

Olmsted, Frederick Law. *A Journey through Texas or, a Saddle-Trip on the Southwestern Frontier.* New York: Dix, Edwards and Co., 1857. Reprint, Austin: Univ. of Texas Press, 1978.

Paredes, Raymond. "The Evolution of Chicano Literature." In *Three American Literatures.* Edited by Houston A. Baker. New York: Modern Language Association, 1982, pp. 33–79.

Parr, Carmen Salazar, and Genevieve M. Ramírez. "The Female Hero in Chicano Literature." In *Beyond Stereotypes: The Critical Analysis of Chicana Literature.* Binghamton, N.Y.: Bilingual Press, 1985, pp. 47–59.

Payne, Leonidas Warren, Jr. *A Survey of Texas Literature.* New York: Rand McNally and Co., 1928.

Pearce, Bessie Malvina. "Texas Through Women's Eyes, 1823–1868." Ph.D. diss., University of Texas at Austin, 1965.

Peery, William, ed. *21 Texas Short Stories.* Austin: Univ. of Texas Press, 1954. Reprint, Austin: Univ. of Texas Press, 1980.

Perry, George Sessions. *My Granny Van: The Running Battle of Rockdale, Texas.* New York: Whittlesey House, 1949.

———. *Roundup Time.* New York: Whittlesey House, 1943.

Pilkington, William T., ed. *Careless Weeds: Six Texas Novellas.* Dallas: Southern Methodist Univ. Press, 1993.

———. *Imagining Texas: The Literature of the Lone Star State.* Boston: American Press, 1981.

Platt, Randall Beth. *The Four Arrows of Fe-As-Ko.* Highland Park, N.J.: Catbird Press, 1991.

Posey, John, ed. *Kentecloth: African American Voices in Texas*. Denton: Center for Texas Studies, 1995.

Pound, Ezra. *A Draft of XVI Cantos of Ezra Pound: For the Beginning of a Poem of Some Length*. Paris: Three Mountains Press, 1925.

Proctor, Adelaide. *Legends and Lyrics: A Book of Verses*. London: G. Bell, 1877.

Raines, C. W. *Bibliography of Texas*. Austin: Gammel Book Co., 1896.

Ramos-Garcia, Luis A., ed. *Cuentos de Austin/Tales from Austin*. Austin: Studia Hispanica Editions, 1980.

Raymond, Ida. *Southland Writers: Biographical and Critical Sketches of the Living Female Authors of the South*. Philadelphia: Claxton, Remsen and Haffelfinger, 1870.

Rogers, John William, and J. Frank Dobie. *Finding Literature on the Texas Plains*. Dallas: Southwest Press, 1931.

Rubin, Louis D., ed. *A Bibliographic Guide to the Study of Southern Literature*. Baton Rouge: Louisiana State Univ. Press, 1969.

Rush, Theressa Gunnels, et al. *Black American Writers Past and Present*. Vols. 1 and 2. Metuchen, N.Y.: Scarecrow, 1975.

Sage, Fannie Mae. "Contemporary Women Poets of Texas." *The Texas Quarterly* 21, no. 2 (Summer, 1978): 84–108.

Saldivar, Ramón. "Where the Sun Cuts a Thinner Shadow: The Fate of Chicano Poetry." *Pawn Review* 7, no. 3 (1983): 1–8.

Sánchez, Rosaura, and Rosa Martínez Cruz, eds. *Essays on la mujer*. Los Angeles: UCLA/Chicano Studies Center Publications, 1977.

Seligman, Claudia Dee. *Texas Women: Legends in Their Own Time*. Dallas: Hendrick-Long Publishing Co., 1989.

Simmen, Edward, ed. *North of the Rio Grande: The Mexican-American Experience in Short Fiction*. New York: Mentor, 1992.

Snapp, Elizabeth, and Harry F. Snapp. *Read All About Her! Texas Woman's History: A Working Bibliography*. Denton: Texas Woman's Univ. Press, 1995.

Sonnichsen, C. L. *From Hopalong to Hud: Thoughts on Western Fiction*. College Station: Texas A&M Univ. Press, 1978.

Steuart, Ella Hutchins, ed. *Gems from a Texas Quarry: Or, Literary Offerings By and Selections from Leading Writers and Prominent Characters of Texas: Being a Texas Contribution to the World's Industrial Exposition at New Orleans, La., 1884–5*. New Orleans: J. S. Rivers, 1885.

Tatum, Charles. *Mexican American Literature*. New York: Harcourt, Brace, Jovanovich, 1990.

Terry, Marshall, ed. *Prize Stories: Texas Institute of Letters*. Dallas: Still Point Press, 1986.

Texas State Historical Association. *Handbook of Texas*. 3 vols. Austin: Texas State Historical Association, 1952.

———. *The New Handbook of Texas*. 6 vols. Austin: Texas State Historical Association, 1996.

Thomas, Lorenzo. "Gathering Like Heat: Black Writing in Texas." *Texas Humanist* 2, no. 7 (April, 1980): 4–5, 9.

Tyson, Eleanore Ely Smith. "Texas Writers of Children's Literature: A Collection of Interviews and a Critical Examination of Their Work." Master's thesis, University of Houston, 1973.

Vann, William H. *The Texas Institute of Letters 1936–1966*. Austin: Encino Press, 1967.

Walton, Mrs. M. R. *A History of the Texas Woman's Press Association from the Year of Its Organization, 1893, until the Celebration of the Fifteenth Anniversary*. N.p., 1908.

White, James P. ed. *The Bicentennial Collection of Texas Short Stories*. Dallas: Texas Center for Writers Press, 1974.

White, Janice L., ed. *Fiction and Poetry by Texas Women*. Midland: Texas Center for Writers Press, 1975.

Wiesepape, Betty. "The Manuscript Club of Wichita Falls: A Noteworthy Texas Literary Club." *Southwestern Historical Quarterly* 97 (April, 1994): 643–59.

Winfrey, Dorman H. *Seventy-five Years of Texas History: The Texas State Historical Association, 1897–1972*. Austin: Jenkins Publishing Co., 1975.

Wister, Owen. *The Virginian: A Horseman of the Plains*. New York: Macmillan, 1902.

Wolf, Carole. "A Study of Prose by Nineteenth Century Texas Women." Ph.D. diss., Texas Tech University, 1982.

"Women's Voices." Special Issue of *The Texas Observer*, September 25, 1987.

Woods, Gary Doyle. *The Hicks-Adams-Bass-Floyd-Patillo and Collateral Lines with Family Letters, 1840–1868*. Salado, Tex.: Anson-Jones Press. 1963.

AUTHOR WORKS

Aaker, Linda. *A Woman's Odyssey: Journals 1976–1992*. Denton: Univ. of North Texas Press, 1994.

Adair, Cornelia R. *My Diary: August 30th to November 5th, 1874*. N.p., 1918. Reprint, Austin: Univ. of Texas Press, 1965.

Adams, Gail Galloway. *The Purchase of Order*. Athens: Univ. of Georgia Press, 1988.

Agatha, Sister M. *See* Sheehan, Sister M. Agatha.

Albert, Susan Wittig. *Hangman's Root*. New York: Scribner's, 1994.

———. *Rosemary Remembered: A China Bayles Mystery*. New York: Berkley Prime Crime, 1995.

———. *Steps to Structure: An Introduction to Composition and Rhetoric*. Cambridge, Mass.: Winthrop, 1975.

———, ed. *Structuralism: An Interdisciplinary Study*. Pittsburgh: Pickwick Press, 1975.

———. *Stylistic and Narrative Structure in the Middle English Romances*. Austin: Univ. of Texas Press, 1978.

———. *Thyme of Death: A Mystery Introducing China Bayles*. New York: Scribners, 1992.

———. *Witches' Bane*. New York: Scribners, 1993.

———. *Work of Her Own: How Women Create Success and Fulfillment off the Traditional Career Track*. New York: G. P. Putnam's, 1992.

Alexander, Frances. *Choc, The Chachalaca*. Austin: Von Boeckmann-Jones, 1969.
———. *Conversation with a Lamb*. Austin: n.p., 1955.
———. *The Diamond Tree*. Austin: Von Boeckmann-Jones, 1970.
———. *A Handbook of Chinese Art Symbols*. Austin: Von Boeckmann-Jones, 1958.
———. *Mary Charlotte Alexander (Au Mo Ling), Missionary to China*. Austin: Von Boeckmann-Jones, 1968.
———. *Miss Chou: The Biography of Inez Lung Lee, Missionary-Teacher in China, 1927 to 1958*. Austin: W. Frank Evans, 1974.
———. *Mother Goose on the Rio Grande*. Dallas: Banks, 1944.
———. *Orphans on the Guadalupe*. Wichita Falls: Nortex Offset Pub., 1971.
———. *Pebbles from a Broken Jar: Fables and Stories from Old China*. Indianapolis: Bobbs, 1969.
———. *Time at the Window*. Dallas: Kaleidograph Press, 1948.
———. *Seven White Birds*. Dallas: Kaleidograph Press, 1938.
Alonzo, Adela. "*Sabor a Mi/Savor Me*." In *Common Bonds: Stories by and about Modern Texas Women*. Edited by Suzanne Comer. Dallas: Southern Methodist Univ. Press, 1990, pp. 177–78.
Alter, Judy. *After Pa Was Shot*. New York: Morrow, 1978.
———. *A Ballad for Sallie*. New York: Doubleday, 1992.
———. *Dorothy Johnson*. Boise, Idaho: Boise State University Western Writers Series, no. 44, 1980.
———. *Elmer Kelton and West Texas: A Literary Relationship*. Denton: North Texas Univ. Press, 1989.
———. *Jeanne Williams*. Boise, Idaho: Boise State University Western Writers Series, no. 98, 1991.
———. *Jessie*. New York: Bantam Books, 1995.
———. *Katie and the Recluse*. Lufkin, Tex.: E-Heart, 1991.
———. *Libbie*. New York: Bantam Books, 1994.
———. *Luke and the Van Zandt County War*. Fort Worth: Texas Christian Univ. Press, 1984.
———. *Maggie and Devildust Ridin' High*! Lufkin, Tex.: E-Heart, 1990.
———. *Maggie and a Horse Named Devildust*. Lufkin, Tex.: E-Heart, 1989.
———. *Maggie and the Search for Devildust*. Lufkin, Tex.: E-Heart, 1989.
———. *Mattie*. New York: Doubleday, 1988.
———. *The Quack Doctor*. Fort Worth: Branch-Smith, 1974.
———. *Stewart Edward White*. Boise, Idaho: Boise State University Western Writers Series, no. 18, 1975.
———. *Stretch and Strengthen*. Boston: Houghton-Mifflin, 1986.
———. *The Texas ABC Book*. Fort Worth: Picnic Press, 1981.
———. *Texas College of Osteopathic Medicine: The First Twenty Years*. Fort Worth: Texas College of Osteopathic Medicine with the Univ. of North Texas Press, 1990.
———. *Thistle Hill: The History and the House*. Fort Worth: Texas Christian Univ. Press, 1988.
———. *Unbridled Spirits: Short Fiction about Women in the Old West*. Fort Worth: Texas Christian Univ. Press, 1994.

————, and Joyce Gibson Roach, eds. *Texas and Christmas: A Collection of Traditions, Memories, and Folklore.* Fort Worth: Texas Christian Univ. Press, 1983.

Altgelt, Emma. "Emma Altgelt's Sketches of Life in Texas." Edited by Henry B. Dielmann. *Southwestern Historical Quarterly* 63 (1959–60): 363–84.

Anzaldúa, Gloria. *Borderlands/La Frontera: The New Mestiza.* San Francisco: Spinsters/Aunt Lute, 1987.

Arnold, Janis. *Daughters of Memory.* Chapel Hill, N.C.: Algonquin Books, 1991.

————. *Excuse Me for Asking.* Chapel Hill, N.C.: Algonquin Books, 1994.

Arnold, June. *Applesauce.* New York: Daughters, 1977.

————. *Baby Houston.* Austin: Texas Monthly Press, 1987.

————. *Sister Gin.* Plainfield, Vt.: Daughters, 1975.

Arthur, Dora Fowler. "Jottings from the Old Journal of Littleton Fowler." *Quarterly of the Texas State Historical Association* 2 (1898–99): 73–84.

Austin, Anne. *The Black Pigeon.* New York: Grosset, 1929.

————. *Jackson Street.* New York: Greenberg, 1927.

————. *Murder at Bridge: A Mystery Novel.* New York: Macmillan, 1931.

————. *Murdered but Not Dead.* New York: Macmillan, 1939.

————. *One Drop of Blood.* New York: Macmillan, 1932.

————. *A Wicked Woman.* New York: Macmillan, 1933.

Austin, Maud Mason. *'Cension: A Sketch from Paso del Norte.* New York: Harper and Bros., 1896.

Averitte, Ruth Humphrey. *Carols in Flower.* Dallas: Avalon, 1946.

————. *Cowboy over Kiska.* Dallas. Avalon Press, 1945.

————. *Let's Review a Book: A Practical Analysis of Reading and Reviewing Designed for the Common Reader.* Dallas: Tardy Publishing, 1938.

————. *Salute to the Dawn.* Dallas: Tardy Publishing Co., 1936.

Ayers, Vivian. *The Marriage Ceremony.* Houston: Adept Publications, 1973.

Bachmann, Evelyn Trent. *New Town in Texas.* New York: Longmans, 1942.

————. *Rabbit Fires.* Boerne, Tex.: Highland, 1951.

————. *Susan's Year.* New York: Longman's, 1948.

————. *Texas, the Land of the Tejas.* New York: Random, 1943.

————. *Tressa.* New York: Viking, 1966.

Baines, Mrs. W. M., ed. *Historic Souvenir Dedicated to Texas Centennial, 1936.* Houston: Houston Pen Women, 1936.

Baker, Elizabeth. *Sonny-Boy Sim.* Chicago: Rand, 1948.

Baker, Karle Wilson [Charlotte Wilson]. "The Accidental Saint." *Collier's* 40 (December 21, 1907): 14–16.

————. *The Birds of Tanglewood.* Dallas: Southwest Press, 1930.

————. *Blue Smoke: A Book of Verses.* New Haven: Yale Univ. Press, 1919.

————. *Burning Bush.* New Haven: Yale Univ. Press, 1922.

————. *Dreamers on Horseback (Collected Verse).* Dallas: Southwest Press, 1931.

————. *Family Style.* New York: Coward-McCann, 1937.

————. *The Garden of the Plynck.* New Haven: Yale Univ. Press, 1920.

————. *Old Coins.* New Haven: Yale Univ. Press, 1923.

———. *The Reindeer's Shoe and Other Stories.* Austin: Ellen C. Temple Publisher, in cooperation with Stephen F. Austin State University, 1988.

———. *Star of the Wilderness: A Novel.* New York: Coward-McCann, 1942.

———. *Texas Flag Primer.* Yonkers-on-Hudson: World Book Co., 1925.

———. *Two Little Texans.* Yonkers-on-Hudson: World Book Co., 1932.

Secondary Sources (Baker, Karle Wilson)

Gaston, Edwin W., Jr. "Karle Wilson Baker: First Woman of Texas Letters." *East Texas Historical Journal* 15 (1977): 45–51.

Palmer, Pamela Lynn. "Dorothy Scarborough and Karle Wilson Baker: A Literary Friendship." *Southwest Historical Quarterly* 91 (July, 1987): 19–32.

———. "Karle Wilson Baker and the East Texas Experience." *East Texas Historical Journal* 24 (1986): 46–58.

Scarborough, Dorothy. "Contemporary American Poets: Karle Wilson Baker of Nacogdoches—Poet of Quiet Things." *Dallas Morning News,* March 16, 1924, sect. 3, p. 6.

———. "Karle Wilson Baker." *In The Library of Southern Literature.* Atlanta: Martin and Hay Co., 1923, pp. 47–52.

Ballou, Ellen B. "Scudder's Journey to Texas, 1859." *Southwestern Historical Quarterly* 63 (1959–60): 1–14.

Banks, Carolyn. *The Adventures of Runcible Spoon.* Etlan, Va.: Ethos Enterprises, 1979.

———. *The Darkroom.* New York: Viking, 1980.

———. *Death by Dressage.* New York: Fawcett, 1993.

———. *The Girls on the Row.* New York: Crown, 1983.

———. *Mr. Right.* New York: Viking Press, 1979.

———. *Patchwork.* New York: Crown, 1986.

———. *Tart Tales: Elegant Erotic Stories.* New York: Carroll and Graff, 1995.

———, and Amy Kwalwasser. *The Horse Lover's Guide to Texas.* Austin: Texas Monthly Press, 1988.

———, and Janis Rizzo, eds. *A Loving Voice—A Caregiver's Book of Read-Aloud Stories for the Elderly.* Philadelphia: The Charles Press, 1992.

Barbour, Martha Isabella Hopkins. *Journals of the Late Brevet Major Philip Norbourne Barbour . . . and his Wife Martha Isabella Hopkins Barbour, Written During the War with Mexico, 1846.* Edited by Rhoda van Bibber Tanner Doubleday. New York: G. P. Putnam's Sons, 1939.

Barker, Wendy. *Let the Ice Speak.* Greenfield Center: Ithaca House Books, 1991.

———. *Winter Chickens and Other Poems.* San Antonio: Corona Publishing Co., 1990.

Barns, Florence Elberta. "The Novel in Texas." *The Southwester* 1 (1935): 12.

———. "Strap Buckner Again." *Publications of the Texas Folklore Society* 10 (1932): 127–30.

———. "Strap Buckner of the Texas Frontier." *Publications of the Texas Folklore Society* 8 (1930): 129–51.

————. *A Texas Calendar.* Dallas: Tardy Publishing, 1935.

————. *Texas Writers of Today.* Foreword by Robert Adger Law. Dallas: Tardy Publishing Co., 1935. Reprint, Detroit: Gale Research Co., 1971.

————. *See also under General listing:* Greer, Hilton Ross.

Barnes, Leola Christie. *Her Majesty Nevertheless.* San Antonio: Naylor, 1968.

————. *Silver Century.* San Antonio: Naylor, 1973.

————. *West to Glory: A Poem.* New York: Exposition Press, 1961.

Barr, Amelia Edith Huddleston. *All the Days of My Life: An Autobiography. The Red Leaves of a Human Heart.* New York and London: Appleton, 1913.

————. *The Beads of Tasmer.* New York: R. Bonner's Sons, 1891.

————. *Bernicia.* New York: Dodd, Mead and Co., 1895.

————. *Between Two Loves.* New York: Dodd, Mead and Co., 1889.

————. *A Border Shepherdess: A Romance of Eskdale.* New York: Dodd, Mead and Co., 1887.

————. *A Bow of Orange Ribbon: A Romance of New York.* New York: Dodd, Mead and Co., 1886.

————. *Christopher, And Other Stories.* New York: Hunt and Eaton, 1888.

————. *A Daughter of Fife.* New York: Dodd, Mead and Co., 1886.

————. *Feet of Clay.* New York: Dodd, Mead and Co., 1889.

————. *The Flower of Gala Water.* New York: R. Bonner and Sons, 1894.

————. *Friend Olivia.* New York: Dodd, Mead and Co., 1889.

————. *Girls of a Feather.* New York: R. Bonner and Sons, 1893.

————. *The Hallam Secession: A Tale of Methodist Life in Two Countries.* New York: Phillips and Hunt, 1885.

————. *The Household of McNeil.* New York: Dodd, Mead and Co., 1890.

————. *I, Thou, and the Other One: A Love Story.* New York: Dodd, Mead and Co., 1898.

————. *Jan Vedder's Wife.* London: J. Clarke, 1888.

————. *The King's Highway.* New York: Dodd, Mead and Co., 1897.

————. *A Knight of the Nets.* New York: Dodd, Mead and Co., 1896.

————. *The Last of the Macallisters.* New York: Dodd, Mead and Co., 1889.

————. *The Lone House.* New York: Dodd, Mead and Co., 1893.

————. *The Lost Silver of Briffault.* New York: Phillips and Hunt, 1895.

————. *Love for an Hour Is Lone Forever.* New York: Dodd, Mead and Co., 1891.

————. *The Maid of Maiden Lane: A Sequel to "The Bow of Orange Ribbon."* New York: Dodd, Mead and Co., 1900.

————. *A Maid of Old New York: A Romance of Peter Stuyvesant's Time.* New York: Dodd, Mead and Co., 1911.

————. *A Master of His Fate.* New York: Dodd, Mead and Co., 1888.

————. *A Mate of the "Easter Bell": And Other Stories.* New York: R. Bonner's Sons, 1893.

————. *Mrs. Barr's Short Stories.* New York: R. Bonner's Sons, 1892.

————. *The Paper Cap: A Story of Love and Labor.* New York: Appleton, 1918.

————. *Paul and Christina.* New York: Dodd, Mead and Co., 1887.

————. *The Preacher's Daughter.* Boston: Bradley and Woodruff, 1892.

———. *Prisoners of Conscience.* New York: The Century Co., 1897.

———. *Remember the Alamo.* New York: Dodd, Mead and Co., 1888.

———. *Romances and Realities: Tales of Truth and Fancy.* New York: J. B. Ford, 1876.

———. *A Rose of a Hundred Leaves: A Love Story.* New York: Dodd, Mead and Co., 1891.

———. *Scottish Sketches.* New York: Dodd, Mead and Co., 1883.

———. *She Loved a Sailor.* New York: Dodd, Mead and Co., 1891.

———. *Shiela Vedder.* New York: Dodd, Mead and Co., 1911.

———. *A Singer from the Sea.* New York: Dodd, Mead and Co., 1893.

———. *A Sister to Esau.* New York: Dodd, Mead and Co., 1891.

———. *A Song of a Single Note: A Love Story.* New York: Dodd, Mead and Co., 1902.

———. *The Squire of Sandal-Side: A Pastoral Romance.* New York: Dodd, Mead and Co., 1887.

———. *Stories of Life and Love.* New York: The Christian Herald, 1897.

———. "Texas Memoirs of Amelia Barr." Edited by Philip Graham. *Southwestern Historical Quarterly* 69 (1966): 473–98.

———. *Trinity Bells: A Tale of Old New York.* London: T. F. Unwin, 1900.

———. *Was It Right to Forgive? A Domestic Romance.* New York: H. S. Stone, 1899.

———. *Winter Evening Tales.* New York: The Christian Herald, 1896.

Secondary Sources (Barr, Amelia Edith Huddleston)

Adams, Paul. "Amelia Barr in Texas, 1856–1868." *Southwestern Historical Quarterly* 49 (1946): 361–73.

Howard, Mary Eby. "The Novels of Amelia Barr." Master's thesis: University of Texas, 1943.

Baylor, Byrd. *Amigo.* New York: Collier Books, 1963.

———. *And It Is Still That Way.* New York: Scribner, 1976.

———. *Before You Came This Way.* New York: Dutton, 1969.

———. *The Best Town in the World.* New York: Scribner, 1983.

———. *The Chinese Bug.* Boston: Houghton Mifflin, 1968.

———. *Coyote Cry.* New York: Lothrop, Lee and Shepard Co., 1972.

———. *The Desert Is Theirs.* New York: Scribner, 1975.

———. *Desert Voices.* New York: Scribner, 1981.

———. *Everybody Needs a Rock.* New York: Scribner, 1974.

———. *Guess Who My Favorite Person Is.* New York: Scribner, 1977.

———. *Hawk, I'm Your Brother.* New York: Scribner, 1976.

———. *If You Are a Hunter of Fossils.* New York: Scribner, 1980.

———. *I'm in Charge of Celebrations.* New York: Scribner, 1986.

———. *The Man Who Talked to a Tree.* New York: Dutton 1968.

———. *One Small Blue Bead.* New York: Macmillan, 1965.

———. *The Other Way to Listen.* New York: Scribner, 1978.

———. *Plink, Plink, Plink.* Boston: Houghton Mifflin, 1971.

———. *Sometimes I Dance Mountains.* New York: Scribner, 1973.

———. *The Table Where Rich People Sit.* New York: Scribner, 1994.

———. *They Put On Masks.* New York: Scribner, 1974.

———. *The Way to Start a Day.* New York: Scribner, 1978.

———. *We Walk in Sandy Places.* New York: Scribner, 1976.

———. *When Clay Sings.* New York: Scribner, 1972.

———. *Yes Is Better than No.* New York: Scribner, 1977.

———. *Your Own Best Secret Place.* New York: Scribner, 1979.

Baylor, Frances Courtenay. *Juan and Juanita.* Boston: Houghton, 1886.

Beasley, Gertrude. *My First Thirty Years.* Paris: Robert McAlmon, 1925. Reprint, Austin: The Book Club of Texas, 1989.

Benedict, Dianne. *Shiny Objects.* Iowa City: Univ. of Iowa Press, 1982.

Secondary Sources (Benedict, Dianne)

Givens, Bettye. "An Interview with Dianne Benedict." *The Pawn Review* 8 (1984): 67–76.

Benson, Elizabeth. *The Younger Generation.* New York: Greenberg, 1927.

Berry, Margaret. *Brick by Golden Brick: A History of Campus Buildings at the University of Texas at Austin, 1883–1993.* Austin: LB Co., 1993.

———. *The University of Texas: A Pictorial Account of Its First Century.* Austin: Univ. of Texas Press, 1980.

———. *UT Austin: Traditions and Nostalgia.* Austin: Shoal Creek Publishers, 1975.

Biddle, Ellen McGowan. *Reminiscences of a Soldier's Wife.* Philadelphia: J. B. Lippincott Co., 1907.

Bird, Sarah. *Alamo House: Women without Men, Men without Brains.* New York: W. W. Norton and Co., 1986.

———. *The Boyfriend School.* New York: Doubleday, 1989.

———. *Do Evil Cheerfully.* New York: Avon Paperbacks, 1983.

———. *The Mommy Club.* New York: Doubleday, 1991.

———. *Virgin of the Rodeo.* New York: Doubleday, 1993.

Secondary Sources (Bird, Sarah)

Bronk, Ray. "Sarah Bird: A Soaring Imagination, A Rising Career." *Writer's News* 1 (1990): 12–13.

Root, Amy L. "Sarah Bird Blends Wit with Insight." *Texas Libraries* 52 (1991): 14–16.

Bishop, Julia Truitt. *Kathleen Douglas.* New York: Street and Smith Publishers, 1890.

Blackwelder, Julia Kirk. *Women of the Depression: Caste and Culture in San Antonio, 1929–1939.* College Station: Texas A&M Univ. Press, 1984.

Bonner, Cindy. *Lily.* Chapel Hill, N.C.: Algonquin Books, 1992.

———. *Looking After Lily.* Chapel Hill, N.C.: Algonquin Books, 1994.

———. *The Passion of Dellie O'Barr.* Chapel Hill, N.C.: Algonquin Books, 1996.

Brandimarte, Cynthia A. *Inside Texas: Culture, Identity, and Houses, 1878–1920.* Fort Worth: Texas Christian Univ. Press, 1991.

Brannon, Ada Cornelius. *A Noble Girl. A Book Devoted to The Uplift of Character and Modern Society.* Cisco, Tex.: Collie Printing Co., 1905.

Brans, Jo. *Listen to the Voices: Conversations with Contemporary Writers.* Dallas: Southern Methodist Univ. Press, 1988.

———. *Mother, I Have Something to Tell You.* Research by Margaret Taylor Smith. New York: Doubleday, 1987.

Breeze, Katie. *Nekkid Cowboy.* San Antonio: Corona Publishing Co., 1982.

Brenner, Anita. *The Boy Who Could Do Anything and Other Mexican Folk Tales.* New York: W. R. Scott, 1942.

———. *The Influence of Technique on the Decorative Style in the Domestic Pottery of Culhuacan.* New York: AMS Press, 1969.

———. *A Hero by Mistake.* New York: W. R. Scott, 1953.

———. *Idols Behind Altars.* New York: Harcourt, Brace, 1929.

———. *Tales from the Argentine.* New York: Farrar and Rinehart, 1930.

———. *The Timid Ghost, or, What Would You Do With a Sackful of Gold?* New York: W. R. Scott, 1966.

———. *The Wind that Swept Mexico: The History of the Mexican Revolution, 1910–1942.* Austin: Univ. of Texas Press, 1971.

———. *Your Mexican Holiday, a Modern Guide.* New York: C. P. Putnam's Sons, 1932.

Bresenhan, Karoline Patterson, and Nancy O'Bryant Puentes. *Lone Stars: A Legacy of Texas Quilts 1836–1936.* Austin: Univ. of Texas Press, 1986.

———. *Lone Stars, Volume II: A Legacy of Texas Quilts 1936–1986.* Austin: Univ. of Texas Press, 1990.

Bright, Susan. *Altar.* Austin: Plain View Press, 1984.

———. *Atomic Basket: Occasional Poems.* Sausalito, Calif.: In Between Books, 1985.

———. *Bunny.* Austin: Plain View Press, 1990.

———. *Colors.* Austin: Plain View Press, 1979.

———. *Eulogy for the ERA.* Austin: Plain View Press, 1982.

———. *Far Side of the Word.* Austin: Plain View Press, 1986.

———. *House of the Mother.* Austin: Plain View Press, 199[?].

———. *Images.* Austin: Plain View Press, 1982.

———. *Julia.* Houston: Wings Press, 1977.

———. *Pewter Wheel.* Austin: Plain View Press, 1982.

Brooks, Elizabeth. *Prominent Women of Texas.* Akron, Ohio: Werner Co., 1896.

Brown, Marion T. *Letters from Fort Sill, 1886–1887.* Edited by C. Richard King. Austin: Encino Press, 1970.

Brown, Mary M. *A School History of Texas from its Discovery in 1685 to 1893, for the use of Schools, Academies, Convents, Seminaries, and all Institutions of Learning.* Dallas: by the author, 1894.

Brown, Rosellen. *The Autobiography of My Mother.* Garden City, N.Y.: Doubleday, 1976.

———. *Banquet: Five Short Stories.* Lincoln, Mass.: Penmaen Press, 1978.

———. *Before and After.* New York: Farrar, Straus and Giroux, 1992.

———. *Civil Wars.* New York: Alfred A. Knopf, 1984.

———. *Cora Fry.* New York: W. W. Norton, 1977.

———. *Cora Fry's Pillow Book.* New York: Farrar, Straus and Giroux, 1994.

———. *A Rosellen Brown Reader: Selected Poetry and Prose.* Middlebury, Vt.: Middlebury College Press, 1992.

———. *Some Deaths in the Delta and Other Poems.* Amherst: Univ. of Massachusetts Press, 1970.

———. *Street Games.* Garden City, N.Y.: Doubleday, 1974.

———. *Tender Mercies.* New York: Alfred A. Knopf, 1978.

Brown-Guillory, Elizabeth. *Their Place on the Stage: Black Women Playwrights in America.* New York: Greenwood Press, 1988.

———. *Wines in the Wilderness: Plays by African American Women from the Harlem Renaissance to the Present.* New York: Greenwood Press, 1990.

Bunkley, Anita Richmond. *Black Gold.* New York: Dutton, 1994.

———. *Emily: The Yellow Rose.* Houston: Rinard Publishing, 1989.

———. *Wild Embers.* New York: Dutton, 1995.

Secondary Sources (Bunkley, Anita Richmond)

Harris, Trudier. "'The Yellow Rose of Texas': A Different Cultural View." *Publications of the Texas Folklore Society* 44 (1996): 315–31.

Bunton, Mary Taylor. *A Bride on the Old Chisholm Trail in 1886.* San Antonio: Naylor, 1939.

Burkhalter, Lois Wood. *Gideon Lincecum, 1793–1874: A Biography.* Austin: Univ. of Texas Press, 1965.

———. *Marion Koogler McNay: A Biography.* San Antonio: Marion Koogler McNay Art Institute, 1968.

Burleson, Elizabeth Morris. *A Man of the Family.* Chicago: Follett, 1965.

Burnett, Georgellen. *We Just Toughed It Out: Women in the Llano Estacado.* El Paso: Texas Western Univ. Press, 1990.

Burns, Mamie Sypert. *This I Can Leave You: A Woman's Days on the Pitchfork Ranch.* College Station: Texas A&M Univ. Press, 1986.

Byrd, Lee Merrill. *My Sister Disappears.* Dallas: Southern Methodist Univ. Press, 1993.

Campbell, Camilla. *Bartletts of Box B Ranch.* New York: Whittlesey, 1949.

———. *Coronado and His Captains.* Chicago: Follett, 1958.

———. *Galleons Sail Westward.* Dallas: Mathis, 1939.

———. *Star Mountain and Other Legends of Mexico.* New York: Whittlesey, 1946.

Campbell, Trini. *Canto indio mexicano.* New York: Ediciones Abra, 1977.

Campbell, Wanda Jay. *The Mystery of McClellan Creek.* New York: Dutton, 1958.

———. *The Mystery of Old Mobeetie.* New York: Dutton, 1960.

———. *The Museum Mystery.* New York: Dutton, 1957.

———. *Ten Cousins.* New York: Dutton, 1960.

Cardelle, Cara [Emaretta C. Kimball]. *Letters from an Early Texas Settler.* Edited by William B. DeWees. Louisville, Ky.: Morton & Griswold, 1852. Reprint, Waco: Texian Press, 1968.

Cardenas, Reyes. *Get Your Tortillas Together*. San Antonio: M&A Editions, 1976.

Carmichael, Ida. *Beware! or, Irma's Life*. Houston: n.p., 1901.

Carpenter, Liz. *Getting Better All the Time*. New York: Simon and Schuster, 1987. Reprint, College Station: Texas A&M Univ. Press, 1993.

———. *Ruffles and Flourishes: The Warm and Tender Story of a Simple Girl Who Found Adventure in the White House*. New York: Doubleday, 1970. Reprint, with a new foreword by the author, College Station: Texas A&M Univ. Press, 1993.

———. *Unplanned Parenthood: The Confessions of a Seventysomething Surrogate Mother*. New York: Random, 1994

Carr, Pat. *Bernard Shaw*. New York: Ungar, 1976.

———. *Grass Creek Chronicle*. El Paso: Endeavors in Humanity Press, 1976.

———. *In Fine Spirits: The Civil War Letters of Ras Stirman with Historical Comments*. Fayetteville, Ark.: Washington County Historical Society, 1986.

———. *Mimbres Mythology*. El Paso: Texas Western Univ. Press, 1979.

———. *Night of the Luminarias*. Austin: Slough Press, 1986.

———. *Sonahchi: A Collection of Myth-Tales*. El Paso: Cinco Puntos Press, 1988.

———. *The Women in the Mirror*. Iowa City: Univ. of Iowa Press, 1977.

Carrington, Evelyn M., ed. *Women in Early Texas*. Austin: Jenkins Publishing, 1975. Reprint, Austin: Texas State Historical Association, 1994.

Catacalos, Rosemary. *Again for the First Time*. Santa Fe: Tooth of Time Press, 1984.

———. *As Long as It Takes*. Springfield, Mo.: Iguana Press, 1984.

Secondary Sources (Catacalos, Rosemary)

Bennett, Steve. "Catacalos versed in hardships of poetry 'job.'" *San Antonio Light,* May 12, 1985.

Oliphant, Dave. "Three San Antonio Poets." *Cedar Rock* 10:1 (Winter, 1985): 6–8.

Catlin, Wynelle. *Old Wattles*. Garden City, N.Y.: Doubleday, 1975.

Cazneau, Jane. *See:* Montgomery, Cora

Chastain, Madye Lee. *Bright Days*. New York: Harcourt, Brace, 1952.

———. *Emmy Keeps a Promise*. New York: Harcourt, Brace, 1956.

———. *Fripsey Summer*. New York: Harcourt, 1953.

———. *Loblolly Farm*. New York: Harcourt, 1950.

———. *Steamboat South*. New York: Harcourt, Brace, 1951.

Chávez, Denise. *Face of an Angel*. Houston: Arte Público Press, 1991. Reprint, New York: Farrar, Straus and Giroux, 1994.

———. "The Flying Tortilla Man." In *Mexican American Literature*. Edited by Charles Tatum. Orlando: Harcourt Press, 1990, pp. 642–87.

———. *The Last of the Menu Girls*. Houston: Arte Público Press, 1986.

———. "Novena Narritivas y Offrendas." In *Chicana Creativity and Criticism: Charting New Frontiers in American Literature*. Edited by Maria Hererra-Sobek and Helena Maria Viramontes. Houston: Arte Público Press, 1988, pp. 85–100.

————.."Plaza." In *New Mexico Plays*. Edited by David Richard Jones. Albuquerque: Univ. Of New Mexico Press, 1989, pp. 79–106.

————. *Shattering the Myth: Plays by Hispanic Women*. Houston: Arte Público Press, 1992.

Christian, Mary Blount. *Go West, Swamp Monsters!* New York: Dial Books for Young Readers, 1985.

————. *Goody Sherman's Pig*. New York: Macmillan, 1991.

————. *The Goosehill Gang and the Christmas Shoe Thief*. St. Louis: Concordia Pub. House, 1977.

————. *The Goosehill Gang and the Disappearing Dues*. St. Louis: Concordia Pub. House, 1976.

————. *The Goosehill Gang and the Ghost in the Garage*. St. Louis: Concordia Pub. House, 1978.

————. *Hats Are for Watering Horses*. New York: Rand, 1976.

————. *Murder on the Orient Expressway*. New York: E. P. Dutton, 1986.

————. *The Mysterious Case Case*. New York: E. P. Dutton, 1985.

Cisneros, Sandra. *Bad Boys*. San Jose, Calif.: Mango Press, 1980.

————. "Cactus Flowers: In Search of Tejana Feminist Poetry." *Third Woman* 3, nos. 1–2 (1986): 73–80.

————. *The House on Mango Street*. Houston: Arte Público Press, 1984. Reprint, New York: Vintage Books, 1991.

————. *Loose Woman: Poems*. New York: Alfred A. Knopf, 1994.

————. *My Wicked Wicked Ways*. Bloomington: Third Woman Press, 1987.

————. *Woman Hollering Creek and Other Stories*. New York: Random House, 1991.

Secondary Sources (Cisneros, Sandra)

Hadari, Atar. "The Profession of Pain." *Borderlands: Texas Poetry Review* (Spring/Summer, 1996): 97–104.

Clark, LaVerne Harrell. *The Deadly Swarm and Other Stories*. New York: Hermes House Press, 1985.

————. *They Sang for Horses: The Impact of the Horse on the Folklore of the Navajo and Apache*. Tucson: Univ. of Arizona Press, 1966.

Secondary Sources (Clark, LaVerne Harrell)

Woods, Christopher. "An Interview with LaVerne Harrell Clark." *Cross Timbers Review* 4 (1987): 6–17.

Clarke, Fannie McAlpine. "The Indians of Young Territory." *Quarterly of the Texas State Historical Association* 9 (1905): 51–62.

Clarke, Mary Whatley. *A Century of Cow Business*. Fort Worth: Texas and Southwestern Cattle Raisers Association, 1976.

————. *Chief Bowles and the Texas Cherokees*. Norman: Univ. of Oklahoma Press, 1971.

————. *David G. Burnet*. Austin: Pemberton Press, 1969.

———. *John Simpson Chisum: Jinglebob King of the Pecos*. Austin: Eakin Press, 1984.

———. *The Palo Pinto Story*. Ft. Worth: Printed by the Manney Co., 1956.

———. *Thomas J. Rusk, Soldier, Statesman, Jurist*. Austin: Jenkins Publishing, 1971.

———. *The Slaughter Ranches and Their Makers*. Austin: Jenkins Publishing, 1979.

———. *The Swenson Saga and the SMS Ranches*. Austin: Jenkins Publishing, 1976.

Cleveland, Alice. *Grace Loveland, or, The Blind Man's Dream: A Tale of Love*. Boston: Gleason's, 1846.

———. *The Haunted Castle*. Boston: Gleason's, 1846.

———. *Lucy Morley, or, The Young Officer: A Tale of the Texan Revolution*. Boston: Gleason's, 1846.

Cole, Maude E. *Wind Against Stone: A Texas Novel*. Los Angeles: Lymanhouse, 1941.

[Coleman, Anne Raney]. *Victorian Lady on the Texas Frontier: The Journal of Anne Raney Coleman*. Edited by Richard C. King. Norman: Univ. of Oklahoma Press, 1971.

Collins, Hilda C. *My Guardian Angel: A Novel*. San Antonio: F. Tennyson Neely, 1899. Reprint, San Antonio: W. L. Winters, 1902.

Collins, Hilda C. *Nadia Grey, A Novel*. San Antonio: n.p., 1909.

Colquitt, Betsy, *Honor Card & Other Poems*. Socorro, N.M.: Saurian Press, 1980.

———, ed. *A Part of Space: Ten Texas Writers: John Howard Griffin and Others*. Ft. Worth: Texas Christian Univ. Press, 1969.

Colson, Celeste. *See:* Colson-Walker, Celeste

Colson-Walker, Celeste

Secondary Sources

McIntosh, Barbara. "Celeste Colson: Writer Seeks 'To Go as High as I Can Go.'" *Houston Post,* July 12, 1981, p. 7BB.

Walker, Margie. "Celeste Walker: Look for the Last Line First." *Houston Defender*. December 11–17, 1986, p. 9B.

Comer, Suzanne, ed. *Common Bonds: Stories by and about Modern Texas Women*. Dallas: Southern Methodist Univ. Press, 1990.

Cooper, J. California. *Family*. New York: Doubleday, 1991.

———. *Homemade Love*. New York: St. Martin's 1986.

———. *In Search of Satisfaction*. New York: Doubleday, 1994.

———. *The Matter Is Life*. New York: Doubleday, 1991.

———. *A Piece of Mine*. Navarro, Calif.: Wild Trees Press, 1984. Reprint, New York: St. Martin's, 1986.

———. *Some Love, Some Pain, Sometime*. New York: Doubleday, 1995.

———. *Some Soul to Keep*. New York: St. Martin's, 1987.

Cotera, Marta. *Diosa y Hembra: The History and Heritage of Chicanas in the United States*. Austin: Informations Systems Dev., 1976.

———. *Profile of the Mexican American Woman*. Austin: National Education Laboratory, 1976.

Cottrell, Debbie Mauldin. *Pioneer Woman Educator: The Progressive Spirit of Annie Webb Blanton*. College Station: Texas A&M Univ. Press, 1993.

Cousins, Margaret. *Ben Franklin of Old Philadelphia*. New York: Random House, 1952.

———. *The Boy in the Alamo*. San Antonio: Corona, 1983.

———. *Christmas Gift*. Garden City, N. Y.: Doubleday, 1952.

———, ed. *Love and Marriage: 22 Stories*. Garden City, N.Y.: Doubleday, 1961.

———. *We Were There at the Battle of the Alamo*. New York: Grosset, 1958.

Crawford, Ann Fears. *A Boy Like You*. Austin: Pemberton Press, 1996.

———. *The Eagle: The Autobiography of Santa Anna*. Austin: Pemberton Press, 1967. Reprint, Austin: Statehouse Books, 1988.

———. *Jane Long: Frontier Woman*. Austin: W. S. Benson, 1990.

———. *Lizzie, Queen of the Cattle Trails*. Austin: W. S. Benson, 1990.

———. *New Life—New Land: Women in Early Texas*. Austin: Eakin Press, 1986.

———. *Sam Houston: American Hero*. Austin: Eakin Press, 1988.

———. *Texas, Lone Star Land: Its History, Its Geography, Its Government, Its People*. Austin: W. S. Benson, 1993.

———. *Viva! Famous Mexican Americans*. Austin: Steck-Vaughn, 1976.

———, and Jack Keever. *John B. Connally, Portrait in Power*. Austin: Jenkins Publishing Co., 1973.

———, and Crystal Sasse Ragsdale. *Women in Texas: Their Lives, Their Experiences, Their Accomplishments*. Austin: Eakin Press, 1982.

Crook, Elizabeth. *Promised Lands: A Novel of the Texas Rebellion*. New York: Doubleday, 1994.

———. *The Raven's Bride*. New York: Doubleday, 1991. Reprint, Dallas: Southern Methodist Univ. Press, 1991. Includes "Sam Houston and Eliza Allen: The Marriage and the Mystery." First published in *Southwestern Historical Quarterly* 94 (July, 1990): 1–36.

Cross, Ruth. *Back Door to Happiness*. New York: John H. Hopkins and Son, 1937.

———. *The Beautiful and the Doomed: A Novel in Defense of Natural Beauty*. Natchitoches: Northwestern State University of Louisiana, Special Collections, 1976.

———. *The Big Road*. New York: Longmans, Green, 1931.

———. *Eden on a Country Hill*. New York: H. C. Kinsey and Co., 1938.

———. *Enchantment*. New York: Longmans, Green and Co., 1930.

———. *The Golden Cocoon*. New York: Harper and Brothers, 1924.

———. *Soldier of Good Fortune*. Dallas: Banks Upshaw and Co., 1936.

———. *The Unknown Goddess*. New York: Harper and Brothers, 1926.

———. *Wake Up and Garden! The Complete Month-by-Month Gardener's Manual*. New York: Prentice-Hall, 1942.

Secondary Sources (Cross, Ruth)

Jones, Pamela Webster. "Portrait of a Melrose Writer: A Critical Analysis of Ruth Cross." Master's thesis, Northwestern State University of Louisiana, 1986.

Crowell, Evelyn Miller Pierce. *Hilltop*. New York: Alfred H. King, 1931.

Crowell, Grace Noll. *Apples of Gold*. New York: Harper, 1950.

———. *Between Eternities*. New York: Harper, 1944.

———. *Beyond All Price*. Elgin, Ill.: Cook, 1945.

———. *Bright Destiny: A Book of Texas Verse*. Dallas: Turner Co., 1936.

———. *Bright Harvest*. New York: Harper, 1952.

———. *A Child Kneels to Pray*. Minneapolis: Augsburg Pub. House, 1950.

———. *The Crystal Fountain*. New York: Harper, 1948.

———. *The Eternal Things: The Best of Grace Noll Crowell*. New York: Harper, 1965.

———. *Facing the Stars*. New York: Harper, 1941.

———. *Flame in the Wind*. Dallas: Southwest Press, 1930.

———. *God's Masterpieces*. New York: Abingdon Press, 1963.

———. *Happiness for Sale*. Minneapolis: Augsburg Pub. House, 1943.

———. *Journey into Dawn*. New York: Harper, 1955.

———. *Let the Sun Shine In*. Old Tappan, N.J.: F. H. Revell Co., 1970.

———. *The Lifted Lamp*. New York: Harper, 1942.

———. *Light of the Years*. New York: Harper, 1936.

———. *Little Boy Down the Lane*. Minneapolis: Augsburg Pub. House, 1952.

———. *The Little Serving Maid*. Minneapolis: Augsburg Pub. House, 1953.

———. *Meditations: Devotions for Women*. Nashville: Abingdon, 1951.

———. *My Book of Prayer and Praise*. Minneapolis: Augsburg Pub. House, 1955.

———. *The Radiant Quest*. New York: Harper, 1940.

———. *Riches of the Kingdom*. Nashville: Abingdon Press, 1954.

———. *The Shining Hour*. Minneapolis: Augsburg Pub. House, 1944.

———. *Silver in the Sun*. Dallas: P. L. Turner Co., 1928.

———. *Some Brighter Dawn*. New York: Harper, 1943.

———. *Songs for Comfort*. New York: Harper, 1947.

———. *Songs for Courage*. New York: Harper, 1938.

———. *Songs of Faith*. New York: Harper, 1939.

———. *Songs of Hope*. New York: Harper, 1938.

———. *Songs of Triumph*. New York: Harper, 1959.

———. *Splendor Ahead*. New York: Harper, 1940.

———. *This Golden Summit*. New York: Harper, 1937.

———. *Vital Possessions*. Nashville: Abingdon Press, 1960.

———. *The Wind-Swept Harp*. New York: Harper, 1946.

———. *The Wood Carver*. Minneapolis: Augsburg Pub. House, 1954.

Secondary Sources (Crowell, Grace Noll)

Plumb, Beatrice. *Grace Noll Crowell: The Poet and the Woman*. New York and London: Harper and Brothers, 1938.

Cumming, Marian. *All About Marjory*. New York: Harcourt, 1950.

———. *Clan Texas*. New York: Harcourt, 1955.

————. *Just Like Nancy.* New York: Harcourt, 1953.

————. *A Valentine for Candy.* New York: Harcourt, 1959.

Cuney-Hare, Maud. *Creole Songs.* New York: Carl Fischer and Co., 1921.

————. *Morris Wright Cuney: A Tribune of the Black People.* Austin: Steck, 1968. Reprint, New York: G.K. Hall; London: Prentice Hall International, 1995.

————. *Negro Musicians and Their Music.* Washington, D.C.: Associated Publishers, 1936. Reprint, New York: De Capo Press, 1974.

Secondary Sources (Cuney-Hare, Maud)

Ayars, Christie Herrick. *Contribution to the Art of Music in America by the Music Industries of Boston.* New York: H. W. Wilson, 1937.

Dannett, Sylvia G. *Profiles of Negro Womanhood.* Vol. 1. Yonkers, N.Y.: Educational Heritage, 1964.

Jones, LeRoi. *Blues People.* New York: William Morrow and Co., 1963.

Lovell, John, Jr. *Black Song: The Forge and the Flame.* New York: Macmillan, 1972.

Richardson, W., ed. *Plays and Pageants from the Life of the Negro.* Washington, D.C.: 1929.

Custer, Elizabeth Bacon. *Boots and Saddles: or, Life in Dakota with General Custer.* Norman: Univ. of Oklahoma Press, 1961.

————. *The Civil War Memories of Elizabeth Bacon Custer: Reconstructed from Her Notes and Diaries.* Edited by Arlene Reynolds. Austin: Univ. of Texas Press, 1994.

————. *Following the Guidon.* New York: Harper, 1890.

————. *Tenting on the Plains: or General Custer in Kansas and Texas.* New York: C. L. Webster and Co., 1887.

Secondary Sources (Custer, Elizabeth Bacon)

Frost, Lawrence. *General Custer's Libbie.* Seattle: Superior Publishing Co., 1976.

Leckie, Shirley A. *Elizabeth Bacon Custer and the Making of a Myth.* Norman: Univ. of Oklahoma Press, 1993.

Cutrer, Emily Fourmy. *The Art of the Woman: The Life and Work of Elizabet Ney.* Lincoln: Univ. of Nebraska Press, 1988.

Daffan, Katie. *As Thinketh a Woman: Poems.* Houston: SW Pub. Co., 1912.

————. *History of the United States.* Ennis, Tex.: Katie Daffan, Publisher, 1924.

————. *My Father, As I Remember Him.* Houston: Gray and Dillaye, n.d.

————. *New Orleans.* Houston: Cumming and Sons, 1906.

————. *Texas Hero Stories: an Historical Reader for the Grades.* Boston and New York: B. H. Sanborn and Co., 1908.

————. *Texas Heroes: A Reader for the Schools.* Boston: Benjamin H. Sanborn and Co., 1912.

————. "United Daughters of the Confederacy." *The Texas Magazine* 1 (1909): 27–29.

———. *The Woman on the Pine Springs Road*. New York: Neale Publishing Co., 1910

———. *Women in History*. New York and Washington: Neale Publishing Co., 1908.

Darden, Fannie Baker. *Romances of the Texas Revolution*. N.p., n.d.

Secondary Sources (Darden, Fannie Baker)

Flachmeier, Jeanette Hastedt. "Fannie Baker Darden (1829–1890)." In *Women in Early Texas*. Edited by Evelyn M. Carrington. Austin: Jenkins Publishing Co./The Pemberton Press, 1975, pp. 59–70.

Davis, Anne Pence. *The Customer Is Always Right*. New York: Macmillan, 1940.

———. *Mimi at Camp: The Adventures of a Cowboy*. Chicago: Goldsmith Publishing Co., 1935.

———. *Mimi at Sheridan School*. Chicago: Goldsmith, 1935.

———. *Mimi's House Party*. Chicago: Goldsmith, 1936.

———. *So Swift the Stone: Collected Poems*. Wichita Falls, Tex.: Humphrey Printing Co., 1978.

———. *Top Hand of Lone Tree Ranch*. New York: Crowell, 1960.

Davis, Clare Ogden. *The Woman of It*. New York: J. H. Sears, 1929.

Secondary Sources (Davis, Clare Ogden)

Paulissen, Mary Nelson and Addie Busfield. "Clare Ogden Davis, Newspaper Reporter Extraordinaire." *Texas Studies Annual* 2 (1995): 77–86.

Davis, Mollie (Mary) Evelyn Moore. *A Bunch of Roses, and Other Plays*. Boston: Small, Maynard & Company, 1903.

———. *An Elephant's Track and Other Stories*. New York: Houghton, Mifflin and Co., 1897.

———. *Christmas Boxes: Comedy for 4 Males and 4 Females*. New York: E. S. Werner, 1907.

———. *A Christmas Masque of Saint Roche, Pere Dagobert, and Throwing the Wanga*. Chicago: McClurg, 1896.

———. *A Dress Rehearsal: A Comedy for 4 Males and 4 Females*. New York: E. S. Werner, 1907.

———. *In War Times at La Rose Blanche*. New York: Houghton, Mifflin and Co., 1888.

———. *Jaconetta: Her Loves*. New York: Houghton, Mifflin and Co., 1901.

———. *The Little Chevalier*. New York: Houghton, Mifflin and Co., 1903.

———. *Minding the Gap, And Other Poems*. Houston: Cushing and Cove, 1867.

———. *The New System: Comedy for 4 Males and 4 Females*. New York: E. S. Werner & Company, 1907.

———. *Poems*. Houston: E. H. Cushing, 1869.

———. *The Price of Silence*. New York: Houghton, Mifflin and Co., 1907.

———. *Selected Poems*. New Orleans: The Green Shutter Book Shop, 1927.

———. *Under Six Flags: The Story of Texas*. Boston and London: Ginn and Co., Publishing, 1897.

———. *Under the Man-Fig*. New York: Houghton, Mifflin and Co., 1895.

———. *The Wire-Cutters*. New York: Houghton, Mifflin and Co., 1899.

Secondary Sources (Davis, Mollie [Mary] Evelyn Moore)

Simmons, J. P. "Mollie E. M. Davis's Fiction." *Texas Monthly* 5 (1931): 565–75.

Sneller, Judy E. "Saints, Hell-Raisers, and Other 'Typical Texans': Frontier Women and the Humor of Mollie Moore Davis." *Journal of the American Studies Association of Texas* 25 (1994): 15–31.

Wilkinson, C. W. "The Broadening Stream: The Life and Literary Career of Mollie E. Moore Davis." Ph.D. diss., University of Illinois, 1947.

Davis, Olga Samples. *A Time to Be Born*. San Antonio: Pecan Grove Press, 1991.

Dawson, Carol. *Body of Knowledge*. Chapel Hill, N.C.: Algonquin Books, 1994.

———. *The Waking Spell*. Chapel Hill, N.C.: Algonquin Books, 1992.

Dawson, Cleo. *She Came to the Valley: A Novel of the Lower Rio Grande Valley, Mission, Texas*. New York: William Morrow and Co., 1943. Reprint, Austin: Jenkins Publishing Co., 1972.

De Hoyos, Angela. *Arise Chicano!* Bloomington: Back Stage Books, 1975.

———. *Chicano Poems: For the Barrio*. Bloomington: Backstage Books, 1975.

———. *Selecciones*. Translated by Mireya Robles. Xalapa, Mexico: Cuadernos del Caballo Verde, Universidad Veracruzana, 1976.

———. *Selected Poems/Selecciones*. San Antonio: Dezkalzo Press, 1979.

———. *Woman, Woman*. Houston: Arte Público Press, 1985.

———, ed. *See also under*: Milligan, Bryce, ed.

Secondary Sources (De Hoyos, Angela)

Aguilar-Henson, Marcella. *The Multi-faceted Poetic World of Angela de Hoyos*. Austin: Relámpago Press, 1985.

Cisneros, Sandra. "Cactus Flowers: In Search of Tejana Feminist Poetry." *Third Woman* 3, nos. 1–2 (1986): 73–80.

Islas, Maya. "Mecanismos redentores en la poesía de Angela de Hoyos." In *Calandrajas: Papeles de arte y pensamiento*. Toledo, Spain: Junio, 1987, n.p.

Lindstrom, Naomi. "Four Representative Hispanic Women Poets of Central Texas: A Portrait of Plurality." *Third Woman* 2, no. 1 (1984): 64–70.

Ramos, Luis Arturo. *Angela de Hoyos: A Critical Look*. Albuquerque: Pajarito, 1979.

De la Garza, Beatriz. *The Candy Vendor's Boy and Other Stories*. Houston: Arte Público Press, 1994.

De Sanders, Diane. "When He Saw Me." In *Texas Bound: 19 Texas Stories*. Edited by Kay Cattarulla. Dallas: Southern Methodist Univ. Press, 1994, pp. 39–47.

de Zavala, Adina. *History and Legends of the Alamo and Other Missions in and around San Antonio.* N.p., 1917.

———. *The Margil Vine: Legend of the First Christmas at the Alamo.* San Antonio: n.p., 1916.

———. "Religious Beliefs of the Tejas or Hasanias Indians." *Publications of the Texas Folklore Society* 1 (1916): 39–43.

Dickey, Imogene Bentley. *Early Literary Magazines of Texas.* Austin: Steck-Vaughn Co., 1970.

Dill, Minnie. *Footprints of Texas History.* 4th ed. Austin: Von Boeckmann-Jones Co., 1908.

———, and Elma Dill. *Texas Stories for Reading and Acting.* Austin: n.p., 1925.

Dingus, Anne. *The Book of Texas Lists.* Austin: Texas Monthly Press, 1981.

———. *The Dictionary of Texas Misinformation.* Austin: Texas Monthly Press, 1987.

Dobie, Bertha McKee. "The Death Bell of the Brazos." *Publications of the Texas Folklore Society* 3 (1924): 141–42.

———. "The Eagle Lover." *Publications of the Texas Folklore Society* 12 (1935): 159–61.

———. "From a Texas Household: Mrs. Russell's Stories." *Publications of the Texas Folklore Society* 26 (1954): 67–77.

———. "The Ghosts of Lake Jackson." *Publications of the Texas Folklore Society* 7 (1928): 135–36.

———. "The Legend of the Salt Marshes (San Luis Pass, Brazoria County)." *Publications of the Texas Folklore Society* 3 (1924): 143.

———. "Mysterious Music in the San Barnard River." *Publications of the Texas Folklore Society* 3 (1924): 137–41.

———. "Old Alf: Yardman by the Day." *Southwest Review* 27 (1942): 463–69.

———. "Tales and Rhymes of a Texas Household." *Publications of the Texas Folklore Society* 6 (1927): 23–71.

———, and others. *Growing Up in Texas: Recollections of Childhood.* Austin: Encino Press, 1972.

Dodson, Ruth. *Don Pedrito Jaramillo, "Curandero."* San Antonio: Casa Editorial Lozano, 1934.

Douglas, Carole Nelson. *Cat in a Crimson Haze.* New York: Forge, 1995.

———. *Catnip: A Midnight Louie Mystery.* New York: Tor, 1992.

———. *Counterprobe.* New York: T. Doherty Assoc., 1988.

———. *Cup of Clay.* New York: T. Doherty Assoc., 1991.

———. *Exiles of the Rynth.* New York: Ballantine Books, 1984.

———. *Good Morning, Irene.* New York: Tor, 1991.

———. *Good Night, Mr. Holmes.* New York: T. Doherty Assoc., 1990.

———. *Heir of Rengarth.* New York: T. Doherty Assoc., 1988.

———. *Irene at Large.* New York: Tor, 1992.

———. *Irene's Last Waltz.* New York: Forge, 1994.

———. *Keepers of Edanvant.* New York: T. Doherty Assoc., 1987.

———. *Probe.* New York: T. Doherty Assoc., 1985.

———. *Seed Upon the Wind*. New York: Tor Fantasy, 1992.

———. *Seven of Swords*. New York: T. Doherty, 1989.

———. *Six of Swords*. New York: Ballantine, 1982.

Drago, Gail, and Ann Ruff. *Outlaws in Petticoats and Other Notorious Texas Women*. Plano: Republic of Texas Press, 1995.

Driscoll, Clara. *The Girl of La Gloria*. New York: G. P. Putnam's Sons, 1905.

———. *In the Shadow of the Alamo, and Other Texas Tales*. New York: G. P. Putnam's Sons, 1906.

———. *Mexicana*. New York: n.p., 1905.

Secondary Sources (Driscoll, Clara)

Turner, Martha Anne. *Clara Driscoll: An American Tradition*. Austin: Madrona Press, 1979.

Dumont, Ella Elgar Bird. *Ella Elgar Bird Dumont: An Autobiography of a West Texas Pioneer*. Tommy J. Boley. ed. Austin: Univ. of Texas Press, 1988.

Dunn, Mary Lois. *The Man in the Box: A Story from Vietnam*. New York: McGraw, 1965.

———, and Ardath Mahar. *The Absolutely Perfect Horse*. New York: Harper, 1983.

Durst, Harriet. *Early Days in Texas*. N.p. 1888. Reprint, Oklahoma City: Perry Printing Co., 1903.

Eberle, Irmengarde. *The Bands Play On: The Story of Bands and Orchestras*. New York: R. M. McBride, 1942.

———. *Basketful, The Story of Our Foods*. New York: Thomas Y. Crowell, 1946.

———. *Beavers Live Here*. Garden City, N.Y.: Doubleday, 1972.

———. *The Dog Who Came to Visit*. New York: Abelard-Schuman, 1967.

———. *Evie and Cookie*. New York: Knopf, 1957.

———. *A Family to Raise*. New York: Holiday House, 1939.

———. *Hop, Skip, and Fly: Stories of Small Creatures*. New York: Holiday House, 1950.

———. *Koalas Live Here*. Garden City, N.Y.: Doubleday, 1967.

———. *Lone Star Fight*. New York: Dodd, 1954.

———. *Modern Medical Discoveries*. New York: T. Y. Crowell, 1948.

———. *Moose Live Here*. Garden City, N.Y.: Doubleday, 1971.

———. *Mountain Holiday*. New York: Abelard-Schuman, 1971.

———. *Mustang on the Prairie*. Garden City, N.Y.: Doubleday, 1968.

———. *The New World of Paper*. New York: Dodd, Mead and Co., 1969.

———. *The New World of Rubber*. New York: Dodd, Mead and Co., 1966.

———. *Pandas Live Here*. Garden City, N.Y.: Doubleday, 1973.

———. *Penguins Live Here*. Garden City, N.Y.: Doubleday, 1974.

———. *Prairie Dogs in Prairie Dog Town*. New York: Crowell, 1974.

———. *Radium Treasure and the Curies*. New York: Crowell, 1942.

———. *Rosemary's Secret*. New York: Random House, 1958.

———. *The Very Good Neighbors*. New York: J. B. Lipppincott, 1945.

Eckhardt, Celia Morris. *See*: Morris, Celia

Egbert, Kathlyn Whitsit. *The 23rd Dream*. Dallas: Southern Methodist Univ. Press, 1993.

Elder, Iva Nell. *Gentle Giants: Women Writers in Texas*. Austin: Eakin, 1983.

Embree, Emily Davant. *A Lesser Light*. Belton: Baylor College, 1904.

———. *Mine Inheritance*. Belton: The Cottage Home, 1907.

Emmons, Martha. *Deep Like the Rivers: Stories of My Negro Friends*. Austin: Encino Press, 1969.

———. *I Come Runnin'*. Waco: Texian Press, 1976.

Erdman, Loula Grace. *Another Spring*. New York: Dodd, Mead, 1966.

———. *A Bluebird Will Do*. New York: Dodd, Mead, 1973.

———. *The Edge of Time*. New York: Dodd, Mead, 1950. Reprint, Ft. Worth: Texas Christian Univ. Press, 1989.

———. *Fair Is the Morning*. New York: Longmans, Green, 1945.

———. *The Far Journey*. New York: Dodd, Mead, 1955.

———. *The Good Land*. New York: Dodd, Mead, 1959.

———. *Life Was Simpler Then*. New York: Dodd, Mead, 1963.

———. *Lonely Passage*. New York: Dodd, Mead, 1948.

———. *The Man Who Told the Truth with Six Short Stories*. New York: Dodd, Mead, 1962.

———. *Many a Voyage*. New York: Dodd, Mead, 1960.

———. *My Sky is Blue*. New York: Longmans, Green, 1953.

———. *Room to Grow*. New York: Dodd, Mead, 1962.

———. *Save Weeping for the Night*. New York: Dodd Mead, 1975.

———. *Separate Star*. New York: Longmans, Green, 1944.

———. *Short Summer*. New York: Dodd, Mead, 1958.

———. *Three at the Wedding*. New York: Dodd, Mead, 1953.

———. *A Time to Write*. New York: Dodd, Mead, 1969.

———. *The Wind Blows Free*. New York: Dodd, Mead, 1952.

———. *The Wide Horizon: A Story of the Texas Panhandle*. New York: Dodd, Mead, 1956.

———. *A Wonderful Thing and Other Stories*. New York: Dodd, Mead, 1940.

———. *The Years of the Locust*. New York: Dodd, Mead, 1947.

Secondary Sources (Erdman, Loula Grace)

Sewell, Ernestine P. "Afterword." In *The Edge of Time*. By Loula Grace Erdman. Fort Worth: Texas Christian Univ. Press, 1989, pp. 276–80.

———. "An Interview with Loula Grace Erdman." *Southwestern American Literature* 2 (1972): 33–42.

———. Loula Grace Erdman. *Southwest Writers Series* 33. Austin: Steck-Vaughn, 1970.

Esslinger, Pat M. [Pat Carr]. *From beneath the Hill of the Three Crosses: Procesion de Navidad*. Ft. Smith, Ark.: South and West Press, 1970.

Evans, Augusta Jane. *At the Mercy of Tiberius*. New York: G. W. Dillingham, 1887.

———. *Beulah*. New York: Derby and Jackson, 1859.

————. *Devorta.* New York: G. W. Dillingham, 1907.

————. *Inez: A Tale of the Alamo.* New York: Harper and Brothers, Publishers, 1855.

————. *Infelice.* New York: A. L. Burt, 1875.

————. *Macaria, or, Altars of Sacrifice.* New York: Co-Operative Publishing Society, 1896. Reprint, Baton Rouge: Louisiana State Univ. Press, 1992.

————. *St. Elmo.* New York: Carleton, 1857.

————. *A Speckled Bird.* Austin: Von Boeckmann–Jones Co., 1902.

————. *Vashti: or "Until Death Do Us Part."* New York: Carleton, 1869.

Secondary Sources (Evans, Augusta Jane)

Fidler, William Perry. *Augusta Evans Wilson 1835–1909: A Biography.* Birmingham: Univ. of Alabama Press, 1951.

Exley, Jo Ella Powell, ed. *Texas Tears and Texas Sunshine: Voices of Frontier Women.* College Station: Texas A&M Univ. Press, 1985.

Fernandez, Roberta, ed. *Literature of Latinas of the United States.* Houston: Arte Público, 1994.

————. *Intaglio: A Novel in Six Stories.* Houston: Arte Público Press, 1990.

————. *In Other Words: Literature by Latinas of the United States.* Houston: Arte Público Press, 1995.

Fields, Helen Mangum. *Walking Backward in the Wind.* Fort Worth: Texas Christian Univ. Press, 1995.

Fisher, J. E.

Secondary Sources

Brukenfeld, Dick. "Off-Off Broadway." *Theatre* 4: The American Theatre (1970–71), 51.

————. "The Unfortunate Sag." *Village Voice* 19 (18 July 1974), 51.

Gill, Brendon. "Off Broadway: The Second Time Around." *New Yorker* 50 (December 9, 1974): 69–70.

Fisher, Mrs. Rebecca J. [Gilleland]. "Capture and Rescue of Mrs. Rebecca J. Fisher, nee Gilleland." *Quarterly of the Texas State Historical Association* 3 (1900): 209–13.

————. *Captured by Comanches.* Austin: n.p., 1906.

Fisher, Mrs. Wm. E. *Women's Right to Preach: A Sermon.* Dallas: Berachah Printing Co., 1904.

Fitze, Shelley. "An Ordinary Crime." *The Pawn Review* 9 (1985): 116–43.

Flatten, Mary K. "Old Enough." In *Texas Bound: 19 Texas Stories.* Edited by Kay Cattarulla. Dallas: Southern Methodist Univ. Press, 1994, pp. 49–60.

Flowers, Betty Sue. *Browning and the Modern Tradition.* London: Macmillan, 1976.

————. *Extending the Shade.* Austin: Plain View Press, 1990.

————, ed. *Joseph Campbell and the Power of Myth: Bill Moyers and Joseph Campbell in Conversation.* New York: Doubleday, 1981.

———, with Lynn Gilbert, Elaine Sullender, and Peggy Kelly. *Four Shields of Power.* Austin: Plain View Press, 1987.

Flynn, Jean. *James Butler Bonham: The Rebel Hero.* Austin: Eakin, 1984.

———. *Jim Bowie: A Texas Legend.* Burnet: Eakin, 1980.

———. *Lady: The Story of Claudia Alta (Lady Bird) Johnson.* Austin: Eakin Press, 1991.

———. *Remember Goliad: James W. Fannin.* Austin: Eakin, 1984.

———. *Stephen F. Austin, The Father of Texas.* Burnet: Eakin, 1981.

———. *William Barret Travis: "Victory or Death."* Austin: Eakin, 1982.

Fortune, Jan Isbelle. *Black Poppies.* Dallas: Southwest Press, 1929.

———. *Elisabet Ney.* New York: A. A. Knopf, 1943.

———, ed. *Fugitive: The Story of Clyde Barrow and Bonnie Parker.* Dallas: Ranger Press, 1934.

———. *Tower to the East, a Sonnet Sequence.* Dallas: Southwest Press, 1934.

Franklin, J. E. *"Black Girl": From Genesis to Revelations.* Washington, D.C.: Howard Univ. Press, 1973.

Secondary Sources (Franklin, J. E.)

Bailey, Peter. "Annual Round-Up: Black Theatre in America." *Black World* 24 (1975): 22–23.

Garnett, Richard. "Black Drama Finds New Audience." *Race Relations Reporter* 3 (February 7, 1972): 4–6.

Kupa, Kushawi. "Closeup: The New York Scene—Black Theatre in New York, 1970–1971." *Black Theatre* 6 (1972): 48–50.

Lamb, Margaret. "Feminist Criticism." *Drama Review* 18 (September, 1974): 49.

Parks, Carole A. "Perspectives: J. E. Franklin, Playwright." *Black World* 21 (April, 1972): 49–50.

Salaam, Kalamu Ya. "Making the Image Real." *The Black Collegian* 7 (March–April, 1977): 54, 57.

Simon, John. "Mad, Bad, Sad and Glad." *New York Magazine* 7 (December 16, 1974): 96.

Fraser, Margot. *The Laying Out of Gussie Hoot.* Dallas: Southern Methodist Univ. Press, 1990.

Friend, Llerena. "The Life of Thomas Jefferson Chambers." Master's thesis, University of Texas, 1928.

———, ed. *M. K. Kellogg's Texas Journal.* Austin: Univ. of Texas Press, 1967.

———. *Sam Houston: The Great Designer.* Austin: Univ. of Texas Press, 1954. Reprint, Austin: Univ. of Texas Press, 1969.

———. "The Texan of 1860." *Southwest Historical Quarterly* 52 (July, 1958): 1–17.

———. [Untitled]. In *Growing Up in Texas: Recollections of Childhood.* By Bertha McKee Dobie, and others. Austin: Encino Press, 1972, pp. 27–37.

Furman, Laura. *The Glass House: A Novella and Stories.* New York: Viking, 1980.

———. *The Shadow Line.* New York: Viking, 1982.

———. *Tuxedo Park*. New York: Summit Books, 1986.
———. *Watch Time Fly*. New York: Viking, 1983.

Secondary Sources (Furman, Laura)

Root, Amy. "Laura Furman." *Texas Libraries* (Summer, 1990): 54–55.
Unger, Jeffry S. "A Novel Look at the Needs of the Psyche." *Dallas Times Herald*. September 28, 1986.

Galaviz, Victoria García. In *This Promiscuous Light: Young Women Poets of San Antonio*. Edited by Bryce Milligan. San Antonio: Wings Press, 1996, pp. 15–28.
Galloway, Terry. *Buncha Crocs in Surch of Snac and Other Poems*. Austin: Curbstone Press, 1980.
———. "Heart of a Dog." In *The Women's Project: 2*. Edited by Julia Miles. New York: Performing Arts Journal Publications, 1984, pp. 135–54.
———. *Out All Night and Lost My Shoes*. Tallahassee: Opalachee, 1993.
Gámez, Rocky. "Enedina Pascasio." In *Common Bonds: Stories by and about Modern Texas Women*. Edited Suzanne Comer. Dallas: Southern Methodist Univ. Press, 1990, pp. 179–82.
Gardner, Mary. *Boat People*. New York: W. W. Norton and Co., 1995.
———. *Keeping Warm*. New York: Atheneum, 1987.
Garland, Sherry. *Lotus Seed*. San Diego: Harcourt Brace, 1993.
———. *I Never Knew Your Name*. New York: Ticknor and Fields, 1994.
———. *Indio*. San Diego: Harcourt Brace, 1995.
———. *Shadow of the Dragon*. San Diego: Harcourt Brace, 1993.
———. *Silent Storm*. San Diego: Harcourt Brace Jovanovich, 1993.
———. *Song of the Buffalo Boy*. San Diego: Harcourt Brace, 1992.
———. *Vietnam: Rebuilding a Nation*. Minneapolis: Dillon Press, 1990.
———. *Why Ducks Sleep on One Leg*. New York: Scholastic, 1993.
Garrett, Julia Kathryn. *Fort Worth: A Frontier Triumph*. Ft. Worth: Texas Christian Univ. Press, 1996.
———. *Green Flag over Texas: A Story of the Last Years of Spain in Texas*. New York and Dallas: The Cordova Press, 1939. Reprint, Austin: Jenkins Publishing Co., The Pemberton Press, 1969.
———. *Our American Constitution: The Story of a Great Document*. Austin: Steck-Vaughn, 1966.
Garwood, Ellen. *Come to Me, Megan: An American Saga*. Alexandria, Va.: Cameron Press, 1984.
———. *No Other Time for Austin: A Play in One Act about Stephen F. Austin and Mary Holley*. Austin: n. p., 1953.
———. *The Tune on the Stairs*. Washington, D.C.: Regnery Gateway, 1987.
———. *The Undying Flame: Mariano Moreno of Buenos Aires*. Washington, D.C.: American Studies Center, 1986.
———. *Will Clayton: A Short Biography*. Austin: Univ. of Texas Press, 1958.
Gaspar de Alba, Alicia. *The Mystery of Survival and Other Stories*. Tempe, Ariz.: Bilingual Press, 1993.

———. *Three Times a Woman: Chicana Poetry.* Tempe, Ariz.: Bilingual Press, 1989.
Gerald, Florence M. *Adenheim, and Other Poems.* Waco: n. p., 1880.
Gibson, Jewel. *Black Gold.* New York: Random House, 1950.
———. *Joshua Beene and God.* New York: Random House, 1946.

Secondary Sources (Gibson, Jewel)

Mason, Melvin R. "The Girl with the Blue-Handled Hoe: Regional Backgrounds in the Writings of Jewel Gibson." *Texas College English* 3 (October, 1968).
———. "What Even Happened to Joshua Beene?" *Journal of the American Studies Association of Texas* 1 (June, 1970): 74–80.
Turner, Martha Anne. "Joshua Beene and Jewel Gibson." In *Dan Rather and Other Rough Drafts.* Austin: Eakin Press, 1987, pp. 11–28.

Gilliland, Maude Truitt. *Horsebackers of the Brush Country: A Story of Texas Rangers and Mexican Liquor Smugglers.* Brownsville, Tex.: Springman-King, 1968.
———. *Wilson County Texas Rangers, 1837–1977.* N.p., 1977.
Gilstrap, Barbara. *The Alto Part.* New York: Samuel French, 1987.
Glasscock, Sarah. *Anna L.M.N.O.* New York: Random House, 1988.
Godbold, Mollie Moore. *The Flapper Grandmother.* New York: Samuel French, 1926.
———. *Gun-Shy: A Comedy in Three Acts.* Dallas: Bradford Printing Co., 1930.
———. *Help Yourself: A Farce Comedy with Musical Numbers.* Dallas: Bradford Printing Co., 1926.
———. *The Love Bug: A Three Act Farce-Comedy with Musical Numbers.* Dallas: Bradford Printing Co., 1930.
———. *The Love Cure: A Comedy in One Act.* New York: Samuel French, 1926. Reprint, Dallas: Bradford Printing Co., 1930.
Goeth, Ottilie Fuchs. *Memoirs of a Pioneer Grandmother, 1805–1915.* Translated by Irma G. Guenther. Austin: Eakin, 1982.
Gonzáles, Jovíta Guerra (de Mireles). "After the Barbed Wire Came Hunger." In *Aztlan: An Anthology of Mexican American Literature.* Edited by Stan Steiner. New York: Knopf, 1972, pp. 81–83. Reprinted in *Mexican American Literature.* Edited by Charles Tatum. San Diego: Harcourt, Brace, Jovanovich, 1990, pp. 225–33.
———. "Among My People." *Publications of the Texas Folklore Society* 10 (1932): 99–108.
———. "The Bullet-Swallower." *Publications of the Texas Folklore Society* 12 (1935): 107–14.
———. *Dew on the Thorn.* Edited by José Limón. Houston: Arte Público Press, 1996.
———. "Folk-Lore of the Texas-Mexican Vaquero." *Publications of the Texas Folklore Society* 6 (1927): 7–22.
———. "Stories of My People." *Publications of the Texas Folklore Society* 26 (1954): 19–45.
———. "Tales and Songs of the Texas-Mexicans." *Publications of the Texas Folklore Society* 8 (1930): 86–116.

—————, and Eve Raleigh. *Caballero: A Historical Novel.* College Station: Texas A&M Univ. Press, 1996.

—————. *See also under:* Mireles, E. E.

Gonzales, Rebecca. *Slow Work to the Rhythm of Cicadas.* Fort Worth: Prickly Pear Press, 1985.

Gooch[-Iglehart], Fanny Chambers. *The Boy Captive of the Texas Mier Expedition.* San Antonio: J. R. Wood Printing Co., 1909.

—————. *Face to Face with the Mexicans: the Domestic Life, Educational, Social, and Business Ways, Statesmanship and Literature, Legendary and General History of the Mexican People.* New York: Fords, Howard, and Hulbert, 1887. Reprint, Carbondale: Southern Illinois Univ. Press, 1966.

Gorham, Iona Oakley. *Naval Cadet Carlyle's Glove.* New York: J. Selwin Tait and Sons, 1894.

Gorman, Mrs. H. C. L. [Clara LeClerc]. *Uncle Plenty.* Ft. Worth: Texas Printing and Lithographing Co., 1892.

Gray, Millie Richards. *The Diary of Millie Gray, 1832–1840.* Houston: Printed in the name of the Rosenberg Library Press, Galveston: F. Young, 1967.

Greenwood, Kathy L. *Heart-Diamond.* Denton: Univ. of North Texas Press, 1990.

Grider, Sylvia Ann. *The Wendish Texans.* San Antonio: Institute of Texan Cultures, 1982.

—————. "Women's Literature and History in Texas: A Confluence of Traditions." In *Women and Texas History: Selected Essays.* Edited by Fane Downs and Nancy Baker Jones. Austin: Texas State Historical Association, 1993, pp. 168–76.

—————, and Lou Rodenberger. "Women and Literature." In *The New Handbook of Texas.* Vol. 6. Austin: Texas State Historical Association, 1996, pp. 1049–51.

Griffin, Peni. *A Dig in Time.* New York: Puffin Books, 1991.

—————. *Hobkin.* New York: Maxwell Macmillan International, 1982.

—————. *The Switching Well.* New York: Maxwell Macmillan International, 1993.

Griffith, Patricia Browning. *The Future Is Not What It Used to Be.* New York: Simon and Schuster, 1978.

—————. *Tennessee Blue.* New York: C. N. Potter/Crown Publishers, 1981.

—————. *The World Around Midnight.* New York: G. P. Putnam's Sons, 1991.

Gurasich, Marj. *Benito and the White Dove: A Story of Jose Antonio Navarro.* Austin: Eakin, 1989.

—————. *A House Divided.* Fort Worth: Texas Christian Univ. Press, 1994.

—————. *Letters to Oma: A Young Girl's Account of Her First Year in Texas 1847.* Forth Worth: Texas Christian Univ. Press, 1989.

—————. *Red Wagons and White Canvas: A Story of the Mollie Bailey Circus.* Austin: Eakin, 1988.

Hacker, Margaret Schmidt. *Cynthia Ann Parker: The Life and the Legend.* El Paso: Texas Western Press, Southwestern Studies, no. 92, 1990.

Hadlock, Adah. *My Life in the Southwest.* El Paso: Texas Western Press, 1969.

Hailey, Elizabeth Forsythe. *Joanna's Husband and David's Wife.* New York: Delacorte, 1986.

—————. *Life Sentences.* New York: Delacorte, 1982.

———. *A Woman of Independent Means*. New York: Knopf, 1978.

Halsell, Grace. *Bessie Yellowhair*. New York: Morrow, 1973.

———. *Black/White Sex*. New York: Morrow, 1972.

———. *Getting to Know Peru*. New York: Coward-McCann, 1964.

———. *The Illegals*. New York: Stein and Day, 1978.

———. *In Their Shoes: A White Woman's Journey Living as a Black, Navajo, and Mexican Illegal*. Ft. Worth: Texas Christian Univ. Press, 1996.

———. *Journey to Jerusalem*. New York: Macmillan, 1981.

———. *Los Viejos: Secrets of Long Life from the Sacred Valley*. Emmaus, Pa.: Rodale Press, 1976.

———. *Peru*. New York: Macmillan, 1969.

———. *Prophecy and Politics: Militant Evangelist on the Road to Nuclear War*. Westpoint, Conn.: Lawrence Hill and Co., 1986.

———. *Soul Sister*. New York: World Pub. Co, 1969. Reprint, Fort Worth: Texas Christian Univ. Press, 1996.

Hamner, Laura V. *Light 'N Hitch: A Collection of Historical Writing Depicting Life on the High Plains*. Dallas: American Guild Press, 1958.

———. *My Mother Talks of Substitutes: Echoes of the Civil War that Are Most Interesting in These Times of High Prices*. New Orleans: H. McCullough, 1919.

———. *The No-Gun Man of Texas: A Century of Achievement, 1835–1929*. Amarillo: Privately Printed, 1935.

———. *Prairie Vagabonds*. San Antonio: Naylor, 1955.

———. *Short Grass and Long Horns*. Norman: Univ. of Oklahoma Press, 1943.

———. *Somebody Might Come: A Story of Modern Southern Hospitality in the Hills of Alabama*. Dallas: American Guild Press, 1958.

Secondary Sources (Hamner, Laura V.)

Hall, Myra Dorris. "Laura V. Hamner: A Woman Before Her Time." Ph.D. diss., University of Houston, 1988.

Hancock, Sibyl. *Bill Pickett: First Black Rodeo Star*. New York: Harcourt Brace Jovanovich, 1977.

———. *The Blazing Hills*. New York: Putnam, 1975.

———. *Esteban and the Ghost*. New York: Dial, 1983.

———. *Mosshaven*. New York: Beagle Books, 1973.

———. *Old Blue*. New York: Putnam, 1980.

———. *Spindletop*. Burnet: Eakin, 1980.

———. *Texas, Yesterday and Today*. Burnet: Eakin, 1982.

Harby, Mrs. Lee Cohen. "City of the Prince." *Magazine of American History*. (October/November, 1888).

———. "The Earliest Texas." *Annual Report for 1891*. American Historical Association, 1892.

———. "The Old Stone Fort at Nacogdoches." *American Magazine*. (April, 1888).

Hare, Maud Cuney. *See:* Cuney-Hare, Maud

Harris, Dilue. "The Reminiscences of Mrs. Dilue Harris." *Quarterly of the Texas*

State Historical Association 4 (1900–1901), 85–127, 155–89; 7 (1903–1904),
214–22.

Harris, Elizabeth. *The Ant Generator.* Iowa City: Univ. of Iowa Press, 1991.

Hatch, Sheila Sánchez. *Guadalupe and the Kaleidoscopic Screamer.* San Antonio:
Wings Press, 1996.

———, ed. *Tierra Norte: A Collection of Works from North Tejas.* San Antonio:
M&A Editions, 1994.

Hatcher, Mattie Austin. *The Expedition of Don Domingo Teran de los Rios into
Texas.* Austin: Catholic Historical Society Preliminary Studies 2, no. 1, 1932.

———. "The Municipal Government of San Fernando de Bexar, 1731–1800."
Master's thesis, University of Texas, 1903.

———. *The Opening of Texas to Foreign Settlement.* Austin: Univ. of Texas Press, 1927.

Hawthorne, Dorothy. *Chocolate Wildcat.* San Antonio: Corona, 1987.

———. *A Wish for Lutie.* New York: Longmans, 1955.

Hearon, Shelby. *Afternoon of a Faun.* New York: Atheneum, 1983.

———. *Armadillo in the Grass.* New York: Knopf, 1968. Reprint, Dallas: Pressworks Publishing, 1983.

———. *Five Hundred Scorpions.* New York: Atheneum, 1987.

———. *Footprints.* New York: Knopf, 1996.

———. *Group Therapy.* New York: Atheneum, 1984.

———. *Hannah's House.* Garden City, N.Y.: Doubleday, 1975.

———. *Hug Dancing.* New York: Knopf, 1991.

———. *Life Estates.* New York: Knopf, 1994.

———. *Now and Another Time.* Garden City, N.Y.: Doubleday, 1976.

———. *Owning Jolene.* New York: Knopf, 1989.

———. *Painted Dresses.* New York: Atheneum, 1981.

———. *A Prince of a Fellow.* Garden City, N.Y.: Doubleday, 1978.

———. *The Second Dune.* New York: Knopf, 1973.

———. *A Small Town.* New York: Atheneum, 1985.

———, and Barbara Jordan. *Barbara Jordan: A Self-Portrait.* Garden City, N.Y.:
Doubleday, 1979.

Secondary Sources (Hearon, Shelby)

Bennett, Patrick. "Shelby Hearon: Time, Sex, and God." In *Talking with
Texas Writers: Twelve Interviews.* College Station: Texas A&M Univ.
Press, 1980, pp. 111–34.

Compton, Robert. "Hug Dancing with Fame." *Dallas Morning News,*
December 3, 1991.

Dunn, Si. "Shelby Hearon Is Alive and Well Living It Up in New York."
Dallas Morning News, June 24, 1984.

Furtado, Ted. "Shelby Hearon." *Alcade* 75 (March/April, 1987): 21.

Levine, Beth. "PW Interviews." *Publishers Weekly* (April 3, 1987): 56–57.

McFarland, Gay E. "Shelby Hearon, a 'Total Immersion' Novelist, Has
Great Reverence for the Hours of Her Day." *Houston Chronicle,* October 16, 1977.

Morris, Anne. "Character Study." *Dallas Morning News,* November 9, 1992.

Strutton, Kelley. "A Journey of Self-Discovery." *Texas Libraries* 52 (Fall, 1991): 64–67.

Helm, Mary Sherwood. *Scraps of Early Texas History, by Mrs. Mary S. Helm who with her First Husband, Elias R. Wightman, Founded the City of Matagorda, in 1828–29.* Austin: Published for the author, 1884. Reprint, Austin: Eakin Press, 1987.

Henson, Margaret Swett. *Anglo-American Women in Texas, 1820–1850.* Boston: American Press, 1982.

———. *Cartwrights of San Augustine: Three Generations of Agrarian Entrepreneurs in Nineteenth-Century Texas.* Austin: Texas State Historical Association, 1993.

———. *Chambers County: A Pictorial History.* Norfolk, Va.: Donning Co., 1988.

———. *Juan Davis Bradburn: A Reappraisal of the Mexican Commander of Anahuac.* College Station: Texas A&M Univ. Press, 1982.

———. *Lorenzo de Zavala: The Pragmatic Idealist.* Ft. Worth: Texas Christian Univ. Press, 1996.

———. *Samuel May Williams, Early Texas Entrepreneur.* College Station: Texas A&M Univ. Press, 1976.

———. *The Samuel May Williams Home: The Life and Neighborhood of an Early Galveston Entrepreneur.* Austin: Texas State Historical Association, 1992.

Hernández, Irene Beltrán. *Across the Great River.* Houston: Arte Público Press, 1989.

———. *Heartbeat, Drumbeat.* Houston: Arte Público Press, 1992.

———. *The Secret of the Brothers.* Houston: Piñata Books, 1995.

Hernández-Tovar, Inés. *Con razón Corazón.* San Antonio: Caracol, n.d. New ed., San Antonio: M&A Editions, 1987.

Herrera-Sobek, María, ed. *Beyond Stereotypes: The Critical Analysis of Chicana Literature.* Binghamton: Bilingual Press, 1985.

———. *The Bracero Experience: Elitelore versus Folklore.* Los Angeles: UCLA Latin American Center Publications, 1979.

———. *Chicana Creativity and Criticism: Charting New Frontiers in American Literature.* Houston: Arte Público Press, 1988.

———. *Chicana (W)rites: On Word and Film.* Berkeley, Ca.: Third Woman Press, 1995.

———. *The Mexican Corrido: A Feminist Analysis.* Bloomington: Indiana Univ. Press, 1990.

———. *Northward Bound: The Mexican Immigrant Experience in Ballad and Song.* Bloomington: Indiana Univ. Press, 1993.

———. *Reconstructing a Chicano/a Literary Heritage: Hispanic Colonial Literature of the Southwest.* Tucson: Univ. of Arizona Press, 1993.

———, and Helena Maria Viramontes, eds. *Chicana Creativity and Criticism.* Albuquerque: Univ. of New Mexico Press, 1987.

Hershey, Olive. *Floating Face Up.* Austin: Thorp Springs Press, 1984.

———. *Truck Dance.* New York: Harper and Row, 1989.

Hiller, Ilo. *Introducing Birds to Young Naturalists: From Texas Parks and Wildlife Magazine.* College Station: Texas A&M Univ. Press, 1989.

———. *Introducing Mammals to Young Naturalists: From Texas Parks and Wildlife Magazine.* College Station: Texas A&M Univ. Press, 1990.

———. *The White-Tailed Deer.* College Station: Texas A&M Univ. Press, 1996.

———. *Young Naturalist: From Texas Parks and Wildlife Magazine.* College Station: Texas A&M Univ. Press, 1983.

Hinueber, Caroline von. "Life of German Pioneers in Early Texas." *Quarterly of the Texas State Historical Association* 2 (1898–99), 227–32.

Hoff, Carol. *Chris.* Chicago: Follett, 1960.

———. *The Four Friends.* Chicago: Follett, 1958.

———. *Head to the West.* Chicago: Follett, 1957.

———. *Johnny Texas.* Chicago: Wilcox, 1950.

———. *Johnny Texas on the San Antonio Road.* Chicago: Wilcox, 1953.

———. *They Served America.* Austin: Steck-Vaughn, 1966.

———. *Wilderness Pioneer: Stephen F. Austin of Texas.* Chicago: Follett, 1955.

Holden, Frances Mayhugh. *Lambshead before Interwoven: A Texas Range Chronicle, 1848–1878,* College Station: Texas A&M Univ. Press, 1982.

Holland, Ada Morehead. *Brush Country Woman.* College Station: Texas A&M Univ. Press, 1988.

———. *Mr. Claude.* College Station, Texas A&M Univ. Press, 1984.

———. *No Quittin' Sense.* Austin: Univ. of Texas Press, 1969.

Holland, Annie Jefferson. *The Refugees: A Sequel to "Uncle Tom's Cabin".* Austin: Press of Ben C. Jones and Co., 1892.

Holland, Ellen Bowie. *Gay as a Grig: Memories of a North Texas Girlhood.* Austin: Univ. of Texas Press, 1963.

Holley, Mary Austin. *Letters of an Early American Traveller: Mary Austin Holley, Her Life and Her Works, 1784–1846.* Edited by Mattie Austin Hatcher. Dallas: Southwest Press, 1933.

———. *Texas.* Lexington: P. Clarke, 1836. Reprint, Austin: Texas State Historical Association, 1985.

———. *The Texas Diary, 1835–1838.* Edited by J. P. Bryan. Austin: The Humanities Research Center, Univ. of Texas at Austin, 1965; *The Texas Quarterly* 8, no. 2 (1965): 7–119.

———. *Texas. Observations, Historical, Geographical and Descriptive. In a Series of Letters, Written during a Visit to Austin's Colony, with a view to a permanent Settlement in that country, in the Autumn of 1831.* Baltimore: Armstrong and Plaskitt, 1833. Reprinted in Mattie Austin Hatcher, ed. *Letters of an Early American Traveller: Mary Austin Holley, Her Life and Works, 1784–1846.* Dallas: Southwest Press, 1933.

Secondary Sources (Holley, Mary Austin)

Lee, Rebecca Smith. *Mary Austin Holley: A Biography.* Austin: Univ. of Texas Press, 1962.

Hood, Emma Nelson. *Bob Dean; or, Our Other Boarder.* Philadelphia: Claxton, 1882.

Horton, Louise. *Houston: A Novel.* Austin: White Cross Press, 1982.

———. *In the Hills of the Pennyroyal: A History of Allen County, Kentucky from 1815–1880.* Austin: White Cross Press, 1975.

———. *A Map for a Journey: An Epic Lyric in Terza Rima.* Granger, Tex.: White Cross Press, 1990.

———. *Samuel Bell Maxey: A Biography.* Austin: Univ. of Texas Press, 1974.

———. *Some of the Ancestors of Thomas Marion Thomas and Alice May Armstrong.* Austin: White Cross Press, 1974.

Houston, Margaret Bell. *Bride's Island.* New York: Corona, 1951.

———. *Collected Poems of Margaret Bell Houston.* San Antonio: Naylor, 1967.

———. *Cottonwoods Grow Tall.* New York: Corona, 1958.

———. *Gypsy Weather.* New York: D. Appleton-Century, 1935.

———. *Hurdy-Gurdy.* New York: Appleton and Co., 1932.

———. *Lanterns in the Dusk.* New York: Dodd, Mead, 1930.

———. *The Little Straw Wife.* New York: H. K. Fly, 1914.

———. *Magic Valley.* New York: D. Appleton-Century, 1934.

———. *Moon of Delight.* New York: Dodd, Mead, 1931.

———. *Prairie Flowers.* Boston: R. G. Badger, 1907.

———. *Window in Heaven.* New York: D. Appleton-Century, 1937.

———. *Yonder.* New York: Crown, 1955.

Houstoun, Matilda Charlotte (Jesse) Fraser. *Hesperos: or Travels in the West.* 2 vols. London: John W. Parker, 1850.

———. *Texas and the Gulf of Mexico: or, Yachting in the New World.* Philadelphia: G. B. Zieber and Co., 1845. Reprint, Austin: Steck-Warlick Co., 1968.

Howard, Dorothy. *Dorothy's World: Childhood in Sabine Bottom, 1902–1910.* Englewood Cliffs, N.J.: Prentice-Hall, 1977.

Secondary Sources (Howard, Dorothy)

Grider, Sylvia Ann. "Dorothy Howard: Pioneer Collector of Children's Folklore." *Children's Folklore Review* 17:1 (Fall, 1994): 3–17.

Huck, Olive. "The Last Hunt of Dorax." In *Writers and Writings of Texas.* Edited by Davis Foute Eagleton. New York: Broadway Publishing Co., 1913, pp. 208–20.

Hughes, Mary Gray. *The Calling.* Urbana: Univ. of Illinois Press, 1980.

———. *The Empty Lot.* Chicago: Another Chicago Press, 1992.

———. *The Thousand Springs.* Puckerbrush Press, 1971.

Hunt, Annie Mae. *See: Winegarten, Ruthe, ed.*

Ivins, Molly. "Lubbock: Seat of Rebellion." *Texas Monthly* 17 (May, 1989): 105–106.

———. *Molly Ivins Can't Say That, Can She?* New York: Random House, 1991.

———. *Nothin' but Good Times Ahead.* New York: Random House, 1993.

Secondary Sources (Ivins, Molly)

Bean, Judith. "True Grit and All the Rest: The Expression of Regional and

Individual Identity in Molly Ivins's Discourse." *Southwestern American Literature* 19 (1993): 35–46.

Schwartz, Mimi. "The Price of Being Molly." *Texas Monthly* (Nov., 1992): 138–42, passim.

Jackson, Guida. *Passing Through*. New York: Simon and Schuster, 1979.

James, Bessie Rowland. *For God, For Country, For Home: The National League for Women's Service*. New York: G. P. Putnam's Sons, 1920.

———. *Gallant the Hour*. Dallas: Kaleidograph Press, 1945.

———. *Six Feet Six: The Heroic Story of Sam Houston*. Indianapolis: Bobbs, 1931.

Jaques, Mary J. *Texas Ranch Life: With Three Months through Mexico in a "Prairie Schooner."* London: Horace Cox, Windsor House, Bream's Buildings, 1894.

John, Elizabeth A. H. *Storms Brewed in Other Men's Worlds: The Confrontation of Indians, Spanish, and French in the Southwest*. College Station: Texas A&M Univ. Press, 1975.

Johnson, Olive McClintic. "De Nation's Bu'ffday." *Collier's* 68 (July 9, 1921): 9–10.

———. "Didja Getcha Feet Wet?" *Collier's* 65 (February 21, 1920): 7–8.

———. "Disagreeable as a Husband." *Collier's* 65 (May 29, 1920): 56.

———. "Doublin' Bank." *Collier's* 69 (April 22, 1922): 13–14.

———. "First Kind Word." *Colllier's* 68 (September 3, 1921): 7–8.

———. "Great Grief!" *Colllier's* 65 (January 22, 1921): 5–6.

———. "Insane Truth." *Collier's* 66 (October 9, 1920): 7–8.

———. "Isn't Nature Wonderful?" *Collier's* 67 (February 26, 1921): 7–8.

———. *Little Tejas: Child of Twilight*. Ft. Worth: The Economy Company, 1937.

———. "Moons—Full, Blue, and Honey." *Collier's* 65 (January 3, 1920): 12–13.

———, ed. *New Declamations for Seniors, Juniors, and Sub-Juniors*. Dallas: Banks Upshaw and Company, 1940.

———. "Relief of Truckrow." *Collier's* 69 (January 14, 1922): 7–8.

———. "Turquoise Skies." *Collier's* 65 (February 7, 1920): 10–11.

Johnson, Siddie Joe. *Agarita Berry*. Dallas: The South-West Press, 1933.

———. *Cat Hotel*. New York: Longmans, 1955.

———. *Cathy*. New York: Longmans, 1945.

———. *Debby*. New York: Longmans, 1940.

———. *Feather in My Hand*. New York: Atheneum, 1967.

———. *The Firebird*. Dallas: Dallas Public Library, 1945.

———. *Gallant the Hour*. Dallas: Kaleidograph Press, 1945.

———. *Joe and Andy Want a Boat*. Austin: Steck, 1951.

———. *A Month of Christmases*. New York: Longmans, 1952.

———. *New Town in Texas*. New York: Longmans, 1942.

———. *Rabbit Fires*. Boerne, Tex.: Highland, 1951.

———. *Susan's Year*. New York: Longmans, 1948.

———. *Texas, the Land of the Tejas*. New York: Random, 1943.

Johnston, Eliza Griffin. "The Diary of Eliza (Mrs. Albert Sidney) Johnston: The Second Cavalry Comes to Texas." Edited by Charles P. Roland and Richard C. Robbins. *Southwestern Historical Quarterly* 60 (1956–57): 463–500.

————. *Texas Wildflowers with a Biography of Mrs. Johnston by Mildred Pickle Mayhall*. Austin: Shoal Creek Publishers, 1972.

Johnston, Marguerite. *Houston: The Unknown City, 1836–1946*. College Station: Texas A&M Univ. Press, 1991.

Jordan, Margaret Olive. *God's Smiles and A Look into His Face*. San Antonio: F. Tennyson Neely Co., 1901.

————. *Scattered Rose Leaves*. San Antonio: T. Ruzman Printer, 1903.

————. *Wine for the Soul in Prose and Verse*. Los Angeles: J. F. Rowny Press, 1919.

Juarez, Tina. *Call No Man Master*. Houston: Arte Público Press, 1995.

Kafka, Sherry. *Hannah Jackson*. New York: Morrow, 1966.

————. "The Man Who Loved God." In *The Best Short Plays 1968*. Edited by Stanley Richards. New York: Chilton, 1969, pp. 361–88.

————, and Robert Coles, eds. *I Will Always Stay Me: Writings of Migrant Children*. Austin: Texas Monthly Press, 1982.

Karr, Mary. *The Liar's Club: A Memoir*. New York: Viking, 1995.

Kimball, Emaretta C. *See:* Cardelle, Cara

Kemp, Augusta Hasslock. *Pegasus Limping*. Waco: Texian Press, 1965.

King, Evelyn. *Women on the Cattle Trail and in the Roundup*. Glendale, Calif.: Brazos Corral of the Westerners/Prosperity Press, 1983.

King, Mary. *Quincie Bolliver*. Boston: Houghton-Mifflin, 1941.

————. *See also under:* O'Donnell, Mary King

Kirkland, Elithe Hamilton. *Divine Average*. Boston: Little, Brown and Co., 1952. Reprint, Bryan, Tex.: Shearer Publishing, 1984.

————. *The Edge of Disrepute*. Bryan, Tex.: Shearer Publishing, 1984.

————. *Leet's Christmas*. Wimberley, Tex.: The White Chapel Press, 1985.

————. *Love Is a Wild Assault*. New York: Doubleday and Co., 1959. Reprint, Bryan, Tex.: Shearer Publishing, 1984.

————, and Jenny Lind Porter. *On the Trellis of Memory: A Psychic Journey into Prehistory*. New York: Carlton Press, 1971.

Kleberg, Rosa. "Some of My Early Experiences in Texas." *Quarterly of the Texas State Historical Association* 1 (1897–98): 297–302; 2 (1989–99): 170–73.

Koch, Polly. *Invisible Borders*. New York: Simon & Schuster, 1991.

Koen, Karleen. *Through a Glass Darkly*. New York: Random House, 1986.

Koenig, Janie Ray Shofner. *Pine Trees and Cotton Fields: Reminiscences of a Childhood, NE Texas—NW Louisiana, 1925–1942*. San Antonio: Piney Woods Productions, 1991.

Krey, Laura. *And Tell of Time*. Boston: Houghton Mifflin, 1938.

————. *On the Long Tide*. Boston: Houghton Mifflin, 1940.

Landry, Wanda. *Boardin' in the Thicket*. Denton: Univ. of North Texas Press, 1989.

Lane, Lydia Spencer (Blaney). *I Married a Soldier: or, Old Days in the Old Army*. Philadelphia: J. B. Lippincott, 1893. Reprint, Albuquerque: Horn and Wallace Publishing, 1964.

Laswell, Mary. *Bread for a Living*. Boston: Houghton Mifflin, 1948.

————. *High Time*. Boston: Houghton Mifflin, 1944.

————. *John Henry Kirby: Prince of the Pines*. Austin: Encino, 1967.

———. *Let's Go for Broke.* Boston: Houghton Mifflin, 1962.

———. *Mrs. Rasmussen's Book of One-Arm Cookery with Second Helpings.* Boston: Houghton Mifflin, 1970.

———. *One on the House.* Boston: Houghton Mifflin, 1949.

———. *Suds in Your Eye.* Boston: Houghton Mifflin, 1942.

———. *Tooner Schooner.* Boston: Houghton Mifflin, 1953.

———. *Tio Pepe.* Boston: Houghton Mifflin, 1963.

———. *Wait for the Wagon.* Boston: Houghton Mifflin, 1951.

———, with Bob Pool. *I'll Take Texas.* Boston: Houghton Mifflin Co., 1958.

Secondary Sources (Laswell, Mary)

Miles, Elton. *Southwest Humorists.* Southwest Writers Series, no. 26. Austin: Steck-Vaughn, 1969.

Leake, Grace Sothcote. *House of Refuge.* New York: W. F. Payson, 1932.

Leaton, Anne. *Good Friends, Just.* London: Chatto and Windus, 1983.

———. *Mayakovsky, My Love.* Woodstock, Vt.: Countryman Press, 1984.

———. *Pearl.* New York: A. A. Knopf, 1985.

LeClerc, Clara. *See:* Gorman, Mrs. H. C. L.

Lee, Mrs. A. J. "Some Recollections of Two Pioneer Texas Women." *The Texas Methodist Quarterly* 1 (1910): 207–13.

Lee, Rebecca Smith. *Mary Austin Holley, A Biography.* Austin: Univ. of Texas Press, 1962.

———. "The Southwest in Fiction." In *Roundup Time.* Edited by George Sessions Perry. New York: Whittlesey House, 1943, pp. 377–84.

———, and Francis Keller Barr [primary au.]. *The Great Elm Tree: Heritage of the Episcopal Diocese of Lexington.* Lexington, Ky.: Faith House Press, 1969.

———. *See also under:* Major, Mabel; Smith, Rebecca W.; *and under General listing:* Duval, John C.

Leedom-Ackerman, Joanne. *The Dark Path to the River.* Dallas: Saybrook Publishing Co., 1988.

———. *No Marble Angels.* Dallas: Saybrook Publishing Co., 1985.

Lehrer, Kate. *Best Intentions.* Boston: Little, Brown, 1987.

———. *When They Took Away the Man in the Moon.* New York: Harmony House, 1993.

Lesesne, Mary Richardson. *Torpedoes: or Dynamite in Society.* Galveston: Press of Saw and Blaylock, 1883.

Leslie, Candace. *From Forge and Anvil: Erich Riesel, Hill Country Ironworker.* Photographs by Diane Hopkins-Hughs. Bryan, Tex.: Insite Press, 1992.

Lewis, Willie Newbury. *Between Sun and Sod: An Informal History of the Texas Panhandle.* College Station: Texas A&M Univ. Press, 1976.

———. *Tapadero: The Making of a Cowboy.* Austin: Univ. of Texas Press, 1972.

———. *Willie, a Girl from a Town Called Dallas.* College Station: Texas A&M Univ. Press, 1984.

Linck, Ernestine Sewell. see Sewell, Ernestine

Lindsey, Therese. *Blue Norther.* New York: Harold Vinal, 1925.

———. *A Tale of the Galveston Storm.* Dallas: The Kaleidograph Press, 1936.

Little Dog, Pat. *See:* Taylor, Pat Ellis

Livingston, Myra Cohn. *Abraham Lincoln: A Man for All the People.* New York: Holiday House, 1993.

———. *Animal, Vegetable, Mineral: Poems about Small Things.* New York: Harper-Collins, 1994.

———. *Birthday Poems.* New York: Holiday House, 1989.

———. *Call Down the Moon: Poems of Music.* New York: M. K. McElderry Books, 1995.

———. *Callooh! Callay! Holiday Poems for Young Readers.* New York: Atheneum, 1978.

———. *Cat Poems.* New York: Holiday House, 1987.

———. *The Child as Poet—Myth or Reality?* Boston: Horn Book, 1984.

———. *A Circle of Seasons.* New York: Holiday House, 1982.

———. *Climb into the Bell Tower: Essays on Poetry.* New York: Harper and Row, 1990.

———. *Come Away.* New York: Atheneum, 1974.

———. *A Crazy Flight and Other Poems.* New York: Harcourt, Brace and World, 1969.

———. *Dog Poems.* New York: Holiday House, 1990.

———. *Earth Songs.* New York: Holiday House, 1986.

———. *Halloween Poems.* New York: Holiday House, 1989.

———. *Happy Birthday!* New York: Harcourt, Brace and World, 1964.

———. *I Like You, If You Like Me.* New York: Margaret K. Elderry Books, 1987.

———. *I'm Hiding.* New York: Harcourt, 1965.

———. *I Never Told and Other Poems.* New York: Maxwell Macmillan International, 1992.

———. *I Talk to Elephants!* New York: Harcourt Brace and World, 1962.

———. *If the Owl Calls Again.* New York: Maxwell Macmillan, 1990.

———. *If You Ever Meet a Whale.* New York: Holiday House, 1992.

———. *I'm Not Me.* New York: Harcourt, Brace 1963.

———. *Keep on Singing: A Ballad of Marian Anderson.* New York: Holiday House, 1994.

———. *Let Freedom Ring: A Ballad of Martin Luther King.* New York: Holiday House, 1992.

———. *Light and Shadow.* New York: Holiday House, 1992.

———. *Listen Children, Listen: An Anthology of Poems for the Very Young.* New York: Harcourt Brace Jovanovich, 1972.

———. *The Malibu and Other Poems.* New York: Atheneum, 1972.

———. *The Moon and a Star.* New York: Harcourt, 1965.

———. *My Head Is Red and Other Riddle Rhymes.* New York: Holiday House, 1990.

———. *No Way of Knowing: Dallas Poems.* New York: Atheneum, 1980.

———. *O Frabjous Day: Poetry for Holidays and Special Occasions.* New York: Atheneum, 1977.

————. *O Sliver of Liver: Together with Other Triolets, Cinquains, Haiku, Verses, and a Dash of Poems*. New York: Atheneum, 1979.

————. *One Little Room, an Everywhere. Poems of Love*. New York: Atheneum, 1975.

————. *Poem Making: Ways to Begin Writing Poetry*. New York: HarperCollins, 1991.

————. *Poems for Brothers, Poems for Sisters*. New York: Holiday House, 1991.

————. *See What I Found*. New York: Harcourt, Brace and World, 1962.

————. *Sky Songs*. New York: Holiday House, 1984.

————. *Space Songs*. New York: Holiday House, 1988.

————. *A Time Beyond Us: A Collection of Poems*. New York: Harcourt, 1968.

————. *Up in the Air*. New York: Holiday House, 1989.

————. *The Way Things Are*. New York: Atheneum, 1974.

————. *What a Wonderful Bird the Frog Are*. New York: Harcourt Brace Jovanovich, 1973.

————. *When You Are Alone/It Keeps You Capone: An Approach to Creative Writing with Children*. New York: Atheneum, 1973.

————. *Whispers*. New York: Harcourt, 1958.

————. *Wide Awake*. New York: Harcourt, 1959.

————. *4-Way Stop and Other Poems*. New York: Atheneum, 1976.

————, and Zena Sutherland, comps. *The Scott, Foresman Anthology of Children's Literature*. Glenville, Ill.: Scott, Foresman, 1984.

Looscan, Adele. "Elizabeth Bullock Huling: A Texas Pioneer." *Quarterly of the Texas State Historical Association* 11 (1907): 66–69.

————. "The History and Evolution of the Texas Flag." In *A Comprehensive History of Texas, 1685–1897*. Edited by Dudley G. Wooten. Dallas: William G. Scarff, 1989, vol. 1, pp. 693–99. Reprint, Austin: Texas State Historical Association, 1986.

————. "Micajah Autry: A Soldier of the Alamo." *Quarterly of the Texas State Historical Association* 14 (1910–11): 315–24.

————. "The Old Mexican Fort at Velasco." *Quarterly of the Texas State Historical Association* 1 (1989): 282–84.

————. "Sketch of the Life of Oliver Jones and of His Wife Rebecca Jones." *Quarterly of the Texas State Historical Association* 10 (1906): 172–80.

————. "Tombs and Monuments of Noted Texans." In *A Comprehensive History of Texas, 1685–1897*. Edited by Dudley G. Wooten. Dallas: William G. Scarff, 1989, vol. 1, pp. 700–16. Reprint, Austin: Texas State Historical Association, 1986.

————. "The Women of Pioneer Days in Texas—Domestic and Social Life in the Periods of the Colonies, the Revolution, and the Republic." In *A Comprehensive History of Texas, 1685–1897*. Edited by Dudley G. Wooten. Dallas: William G. Scarff, 1989, vol. 1, pp. 649–68. Reprint, Austin: Texas State Historical Association, 1986.

————. "The Work of the Daughters of the Republic of Texas on Behalf of the Alamo." *Quarterly of the Texas State Historical Association* 8 (1904): 79–82.

Lowry, Beverly. *Breaking Gentle*. New York: Viking, 1988.

———. *Come Back, Lolly Ray.* Garden City, N.Y.: Doubleday, 1977.

———. *Crossed Over: A Murder, A Memoir.* New York: Knopf, 1992.

———. *Daddy's Girl.* New York: Viking, 1981.

———. *Emma Blue.* Garden City, N.Y.: Doubleday, 1978.

———. *The Perfect Sonya.* New York: Viking, 1987.

———. *The Track of Real Desires.* New York: Knopf, 1994.

Secondary Sources (Lowry, Beverly)

Smith, Wendy. "PW Interviews." *Publisher's Weekly* (April 4, 1994): 51–52.

Lowrey, Janette Sebring. *Annunciata and the Shepherds.* New York: Gentry, 1938.

———. *The Lavender Cat.* New York: Harper, 1944.

———. *Love, Bid Me Welcome.* New York: Harper, 1964.

———. *Margaret.* New York: Harper, 1950.

———. *Mr. Heff and Mr. Ho: The Story of Mr. Flowery Field and the Organ Grinder.* New York: Harper, 1952.

———. *The Poky Little Puppy.* New York: Golden, 1942.

———. *Rings on Her Fingers.* New York: Harper, 1941.

———. *The Silver Dollar.* New York: Harper, 1940.

———. *Six Silver Spoons.* New York: Harper, 1971.

Lynn, Sandra. *I Must Hold These Strangers: Poems by Sandra Lynn.* Fort Worth: Prickly Pear Press, 1980.

———. *Three Texas Poets.* Edited by Dave Oliphant. Fort Worth, Tex.: Prickly Pear Press, 1986.

———. *Where Rainbows Wait for Rain: The Big Bend Country.* Granbury, Tex.: Tangram Press, 1989.

Mackintosh, Prudence. *Just as We Were: A Narrow Slice of Texas Womanhood.* Austin: Univ. of Texas Press, 1996.

———. *Retreads.* Garden City, N.Y.: Doubleday, 1985.

———. *The Soul of East Texas.* Photographs by Keith Carter. Austin: Texas Monthly Press, 1989.

———. *Thundering Sneakers.* Garden City, N.Y.: Doubleday, 1981. Reprint, Austin: Texas Monthly Press, 1987.

Major, Mabel. "British Ballads in Texas." *Publications of the Texas Folklore Society* 10 (1932): 131–68.

———, and Rebecca Smith, eds. *My Foot's in the Stirrup.* Dallas: Dealey and Lowe. 1937.

———, and T. M. Pearce, eds. *Signature of the Sun: Southwest Verse, 1900–1950.* Albuquerque: Univ. of New Mexico Press, 1950.

———, Rebecca W. Smith, and T. M. Pearce. *Southwest Heritage: A Literary History with Bibliographies.* Albuquerque: Univ. of New Mexico Press, 1938. Reprint and revision, Albuquerque: Univ. of New Mexico Press, 1948, 1972.

———, and Rebecca W. Smith, eds. *The Southwest in Literature: An Anthology for High Schools.* New York: Macmillan Co., 1929.

———. *See also under General listing:* Duval, John C.

Malone, Ann Patton. "Women in Texas History." In *A Guide to the History of Texas.* Edited by Light Cummins and Alvin Bailey. New York: Greenwood Press, 1988, 123–35.

———. *Women on the Texas Frontier: A Cross-Cultural Perspective.* El Paso: Texas Western Press, 1983.

Manning, Diane. *Hill Country Teacher: Oral Histories from the One-Room School and Beyond.* Boston: Twayne Publishers, 1990.

Maret, Elizabeth. *Women of the Range: Women's Roles in the Texas Beef Cattle Industry.* College Station: Texas A&M Univ. Press, 1993.

Marks, Paula Mitchell. *And Die in the West: The Story of the O.K. Corral Gunflight.* New York: William Morrow and Co., 1989.

———. *Hands to the Spindle: Texas Women and Home Textile Production, 1822–1880.* College Station: Texas A&M Univ. Press, 1995.

———. *Precious Gold: The American Gold Rush 1848–1900.* New York: William Morrow and Co., 1994.

———. *Turn Your Eyes Toward Texas: Pioneers Sam and Mary Maverick.* College Station: Texas A&M Univ. Press, 1989.

Marshall, Kathryn. *Desert Places.* New York: Harper and Row, 1977.

———. *In the Combat Zone: An Oral History of American Women in Vietnam, 1966–1975.* Boston: Little, Brown, 1987.

———. *My Sister Gone.* New York: Harper and Row, 1975.

———. "On Writing from the Center." *The Texas Observer* 74 (April 9, 1982): 1, 15, 18.

Matthews, Sallie Reynolds. *Interwoven.* Houston: The Anson Jones Press, 1936. Reprints: El Paso: Carl Hertzog, 1958; Austin: Univ. of Texas Press, 1974; College Station: Texas A&M Univ. Press, 1982.

———. *True Tales of the Frontier.* Albany: Venture Press, 1961.

Maverick, Mary A. *Memoirs of Mary A. Maverick, Arranged by Mary A. Maverick and Her Son, Geo. Madison Maverick.* Edited by Rena Maverick Green. San Antonio: Alamo Printing Co., 1921. Reprinted with other documents in Rena Maverick Green, ed. *Samuel Maverick, Texas 1803–1870.* San Antonio: privately printed, 1952.

Secondary Sources (Maverick, Mary A.)

Marks, Paula Mitchell. *Turn Your Eyes Toward Texas: Pioneers Sam and Mary Maverick.* College Station: Texas A&M Univ. Press, 1989.

McCallum, Jane Y. *A Texas Suffragist: Diaries and Writings of Jane Y. McCallum.* Edited by Janet G. Humphrey. Austin: Ellen C. Temple, 1988.

———. *Women Pioneers.* Richmond, N.Y.: Johnson Publishing Co., 1929.

McCann, Janet. *Afterword.* Steubenville, Ohio: Franciscan Univ. Press, 1990.

———. *Dialogue with the Dogcatcher.* Austin: Slough Press, 1987.

———. *Ghosts of Christmas.* Gainesville, Fla.: Chimera Connections Press, 1989.

———. *How They Got There.* Columbus, Ohio: Pudding Publications, 1985.

———. *Looking for Buddha in the Barbed Wire Garden*. Greensboro, N.C.: Avisson Press, 1996.

———. *Wallace Stevens Revisited: "The Celestial Possible."* New York: Twayne, 1995.

McCorquodale, Robin. *Dansville*. New York: Harper and Row, 1986.

———. *Stella Landry*. New York: Morrow, 1992. Reprint, New York: Avondale, 1993.

[McCown, Susan Turnham]. "Early Days in Milam County: Reminiscences of Susan Turnham McCown." Edited by L. W. Kemp. *Southwestern Historical Quarterly* 50 (1947): 367–76.

McDaniel, Douglass Scarborough. *George White McDaniel: By His Wife*. Nashville: Sunday School Board of the Southern Baptist Convention, 1928.

McGaw, Jessie Brewer. *Chief Red Horse Tells About Custer: The Battle of the Little Big Horn*. New York: Elsevier/Nelson Books, 1981.

———. *How Medicine Man Cured Paleface Woman, An Easy-Reading Story in Indian Pictures and Paleface Words*. New York: Scott, 1956.

———. *Little Elk Hunts Buffalo; As Little Elk Tells It in Indian Picture Writing*. New York: Nelson, 1961.

———. *Painted Pony Runs Away; As Little Elk Tells it in Indian Picture Writing*. New York: Nelson, 1958.

McGiffin, Lee. *A Coat for Private Patrick*. New York: Dutton, 1964.

———. *The Fifer of San Jacinto*. New York: Lothrop, 1956.

———. *High Whistle Charlie*. New York: Dutton, 1962.

———. *The Horse Hunters*. New York: Dutton, 1963.

———. *The Mustangers*. New York: Dutton, 1965.

———. *Pony Soldier*. New York: Dutton, 1961.

———. *Rebel Rider*. New York: Dutton, 1959.

———. *Ride for Texas*. New York: Dutton, 1960.

———. *Riders of Enchanted Valley*. New York: Dutton, 1966.

———. *Swords, Stars, and Bars*. New York: Dutton, 1958.

———. *Ten Tall Texans: Tales of the Texas Rangers*. New York: Lothrop, 1956.

———. *Yankee Doodle Dandies: Eight Generals of the American Revolution*. New York: Dutton, 1967.

———. *Yankee of the Yalu: Philo Norton McGiffin, American Captain in the Chinese Navy, 1885–1895*. New York: Dutton, 1968.

[McHenry, Lydia Ann]. "Lydia Ann McHenry and Revolutionary Texas." Edited by George R. Nielson. *Southwestern Historical Quarterly* 74 (1971): 393–408.

McKinley, Georgia. *Follow the Running Grass*. Boston: Houghton Mifflin, 1969.

———. *The Mighty Distance*. Boston: Houghton Mifflin, 1965.

McLeRoy, Sherrie. *Black Land, Red River: A Pictorial History of Grayson County, Texas*. Virginia Beach, Va.: Donning, 1993.

———. *Daughter of Fortune: The Bettie Brown Story*. Plano, Tex.: Republic of Texas Press, 1996.

———. *Mistress of Glen Eden: The Life and Times of Texas Pioneer Sophia Porter*. Sherman, Tex.: White Stone Pub. Group, 1990.

———. *More Passages: A New History of Amherst County.* Bowie, Md.: Heritage Books, 1995.

———. *Passages: A History of Amherst County.* Lynchburg, Va.: S. S. McLeRoy, 1977.

———. *Red River Women.* Plano, Tex.: Republic of Texas Press, 1996.

———. *Strangers in Their Midst: The Free Black Population of Amherst County, Virginia.* Bowie, Md.: Heritage Books, 1993.

———. *Texas: 150 Years of Statehood.* Houston: Pioneer Publications, 1996.

Medearis, Angela Shelf. *The African-American Kitchen: Cooking from Our Heritage.* New York: Dutton, 1994.

———. *Annie's Gifts.* Orange, N.J.: Just Us Books, 1994.

———. *Come This Far to Freedom: A History of African Americans.* New York: Atheneum, 1993.

———. *Dancing with the Indians.* New York: Holiday House, 1991.

———. *Picking Peas for a Penny.* Austin: State House Press, 1990.

———. *Poppa's New Pants.* New York: Holiday House, 1995.

———. *The Singing Man: Adapted from a West African Folktale.* New York: Holiday House, 1994.

———. *Too Much Talk.* Cambridge, Mass.: Candlewick Press, 1995.

Menken, Adah Isaacs. *Infelicia.* Philadelphia: J. B. Lippincott and Co., 1888.

———. "Notes of My Life." *New York Times,* September 6, 1868.

Secondary Sources (Menken, Adah Isaacs)

Davis, Kate Wilson. "Adah Isaacs Menken—Her Life and Poetry." Master's thesis, Southern Methodist University, 1944.

Palmer, Pamela Lynn. "Adah Isaacs Menken: From Texas to Paris." In *Legendary Women of Texas.* Edited by Francis E. Abernethy. Dallas: E-Heart Press, 1981, pp. 84–93.

Tolbert, Frank X. "Glamorous Adah [Menken] Was from 'doches." *Dallas Morning News,* November 9, 1961.

Meredith, D. R. [Doris R.] *The Home Front Murders.* New York: Ballantine Books, 1995.

———. *Murder by Deception.* New York: Ballantine, 1989.

———. *Murder by Impulse.* New York: Ballantine, 1987.

———. *Murder by Masquerade.* New York: Ballantine, 1990.

———. *Murder by Reference.* New York: Ballantine, 1991.

———. *Murder by Sacrilege.* New York: Ballantine, 1993.

———. *The Reckoning.* New York: Harper, 1993.

———. *The Sheriff and the Branding Iron Murders.* New York: Walker and Co., 1985.

———. *The Sheriff and the Folsom Man Murders.* New York: Walker and Co., 1987.

———. *The Sheriff and the Panhandle Murders.* New York: Walker and Co., 1984.

———. *A Time Too Late.* New York: Harper-Collins Publishers, 1993.

Merritt, Miriam. *By Lions, Gladly Eaten.* New York: Harcourt, Brace and World, 1965.

Meyer, Carolyn. *Amish People: Plain Living in a Complex World*. New York: Atheneum, 1976.

———. *C. C. Poindexter*. New York: Atheneum, 1978.

———. *The Center: From a Troubled Past to a New Life*. New York: Atheneum, 1979.

———. *Denny's Tapes*. New York: M. K. McElderry Books, 1987.

———. *Drummers of Jericho*. San Diego: Harcourt Brace, 1995.

———. *Elliott and Win*. New York: Atheneum, 1986.

———. *Eskimos: Growing Up in a Changing Culture*. New York: Atheneum, 1977.

———. *Eulalia's Island*. New York: Atheneum, 1982.

———. *Killing the Kudu*. New York: Margaret K. McElderry Books, 1990.

———. *The Luck of Texas McCoy*. New York: Atheneum, 1984.

———. *The Mystery of the Ancient Maya*. New York: Atheneum, 1985.

———. *Voices of South Africa: Growing Up in a Troubled Land*. San Diego: Harcourt Brace Jovanovich, 1986.

———. *Where the Broken Heart Still Beats: The Story of Cynthia Ann Parker*. San Diego: Harcourt Brace Jovanovich, 1992.

———. *White Lilacs*. New York: Harcourt, 1993.

Miller, Helen Topping. *After the Glory*. New York: Appleton-Century-Crofts, 1958.

———. *April to Remember*. New York: Appleton-Century-Crofts, 1955.

———. *Christmas at Mount Vernon with George and Martha Washington*. New York: Longmans, Green, 1957.

———. *Christmas with Robert E. Lee*. New York: Longmans, Green, 1958.

———. *Dark Lightning*. New York: Appleton-Century-Crofts, 1940.

———. *Horns of Capricorn*. New York: Appleton-Century-Crofts, 1950.

———. *Hunter's Moon*. New York: D. Appleton-Century, 1943.

———. *Mirage*. New York: Appleton, 1949.

———. *Never Another Moon*. New York: Appleton, 1938.

———. *No Tears for Christmas*. New York: Longmans, Green, 1954.

———. *The Proud Young Thing*. New York: Appleton-Century-Crofts, 1952.

———. *Rebellion Road*. Indianapolis: Bobbs-Merrill, 1954.

———. *Sing One Song*. New York: Appleton-Century-Crofts, 1956.

———. *Song After Midnight*. New York: Appleton-Century, 1939.

———. *Storm Over Eden*. New York: Appleton-Century, 1937.

———. *Witch Water*. Indianapolis: Bobbs-Merrill, 1952.

Miller, Vassar. *Adam's Footprint*. New Orleans: The New Orleans Poetry Journal, 1956.

———. *Approaching Nada*. Houston: Wings Press, 1977.

———. *Despite This Flesh: The Disabled in Stories and Poems*. Austin: Univ. of Texas Press, 1985.

———. *If I Could Sleep Deeply Enough: Poems*. New York: Liveright, 1974.

———. *If I Had Wheels or Love: Collected Poems of Vassar Miller*. Dallas: Southern Methodist Univ. Press, 1991.

———. *My Bones Being Wiser: Poems*. Middletown, Conn.: Wesleyan Univ. Press, 1963.

———. *Opinions and Roses: Poems*. Middletown, Conn.: Wesleyan Univ. Press, 1968.

———. *Selected and New Poems: 1950–1980.* Edited by Robert Bonazzi. Austin: Latitudes Press, 1981.

———. *Small Change.* Houston: Wings Press, 1976.

———. *Struggling to Swim on Concrete: Poems.* New Orleans: New Orleans Poetry Journal Press, 1984.

———. *Wage War on Silence: A Book of Poems.* Middletown, Conn.: Wesleyan Press, 1960.

Secondary Sources (Miller, Vassar)

Brown, Stephen Ford, ed. *Heart's Invention: On the Poetry of Vassar Miller.* Houston: Ford-Brown and Co., 1987.

Hammond, Karla M. "An Interview with Vassar Miller." *Pawn Review* 7, no. 1 (1983): 1–18.

Levertov, Denise. "Foreword." In *Vassar Miller: Selected and New Poems: 1950–1980.* Edited by Robert Bonazzi. Austin: Latitudes Press, 1981.

Miner, Sara Isadore (Pauline Periwinkle)

Secondary Sources

McElhaney, Jacquelyn. "Pauline Periwinkle: Prodding Dallas into the Progressive Era." In *Women and Texas History.* Edited by Fane Downs and Nancy Baker Jones. Austin: Texas State Historical Association, 1993, pp. 42–46.

Mireles, E. E., R. B. Fisher, and Jovita G. Mireles. *Mi Libro Español.* Austin: Benson and Co., 1941.

Mireles, E. E., and Jovita G. Mireles. *El Español Elemental.* Austin: W. S. Benson & Co., 1949.

Mohl, Aurelia Hadley. "An Afternoon Nap." *Houston Tri-Weekly Telegraph,* December 25, 1865.

Mojtabai, A. G. *Blessed Assurance: At Home with the Bomb in Amarillo, Texas.* New York: Doubleday, 1986.

———. *Called Out.* New York: Doubleday, 1994.

———. *Autumn.* Boston: Houghton Mifflin, 1982.

———. *Mundome.* New York: Simon and Schuster, 1974.

———. *Ordinary Time.* New York: Doubleday, 1989.

———. *A Stopping Place.* New York: Simon and Schuster, 1979.

———. *The 400 Eels of Sigmund Freud.* New York: Simon and Schuster, 1976.

Montgomery, Charlotte Baker. *An ABC of Dog Care for Young Owners.* New York: McKay, 1959.

———. *The Best of Friends.* New York: McKay, 1966.

———. *Cockleburr Quarters.* Englewood Cliffs, N. J.: Prentice-Hall, 1972.

———. *The Green Poodles.* New York: McKay, 1956.

———. "Hands of Horror." In *Her Work: Stories by Texas Women.* Edited by Lou Rodenberger. Bryan, Tex.: Shearer Publishing, 1982, pp. 182–94.

———. *Hope Hacienda.* New York: Crowell, 1942.

———. *House of the Roses.* New York: Dutton, 1942.

———. *The House on the River.* New York: Coward-McCann, 1948.

———. *Kinnery Camp: A Story of the Oregon Woods.* New York: McKay, 1951.

———. *The Kittens and the Cardinals.* New York: McKay, 1969.

———. *Little Brother.* New York: McKay, 1959.

———. *Magic for Mary M.* New York: McKay, 1953.

———. *Meeting Animal Friends: A Humane Education Handbook.* Waterford, Va.: National Humane Education Center, 1972.

———. *Necessary Nellie.* New York: Coward, 1945.

———. *Nellie and the Mayor's Hat.* New York: Coward, 1947.

———. *The Return of the Thunderbird.* New York: McKay, 1954.

———. *Return to Eden: A Play about Ecology.* Wakefield, Mass.: Parameter Press, 1973.

———. *A Sombrero for Miss Brown.* New York: Dutton, 1941.

———. *Sunrise Island: A Story of the Northwest Coast Indians before the Coming of the White Man.* New York: McKay, 1953.

———. *Thomas, the Ship's Cat.* New York: McKay, 1958.

———. *The Trail North: Stories of Texas' Yesterdays.* Austin: Eakin Press, 1990.

———. *The Venture of the Thunderbird.* New York: McKay, 1954.

———. *A Visit to a Humane Society Animal Shelter: A Teacher's Guide Grades 3–4.* Waterford, Va.: National Humane Education Center, 1967.

Montgomery, Cora [Jane Cazneau]. *Eagle Pass: or Life on the Border.* New York: George P. Putnam and Co., 1852. Reprint, Austin: Pemberton Press, 1966.

———. *The King of the Rivers: With a Chart of Our Slave and Free Soil Territory.* New York: C. Wood, 1850.

———. *Life in Santo Domingo, By a Settler.* New York: G. W. Carleton and Co., 1873.

———. *The Queen of Islands and King of Rivers.* New York: C. Wood, 1850.

Montgomery, Vaida Stewart, ed. *A Century with Texas Poets and Poetry.* Dallas: Kaleidograph Press, 1934.

———. *Hail for Rain.* Dallas: Kaleidograph Press, 1948.

———. *Locoed and Other Poems.* Dallas: Kaleidograph Publishers, 1930.

———, ed. *Merry-Go-Round: A Collection of Poems Selected from Kaleidograph, A National Magazine of Poetry.* Dallas: Kaleidograph Press, 1935.

Moore, Dulce D. *A Place in Mind.* Dallas: Baskerville Publishers, 1992.

Moore, Mollie E. *See:* Davis, Mollie (Mary) Evelyn Moore

Moore-Lanning, Linda. *Breaking the Myth: The Truth about Texas Women.* Austin: Eakin Press, 1986.

Mora, Pat. *Agua, Agua, Agua.* Glenview, Ill.: Good Year Books, 1994.

———. *Agua santa: Holy Water.* Boston: Beacon Press, 1995.

———. *All My Family.* Columbus, Ohio: McGraw-Hill, 1995.

———. *Ana Meets the Wind.* New York: Clarion Books, n.d.

———. *A Birthday Basket for Tía.* New York: Macmillan, 1992.

———. *Borders.* Houston: Arte Público Press, 1986.

———. *Chants.* Houston: Arte Público Press, 1984.

———. *Communion*. Houston: Arte Público Press, 1991.

———. *Confetti*. New York: Lee and Low Books, 1996.

———. *The Desert Is My Mother: El desierto es mi madre*. Houston: Piñata Books/ Arte Público Press, 1994.

———. *The Gift of the Poinsettia: El regalo de la flor de nochebuena*. Houston: Piñata Books, 1995.

———. *Listen to the Desert: Oye al desierto*. New York: Clarion Books, 1994.

———. *Nepantla: Essays from the Land in the Middle*. Albuquerque: Univ. of New Mexico Press, 1993.

———. *Pablo's Tree*. New York: Macmillan, 1994.

———. *The Race of Toad and Deer*. New York: Orchard Books, 1995.

———. *Tomás and the Library Lady*. New York: Knopf, 1992.

———. *Uno, dos, tres: One, Two, Three*. New York: Clarion Books, 1996.

———. *Voices from the Garden*. Boston: Beacon Press, 1996.

Secondary Sources (Mora, Pat)

Alarcon, Norma. "Interview with Pat Mora." *Third Woman* 3, nos. 1–2 (1985–86): 121–26.

Fast, Robin Riley. "Nature and Creative Power: Pat Mora and Patricia Hampl." *San Jose Studies* 14, no. 2 (1989): 29–40.

Nawrocki, Sarah. "Asking Their Own Questions: Chicana Poets in the 1980s." Brown University: Bachelor's thesis, 1989, pp. 28–44.

Morris, Celia. *Bearing Witness: Sexual Harassment and Beyond—Everywoman's Story*. Boston: Little, Brown, 1994.

———. *Fanny Wright: Rebel in America*. Cambridge, Mass.: Harvard Univ. Press, 1984.

———. *Storming the Statehouse: Running for Governor with Ann Richards and Dianne Feinstein*. New York: Scribner's, 1992.

Morris, Suzanne. *Galveston*. Garden City, N.Y.: Doubleday, 1976.

———. *Keeping Secrets*. Garden City, N.Y.: Doubleday, 1979.

———. *Skychild*. Garden City, N.Y.: Doubleday, 1981.

———. *Wives and Mistresses*. Garden City, N.Y.: Doubleday, 1986.

Mossiker, Frances. *An Affair of the Poisons: Louis XIV, Madame de Montespan, and One of History's Great Unsolved Mysteries*. New York: Knopf, 1969.

———. *Madame de Sevigne: A Life and Letters*. New York: Knopf, 1983.

———. *More Than a Queen: The Story of Josephine Bonaparte*. New York: Knopf, 1971.

———. *Napoleon and Josephine: The Biography of a Marriage*. New York: Simon and Schuster, 1964.

———. *Pocahontas: The Life and the Legend*. New York: Knopf, 1976.

———. *Madame de Sevigne: A Life and Letters*. New York: Knopf, 1983.

———. *The Queen's Necklace*. New York: Simon and Schuster, 1961.

Secondary Sources (Mossiker, Frances)

Bennett, Patrick. "Frances Mossiker: The Method of Madame Mossiker."

Talking with Texas Writers: Twelve Interviews. College Station: Texas A&M Univ. Press, 1980, pp. 205–25.

Mullen, Harryette. *Tree Tall Woman.* Galveston: Energy Earth Communications 1981.

Murray, Amelia Matilda. *Letters from the United States, Cuba and Canada.* New York: G. P. Putnam and Co., 1856.

———. *Recollections from 1803 to 1837: With a Conclusion in 1868.* London: Longman, Green, 1868.

Myres, Sandra L., ed. *Force without Fanfare: The Autobiography of K. M. Van Zandt.* Ft. Worth: Texas Christian Univ. Press, 1968.

———, ed. *Ho for California: Women's Overland Diaries from the Huntington Library.* San Marino, Calif.: Huntington Library, 1980.

———. *Native Americans of Texas.* Boston: American Press, 1981.

———. *One Man, One Vote: Gerrymandering vs Reapportionment.* Austin: Steck-Vaughn, 1970.

———. *The Ranch in Spanish Texas, 1691–1800.* El Paso: Texas Western Press, 1969.

———. *S. D. Myres, Saddlemaker.* Kerrville, Tex.: Privately Printed, 1961.

———. *Westering Women and the Frontier Experience 1800–1915.* Albuquerque: Univ. of New Mexico Press, 1982.

Nance, Berta Hart. *Flute in the Distance.* Dallas: Kaleidograph Press, 1935.

———. *Lines from Arizona.* Dallas: Kaleidograph Press, 1938.

———. *The Round-Up.* Cedar Rapids, Iowa: Torch Press, 1926.

Secondary Sources (Nance, Berta Hart)

Turner, Elsa McFarland. *Berta Hart Nance: A Brand of Innocence.* Quanah, Tex.: Nortex Press, 1974.

Nash, Sunny. *Bigmama Didn't Shop at Woolworth's.* College Station: Texas A&M Univ. Press, 1996.

Secondary Sources (Nash, Sunny)

Bevers, Jennifer. "Sunny Nash Recalls Segregated Bryan in Book." *Bryan (Texas) Eagle,* October 6, 1996, p. D7.

Johnstone, Barbara. "Consistency and Individual Style." In *The Linguistic Individual: Self-Expression in Language and Linguistics.* New York: Oxford Univ. Press, 1996, pp. 128–56.

Nelson, Barney, ed. *Here's to the Vinegarroon!: A Collection of Cowboy Poetry.* Alpine, Tex.: Territorial Printer, 1989.

———. *The Last Campfire: The Life Story of Ted Gray, a West Texas Rancher.* College Station: Texas A&M Univ. Press, 1984.

———, ed. *Voices and Visions of the American West.* Austin: Texas Monthly Press, 1986.

Newton, Violette. *All Time Is Now: Poems*. Palestine, Tex.: Harp and Quill Press, 1991.

———. *A Cathedral Singing: Poems of Guatemala*. Quanah, Tex.: Nortex Press, 1976.

———. *Moses in Texas*. Fort Smith, Ark.: South and West, 1967.

———. *The Proxy: Poems*. Quanah, Tex.: Nortex Offset Pub., 1973.

———. *The Shamrock Cross*. Palestine, Tex.: Harp and Quill Press, 1993.

———, and Claire Ottenstein. *Because We Dream*. Spring, Tex.: Counterpoint Publishing Co., 1984.

Niggli, Josefina. "Call Them Dreams." *Pax: A Journal for Peace through Culture* 3, nos. 1–2 (1985–86): 98–102.

———. *Mexican Folk Plays*. Chapel Hill: Univ. of North Carolina Press, 1938.

———. *Mexican Silhouettes*. Hidalgo, N. L. [Mexico]: Silhouette Press, 1928. Reprint, San Antonio: n. p., 1931.

———. *Mexican Village*. Chapel Hill: Univ. of North Carolina Press, 1945.

———. *A Miracle for Mexico*. Greenwich, Conn.: New York Graphic Society Pub., 1964.

———. *New Pointers on Playwriting*. Boston: The Writer, 1967.

———. *Pointers on Playwriting*. Boston: The Writer, 1945.

———. *Pointers on Radio Writing*. Boston: The Writer, 1946.

———. *Step Down, Elder Brother: A Novel*. New York: Rinehart, 1947.

Secondary Sources (Niggli, Josefina)

Igo, John. [Obituary]. *North San Antonio Times*, December 22, 1983.

Lee, Amy Freeman. "Playmaker of Mexico." *San Antonio Express News*, June 4, 1939.

Spearman, Walter, ed. *The Carolina Playmakers: The First 50 Years*. Chapel Hill: Univ. of North Carolina Press, 1970.

Nixon, Joan Lowery. *Alligator under the Bed*. New York: Putnam, 1974.

———. *And Maggie Makes Three*. San Diego: Harcourt Brace Jovanovich, 1986.

———. *Beats Me, Claude*. New York: Viking Kestrel, 1986.

———. *Bigfoot Makes a Movie*. New York: Putnam, 1979.

———. *The Boy Who Could Find Anything*. New York: Harcourt Brace Jovanovich, 1978.

———. *The Butterfly Tree*. Huntington, Ind.: Our Sunday Visitor, 1979.

———. *Casey and the Great Idea*. New York: Dutton, 1980.

———. *Caught in the Act*. (The Orphan Train Quartet.) New York: Bantam, 1988.

———. *Days of Fear*. New York: Dutton, 1983.

———. *A Family Apart*. (The Orphan Train Quartet.) New York: Bantam, 1987.

———. *Fat Chance, Claude*. New York: Viking Kestrel, 1987.

———. *The Ghosts of Now*. New York: Delacorte Press, 1984.

———. *The Gift*. New York: Macmillan, 1983.

———. *The Grandmother's Book*. Nashville: Abingdon, 1979.

———. *The Halloween Mystery*. Chicago: A. Whitman, 1979.

———. *The Happy Birthday Mystery.* Chicago: A. Whitman, 1979.

———. *The House on Hackman's Hill.* New York: Scholastic, 1985.

———. *If You Say So, Claude.* New York: Warne, 1980.

———. *In the Face of Danger.* (The Orphan Train Quartet.) New York: Bantam, 1988.

———. *The Kidnapping of Christina Lattimore.* New York: Harcourt Brace Jovanovich, 1979.

———. *Land under the Sea.* New York: Dodd, Mead, 1985.

———. *Muffie Mouse and the Busy Birthday.* New York: Seabury Press, 1978.

———. *The Mysterious Prowler.* New York: Harcourt Brace Jovanovich, 1976.

———. *The Mystery of Hurricane Castle.* New York: Criterion Books, 1964.

———. *The New Year's Mystery.* Chicago: A. Whitman, 1979.

———. *The Other Side of Dark.* New York: Delacorte, 1986.

———. *A Place to Belong.* (The Orphan Train Quartet.) New York: Bantam, 1989.

———. *The Seance.* New York: Harcourt Brace Jovanovich, 1980.

———. *The Secret Box Mystery.* New York: Putnam, 1974.

———. *Secret, Silent Screams.* New York: Delacorte, 1988.

———. *The Son Who Came Home Again: The Prodigal Son for Beginning Readers.* St. Louis: Concordia Pub. House, 1977.

———. *The Specter.* New York: Delacorte, 1982.

———. *The Stalker.* New York: Delacorte, 1985.

———. *The Statue Walks at Night.* New York: Disney Press, 1995.

———. *The Valentine Mystery.* Chicago: A. Whitman, 1979.

———. *Volcanoes: Nature's Fireworks.* New York: Dodd, Mead, 1978.

———. *When God Listens.* Huntington, Ind.: Our Sunday Visitor, 1978.

———. *When God Speaks.* Huntington, Ind.: Our Sunday Visitor, 1978.

———. *When I Am Eight.* New York: Dial Books for Young Readers, 1994.

———. *Whispers from the Dead.* New York: Delacorte, 1989.

———. *Will You Give Me a Dream?* New York: Four Winds Press, 1994.

———. *Writing Mysteries for Young People.* Boston: The Writer, 1977.

———. *You Bet Your Britches, Claude.* New York: Viking Kestrel, 1989.

Nye, Naomi Shihab. *Benito's Dream Bottle.* New York: Simon and Schuster, 1995.

———. *Different Ways to Pray.* Portland, Oreg.: Breitenbush Books, 1980.

———. *Eye-to-Eye.* Texas City, Tex.: Texas Portfolio Chapbook Series, 1977.

———. *Hugging the Jukebox.* New York: E. P. Dutton, 1982.

———. *I Feel a Little Jumpy around You.* New York: Simon and Schuster, 1996.

———. *Invisible.* Denton, Tex.: Trilobite Press, 1987.

———. *Lullaby Raft.* New York: Simon and Schuster, 1996.

———. *Mint.* Brockport, N.Y.: State Street Press, 1991.

———. *Never in a Hurry: Essays on People and Places.* Columbia: Univ. of South Carolina Press, 1996.

———. *On the Edge of the Sky.* Madison, Wis.: Iguana Press, 1981

———. *Our Own Clues: Poets of the Lake/2.* San Antonio: Our Lady of the Lake University, 1993.

———. *Red Suitcase.* Brockport, N.Y.: BOA Editions, 1994.

———. *Sitti's Secrets.* New York: Four Winds Press, 1994.

———. *The Spoken Page*. Pittsburgh: International Poetry Forum, 1988.

———. *Tattooed Feet*. Texas City, Tex.: Texas Portfolio Chapbook Series, 1976.

———. *This Same Sky: A Collection of Poems from around the World*. New York: Four Winds Press, 1992.

———. *Tomorrow We Smile*. Madison, Wis.: Iguana Press, 1990.

———. *Travel Alarm*. Houston: Wings Press, 1993.

———. *The Tree Is Older Than You Are: A Bilingual Gathering of Poems and Stories from Mexico with Paintings by Mexican Artists*. New York: Simon and Schuster, 1995.

———. *Words under the Words: Selected Poems*. Portland, Oreg.: Eighth Mountain Press, 1994.

———. *Yellow Glove*. Portland, Oreg.: Breitenbush, 1986.

O'Connor, Louise S. *Crying for Daylight: A Ranching Culture in the Coastal Bend*. Austin: Wexford Park, 1989.

O'Donnell, Mary King. *Quincie Bolliver. Those Other People*. Boston: Houghton Mifflin, 1946.

———. *You Can Hear the Echo*. New York: Simon and Schuster, 1965.

See also under: King, Mary

Oppenheimer, Evelyn. *The Articulate Woman*. Anderson, S.C.: Droke House, 1968.

———. *A Book Lover in Texas*. Denton: Univ. of North Texas Press, 1995.

———. *Book Reviewing for an Audience: A Parochial Guide in Technique for Lecture and Broadcast*. Metuchen, N. J.: Scarecrow Books, 1980.

———. *Gilbert Onderdonk, The Nurseryman of Mission Valley: Pioneer Horticulturist*. Denton: Univ. of North Texas Press, 1991.

———. *Legend and Other Poems*. San Antonio: Naylor, 1951.

———. *Texas in Color*. New York: Hastings House, 1971.

———. *Tillie Comes to Texas*. Dallas: Hendrick-Long, 1986.

———. *Tolbert of Texas: The Man and His Work*. Ft. Worth: Texas Christian Univ. Press, 1986.

———, and Eugene W. Bowers. *Red River Dust: True Tales of an American Yesterday*. Waco, Tex.: Word Books, 1968.

———, and Bill Porterfield. *The Book of Dallas*. Garden City, N.Y.: Doubleday, 1976.

Orgain, Kate Alma. *Southern Writers in Poetry and Prose*. New York: Neale Publishing Co., 1908.

———. *Supplementary Reader*. Temple, Tex.: Perry and Denison, Printers, n.d.

———. *A Waif from Texas*. Austin: B. C. Jones and Co., Printers, 1901.

Ornish, Natalie. *Pioneer Jewish Texans: Their Impact on Texas and American History for 400 Years, 1590–1990*. Dallas: Texas Heritage Press, 1989.

Osborn, Carolyn. "'Eunice B.' and Other Stories." Master's thesis, University of Texas at Austin, 1959.

———. *The Fields of Memory*. Bryan, Tex.: Shearer Publishing, 1984.

———. *The Grands*. Austin: The Book Club of Texas, 1990.

———. "The Grands." *Prize Stories 1990: The O. Henry Awards*. Edited by William Abrahams. New York: Doubleday, 1990, pp. 102–21.

———. *A Horse of Another Color.* Urbana-Champaign: Univ. of Illinois Press, 1977.

———. *Warriors and Maidens.* Fort Worth: Texas Christian Univ. Press, 1991.

Secondary Sources (Osborn, Carolyn)

Clayton, Lawrence. "Carolyn Osborn's Cowboy Brother." *Southwestern American Literature* 13 (1987): 5–11.

———. "The Fiction of Carolyn Osborn." *RE: Artes Liberales* 12 (1986): 5–11.

———. "Osborn's Stories Are Significant." *Abilene Reporter News,* December 23, 1984.

Grover, Dorys Crow. "Eudora Welty and Carolyn Osborn." *Southwestern American Literature* 14 (1988): 19–21.

Long, Tanya. "The Real Texas: A Study of Carolyn Osborn's Short Stories." Master's thesis, Texas A&M University, 1988.

Owens, Virginia Stem. *At Point Blank.* Grand Rapids: Baker Publishing, 1992.

———. *Congregation: A Suspense Novel.* Grand Rapids: Baker Publishing, 1992.

———. *If You Do Love Old Men.* New York: William B. Eerdmans Publ., 1990.

———. *A Multitude of Sins.* Grand Rapids: Baker Publishing, 1993.

Paredez, Deborah. "Tia Maria." In *Daughters of the Fifth Sun: A Collection of Latina Fiction and Poetry.* Edited by Bryce Milligan, Angela De Hoyos, and Mary Guerrero-Milligan. New York: Putnam, 1995, pp. 98–102.

———. In *This Promiscuous Light: Young Women Poets of San Antonio.* Edited by Bryce Milligan. San Antonio: Wings Press, 1996, pp. 89–106.

Parks, Annabel. *Big Texas: Centennial Poems.* Dallas: Kaleidograph Press, 1935.

———. *Texas Marches On.* Lancaster, Tex.: Lancaster Printing, 193[?].

Parsons, Lucy. *Life of Albert R. Parsons, with Brief History of the Labor Movement in America.* Chicago: Privately published, 1903.

Secondary Sources (Parsons, Lucy)

Ashbaugh, Carolyn. *Lucy Parsons: American Revolutionary.* Chicago: Charles Herr for the Illinois Labor History Society, 1976.

Paschal, Nancy [Grace Trotter]. *Clover Creek.* New York: Nelson, 1946.

———. *Magnolia Heights.* New York: Nelson, 1947.

———. *Make Way for Lauren.* Philadelphia: The Westminster Press, 1963.

———. *Promise of June.* New York: T. Nelson, 1955.

———. *Sylvan City.* New York: Viking, 1950.

Pate, J' Nell L. *Livestock Legacy: The Fort Worth Stockyards.* College Station: Texas A&M Univ. Press, 1988.

———. *North of the River: A Brief History of Ft. Worth.* Ft. Worth: Texas Christian Univ. Press, 1994.

Patterson, Norma. *Drums of the Night.* New York: Farrar and Rinehart, 1935.

———. *The Gay Procession.* New York: Farrar and Rinehart, 1930.

———. *Give Them Their Dreams.* New York: Farrar and Rinehart, 1938.

———. *Jenny.* New York: Farrar and Rinehart, 1930.

———. *Love is Forever.* Farrar and Rinehart, 1941.

———. *The Man I Love.* New York: Farrar and Rinehart, 1940.

———. *Out of the Ground.* New York: Farrar and Rinehart, 1937

———. *The Sun Shines Bright.* New York: Farrar and Rinehart, 1932.

———. *Try and Hold Me.* New York: Farrar and Rinehart, 1937.

———. *West of the Weather.* New York: Farrar and Rinehart, 1941.

———. *When the Lights Go up Again.* New York: Farrar and Rinehart, 1943.

Pattie, Jane. *Cowboy Spurs and Their Makers.* College Station: Texas A&M Univ. Press, 1991.

———, and Wayne Ingram. *Jasbo.* San Antonio: Naylor, 1959.

Paul, Paula. *Sarah, Sissy Weed and the Ships of the Desert.* Austin: Eakin, 1985.

Paulissen, May Nelson, and Carl McQueary. *Ma's in the Kitchen: You'll Know When It's Done. The Recipes and History of Governor Miriam A. Ferguson, First Woman Governor of Texas.* Austin: Eakin, 1994.

———, and Carl McQueary. *Miriam: The Southern Belle Who Became the First Woman Governor of Texas.* Austin: Eakin, 1995.

[Pease, Lucadia]. *Lucadia Pease and the Governor: Letters, 1850–1857.* Edited by Katherine Hart and Elizabeth Kemp. Austin: Encino Press, 1974.

Peery, Janet. *Alligator Dance.* Dallas: Southern Methodist Univ. Press, 1993.

Pennybacker, Anna J. Hardwick. *A New History of Texas for Schools.* Tyler, Tex: for the author, 1888. Reprinted in numerous editions.

Secondary Sources (Pennybacker, Anna J. Hardwick)

Richmond, Rebecca. *A Woman of Texas: Mrs. Percy V. Pennybacker.* San Antonio: Naylor, 1941.

Periwinkle, Pauline. *See:* Miner, Sara Isadore

Petroski, Catherine. "Beautiful My Mane in the Wind." *Prize Stories: Texas Institute of Letters.* Edited by Marshall Terry. Dallas: Still Point Press, 1986, pp. 118–24.

Pickrell, Annie Doom. *Pioneer Women in Texas.* Austin, Tex., and New York: Steck Co., 1929. Reprint, Austin: Jenkins Publishing Co., The Pemberton Press, 1970.

Pierce, Evelyn Miller. *See:* Crowell, Evelyn Miller Pierce

Pinckney, Susanna Shubrick [Miss McPherson]. *Darcy Pinckney.* New York: Neale Publishing Co., 1906.

———. *Douglas: Tender and True.* St. Louis: Nixon-Jones Printing Co., 1892.

———. *In the Southland.* New York: Neale Publishing Co., 1906.

Secondary Sources (Pinckney, Susanna Shubrick)

Sonnichsen, C. L. "The Private World of Miss Sue Pinckney." From *Hopalong to Hud: Thoughts on Western Fiction.* College Station: Texas A&M Univ. Press., 1978, pp. 129–42.

Pinson, Hermine. *Ashe.* Houston: Wings Press, 1992.

Pirie, Emma Elizabeth. *Science of Home Making.* N. p., 1915.

———. *A Sewing Course.* N. p., 1906.

Plummer, Rachael. *Rachael Plummer's Narrative of Twenty-One Months Servitude as a Prisoner among the Comanchee Indians.* New York: Perry and Cooke, 1838. Reprint, Austin: Jenkins Co., 1977.

Ponton, Bonnie, and Bates H. McFarland. "Alvar Nuñez Cabeza de Vaca: A Preliminary Report on His Wanderings in Texas." *Quarterly of the Texas State Historical Association* 1 (1898): 166–86.

Pollentier, Nicole. "For Ryan, Thanks for the Offer." In *Daughters of the Fifth Sun: A Collection of Latina Fiction and Poetry.* Edited by Bryce Milligan, Angela De Hoyos, and Mary Guerrero-Milligan. New York: Putnam, 1995, pp. 115–16.

———. In *This Promiscuous Light: Young Women Poets of San Antonio.* Edited by Bryce Milligan. San Antonio: Wings Press, 1996, pp. 107–22.

Porter, Katherine Anne. *The Collected Essays and Occasional Writings of Katherine Anne Porter.* New York: Delacorte, 1970.

———. *The Collected Stories of Katherine Anne Porter.* New York: Harcourt, Brace and World, 1965.

———. *The Days Before.* New York: Harcourt, Brace, 1952.

———. *Flowering Judas.* New York: Harcourt, Brace, 1930.

———. *Hacienda.* New York: Harrison, 1934.

———. *Katherine Anne Porter's French Song Book.* Paris: Harrison, 1933.

———. *The Leaning Tower and Other Stories.* New York: Harcourt, Brace, 1944.

———. *Letters of Katherine Anne Porter.* Edited by Isabel Bayler. New York: Atlantic Monthly Press, 1990.

———. *The Never-Ending Wrong.* Boston: Little, Brown, 1977.

———. *Noon Wine.* Detroit: Schuman's 1937.

———. *Pale Horse, Pale Rider: Three Short Novels.* New York: Harcourt, Brace, 1939.

———. *Ship of Fools.* Boston: Little, Brown, 1962.

———. *"This Strange Old World" and Other Book Reviews.* Edited by Darlene Harbour Unrue. Athens: Univ. of Georgia Press, 1991.

———. *Uncollected Early Prose of Katherine Anne Porter.* Edited by Thomas F. Walsh and Ruth M. Alvarez. Austin: Univ. of Texas Press, 1993.

Secondary Sources (Porter, Katherine Anne)

Barnes, Daniel R. and Madeline T. Barnes. "The Secret Sin of Granny Weatherall." *Renascence* 21 (1969): 162–65.

Cheatham, George. "Face and Redemption in Pale Horse, Pale Rider." *Renascence* 39, no. 3 (Spring, 1987): 396–405.

Clark, Bedford and Clinton Machann, eds. *Katherine Anne Porter and Texas: An Uneasy Relationship.* College Station: Texas A&M Univ. Press, 1990.

DeMouy, Jane Krause. *Katherine Anne Porter's Women: The Eye of Her Fiction.* Austin: Univ. of Texas Press, 1983.

Emmons, Winfred J. *Katherine Anne Porter: The Regional Stories.* Southwest Writers Series, no. 6. Austin: Steck-Vaughn, 1967.

Fetterley, Judith. "The Struggle for Authenticity: Growing Up Female in The Old Order." *Kate Chopin Newsletter* 2 (1976): 11–19.

Flanders, Jane. "Katherine Anne Porter and the Ordeal of Southern Womanhood." *Southern Literary Journal* 9 (1976): 47–60.

Gardiner, Judith Kegan. "'The Grave', 'On Not Shooting Sitting Birds', and the Female Esthetic." *Studies in Short Fiction* 20 (1983): 265–70.

Givner, Joan. *Katherine Anne Porter: A Life*. New York: Simon and Schuster, 1982. Reprint, Athens: Univ. of Georgia Press, 1991.

Hardy, John E. *Katherine Anne Porter*. New York: Fredrick Ungar, 1973.

Hendrick, George. *Katherine Anne Porter*. New York: Twayne, 1965. Reprint, New York: Twayne, 1988.

Hilt, Kathryn, and Ruth M. Alvarez. *Katherine Anne Porter: An Annotated Bibliography*. New York: Garland Press, 1990.

Jones, Suzanne W. "Reading the Endings in Katherine Anne Porter's 'Old Mortality.'" *Southern Quarterly* 31 (1993): 29–44.

Liberman, M. M. *Katherine Anne Porter's Fiction*. Detroit: Wayne State Univ. Press, 1971.

Lopez, Enrique Hank. *Conversations with Katherine Anne Porter: Refugee from Indian Creek*. New York: Little, Brown, 1981.

Mooney, Harry John, Jr. *The Fiction and Criticism of Katherine Ann Porter*. Pittsburgh: Univ. of Pittsburgh Press, 1957. Revised, 1962.

Nance, William L. *Katherine Anne Porter and the Art of Rejection*. Chapel Hill: Univ. of North Carolina Press, 1964.

Prater, William. "'The Grave': Form and Symbol." *Studies in Short Fiction* 6 (1969): 336–38.

Schwartz, Edward Greenfield. "The Fictions of Memory." *Southwest Review* 45 (1960): 204–15.

Stout, Janis P. *Katherine Anne Porter: A Sense of the Times*. Charlottesville: Univ. Press of Virginia, 1995.

———. "Miranda's Guarded Speech: Porter and the Problem of Truth-Telling." *Philological Quarterly* 66 (1987): 259–78.

———. "Mr. Hatch's Volubility and Miss Porter's Reserve." *Essays in Literature* 12 (1985): 285–93.

———. *Strategies of Reticence: Silence and Meaning in the Works of Jane Austen, Willa Cather, Katherine Anne Porter, and Joan Didion*. Charlottesville: Univ. Press of Virginia, 1990.

Tanner, James T. F. *The Texas Legacy of Katherine Anne Porter*. Denton: Univ. of North Texas Press, 1991.

Thomas, M. Wynn. "Strangers in a Strange Land: A Reading of 'Noon Wine.'" *American Literature* 47 (1975): 230–46.

Titus, Mary. "Mingled Sweetness and Corruption: 'The Fig Tree' and 'The Grave.'" *South Atlantic Review* 53 (1988): 111–25.

Unrue, Darlene Harbour. *Katherine Anne Porter's Poetry*. Columbia: Univ. of South Carolina Press, 1996.

———. *Truth and Vision in Katherine Anne Porter's Fiction.* Athens: Univ. of Georgia Press, 1985.

———. *Understanding Katherine Anne Porter.* Columbia: Univ. of South Carolina Press, 1988.

Walsh, Thomas F. *Katherine Anne Porter and Mexico: The Illusion of Eden.* Austin: Univ. of Texas Press, 1992.

———. "Miranda's Ghost in 'Old Mortality.'" *College Literature* 6 (1979): 57–63.

Warren, Robert Penn, ed. *Katherine Anne Porter: A Collection of Critical Essays.* Englewood Cliffs, N.J.: Prentice-Hall, 1979.

West, Ray B. *Katherine Anne Porter.* Minneapolis: Univ. of Minnesota Press, 1963.

Youngblood, Sarah. "Structure and Imagery in Katherine Anne Porter's 'Pale Horse, Pale Rider.'" *Modern Fiction Studies* 5 (1959): 344–52.

Portillo, Estela. *See:* Trambley, Estela Portillo

Prather, Patricia Smith, and Jane Clements Monday. *From Slave to Statesman: The Legacy of Joshua Houston, Servant to Sam Houston.* Denton: Univ. of North Texas Press, 1993.

Pryor, LaRita Booth. *The African-American Writer's Digest: How and Where to Sell What You Write.* Austin: Princess Press, 1994.

Rabb, Mary Crownover. *Travels and Adventures in Texas in the 1820s: Being the Reminiscences of Mary Crownover Rabb.* Waco: W. M. Morrison, 1962.

Ragsdale, Crystal Sasse, ed. *The Golden Free Land: The Reminiscences and Letters of Women on an American Frontier.* Austin: Landmark Press, 1976.

———. *Women and Children of the Alamo.* Austin: State House Press, 1994.

———. See also under: Crawford, Ann Fears

Ramirez, Sara Estela

Secondary Sources

Hernandez, Inés. "Sara Estela Ramírez: The Early Twentieth Century Texas Mexican Poet." Ph.D. diss., University of Houston, 1984.

Rankin, Melinda. *Texas in 1850.* Boston: Damrell and Moore, 1850. Reprint, Waco: Texian Press, 1966.

———. *Twenty Years among the Mexicans: A Narrative of Missionary Labor.* Cincinnati: Chase and Hall, 1875.

Ratchford, Fannie Elizabeth. *The Brontes' Web of Childhood.* New York: Russell and Russell, 1941.

———, ed. *L'Heroine du Texas.* By "F__n, M. G__n." Translated by Donald Joseph. Dallas: The Book Club of Texas, 1937.

———, ed. *The Story of Champ d'Asile.* Dallas: Book Club of Texas, 1937. Reprint, Austin: Steck-Vaughn, 1969.

———. *Swinburne at Work.* Sewanee, Tenn.: Univ. Press of Sewanee, 1923.

Raymond, Dora Neill. *British Policy and Opinion During the Franco-Prussian War.*

New York: Columbia Univ. Press/Columbia Studies in the Social Sciences, 1921.

———. *Captain Lee Hall of Texas*. Norman: Univ. of Oklahoma Press, 1940. Reprint, Norman: Univ. of Oklahoma Press, 1982.

———. *Oliver's Secretary: John Milton in an Era of Revolt*. New York: Minton, Balch, 1932.

Rigler, Judyth, and Lewis Rigler [primary au.]. *In the Line of Duty: Reflections of a Texas Ranger Private*. Houston: Larksdale, 1984. Reprint, Denton: Univ. of North Texas Press, 1995.

Roach, Joyce Gibson. *C. L. Sonnichsen*. Boise: Boise State University Western Writers Series, no. 40, 1979.

———. *The Cowgirls*. Houston: Cordovan Corporation, 1977. Reprint, Fort Worth: Texas Christian Univ. Press, 1990.

———, ed. *This Place of Memory: A Texas Perspective*. Denton: Univ. of North Texas Press, 1992.

———. *See also under:* Alter, Judy; Sewell, Ernestine

Roberts, Lou Conway. *Mrs. D. W. Roberts, A Woman's Reminiscences of Six Years in Camp with the Texas Rangers*. Austin: Von Boeckman-Jones, 1928.

Roberts, Madge Thornall. *Star of Destiny, the Private Life of Sam and Margaret Houston*. Denton: Univ. of North Texas Press, 1993.

Robinson, Dorothy Redus. *The Bell Rings at Four: A Black Teacher's Chronicle of Change*. Austin: Madrona Press, 1978.

Robison, Mary. *An Amateur's Guide to the Night: Stories*. New York: Knopf, 1983.

———. *Believe Then: Stories*. New York: Knopf, 1988.

———. *Subtraction*. New York: Knopf, 1991.

Rodenberger, Lou I I. "The Creative Woman in the Works of Southwestern Women Writers." *Southwestern American Literature* 13 (Spring, 1987): 13–30.

———, ed. *Her Work: Stories by Texas Women*. Bryan, Tex.: Shearer Publishing, 1982.

———. *Jane Gilmore Rushing*. Boise, Idaho: Boise State University Western Writers Series, no. 118, 1995.

———. "Presidential Address: Texas Women Writers and Their 'Usable Past.'" *West Texas Historical Association Yearbook* 62 (1996): 201–208.

———. "Texas Women Writers and Their Work: No Longer 'Lady Business,'" *Texas Libraries* 45 (Fall, 1984): 124–28.

———. "Women as Literary Participants in Contemporary Events." In *Women and Texas History: Selected Essays*. Edited by Fane Downs and Nancy Baker Jones. Austin: Texas State Historical Association, 1993, pp. 158–67.

———. *See also under:* Grider, Sylvia Ann

Rogers, Del Marie. *Breaking Free*. Tucson: Ironwood Press, 1977.

———. *Close to the Ground*. San Antonio: Corona Publishing Co., 1990.

———, and Gerald Sewell. *The Story of Texas Public Lands: A Unique Heritage*. Austin: Texas General Land Office, 1973.

Rogers, Mary Beth. *Cold Anger: A Story of Faith and Power Politics*. Denton: Univ. of North Texas Press, 1990.

———. *Texas Women: A Celebration of History*. Austin: Texas Foundation for Women's Resources, 1981.

————, Sherry Smith, and Janelle Scott. *We Can Fly: Stories of Katherine Stinson and Other Gutsy Texas Women.* Austin: Ellen C. Temple/Texas Foundation for Women's Resources, 1983.

Rogers, Pattiann. *The Ark River Review: Three Poet Issue.* N. p.: Ark River Review, 1981.

————. *The Expectations of Light.* Princeton, N. J.: Princeton Univ. Press, 1981.

————. *Firekeeper, New and Selected Poems.* Minneapolis, Min.: Milkweed Editions, 1994.

————. *Geocentric.* Salt Lake City: Gibbs Smith Pub., 1993.

————. *Legendary Performance.* Memphis, Tenn.: Ion Books, 1987.

————. *Lies and Devotions.* Berkeley, Calif.: Tangram Press, 1994.

————. *The Only Holy Window.* Denton, Tex.: Trilobite Press, 1984.

————. *Splitting and Binding.* Middletown, Conn.: Wesleyan Univ. Press, 1989.

————. *The Tattooed Lady in the Garden.* Middletown, Conn.: Wesleyan Univ. Press, 1986.

Secondary Sources (Rogers, Pattiann)

McCann, Richard. "An Interview with Pattiann Rogers." *The Iowa Review* 17 (1987): 25–42.

Seale, Jan Upton. "Interview with Pattiann Rogers." *Concho River Review* 5 (1991): 59–65.

Rohde, Mary. "Ladybug, Ladybug, Fly Away Home." *Texas Plays.* Edited by William B. Martin. Dallas: Southern Methodist Univ. Press, 1990, pp. 353–406.

Rojas-Urista, Xelina. *Ku: poemas de Xelina.* La Jolla, Calif.: Maize Press, 1977.

————, ed. *Southwest Tales: A Contemporary Collection.* Colorado Springs, Colo.: Maize Press, 1986.

Rushing, Jane Gilmore. *Against the Moon.* Garden City, N.Y.: Doubleday and Co., 1968. Reprint, Ft. Worth: Texas Christian Univ. Press, 1991.

————. "Against the Moon." *Virginia Quarterly Review* 37 (1961): 376–90.

————. *Covenant of Grace.* Garden City, N.Y.: Doubleday and Co., 1982.

————. "The Grandmother of West Texas." *Texas Women: The Myth, The Reality.* Edited by Joyce Thompson. Denton, Tex.: Texas Woman's Univ. Press, 1985, pp. 39–45.

————. *Mary Dove: A Love Story.* Garden City, N.Y.: Doubleday and Co., 1974.

————. "People and Place." *Writer* 82 (September, 1969): 9–12.

————. *The Raincrow.* Garden City, N.Y.: Doubleday and Co., 1977.

————. "Roots of a Novel." *Writer* 88 (July, 1975): 9–11.

————. "Setting in the Historical Novel." *Writer* 97 (September, 1984): 13–15.

————. *Starting from Pyron.* Lubbock: Texas Tech Univ. Press, 1992.

————. *Tamzen.* Garden City, N.Y.: Doubleday and Co., 1972.

————. *Walnut Grove.* Garden City, N.Y.: Doubleday and Co., 1964.

————. *Winds of Blame.* Garden City, N.Y.: Doubleday and Co., 1983.

————, and Kline A. Nall. *Evolution of a University: Texas Tech's First Fifty Years.* Austin: Madrona Press, 1975.

Secondary Sources (Rushing, Jane Gilmore)

Bennett, Patrick. "Jane Rushing: Mixing Religion, Writing." *Dallas Morning News,* February 14, 1982, G5.

Jones, Daryl. "Afterword." In *Starting from Pyron.* Lubbock: Texas Tech Univ. Press, 1993, pp. 147–53.

Key, Cheryl. "Jane Gilmore Rushing: Social Historian of West Texas." Master's thesis, Angelo State University, 1988.

Richardson, Hazel. "West Texas Sets Stage for Rushing's Fiction." *The Bryan (Tex.) Eagle,* September 25, 1977.

Rodenberger, Lou H. *Jane Gilmore Rushing.* Boise, Idaho: Boise State University Western Writers Series, no. 118, 1995.

Sandlin, Lisa. *The Famous Thing about Death.* El Paso: Cinco Puntos Press, 1991.

Sanford, Annette. *Lasting Attachments.* Dallas: Southern Methodist Univ. Press, 1989.

Sanford, Winifred M. *Windfall and Other Stories.* Dallas: Sanford, 1980. Reprint, Dallas: Southern Methodist Univ. Press, 1988.

Secondary Sources (Sanford, Winifred M.)

Rodenberger, Lou Halsell. "Afterword." In *Windfall and Other Stories.* Dallas: Southern Methodist Univ. Press, 1989, pp. 173–79.

Wiesepape, Betty Holland. "Winifred Sanford: Her Life and Times." Master's thesis, University of Texas at Dallas, 1991.

Santos, E. D. *Mesquite Sighs.* Hondo, Tex.: La Sombra, 1991.

———. *On the Road Too.* Hondo, Tex.: La Sombra, 1988.

Sayers, Frances Clarke. *Anne Carroll Moore: A Biography.* New York: Atheneum, 1972.

———. *Bluebonnets for Lucinda.* New York: Viking, 1934.

———. *Ginny and Custard.* New York: Viking Press, 1951.

———. *Mr. Tidy Claws.* New York: Viking Press, 1935.

———. *Oscar Lincoln Busby Stokes.* New York: Harcourt, Brace and World, 1970.

———. *Sally Tait.* New York: Viking, 1948.

———. *Summoned by Books: Essays and Speeches by Frances Clarke Sayers.* New York: Viking Press, 1965.

———. *Tag-Along-Tooloo.* New York: Viking, 1941.

———, et al. *Anthology of Children's Literature.* Boston: Houghton Mifflin, 1970.

Scarborough, Dorothy. "The 'Blues' as Folksongs." *Publications of the Texas Folklore Society* 2 (1923): 52–66.

———. *Can't Get a Redbird.* New York: Harper and Brothers, 1929. Reprint, New York: AMS Press/The Labor Movement in Fiction and Non-Fiction, 1977.

———, ed. *Famous Modern Ghost Stories.* New York: G. P. Putnam's Sons/The Knickerbocker Press, 1919.

———. *From a Southern Porch.* New York: G. P. Putnam's Sons/The Knickerbocker Press, 1919.

———. *Fugitive Verses.* Waco: Baylor Univ. Press, 1912.

————, ed. *Humorous Ghost Stories.* New York: G. P. Putnam's Sons. 1921. Reprint, Folcraft, Pa.: Folcraft Library Editions, n.d.

————. *Impatient Griselda.* New York: Harper and Brothers, 1927.

————. *In the Land of Cotton.* New York: The Macmillan Co., 1923.

————. "Karle Wilson Baker." In *The Library of Southern Literature.* Atlanta: Martin and Hay Co., 1923, pp. 47–52.

————. "Negro Folklore." *Encyclopaedia Britannica.* Vol. 16. Chicago: Encyclopaedia, Inc., 1937, p. 200.

————. *On the Trail of Negro Folksong.* Cambridge: Harvard Univ. Press, 1925. Reprint, with a foreword by Roger Abrahams, Hatboro, Pa.: Folklore Associates, 1963.

————, ed. *Selected Short Stories for Today.* New York: Farrar and Rinehart, 1935.

————. *A Song Catcher in Southern Mountains: American Folksongs of British Ancestry.* New York: Columbia Univ. Press, 1937. Reprint, New York: AMS Press, 1966.

————. *The Stretch-Berry Smile.* Indianapolis: Bobbs-Merrill, 1932.

————. *The Story of Cotton.* New York: Harper and Brothers/City and Country Series, 1933.

————. *The Supernatural in Modern English Fiction.* New York: G. P. Putnam's Sons, 1917. Reprint, New York: Octagon Books/Farrar Straus and Giroux, 1967.

————. "Traditions of the Waco Indians." *Publications of the Texas Folklore Society* 1 (1916): 50–54.

————. *The Unfair Sex.* Serialized in *The Women's Viewpoint,* 1925–26.

————. *The Wind.* New York: Harper and Brothers, 1925. Reprint, Austin: Univ. of Texas Press, 1979.

Secondary Sources (Scarborough, Dorothy)

Abrahams, Roger. "Foreword." In *On the Trail of Negro Folksong.* By Dorothy Scarborough. Hatboro, Pa.: Folklore Associates, 1963, pp. i–ix.

Beard, Joyce Juanita. "Dorothy Scarborough: Texas Regionalist." Master's thesis, Texas Christian University, 1965.

Cranfill, Mabel. "Dorothy Scarborough." *Texas Monthly* 4 (1929): 212–27.

Crawford, Anne Fears, and Crystal Sasse Ragsdale. "I Have Books I Must Write: Dorothy Scarborough." In *Women in Texas: Their Lives, Their Experiences, Their Accomplishments.* Edited by Ann Fears Crawford and Crystal Sasse Ragsdale. Austin: Eakin Press, 1982, pp. 235–47.

Dixon, Arline Harris. "The Development of the Novel: Lectures of Dorothy Scarborough." Master's thesis, Baylor University, 1943.

Grider, Sylvia Ann. "The Folksong Scholarship of Dorothy Scarborough." *Publications of the Texas Folklore Society* 49 (1990): 97–103.

————. "Mythic Elements in The Wind." In *Texas Women: The Myth, The Reality.* Edited by Joyce Thompson. Denton: Texas Woman's Univ. Press, 1987, pp. 29–34.

————. "The Showdown Between Dorothy Scarborough and Judge R. C. Crane." *West Texas Historical Association Yearbook* 62 (1986): 5–13.

Heavens, Jean Earl. "Dorothy Scarborough: Fictional Historian." Master's thesis, University of Texas at El Paso, 1968.

Johnson, Ellen L. "The Unpublished Mountain Folk-Songs Collected by Dorothy Scarborough." Master's thesis, Baylor University, 1941.

Leake, Grace Hillary. "Dorothy Scarborough: A Splendid Southerner." *Hollands: The Magazine of the South* 47 (1928): 5, 63, 65.

Maxwell, Mary Rebecca. "Short Story Lectures of Dorothy Scarborough." Master's thesis, Baylor University, 1942.

Middlebrook, Anne. "Dorothy Scarborough's Lectures on the Technique of the Novel." Master's thesis, Baylor University, 1943.

Muncy, Elizabeth Roberta. "Dorthy Scarborough: A Literary Pioneer." Master's thesis, Baylor University, 1940.

Neatherlin, James. "Dorothy Scarborough: Form and Milieu in the Works of a Texas Writer." Ph. D. diss., University of Iowa, 1973.

Palmer, Pamela. "Dorothy Scarborough and Karle Wilson Baker: A Literary Friendship." *Southwest Historical Quarterly* 91 (July, 1987): 19–32.

Quissell, Barbara. "Dorothy Scarborough's Critique of the Frontier Experience in The Wind." In *Women, Women Writers, and the West.* Edited by L. L. Lee and Merrill Lewis. Troy, N.Y.: Whitson Publishing Co., 1979, pp. 173–95.

Scarborough, Sheree. "Feminism in the Life and Work of Emily Dorothy Scarborough." Master's thesis, University of Texas at Austin, 1984.

Slade, Carole. "Authorship and Authority in Dorothy Scarborough's The Wind." *Studies in American Fiction* 14 (1986): 85–91.

Swadley, Don R. "She Never Left Home: Notes on Dorothy Scarborough's Fiction." *English in Texas* 13 (1981): 11–13.

Trantham, Carrie P. "An Investigation of the Unpublished Negro Folk-Songs of Dorothy Scarborough." Master's thesis, Baylor University, 1941.

Truett, Luther J. "The Negro Element in the Life and Work of Dorothy Scarborough." Master's thesis, Baylor University, 1967.

Whitcomb, Virginia Roland. "Dorothy Scarborough: Bibliography and Criticism." Masters thesis, Baylor University, 1945.

Scofield, Sandra. *Beyond Deserving.* Sag Harbor, N.Y.: The Permanent Press, 1991.
————. *A Chance to See Egypt.* New York: HarperCollins, 1996.
————. *Gringa.* Sag Harbor, N.Y.: The Permanent Press, 1989.
————. *More than Allies.* Sag Harbor, N.Y.: Permanent Press, 1993.
————. *Opal on Dry Ground.* New York: Villard Books of Random House, 1994.
————. *Walking Dunes.* Sag Harbor, N.Y.: The Permanent Press, 1992.

Schofield, Susan Clark. *Refugio, They Named You Wrong.* Chapel Hill: Algonquin Books, 1991.

Scott, Bess Whitehead. *You Meet Such Interesting People.* College Station: Texas A&M Univ. Press, 1989.

Seale, Jan Epton. *Airlift*. Fort Worth: Texas Christian Univ. Press, 1992.

———. *Bonds*. 2nd ed. McAllen, Tex.: RiverSedge Press, 1981.

———. *Homeland: Essays beside and beyond the Rio Grande*. Edinburg, Tex.: New Santander Press, 1995.

———. *A Quartet: Texas Poets in Concert*. Denton: Univ. of North Texas Press, 1990.

———. *Sharing the House: Poems by Jan Epton Seale; Illustrations by Carolyn Cammack Seale*. McAllen, Tex.: RiverSedge Press, 1982.

———. *Texas History Classroom Plays: Intermediate*. McAllen, Tex.: Knowing Press, 1986.

———, and Alfonso Ramírez, eds. *¡Tomates, California!* Boston: Houghton-Mifflin, 1993.

Sebestyen, Ouida. *Far from Home*. Boston: Little, 1980.

———. *Out of Nowhere*. New York: Orchard Books, 1994.

———. *IOU'S*. Boston: Little, 1982.

———. *Words by Heart*. Boston: Little, 1979.

Sewell, Ernestine. "Afterword." In *The Edge of Time*. By Loula Grace Erdman. Fort Worth: Texas Christian Univ. Press, 1989, pp. 276–80.

———. "An Interview with Loula Grace Erdman." *Southwestern American Literature* 2 (1972): 33–42.

———, ed. *Confronting Crisis: Teachers in America*. Arlington: Univ. of Texas at Arlington Press, 1979.

———. *How the Cimmaron River Got Its Name and Other Stories about Coffee*. Plano, Tex.: Republic of Texas Press, 1995.

———. *Loula Grace Erdman*. Southwest Writers Series, no 33. Austin: Steck-Vaughn, 1970.

———, and Joyce Gibson Roach. *Eats: A Folk History of Texas Foods*. Fort Worth: Texas Christian Univ. Press, 1989.

Shange, Ntozake. *Betsy Brown*. New York: St. Martin's Press, 1985.

———. *A Daughter's Geography*. New York: St. Martin's Press, 1983.

———. *For Colored Girls Who Have Considered Suicide, When the Rainbow Is Enuf: A Choreopoem*. New York: Macmillan, 1977.

———. *Liliane: Resurrection of the Daughter*. New York: St. Martin's Press, 1994.

———. *The Love Space Demands*. New York: St. Martin's Press, 1991.

———. *Nappy Edges*. New York: St. Martin's Press, 1978.

———. *Ridin' the Moon in Texas: Word Paintings*. New York: St. Martin's Press, 1987.

———. *Sassafras, Cypress and Indigo*. New York: St. Martin's Press, 1982.

———. *See No Evil: Prefaces, Essays and Accounts, 1976–1983*. San Francisco: Momo's Press, 1984.

———. *Spell Number Seven*. London: Methuen, 1985.

———. *Three Pieces*. New York: St. Martin's Press, 1981.

Shaver, Mrs. Lillie T., [Willie Williamson Rogers (primary au.) with]. *Flashlights on Texas*. Austin: A. C. Baldwin & Sons, 1928.

———. *The House by the Side of the Road*. Austin: Von Boeckmann-Jones, 1912.

Sheehan, Sister M. Agatha. *A Study of the First Four Novels of Texas.* Washington, D.C.: by the author, 1939.

———. *Texas Prose Writings: A Reader's Digest.* Foreword by Leonidas Warren Payne, Jr. Dallas: Banks Upshaw and Co., 1936.

Sheehy, Helen. *Margo: The Life and Theatre of Margo Jones.* Dallas: Southern Methodist Univ. Press, 1989.

Shefelman, Janice Jordan. *A Paradise Called Texas.* Austin: Eakin, 1983.

———. *A Peddler's Dream.* Boston: Houghton Mifflin, 1992.

———. *Spirit of Iron.* Austin: Eakin, 1987.

———. *Willow Creek Home.* Austin: Eakin, 1985.

Shindler, Mary Dana. *A Southerner Among the Spirits: A Record of Investigation into the Spiritual Phenomenon.* Memphis: Southern Baptist Publication Society, 1877.

Shipman, Alice Jack Dolan [Mrs. O. L.]. *Taming the Big Bend: A History of the Extreme Western Portion of Texas from Fort Clark to El Paso.* Austin: Von Boeckmann-Jones Co., 1926.

Shortridge, Belle Hunt. "Texas Thanksgiving." *Gulf Messenger.* Nov., 1892. Reprint, in *Writers and Writings of Texas.* Edited by Davis Foute Eagleton. New York: Broadway Publishing, 1913, pp. 141–47.

Shuler, Linda Lay. *She Who Remembers.* New York: Arbor House/William Morrow, 1988.

Sibley, Marilyn McAdams. *George W. Brackenridge: Maverick Philanthropist.* Austin: Univ. of Texas Press, 1973.

———. *Lone Star and State Gazettes: Texas Newspapers before the Civil War.* College Station: Texas A&M Univ. Press, 1983.

———. *The Methodist Hospital of Houston: Serving the World.* Austin: Texas State Historical Association, 1989.

———. *The Port of Houston: A History.* Austin: Univ. of Texas Press, 1968.

———, ed. *Samuel H. Walker's Account of the Mier Expedition.* Austin: Texas State Historical Association, 1978.

———. *Travelers in Texas, 1761–1860.* Austin: Univ. of Texas Press, 1967.

Silverthorne, Elizabeth. *Ashbel Smith of Texas: Pioneer, Patriot, Statesman.* College Station: Texas A&M Univ. Press, 1982.

———. *Christmas in Texas.* College Station: Texas A&M Univ. Press, 1990.

———. *The Ghost of Padre Island.* Nashville: Abingdon Press, 1975.

———. *I, Heracles.* Nashville: Abingdon Press, 1975.

———. *Legends and Lore of Texas Wildflowers.* College Station: Texas A&M Univ. Press, 1996.

———. *Marjorie Kinnan Rawlins: Sojourner at Cross Creek.* Woodstock, N.Y.: Overlook Press, 1988.

———. *Plantation Life in Texas.* College Station: Texas A&M Univ. Press, 1986.

———. *Sarah Orne Jewett: A Writer's Life.* Woodstock, N.Y.: Overlook Press, 1993.

———, and Mary D. Farrell. *First Ladies of Texas: The First One Hundred Years, A History.* Belton, Tex.: Stillhouse Hollow Pub., 1976.

Simond, Ada DeBlanc. "The Discovery of Being Black: A Recollection." *Southwestern Historical Quarterly* 76 (April 1973): 440–47.

———. *Let's Pretend: Mae Dee and Her Family and the First Wedding of the Year.* Austin: Stevenson Press, 1979.

———. *Let's Pretend: Mae Dee and Her Family Go to Town.* Austin: Stevenson Press, 1977.

———. *Let's Pretend: Mae Dee and Her Family in the Merry, Merry Season.* Austin: Stevenson Press, 1978.

———. *Let's Pretend: Mae Dee and Her Family Join the Juneteenth Celebration.* Austin: Stevenson Press, 1978.

———. *Let's Pretend: Mae Dee and Her Family on a Weekend in May.* Austin: Stevenson Press, 1977.

———. *Let's Pretend: Mae Dee and Her Family Ten Years Later.* Austin: Stevenson Press, 1980.

Sinks, Julia Lee. *Chronicles of Fayette: The Reminiscences of Julia Lee Sinks.* Edited by Walter P. Freytag. LaGrange, Tex.: LaGrange Bicentennial Commission, 1975.

———. "Editors and Newspapers of Fayette County." *Quarterly of the Texas State Historical Association* 1 (1897): 35–37.

———. *Heroes of Texas: Jesse Burnam.* Houston: The Union National Bank, 193[?].

Sizemore, Deborah Lightfoot. *A Century in the Works: Freese and Nichols Consulting Engineers, 1894–1994.* College Station: Texas A&M Univ. Press, 1994.

———. *The LH7 Ranch: In Houston's Shadow.* Denton: Univ. of North Texas Press, 1991.

Slayden, Ellen Maury. *Washington Wife: Journal of Ellen Maury Slayden from 1897–1919.* Edited by Walter P. Webb and Terrell Maverick Webb. New York: Harper and Row, 1962.

Smith, Goldie Capers. *The Creative Arts in Texas: A Handbook of Biography.* Nashville and Dallas: Cokesbury Press, 1926.

Smith, Rebecca W. "Finding Folk-Lorists." *Publications of the Texas Folklore Society* 8 (1930): 155–59.

———. *"Following the Lone Star": A Pageant of Texas Independence, Written for the School Children of Texas.* Fort Worth: n.p., 1924.

———. *See:* Lee, Rebecca Smith; Major, Mabel; *and under General listing:* Duval, John C.

Spell, Lota Mae. *Music in Texas: A Survey of One Aspect of Cultural Progress.* Austin: n.p., 1936. Reprint, New York: AMS Press, 1973.

St. Germain, Sheryl. *Going Home.* Van Nuys, Calif.: Perivale Press, 1989.

———. *How Heavy the Breath of God.* Denton: Univ. of North Texas Press, 1994.

———. *Making Bread at Midnight.* Austin: Slough Press, 1992.

———. *The Mask of Medusa.* Merrick, N.Y.: Cross-Cultural Communications, 1987.

Stanley, Diane. *Bard of Avon: The Story of William Shakespeare.* New York: Morrow Junior Books, 1992.

———. *Birdsong Lullaby: Story and Pictures.* New York: Morrow, 1985.

———. *Captain Whiz-Bang.* New York: W. Morrow, 1987.

———. *Cleopatra.* New York: Morrow Junior Books, 1994.

———. *The Conversation Club.* New York: Macmillan, 1983.

———. *A Country Tale.* New York: Macmillan, 1985.

———. *The Good Luck Pencil*. New York: Four Winds Press, 1986.

———. *The Good Queen Bess: The Story of Elizabeth I of England*. New York: Four Winds Press, 1990.

———. *Half-a-ball-of-kenki: An Ashanti Tale Retold*. New York: F. Warne, 1979.

———. *Peter the Great*. New York: Four Winds Press, 1986.

———. *Petrosinella: A Neopolitan Rapunzel*. New York: Dial Books for Young Readers, 1995.

———. *Shaka: King of the Zulus*. New York: Morrow Junior Books, 1988.

———. *The True Adventure of Daniel Hall*. New York: Dial Books for Young Readers, 1995.

Stevens, Mary Ellen. *Little Cloud and the Great Plains Hunters*. Chicago: Reilly, 1962.

———. *Throw Stone: The First American Boy, 25,000 Years Ago*. Chicago: Reilly, 1960.

Stillwell, Hallie, and Virginia Madison. *How Come It's Called That? Place Names in the Big Bend Country*. Albuquerque: Univ. of New Mexico Press, 1958. Rev. ed., New York: October House, 1968.

———. *I'll Gather My Geese*. College Station: Texas A&M Univ. Press, 1991.

Stone, Alma. *The Banishment, and Three Stories*. Garden City, N.Y.: Doubleday, 1973.

———. *The Bible Salesman*. Garden City, N.Y.: Doubleday, 1962.

———. *The Harvard Tree*. Boston: Houghton Mifflin, 1954.

———. *Now for the Turbulence*. Garden City, N.Y.: Doubleday, 1983.

Storey, Gail Donohue. *God's Country Club*. New York: Persea Books, 1996

———. *The Lord's Motel*. New York: Persea Books, 1992.

Story, Rosalyn M. *And So I Sing: African-American Divas of Opera and Concert*. New York: Warner Books, 1990.

[Storm, Jane McManus]. "Jane McManus Storm: Letters from the Mexican War, 1846–1848." Edited by Tom Reilly. *Southwestern Historical Quarterly* 85 (July, 1981): 21–44.

Stout, Janis P. *Eighteen Holes*. San Antonio: Corona Publishing, 1985.

———. *A Family Likeness*. Austin: Texas Monthly Press, 1982.

———. *Home Truth*. New York: Soho Press, 1992.

———. *The Journey Narration in American Literature: Patterns and Departures*. Westport, Conn.: Greenwood Press, 1983.

———. *Katherine Anne Porter: A Sense of the Times*. Charlottesville: Univ. Press of Virginia, 1995.

———. *Sodoms in Eden: The City in American Fiction Before 1860*. Westport, Conn.: Greenwood Press, 1976.

———. *Strategies of Reticence: Silence and Meaning in the Works of Jane Austen, Willa Cather, Katherine Anne Porter, and Joan Didion*. Charlottesville: Univ. Press of Virginia, 1990.

Stowe, Estha Briscoe. *Oil Field Child*. Fort Worth: Texas Christian Univ. Press, 1989.

Stuart, Dee. *The Astonishing Armadillo*. Minneapolis: Carolrhoda, 1993.

Sullivan, Dulcie. *The L. S. Brand: The Story of a Texas Panhandle Ranch*. Austin: Univ. of Texas Press, 1968.

Swisher, Bella French. *Florecita*. New York: J. B. Alden, 1889.

——, ed. *History of Austin, Travis County, Texas, with a Description of its Resources*. Austin: American Sketch Book Pub. House, 1880.

——. *Rocks and Shoals in the River of Life: A Novel*. New York: G. W. Dillingham (successor to G. W. Careton and Co.), 1889.

——. *The Sin of Edith Dean*. New York: J. B. Alden, 1890.

——. *Struggling up to the Light*. Chicago: W. B. Keen, Cooke and Co., 1876.

Tafolla, Carmen. *Curandera*. San Antonio: M&A Editions, 1983.

——. *Patchwork Colcha*. Flagstaff: Creative Educational Enterprises, 1987.

——. *Sonnets to Human Beings and Other Selected Works*. Edited by Ernesto Padillo. Santa Monica, Calif.: Lalo Press, 1992.

——. *To Split a Human: Mitos, Machos y la Mujer Chicana*. San Antonio: Mexican American Cultural Center, 1984.

Secondary Sources (Tafolla, Carmen)

Ordoñez, Elizabeth J. "The Concept of Cultural Identity in Chicana Poetry." *Third Woman* 2, no. 1 (1984): 75–82.

Taylor, A. Elizabeth. *Citizens At Last: The Women's Suffrage Movement in Texas*. Austin: Ellen C. Temple Publishing, 1987.

Taylor, Bride Neill. *Elisabet Ney, Sculptor*. New York: Devin-Adair Co., 1916.

——. "The Women Writers of Texas." *Galveston Daily News*, June 18, 25, 1893.

Taylor, Pat Ellis. *Afoot in a Field of Men*. Austin: Slough Press, 1983. Reprint, New York: Atlantic Monthly Press, 1988.

——. *Border Healing Woman: The Story of Jewell Babb*. Austin: Univ. of Texas Press, 1981.

——. *The God Chaser: A Spirited Assortment of Tales*. Austin: Slough Press, 1986.

——. *In Search of the Holy Mother of Jobs*. El Paso: Cinco Puntos Press, 1991.

——. *Tonics, Teas, Roots and Remedies: Selected Poems*. Austin: Slough Press, 1982.

Terrell, Kate Scurry. "The 'Runaway Scrape.'" In *A Comprehensive History of Texas, 1685–1897*. Edited by Dudley G. Wooten. Dallas: William G. Scarff, 1989, vol. 1, pp. 651–71. Reprint, Austin: Texas State Historical Association, 1986.

——. "Terry's Texas Rangers." In *A Comprehensive History of Texas, 1685–1897*. Edited by Dudley G. Wooten. Dallas: William G. Scarff, 1989, vol. 2, pp. 682–94. Reprint, Austin: Texas State Historical Association, 1986.

Thompson, Joyce. *Making a Trail: A History of the Texas Woman's University*. Denton: Texas Woman's Univ. Press, 1982.

Tolleson-Rinehart, Sue, and Jeanie R. Stanley. *Claytie and the Lady: Anne Richards, Gender, and Politics of Texas*. Austin: Univ. of Texas Press, 1994.

——. *Gender Consciousness and Politics*. New York: Routledge, 1992.

Tolliver, Ruby C. *Blind Bess, Buddy, and Me*. Dallas: Hendrick-Long, 1990.

——. *Have Gun, Need Bullets*. Ft. Worth: Texas Christian Univ. Press, 1991.

——. *Muddy Banks*. Fort Worth: Texas Christian Univ. Press, 1987.

——. *Santa Anna: Patriot or Scoundrel?* Dallas: Hendrick-Long, 1993.

Trambley, Estela Portillo. "Day of the Swallows." In *Contemporary Chicana Theater*. Edited by Robert J. Garza. Notre Dame: Notre Dame Univ. Press, 1976.

———. *Rain of Scorpions and Other Writings*. Berkeley, Calif.: Tonatiuh-Quinto Sol International, 1975.

———. *Sor Juana and Other Plays*. Ypsilanti, Mich.: Bilingual Press, 1983.

———. *Trini*. Binghamton: Bilingual Press, 1986.

Trotter, Grace. *See:* Paschal, Nancy

Tucker, Dianne. *The Grand and Glorious Dance of Magical Miss Shoes: An Allegory*. Dallas: Dallas Printing and Graphics Center, 1985.

Turner, Martha Anne. *Clara Driscoll: An American Tradition*. Austin: Madrona Press, 1979.

———. *Dan Rather and Other Rough Drafts*. Austin: Eakin Press, 1987.

———. *The Life and Times of Jane Long*. Waco, Tex.: Texian Press, 1969.

———. *Old Nacogdoches in the Jazz Age*. Austin: Madrona Press, 1976.

———. *Richard Bennett Hubbard: An American Life*. Austin: Shoal Creek Publishers, 1979.

———. *Sam Houston and His Twelve Women: The Ladies Who Influenced the Life of Texas' Greatest Statesman*. Austin: Pemberton Press, 1966.

———. *Texas Epic: An American Story*. Quanah, Tex.: Nortex Press, 1974.

———. *White Dawn Salutes Tomorrow*. Philadelphia: Dorrance and Co., 1943.

———. *William Barret Travis: His Sword and His Pen*. Waco, Tex.: Texian Press, 1972.

———. *The World of Colonel John W. Thomason, USMC*. Austin: Eakin Press, 1984.

———. *The Yellow Rose of Texas: Her Saga and Her Song*. Austin: Shoal Creek Publishers, 1976.

Urwitz, Marie Bennett. "Early Days in Texas." *Quarterly of the Texas State Historical Association* 9 (1906): 145–56.

Urista, Xelina. *See:* Rojas-Urista, Xelina

Vander Voort, Jo. *The Wisteria Bush*. New York: Samuel French, 1987.

Vásquez, Enedina Cásarez. *Recuerdos de una niña*. San Antonio: Centro de Comunicación Misioneros Oblatos de María Vasquez, Enedina C., 1980.

Viele, Teresa (Griffin). *"Following the Drum": a Glimpse of Frontier Life*. New York: Rudd and Carleton, 1858. Reprint, Lincoln: Univ. of Nebraska Press, 1984.

Vigil-Piñón, Evangelina. *The Computer Is Down*. Houston: Arte Público Press, 1987.

———. *nade y nade*. San Antonio: M&A Editions, 1978.

———. *Thirty an' Seen a Lot*. Houston: Arte Público Press, 1982.

———, ed. "Woman of Her Word: Hispanic Women Write." Special Issue of *Revísta Chicano-Riqueña* 11, nos. 3–4 (1983).

Secondary Sources (Vigil-Piñón, Evangelina)

Cisneros, Sandra. "Cactus Flowers: In Search of Tejana Feminist Poetry." *Third Woman* 3, nos. 1–2 (1986): 73–80.

Villegas de Magnon, Leonor. *The Rebel*. Edited by Clara Lomas. Houston: Arte Público Press, 1994.

Von Herzen, Lane. *Copper Crown*. New York: William Morrow, 1991.

Waerenskjold, Elise. *The Lady with the Pen.* Edited by C. A. Clausen. Northfield, Minn: Norwegian-American Historical Association, 1961. Reprint, New York: Arno Press, 1979.

Secondary Sources (Waerenskjold, Elise)

Nelson, Estelle O. "A First Lady of Texas." From *Our Church in Texas, Program E of the 1943 Program Series.* Minneapolis: Our Lutheran Heritage, 1943.

Smith, Sherry A. "Elise Waerenskjold: A Modern on the Prairie." In *Legendary Ladies of Texas.* Edited by Francis E. Abernethy. Dallas: E-Heart Press, 1981, pp. 79–82.

Wagner, Shelly. *The Andrew Poems.* Lubbock: Texas Tech Univ. Press, 1994.

Walker, Celeste. *See:* Colson-Walker, Celeste

Walker, Mary Willis. *The Red Scream.* New York: Doubleday, 1994.

———. *Under the Beetle's Collar.* New York: Doubleday, 1995.

———. *Zero at the Bone.* New York: St. Martin's, 1991.

Wall, Judith Henry. *Handsome Women.* New York: Viking, 1990.

———. *Love and Duty.* New York: Viking, 1988.

Warren, Betsy. *The Donkey Sat Down.* Austin: Steck-Vaughn, 1955.

———. *Explorers in Early Texas.* Dallas: Hendrick-Long, 1992.

———. *Indians of Texas.* Dallas: Hendrick-Long, 1981.

———. *Indians Who Lived in Texas.* Austin: Steck, 1970.

———. *Papacito and His Family.* Austin: Steck-Vaughn, 1969.

———. *The Queen Cat.* Austin: Steck-Vaughn, 1972.

———. *Right Foot, Wrong Foot.* Austin: Steck-Vaughn, 1968.

———. *Texas: The 28th State.* Dallas: Hendrick-Long, 1984.

———. *Texas: In Historic Sites and Symbols.* Dallas: Hendrick-Long, 1982.

———. *Twenty Texans: Historic Lives for Young Readers.* Dallas: Hendrick-Long, 1985.

———. *When Texas Belonged to Mexico.* Dallas: Hendrick-Long, 1982.

———. *When Texas Belonged to Spain.* Dallas: Hendrick-Long, 1982.

———. *When Texas Was a Republic.* Dallas: Hendrick-Long, 1983.

———. *Wilderness Walkers: Naturalists in Early Texas.* Dallas: Hendrick-Long, 1987.

Washburn, L. J. *Bandera Pass.* New York: M. Evans and Co., 1899.

Waugh, Julia Nott. *Castro-ville and Henry Castro.* San Antonio: Standard Printing Co., 1934. Reprint, Austin: Nortex Press, 1986.

———. *The Silver Cradle: Las Posadas, Los Pastores, and Other Mexican American Traditions.* 1955. Reprint, Austin: Univ. of Texas Press, 1955.

West, Elizabeth Howard. *Calendar of the Papers of Martin Van Buren.* Washington, D.C.: U.S. Government Printing Office, 1910.

———. *Texas Library Manual.* Austin: Texas State Library, 1924.

Wheaton, Elizabeth Lee. *Mr. George's Joint.* New York: Dutton, 1941.

———. *Texas City Remembers.* San Antonio: Naylor, 1948.

White, Brenda Black. *Callahan County.* Austin: Plain View Press, 1988.

Whitebird, J., and Paul Foreman. *Travois: An Anthology of Texas Poets.* Houston: Contemporary Arts Museum and Thorp Springs Press, 1976.

Whitehead, Ruth. *The Mother Tree.* New York: Seabury, 1971.

Williams, Amelia. "A Critical Study of the Siege of the Alamo and the Personnel of its Defenders." *Southwestern Historical Quarterly* 36 (April, 1933): 251–87; 37 (October, 1933): 79–115; 37 (January, 1934): 157–84; 37 (April, 1934): 237–312.

———. *Following General Sam Houston from 1793–1863.* Austin: Steck, 1935.

Williams, J. R. (Jeanne), ed. *Animal Rights and Welfare.* New York: H. W. Wilson, 1991.

———. *Beasts with Music.* New York: Meredith Press, 1967.

———. *The Confederate Fiddle.* Englewood Cliffs, N.J.: Prentice-Hall, 1962.

———. *Coyote Winter.* New York: Norton, 1965.

———. *Daughter of the Sword.* New York: Pocket Books, 1979.

———. *The Horse Talker.* Englewood Cliffs, N.J.: Prentice-Hall, 1960.

———. *Lady of No Man's Land.* New York: St. Martin's Press, 1988.

———. *New Medicine.* New York: Putnam, 1971. Reprint, Dallas: Hendrick-Long Publishing Co., 1994.

———. *No Roof but Heaven.* New York: St. Martin's Press, 1990.

———. *Tame the Wild Stallion.* Englewood Cliffs, N. J.: Prentice-Hall, 1957. Reprint, Ft. Worth: Texas Christian Univ. Press, 1985.

———. *To Buy a Dream.* New York: Messner, 1958.

———. *Trails of Tears: American Indians Driven from Their Lands.* Dallas: Hendrick-Long, 1992.

———. *Winter Wheat.* New York: Putnam, 1975.

———. *A Woman Clothed in Sun.* New York: Coward, McCann and Geoghegan, 1977.

Secondary Sources (Williams, J. R.)

Alter, Judy. *Jeanne Williams.* Boise, Idaho: Boise State University, Western Writers Series, no. 98, 1991.

Williams, Lorece. [Untitled]. In *Growing Up in Texas: Recollections of Childhood.* By Bertha McKee Dobie, and others. Austin: Encino, 1972, pp. 111–18.

Williams, Lynna. *Things Not Seen and Other Stories.* Boston: Little, Brown and Co., 1992.

Wilson, Augusta Evans. *See:* Evans, Augusta

Wilson, Charlotte. *See:* Baker, Karle Wilson

Windle, Janis Woods. *True Women.* New York: G. P. Putnam's Sons, 1993.

Winegarten, Ruthe. *Black Texas Women: 150 Years of Trial and Triumph.* Austin: Univ. of Texas Press, 1995.

———. *Black Texas Women: A Sourcebook: Documents, Biographies, Time Line.* Austin: Univ. of Texas Press, 1996.

———. *Finder's Guide to Texas Women: A Celebration of History Exhibit Archives.* Denton: Texas Women's University Library, 1984.

———, ed. *I Am Annie Mae: An Extraordinary Woman in Her Own Words.* By Annie Mae Hunt. Austin: Rosegarden Press, 1983. Reprinted as *I Am Annie Mae: An Extraordinary Black Texas Woman in Her Own Words.* Austin: Univ. of Texas Press, 1996.

———, ed. *Texas Women's History Project Bibliography.* Austin: Texas Foundation for Women's Resources, 1980.

———. *Texas Women: A Pictorial History From Indians to Astronauts.* Austin: Eakin Press, 1985.

———, and Cathy Schechter. *Deep in the Heart: The Lives and Legends of Texas Jews.* Austin: Eakin Press, 1990.

Winik, Marion. *Boy Crazy and Other Stories.* Austin: Slough, 1986.

———. *First Comes Love.* New York: Pantheon Books, 1996.

———. *Nonstop.* Austin: Cedar Rock, 1980.

———. *Telling: Confessions, Concessions, and Other Flashes of Light.* New York: Villard, 1994.

Winkler, Mrs. A. V. "Hood's Texas Brigade." In *A Comprehensive History of Texas, 1685–1897.* Edited by Dudley G. Wooten. Dallas: William G. Scarff, 1989, vol. 2, pp. 651–81. Reprint, Austin: Texas State Historical Association, 1986.

Witherspoon, Kathleen. "Jute." In *Three Southwest Plays.* Dallas: Southwest Press, 1942, pp. 253–322. Reprint, Freeport, N.Y.: Books for Libraries Press, 1970.

Wood, Jane Roberts. *Dance a Little Longer.* New York: Delacorte Press, 1993.

———. *A Place Called Sweet Shrub.* New York: Dell/Delacorte, 1990.

———. *The Train to Estelline.* Austin: Ellen Temple Publishing, 1987.

———, Donna Dysart Gormly, and Salllye Schrup, eds. *Out of Dallas: 14 Stories.* Univ. of North Texas Press, 1989.

Woodworth, Maria Beulah. *Acts of the Holy Ghost, or the Life, Work, and Experiences of Mrs. M. B. Woodworth-Etter, Evangelist.* Dallas: n.p., 1912.

Wooten, Mattie Lloyd. *Women Tell the Story of the Southwest.* San Antonio: Naylor, 1940.

Wozencraft, Kim. *Notes from the Country Club.* Boston: Houghton Mifflin Co., 1993.

———. *Rush.* New York: Random House, 1990.

Wright, Charlotte M. *Crazy Horse and Walt Whitman's Hands.* Milwaukee: Red Neck Press, 1993.

Wright, Rosalind. *Rocking.* New York: Harper and Row, 1975.

———. *Veracruz.* New York: Harper and Row, 1986.

Young, Maude J. *Familiar Lessons in Botany with Flora of Texas.* New York: A. S. Barnes and Co., 1873.

———. "Stephen F. Austin, the Father of Texas." In *Writers and Writings of Texas.* Edited by Davis Foute Eagleton. New York: Broadway Co., 1913, pp. 43–50.

CONTRIBUTORS

JUDY ALTER, director of Texas Christian University Press, is an award-winning novelist. A former president of Western Writers of America, she has also written juvenile fiction, short stories, and articles. Her novel *Luke and the Van Zandt County War* received the Texas Institute of Letters award for best juvenile fiction in 1984. In 1988 she received a Spur Award from the Western Writers of America for her novel *Mattie*. The National Cowboy Hall of Fame presented her with a Western Heritage Award for her short story "Fool Girl" in 1992. Her most recent novels are *Libbie,* based on the life of Elizabeth Bacon Custer, and *Jessie,* a fictionalized version of the life of Jessie Benton Fremont.

PATRICK BENNETT teaches English and creative writing at McMurry University in Abilene. He has published short stories and poetry and is the author of *Talking with Texas Writers: Twelve Interviews* and *Rough and Rowdy Ways: The Life and Hard Times of Edward Anderson,* the biography of a depression-era Texas writer. His most recent publication, coedited with his wife, Shay, is *Culture on the Catclaw: A List of Published Books and Produced Dramas by Abilene Authors.*

TANYA LONG BENNETT holds a master's degree in English from Texas A&M University. The title of her thesis, which she completed in 1988, is "The Real Texas: A Study of Carolyn Osborn's Short Stories." A native of West Texas, she earned a Ph.D. in 1996 at the University of Tennessee in Knoxville.

BETSY FEAGAN COLQUITT recently retired as professor of English at

Texas Christian University, where she had edited the literary journal *Descant* for more than thirty years. Her poetry has appeared in numerous literary journals and in several anthologies. *Honor Card,* a collection of her poetry was published in 1980.

PAUL CHRISTENSEN, who teaches English at Texas A&M University, is a poet who also has published critical essays on southwestern literature. He is the founder and editor of Cedarhouse Press.

FANE DOWNS is pastor of Trinity Presbyterian Church in Midland. A former chair of the Department of History at McMurry University, she served as an advisory editor for women's history for the *Handbook of Texas* revision project. She has been a member of the Executive Council of the Texas State Historical Association and of the Editorial Advisory Board of the *Southwestern Historical Quarterly.* She has published articles on Texas history and is coeditor of *Women and Texas History,* a collection of essays on Texas women.

LAURIE DUDLEY holds a B.A. from Baylor University and a master's degree in library science from North Texas State University (now the University of North Texas). A former elementary school teacher and public school librarian, she has served as coordinator of Children's Services at the Dallas Public Library for a number of years. She has reviewed books for the *School Library Journal* and was consultant for the H. W. Wilson *Children's Catalog* for many years. In 1993 she retired as reference and special services librarian at the Abilene Public Library.

BETTY SUE FLOWERS, a professor of English at the University of Texas, has published poetry in such journals as *Rocky Mountain Review, New Letters,* and *Thicket,* as well as in several anthologies. She is editor of *Joseph Campbell and the Power of Myth: Bill Moyers and Joseph Campbell in Conversation* and *A World of Ideas: Conversations with Thoughtful Men and Women about American Life Today and the Ideas Shaping Our Future.* She earned a B.A. and an M.A. at the University of Texas and holds a Ph.D. from the University of London. She has served as associate dean of the University of Texas Graduate School and director of the Plan II program.

SYLVIA GRIDER, whose academic background includes degrees in Latin, history, and archaeology, also holds a Ph.D. in folklore from Indiana University. She is associate professor in the Department of Anthropology at Texas A&M University. A former president of the American Folklore Society, she also has been president of the Texas Folklore Society and has published numerous essays on Texas culture and folklore. Her books include *The Wendish Texans* and a biography in progress of Dorothy Scarborough, an early-day Texas folklorist and novelist.

NANCY BAKER JONES holds a Ph.D. in American civilization from the University of Texas. Coordinator of the 1990 conference "Women and Texas History" at the University of Texas, she is coeditor of the essay collection *Women and Texas History.* She served as associate editor for the *Handbook of Texas* revision project.

CHERYL LANCASTER KEY, a native of San Angelo, holds both a B.A. and an M.A. from Angelo State University. For her thesis study, she wrote on the work of Jane Gilmore Rushing. A high-school English teacher, she served on the board of trustees of the Grape-Pulliam Independent School District for several years. The mother of one daughter, she is married to Ralph C. Key.

WILLIAM B. MARTIN is a professor of English at Tarleton State University. He is a longtime teacher of drama in Texas colleges and universities and is editor of *Texas Plays,* the first published anthology of plays by Texans since the 1940s.

MELVIN MASON, a former president of the Texas Folklore Society, has taught English at Sam Houston State University for a number of years. He is producer of several documentary films on Texas folk culture and has written a number of articles on Texas folklore and literature.

BRYCE MILLIGAN has published young adult historical novels and short story collections, including the award winning *With the Wind, Kevin Dolan,* recently republished in Germany. He is also author of three collections of poetry and numerous articles and reviews, serving for several years as book critic for the *San Antonio Light.* He edited *Vortex,* a critical review journal, and founded *Pax: A Journal for Peace Through Culture,* both of which were published for several years. He founded and co-directed for three years what is now the San Antonio Inter-American Bookfair. He is associated at present with the Guadalupe Cultural Arts Center. His most recent work is the anthology *Daughters of the Fifth Sun: A Collection of Latina Fiction and Poetry,* which he edited with Angela De Hoyos and his wife, Mary Guerrero Milligan.

PAMELA LYNN PALMER, a librarian at the Ralph W. Steen Library, Stephen F. Austin State University, has published historical articles, poetry, and fiction in a number of periodicals. Her essays have appeared in the *Southwestern Historical Quarterly* and in *Legendary Ladies of Texas,* a Texas Folklore Society publication. She has received the C. K. Chamberlain Award for best article in the *East Texas Historical Journal.*

JUDYTH RIGLER is book editor of the *San Antonio Express-News.* Since 1981 she has written "Lone Star Library," a column on Texas books that appears in a dozen newspapers. She speaks on Texas books and Texas authors throughout the state and is a contributing editor to *Texas*

Books in Review. She is coauthor of *In the Line of Duty: Reflections of a Texas Ranger Private.* In 1986 she received the first Media Award from the Book Publishers of Texas for excellence in reviewing books. Her works in progress are a critical biography of George Sessions Perry and a novel.

JOYCE ROACH, author of fiction, nonfiction, and musical drama, has won the Spur Award from the Western Writers of America twice. *Eats: A Folk History of Texas Foods,* which she coauthored, won best book of the year award from the Texas Institute of Letters in 1989. She speaks frequently on Texas folklore and southwestern life and letters and is a former president of the Texas Folklore Society. She also teaches courses in southwestern and western literature at Texas Christian University.

LOU HALSELL RODENBERGER, a professor of English at McMurry University, has published articles on Texas women writers and is editor of *Her Work: Stories by Texas Women.* She holds a Ph.D. in English from Texas A&M University. She is a former president of the Texas Folklore Society and of the West Texas Historical Association. Her most recent work is *Jane Gilmore Rushing,* a monograph-length study of a Texas woman writer published as one of the Boise State University Press Western Writers Series.

JAN EPTON SEALE is the author of two collections of poetry, *Bonds* and *Sharing the House.* She also is featured in *Texas Poets in Concert.* Her fiction has appeared in numerous periodicals and is collected in *Airlift.* Her nonfiction has been published in *Texas Monthly* and other magazines, and she has edited textbooks, written radio drama, taught courses on magazine writing and writing autobiography, and given workshops on creative writing. A resident of McAllen, she most recently published a collection of essays entitled *Homeland: Essays Beside and Beyond the Rio Grande.*

ERNESTINE SEWELL was a professor of English at the University of Texas at Arlington before she retired to live in Commerce, where she and her husband, Charles Linck, are founders of Cow Hill Press. She has published widely on subjects ranging from education to southwestern life, literature, and folklore. In 1989 she received the Texas Institute of Letters best book award as coauthor of *Eats: A Folk History of Texas Foods.* Her most recent work is *How the Cimarron River Got Its Name and Other Stories about Coffee,* a collection of stories, lore, and recipes about coffee.

PEGGY SKAGGS, who holds a Ph.D. in English from Texas A&M University, recently retired as dean of the Graduate School at Angelo State University. A professor of English, she teaches courses in southwestern life, literature, and folklore and American realism and has published numerous articles in scholarly journals. She is the author of the critical study *Kate Chopin* and is listed in *Outstanding Educators of America.*

JANIS STOUT, professor of English at Texas A&M University, has published three novels as well as book-length studies of Jane Austen, Willa Cather, Joan Didion, and Katherine Anne Porter. Her most recent scholarly study is *Katherine Anne Porter: A Sense of the Times.* She received her Ph.D. in English at Rice University and has served as associate dean of Liberal Arts at Texas A&M.

JANE TANNER is former editor of *Texas Books in Review,* a quarterly review journal published until recently by the Center for Texas Studies at the University of North Texas. She holds a Ph.D. from the University of North Texas, where she now teaches.

JOYCE THOMPSON was a professor of English at Texas Woman's University, where her interest in Texas women writers led her to direct a conference, "Texas Women: The Myth the Reality," in 1985. She is the author of *Marking a Trail: A History of Texas Woman's University.* A graduate of Texas Tech, where she earned her B.A., M.A., and Ph.D., she presented a number of conference papers on women writers. *Ladies' Firsts,* a miscellany of her research findings on women's achievements and on cultural patterns influencing women's lives, was published after her untimely death from cancer in February 1992.

FRAN VICK is director of the University of North Texas Press. A former English teacher and journalist, she was founder and publisher of E-Heart Press before assuming her present position.

SYLVIA WHITMAN, a free-lance writer, has published articles in numerous magazines, including *Ladies' Home Journal, Redbook, Southern Magazine,* and *Harvard Magazine.* The author of three nonfiction books, she has received several writing awards. She now resides in Charlottesville, Virginia.

PATRICIA WILLIAMS, who received a degree in English at the University of Illinois at Urbana-Champaign, is a professor at Texas Southern University, where she has served as dean of the College of Arts and Sciences and director of the Douglass Institute of Instructional Support and Honors Program. A published poet, she was selected Poet of Merit by the American Poetry Association Panel of Judges in 1989, and her poetry has been published in several anthologies, including *Of Hide and Horn: An Anthology of Texas Poets.*

CAROLE WOLF teaches English at Texas Tech University, where she received her Ph.D. Her dissertation is entitled "A Study of Prose by Nineteenth Century Texas Women." She has served as an archivist in the

Southwest Collection at Texas Tech, and she has taught English in several Texas public schools.

MALLORY YOUNG, head of the Department of English at Tarleton State University, has served as director of the Presidential Honors Program there. She earned her Ph.D. in comparative literature at the State University of New York at Buffalo. She has published essays, poems, and reviews in a number of journals nationwide and has presented conference papers on Texas women writers. She is a recipient of the Distinguished Faculty Award for Excellence in Teaching at Tarleton State University.

INDEX

Bennett, Patrick, 164
Benson, Elizabeth, 10
Bentley, Beverly, 43
Berryhill, Michael, 184
Best American Short Stories, 176, 180, 181, 183, 184
Best Intentions (Lehrer), 31
Best of Friends, The (Montgomery), 92
Best Short Stories of the Southwest (Greer), 22, 175
Best Short Stories, second series (Greer), 176
Betancour, Maria, 209
Between Sun and Sod (Lewis), 40
Beulah (Evans), 73
Beware! or Irma's Life (Carmichael), 7, 72
Beyond Deserving (Scofield), 36
Beyond Stereotypes (Herrera-Sobek), 208, 216, 241
bibliography, 44–45, 288. *See also specific titles*
Bibliography of Texas (Raines), 7
Bibliography of Texas Poetry, A (Adams), 288
Biddle, Ellen McGowan, 62
Big Bend, 13, 16, 29, 31, 39, 41, 305
Bigmamma Didn't Shop at Woolworth's (Nash), 250
Big Road, The (Cross), 97, 98
"Bilingual Christmas" (Mora), 226
bilingualism, in drama, 337. *See also* code switching
Billings, Mary C., 65
biography, 7, 26, 39–44, 53, 55, 57, 61, 161; of famous women, 59; of Sam Houston, 17; of writers, 18, 19, 259, 270, 273–75. *See also specific titles*
Bird, Sarah, 32–33, 142, 196, 344, 353
Birds of Passage (Bishop), 76
Birds of Tanglewood, The (Baker), 89, 93
"Birth of Venus in the Gulf of Mexico, The" (Lynn), 305
Bishop, Julia Truitt, 76
Black, Louis, 195
"Black Antigone" (Deverell), 206
Black Girl (Franklin), 249, 254
Black Gold (Bunkley), 251
Black Gold (Gibson), 106, 107, 110, 115
Black Texas Women (Winegarten), 251
Blessed Assurance (Mojtabai), 29
Bloomsbury Review, 170
bluebonnets, 267–69, 284
Bluebonnets for Lucinda (Sayers), 198
"'Blues' as Folksongs, The" (Scarborough), 136
Blue Smoke (Baker), 88, 89, 90
Boardin' in the Thicket (Landrey), 40
Boas, Frank, 15
Boatright, Mody, 349
Bob Dean (Hood), 75
Bode, Elroy, 317
Body of Knowledge (Dawson), 35, 353
"Body Remembers an Old Grammar, The" (Lynn), 307–308
Boley, Tommy J., 39

Bonds (Seale), 300–302, 308
Boner, Sally, 63
Bonner, Cindy, 36, 344
Book Club of Texas, 14, 17, 170
Booklist, 311, 313
Book Lover of Texas (Oppenheimer), 43
Book Publishers of Texas, 348, 350, 351
"Books and Branding Irons" (Smith), 79
"Book Talk," 43
Book Week, 109
Border Healing Woman (Taylor), 185
Borderlands/La Frontera (Anzaldúa), 241
Borders (Mora), 225, 227
Boston Sunday Herald, 121
Boston Traveler, 119
Bow Boly (Ayers), 253
Bower, B. M., 346
Box Church (Vander Voort), 335
Boy Captive of the Texas Mier Expedition, The (Gooch), 61, 74
Boy Crazy and Other Stories (Winik), 195
Boyfriend School, The (Bird), 32
"Boy Who Couldn't Be Saved, The" (Patterson), 175
Bradstreet, Anne, 295
Brand, Anna, 175
Brann, William Cowper, 112, 327
Brann and the Iconoclast (Gibson), 112, 327
Brannon, Ada Cornelius, 72–73
Brazos River, 11
Breaking Gentle (Lowry), 152, 154
Breeze, Katie, 29
Brenham, Tex., 64
Brenner, Anita, 14–15
Brenner, Marie, 15
Brewer, John Mason, 248
"Bride on the Old Chisholm Trail in 1886, A" (Bunton), 55
Bridges, Annie C., 63
Bright, Susan, 261
"British Ballads in Texas" (Major), 82
Brooks, Elizabeth, 4, 7, 58
Brothers, Debbie, 351
Brown, John Henry, 55, 58
Brown, Larry, 184
Brown, Marion T., 55
Brown, Mary M., 55, 58
Brown, Pat, 326
Brown-Guillory, Elizabeth, 252
Brownsville, Tex., 13, 15, 183
Brownwood, Tex., 24, 30
Bruce-Novoa, Juan, 216, 243
"Bruja: Witch" (Mora), 225
Brush Country Woman (Holland), 40
Bryan, J. P., 53
Bryan, Tex., 346
Buncha Crocs in Surch of Snac and Other Poems (Galloway), 329